Billy Graham

Billy Graham

American Pilgrim

Edited by

ANDREW FINSTUEN
ANNE BLUE WILLS
GRANT WACKER

OXFORD
UNIVERSITY PRESS

OXFORD
UNIVERSITY PRESS

Oxford University Press is a department of the University of Oxford. It furthers the University's objective of excellence in research, scholarship, and education by publishing worldwide. Oxford is a registered trade mark of Oxford University Press in the UK and certain other countries.

Published in the United States of America by Oxford University Press
198 Madison Avenue, New York, NY 10016, United States of America.

Library of Congress Cataloging-in-Publication Data
Names: Finstuen, Andrew | Wills, Anne Blue | Wacker, Grant, editor.
Title: Billy Graham : American pilgrim /
edited by Andrew Finstuen, Anne Blue Wills and Grant Wacker.
Description: New York : Oxford University Press, 2017. |
Includes bibliographical references and index. |
Identifiers: LCCN 2016050920 (print) | LCCN 2017012227 (ebook) |
ISBN 9780190683528 (hardback) | ISBN 9780190683535 (ebook) |
ISBN 9780190683542 (updf) | ISBN 9780190683559 (online content)
Subjects: LCSH: Graham, Billy, 1918– |
United States—Church history—20th century. | Evangelism—United States.
Classification: LCC BV3785.G69 (ebook) |
LCC BV3785.G69 B495 2017 (print) | DDC 269/.2092—dc23
LC record available at https://lccn.loc.gov/2016050920

1 3 5 7 9 8 6 4 2
Printed by Sheridan Books, Inc., United States of America

For

Edith L. Blumhofer

Contents

PART THREE: *Culture*

Preface

IN 2011 THE Lilly Endowment Inc. awarded the Institute for the Study of American Evangelicals (ISAE) at Wheaton College in Illinois a major grant to examine the life and influence of the American evangelist Billy Graham (b. 1918). The ISAE used the award to fund planning meetings, research grants, public lectures, course offerings, two conferences (one academic, one popular), a DVD about the history of Graham's crusades (*A Gathering of Souls: The Billy Graham Crusades,* from Tim Frakes Productions), three spin-off volumes now under contract with Eerdmans Publishing Company, and the scholarly essays that appear in this book. All are published here for the first time. The editors thank the endowment for its generous support.

Many people helped bring this book to completion. First, we wish to thank Paul Ericksen and Bob Shuster of the Billy Graham Center Archives. Their knowledge of the Graham materials and eagerness to assist researchers is legendary. We also wish to thank John Akers and David Bruce of the Billy Graham Evangelistic Association, who helped the authors make sense of the complexity of Graham's story, as well as offering tips about elusive resources to check out and encouragement for carrying the book to publication. At an early planning meeting in Maine, James Bratt astutely critiqued the papers that eventually formed the book's chapters. Larry Eskridge ably handled planning details, and Joan Eskridge provided technical support. Leighton Ford, Martin Marty, and Kenneth L. Woodward participated in a lively and perceptive public discussion about the project at Wheaton College in 2013. Matthew Sutton and an anonymous reader for Oxford University Press offered valuable suggestions for improving the manuscript. Their carefulness established a gold standard for reviewers of manuscripts. As always, Mark Noll staked out a spot on the sidelines, where he brought keen perceptions about American evangelical history (and much else) to bear on our work. Katherine Wacker suggested the book's title. Most important, we wish to thank Ingrid Finstuen for her expert management of the project, for turning gnarled manuscript pages into smooth ones, and for handling the countless details of communication with the volume's authors and agents of Oxford University Press. Ingrid toiled with wit and grace. The dedication to Edith L. Blumhofer betokens our profound appreciation for a scholar, colleague, and friend.

October 2016
Boise, Idaho
Davidson, North Carolina
Chapel Hill, North Carolina

List of Contributors

Margaret Bendroth is the executive director of the Congregational Library and Archives in Boston. She is the author of several books, including *Fundamentalism and Gender, 1875 to the Present* (Yale University Press, 1993), *The Spiritual Practice of Remembering* (Eerdmans, 2013), and *The Last Puritans: Mainline Protestants and the Power of the Past* (University of North Carolina Press, 2015).

Edith L. Blumhofer, professor and director of the Institute for the Study of American Evangelicals at Wheaton College, is the author of several books, including *Her Heart Can See* (Eerdmans, 2005), a biography of hymn writer Fanny Crosby; *Restoring the Faith: the Assemblies of God, Pentecostalism, and American Culture* (Illinois, 1993); and *Aimee Semple McPherson: Everybody's Sister* (Eerdmans, 1992).

Elesha Coffman is an assistant professor of history at Baylor University. She is the author of *The Christian Century and the Rise of the Protestant Mainline* (Oxford University Press, 2013). Her work has also appeared in *American Catholic Studies, Religion and American Culture, Books & Culture,* and *Christianity Today*.

Darren Dochuk, associate professor in the Department of History at the University of Notre Dame, is the author of *From Bible Belt to Sunbelt: Plain-Folk Religion, Grassroots Politics, and the Rise of Evangelical Conservatism* (Norton). He has also co-edited a number of essay collections, including *Sunbelt Rising: The Politics of Space, Place, and Region* (University of Pennsylvania Press, 2011), *American Evangelicalism: George Marsden and the State of American History* (University of Notre Dame Press, 2014), *Faith in the New Millennium: The Future of Religion and American Politics* (Oxford University Press, 2016), and *The Routledge History of the Twentieth-Century United States* (Routledge, forthcoming 2017).

Seth Dowland is an associate professor of religion at Pacific Lutheran University. He is the author of *Family Values and the Rise of the Christian Right* (University of Pennsylvania Press, 2015).

Curtis J. Evans, associate professor of American religions and the history of Christianity at the University of Chicago Divinity School, is the author of *The Burden of Black Religion* (Oxford University Press, 2008) and *A Theology of Brotherhood: The Federal Council of Churches and the Problem of Race* (Oxford, forthcoming).

Andrew Finstuen is dean of the Honors College at Boise State University and an associate professor in the Department of History. His first book, *Original Sin and Everyday Protestants: The Theology of Reinhold Niebuhr, Billy Graham, and Paul Tillich in an Age of Anxiety* (University of North Carolina Press, 2009), won the 2010 American Society of Church History's Brewer Prize. In 2017, he coproduced the documentary film *An American Conscience: The Reinhold Niebuhr Story*, which aired on Public Television.

Ken Garfield is the former religion editor of the *Charlotte Observer*. He has also written for the Duke Divinity School (Faith & Leadership resource), *New York Times, Christian Century*, and Religion News Service. He has written four books, including *Billy Graham: A Life in Pictures* (Triumph Books).

Michael S. Hamilton, Vice President for Programs and Special Initiatives at the Issachar Fund, is currently working on the book *Calvin College and the Revival of Christian Learning in America* (Eerdmans, forthcoming).

David P. King is the Karen Lake Buttrey Director of the Lake Institute on Faith and Giving as well as assistant professor of philanthropic studies within the Indiana University Lilly Family School of Philanthropy. He is currently writing a history of the Christian humanitarian organization World Vision (University of Pennsylvania Press, forthcoming).

William Martin, author of *A Prophet with Honor: The Billy Graham Story* (William Morrow, 1991), is considered the pioneering authority on the subject of Billy Graham. He is the Harry and Hazel Chavanne Professor Emeritus of Sociology at Rice University and Chavanne Senior Fellow for Religion and Public Policy at Rice's Baker Institute.

Steven P. Miller is the author of *Billy Graham and the Rise of the Republican South* (University of Pennsylvania Press, 2009) and *The Age of Evangelicalism: America's Born-Again Years* (Oxford University Press, 2014).

Grant Wacker is the Gilbert T. Rowe Professor Emeritus of Christian History at Duke Divinity School. He is the author of *Heaven Below: Early Pentecostals and American Culture* (2001) and *America's Pastor: Billy Graham and the Shaping of a Nation* (2014), both published by Harvard University Press. Wacker is past president of the American Society of Church History.

Anne Blue Wills is an associate professor of religion at Davidson College. She is currently writing a biography of Ruth Bell Graham. Her work has appeared in such publications as *Religion and American Culture: A Journal of Interpretation* and *Women in American History: An Encyclopedia.*

Billy Graham

Introduction

Grant Wacker

I. "He Brought the Storm Down"

One of the most important parts of Billy Graham's story lies in the letters ordinary people sent him. No one knows exactly how many, since the Billy Graham Evangelistic Association (BGEA) did not keep track. But between 1950, when the BGEA was formed, and 2005, when Graham retired from public ministry, the number easily soared into the millions. All those who wrote to him received personal answers, written by associates following boilerplate formats approved by Graham. For reasons of space and confidentiality, the BGEA destroyed nearly all of the letters. But several thousand, mostly posted in the early 1960s and throughout the 1980s, somehow survived.[1]

The letters show how powerfully Graham influenced Americans' daily lives. People wrote about addictions, sexual lapses, spiritual back-sliding, marriages on the rocks, kids gone astray, and countless other failures and disappointments. They also wrote about loneliness. Graham once said that the second-most frequent topic of the letters was loneliness. Some argued with him about his theology, some invited him to drop by for coffee, some complimented him on his looks, and some offered appreciation for his wife, Ruth Bell Graham, or his choir director, Cliff Barrows, or his beloved songster, George Beverly Shea. At the same time, some asked him not to share their letter with Ruth or Cliff or George—or anyone else. Some asked for a personal response, the sooner the better, yet most seemed to understand that assistants would read the letters, and write responses, and they were okay with that.

But most of the letters just thanked him. They did it in multiple ways, and almost always with transparent earnestness. Most often, writers said they appreciated his preaching, and how it helped them grasp that they had to repent, change their ways, and set a new direction for their lives. He helped them see how they could find peace in Christ, or win a second chance after straying from the law or their spouses or the church. They said he gave them renewed courage.

The letters show too that Graham spoke to the fears and joys of a defined constituency. The names, addresses, and comments indicate that the typical writer was a white female high school graduate between twenty and thirty years old. She worshipped in a Baptist church, occupied a lower middle rung on the social ladder, held a service or skilled job, and lived in a small town in the South or Midwest. Though the demographic profile of that constituency changed over the years, becoming steadily more racially, ethnically, occupationally, educationally, geographically, and, especially, denominationally diverse, the basic configuration remained pretty much the same. Writers with racially or ethnically distinctive names, or names with tags like SJ, MD, or PhD, or with mailing addresses in the tony parts of big cities, never amounted to more than a trace. [2]

Besides the letters, evidence of Graham's importance on the American religious landscape abounds. Between 1949 and 1971, he rose from the rank of a religious leader with a regional following to a celebrity with a national following to an icon with an international following. He retained that iconic status for the rest of the century and well into the first decade of the next. Nearly 215 million people on six continents and in nearly one hundred countries heard him preach in person, and millions—perhaps billions—more encountered him via electronic media. [3]

Although those statistics likely saw some inflation along the way, Graham may have preached to more people face-to-face than any other figure in history. Many of Graham's endeavors set records, including the sermon he delivered on an airport tarmac in Seoul, South Korea, in 1973 to 1,120,000 people (at the time almost certainly the largest gathering of Christians ever recorded). Between 1955 and 2016, Graham scored a spot on Gallup's list of the "Ten Most Admired Men" in the world sixty times. President Ronald Reagan, his closest rival on the list, appeared "only" thirty-one times. Graham authored or authorized under his name more than thirty books. All together, they were translated into at least fifty languages and sold millions of copies. HarperCollins's first printing of his memoir, *Just As I Am*, ran one million copies alone.

Stalwarts saw God's hand in all this, but historians saw Graham's own tireless hands hard at work, too. His syndicated national weekly radio program, *The Hour of Decision*, launched in 1950, quickly ranked as the most widely heard religious broadcast in the country. His daily newspaper column, "My Answer," birthed in 1952, reached a potential readership of twenty million. *Christianity Today*, which Graham established in 1956, soon won recognition as the normative voice of mainstream evangelicalism. The popular monthly *Decision*, which started landing in readers' mailboxes in 1960, became the most widely circulated Christian magazine in the world. Whatever else Graham was, he was a man of bold ambitions.

While Graham touched the lives of millions of everyday people, he also likely enjoyed closer proximity to the top echelons of power than any other religious leader in American history. Among the multitude of awards that he received, two stand out: in 1983 the Presidential Medal of Freedom, and in 1996, with his wife, Ruth Bell Graham, the Congressional Gold Medal (the two highest awards for which civilians are eligible). Graham personally knew all twelve presidents from Harry S. Truman to Barack Obama. Except for Truman, who disliked him, and Obama, who spent only an hour with him, all of the presidents ranked as friends. Four—Johnson, Nixon, Reagan, and Bush I, as well as their First Ladies—ranked as close friends.[4]

Yet Graham's influence is perhaps best represented anecdotally. Five of these anecdotes—what we might call cultural snapshots—symbolize countless others. First, except for elected officials, Graham may have been the only person in the United States who needed no mailing address beyond his name. Just "Billy Graham" would do. Second, among the countless letters children sent to him, a first- or second-grader's 1971 letter seemed to sum up all of them. After asking for a free book, the child closed with one final—telling—request: "Tell Mr. Jesus hi." Third, Harold Bloom, the Yale literary critic, described Graham's influence with brilliant succinctness in a 1999 *Time* cover article on the "100 Most Important People of the Century": "You don't run for office among us by proclaiming your skepticism or deprecating Billy Graham." Fourth, at a public symposium at Wheaton College (IL) in 2013, the American historian Martin E. Marty—as famous in his sphere as Graham was in his—judged that the Mount Rushmore of American religious icons would include Jonathan Edwards, Martin Luther King Jr., and Billy Graham. (With a wink, Marty added that he had not yet decided on the fourth.)[5]

The fifth cultural snapshot is worth quoting at length because of the fame of its author. In 2014, in a long retrospective on his own storied career, the folk musician Bob Dylan recalled his youthful impressions of Graham.

> [He was] the greatest preacher and evangelist of my time—that guy could save souls and did. I went to two or three of his rallies in the '50s or '60s. This guy was like rock 'n' roll personified—volatile, explosive. He had the hair, the tone, the elocution—when he spoke, he brought the storm down. Clouds parted. Souls got saved, sometimes 30- or 40,000 of them. If you ever went to a Billy Graham rally back then, you were changed forever. There's never been a preacher like him. He could fill football stadiums before anybody. He could fill Giants Stadium more than even the Giants football team. Seems like a long time ago. Long before Mick Jagger sang his first note or Bruce strapped on his first guitar—that's some of the part of rock 'n' roll that I retained. I had to. I saw Billy Graham in the flesh and heard him loud and clear.[6]

Not everyone saw Graham in such a glowing light, however. At a time when mainline leaders and academic theologians found dialogue more congenial than proclamation, Graham's unflinching presentation of his interpretation of the gospel stirred resistance. To many, he came across as just another itinerant evangelist, firing 240 words a minute. The sight of Graham fraternizing with the rich and the famous worried friends and delighted foes. For all but the most loyal supporters, his political stances in the 1960s and early 1970s seemed the most troubling of all. The fallout from Graham's unsteady support for the Vietnam War (initially hawkish, later waffling, later neutral) and his dogged defense of Nixon during Watergate persisted long after the public had soured on both causes. Suspicions deepened when his noxious comments about Jews and the media, secretly recorded in President Nixon's office in February 1972, surfaced in February 2002. Graham's repeated apologies to Jews in person and in the media did not erase the damage. Though there was no clear evidence of anti-Semitism in Graham's thinking before or after the 1972 incident,[7] his compliance with Nixon's bigotry on that occasion, and obsequiousness toward Nixon throughout most of his presidency, clouded Graham's reputation.

Public censure came from all sides: left, right, church, academy, and media. President Harry S. Truman stood at the front of the line. Graham botched a meeting with the president in 1950, when the callow thirty-year-old preacher blabbed to reporters about the content of the meeting. Truman never forgave him. Calling Graham a "counterfeit" two decades later, the president groused, "I just don't go for people like that. All he's interested in is getting his name in the paper." In 1970, after Graham invited President Nixon to speak at a crusade at the University of Tennessee, a student paper dismissed the event as a "one-man circus." Shortly afterward, the novelist-satirist Philip Roth ripped him as the "Reverend Billy Cupcake." In 1966, Bob Jones Sr., president of Bob Jones University, angered by Graham's ecumenical leanings, declared that Graham was "doing more harm to the cause of Jesus Christ than any other living man." All of this arrived along with a constant river of hate mail and occasional death threats.

Graham softened with age, and so did the quantity of such critiques, but the acidity level remained. Graham visited a Moscow peace conference in 1982, where he called not only for the elimination of nuclear weapons but also seemed to go out of his way not to offend his Russian hosts. His apparent naiveté about Soviet militarism and acquiescence to the repression of religious liberty in the Soviet bloc prompted the conservative columnist George Will to slam him as "America's most embarrassing export." Will admonished the preacher to "stop acting as though pious intentions are substitutes for intelligence, and excuses for irresponsibility."[8] Graham's anti-Semitic rant to Nixon prompted the secular essayist Christopher Hitchens to excoriate the preacher as "an avid bigot as well as a cheap liar," and "a gaping and mendacious anti-Jewish peasant." Age provided little security.

Yet Graham's legacy, like that of his contemporaries Martin Luther King Jr. and Reinhold Niebuhr, proved to be one of lasting influence. Though it is hard to know exactly how to separate influence from celebrity, the variety and persistence of the kind of indicators noted above leave little doubt that Graham's presence transcended celebrity. And so it was that for millions of "heartland" Americans, Graham thrived as a Protestant saint. By the mid-1950s, he overshadowed all Protestant evangelists of the postwar era. By the mid-1960s, he served as the "Great Legitimator." Graham's approval conferred authority on presidents and legitimacy on wars. His words made events sacred, decency desirable, and indecency shameful. With the possible exception of the itinerant preacher George Whitefield and the hymn writer Charles Wesley, both eighteenth-century luminaries, Graham's public recognition surpassed all evangelicals in American history.

In 2007, at the dedication of the Billy Graham Library in Graham's hometown of Charlotte, North Carolina, former presidents Jimmy Carter and Bill Clinton listened as former president George H. W. Bush publically labeled him "America's pastor." As America's pastor, he appeared to rise above the discord of partisan struggle, theological controversy, and denominational division. He personified the commitment to "fundamental verities" that Americans wanted to see in themselves. In the words of Graham's premier biographer, William Martin, Graham symbolized their "best selves." That many Americans failed to live up to their best selves was beside the point. In their minds Graham did.

II: Billy Graham and American Culture

The literature by and about Graham is vast.[9] This is hardly surprising, given the BGEA's skill in marketing his image, the number of decades he remained in the public eye, the density of his connections with world leaders, the extent of his involvement in the social and political movements of the age, and his indirect evangelistic and pastoral relationships with millions of ordinary people. Even so, Graham's story is far from fully told. Important questions remain unasked, and many of the answers that observers have offered so far have proved inadequate. *Billy Graham: American Pilgrim* seeks to address this need.

The volume does not advance an overarching thesis. The editors selected established scholars and simply asked them to explore broad topics of general interest and see what they came up with. Yet after the authors submitted their chapters, it quickly became clear that two patterns repeatedly surfaced in the research that each one had independently pursued. Those patterns are captured by two words: *change* and *paradox*. More precisely, it would be hard to find a religious leader who changed more over the course of his career, or one who presented more dramatically paradoxical faces at any given stage. Whether those two patterns were intentional or unintentional, or ascribed to him by the media or by the public, or all of the above, remains a matter of debate among Graham scholars. Regardless of the roots, the evidence of both change and paradox across his long life is compelling. It informs the editors' decision to frame Graham as an American pilgrim constantly in motion, and in multiple ways.

How did Graham change over time? All people do, of course, but in his case the development proved distinctive both in degree and in visibility. Between 1949, when Graham's eight-week crusade in Los Angeles catapulted him into national and international attention, and 2005, when he preached his final major crusade in Flushing Meadows, New York, he evinced not only dramatic change, but also, in many respects, progressive change. By "progressive" I mean that he grew more tolerant of differing theological positions, more skeptical of political partisanship, and more assertive in his calls for social justice at home and abroad. Simply put, he became more cognizant of the full implications of the gospel he preached.

To take one of many examples, Graham tracked his own shift on race relations to meeting an African American student when he was an undergraduate transfer student at Wheaton College. That was, he said, the first time in his life he encountered a black person as a peer. Before then, growing up in the South in the 1920s and 1930s, he knew blacks and Hispanics as field hands on his father's farm. He remembered that he treated them politely, but his paternalism did not impress itself on him until he got to Wheaton.[10] By 1982 he would say, in the Patriarchal Cathedral in Moscow, that he had undergone three major conversions in his life: to Christ, to racial justice, and to nuclear disarmament. Later he would say, "I am still a man in process."[11]

And so it was that on most issues—especially political partisanship, global poverty, and, above all, militarism—the evolution from conservative to progressive positions proved both striking and undeniable. The change that probably caught the most attention from the media was his steadily growing willingness to work with Christians of (almost) all stripes, as long as they did not ask him to alter his own message. And the mature Graham's refusal to speculate about the final destiny of Jews and other non-Christians increasingly separated him from his own fundamentalist past.

To be sure, the claim that Graham significantly changed over the years requires crucial qualifications. His core theological convictions altered very little, and the transitions in his social and political views were not uniform. Though his views on racial justice showed impressive development, he moved erratically: two steps forward in the 1950s, one step back in the 1960s and early 1970s, and two steps forward again in the late 1970s and 1980s. His positions on women's rights and ordination were a masterpiece of equivocation. And when it came to his post-Nixon commitment to avoid partisanship, he fell off the wagon more than once, as recently as the Bush election in 2000. Still, taken whole, profound developments appeared across the years. "During most of my life I have been on a pilgrimage in many areas," he told an audience at the John F. Kennedy School of

Government at Harvard in 1982. "I have come to see in deeper ways some of the implications of my faith and message."[12]

Graham's self-description did not, however, reveal much about the reasons for his pilgrimage. He apparently suffered no physical or emotional trauma—such as a life-threatening foxhole experience or a devastating loss of a child—that might help explain fundamental alterations in how he viewed the world. Nor did he reveal an educational crisis, such as reading a life-altering book, of the sort many liberals talk about in their autobiographies.[13] Though he often mentioned evangelists before his time, he rarely spoke of strong mentor figures—other than general references to D. L. Moody—who might have prodded him. And beyond all that, Graham found little support for dramatic change coming from home. His wife, Ruth Bell Graham—always a force of nature (as the historian Anne Blue Wills amply documents in her forthcoming biography of Ruth Graham)—remained steadily conservative in her political and theological views. So we are left to speculate. His continual travels, encounters with international leaders, repeated exposure to the world's suffering, disappointments with friends and himself, and perhaps his reading of the letters that followers and critics posted to him may have played a role.

Changes in the media's perception and representation of Graham were just as important as developments in Graham himself. The press moved from curiosity in 1940s, to critical appreciation in the 1950s, to critical doubt in the 1960s and early 1970s, and finally to steadily growing admiration in the 1980s and 1990s. Granted, in 2002 most journalists were dismayed if not angry when Graham's odious comments to Nixon about Jews came to light. But the media's overall reaction to that incident gradually subsided into disappointment and then a forgiving attitude toward a grievous lapse. To be sure, after the turn of the century, the views attributed to Graham by his culture-warrior son Franklin Graham complicated perceptions. But by then the elder Graham was in his nineties, and most—though certainly not all—journalists seemed to assume that the increasingly progressive positions the father had taken through his eighties should stand.[14]

These considerations bring us to the second recurrent pattern in this volume: *paradox*. The word *irony* might work nearly as well, for it suggests that Graham's self-presentation and mediated presentations bore unexpected and sometimes unwelcome consequences. But paradox provides a more apt description of the complexity of Graham's public images, for it suggests that multiple and often competing impulses simultaneously jockeyed for attention.

In these essays we will see again and again that Graham presented diverse faces to the outside world, and perhaps to himself, too. Numerous descriptive dyads come to mind. Was the pattern one of adroitness— or adeptness? Slipperiness—or flexibility? Calculation—or planning? Shrewdness—or savviness? Manipulation—or skillfulness? Naiveté—or simplicity? Evasiveness—or subtlety? In one sense these dyads were not unique to Graham. Most people present themselves in different ways in different settings. What makes Graham special is that the pattern was so pronounced. What David Brooks said about Dwight Eisenhower may have applied to Graham, too: "He looked simple and straightforward, but his simplicity was a work of art."[15] Whether the slippage originated in him, in the media, in the public's perceptions, or in all three, Graham rarely emerged as a single identity.

The difficulty of pinning Graham down to a single site on the broad cultural map of the era helps make the point. Was he a Southern Baptist Convention loyalist? Or a nondenominational entrepreneur who worked with ease with Christians (and sometimes Jews) of all denominational stripes? Was he a fundamentalist dispensational premillennialist? Or a broadminded "big tent" evangelical who tried to avoid being nailed down to details? Was he a devout churchman who made the proclamation of the gospel his chief passion? Or a pundit of the Nixon White House? Or, to switch the logic of the question, how did it happen that a man universally described as witty and charming and genuinely humble was also so polarizing that he provoked vitriolic smears and even death threats from a small but persistent minority of enemies?

If change and paradox made Graham a pilgrim, the confluences between his life and the great gulf streams of post–World War II US history made him a preeminently American figure, too. Many of the key formative influences in his mature life were deeply rooted in his natal culture. The length of his tenure in the public eye and the breadth of his influence on the cultural landscape of the United States have shaped the scope of the questions this book seeks to address.

So what does Graham's story tell us about America's story? The authors try to help answer that question by exploring the *intersections* between Graham's career and other parts of American culture. Granted, some first-rate books have already taken up that topic, and this work draws on them, but the field remains wide open. Many of the most important questions stand unaddressed, or addressed only lightly, or addressed with ideologically driven agendas.

Billy Graham: American Pilgrim ranges widely, but it does not try to do everything. Some topics, such as Graham's relation to presidents, have received focused treatment elsewhere, and therefore do not win a chapter here. Other topics, such as his tangled relationship with Richard Nixon, or with fundamentalism, turn up one way or another throughout this volume.

A few words about the authors' working assumptions may be helpful. First, all of them (including me) speak only for themselves, and sometimes they disagree. The editors have made no attempt to harmonize, let alone iron out, those differences. The differences show that these materials are so rich and voluminous they can yield a variety of interpretations.

Second, the authors' primary concern is not to determine whether Graham's influence proved good or bad. Countless popular, and not a few academic, studies have fallen into the traps of canonization on one side or demonization on the other. The first approach reduces the evangelist to a saint who could do no wrong. The second reduces him to a scoundrel who could do no good. This volume shows that, in most instances, culture war interpretations of Graham distort the subtleties of the evidence. Some value judgments will inevitably arise—historians are intractable moralizers—but that is not the main aim. The main one is description and analysis.

And finally, the authors are comfortable with a profoundly complicated figure. Graham, like all leaders, was both a product and a producer of his age. Countless variables fed into his story. The challenge is to figure out how Graham's influence emerged, where it flourished (or not), why it persisted, and, most important, what difference it makes for understanding American life.

III: The Landscape
of Billy Graham: American Pilgrim

The chapters in *Billy Graham: American Pilgrim* fall into three parts: Religion, Politics, and Culture. Religion comes first because it came first in Graham's view of his work and in the public's view of him. Graham saw himself primarily as an evangelist called to invite men and women to come to Christ for the first time, or to renew a faith grown cold, or to sustain a faith of long standing. If one could count the number of words he uttered and wrote (or released under his name), a good guess would be that most—at least four-fifths—bore on matters of faith. Whatever the stated text of his sermons, every one of them ultimately stemmed from same one, John 3:16: "For God so loved the world, that he gave his only begotten Son, that whosoever believeth in him should not perish, but have everlasting life." From this premise—that Christ offered everlasting life to all who accepted it—Graham issued the hallmark invitation that concluded virtually every meeting: "Come, you come, we will wait."

Politics constitutes part two of *Billy Graham: American Pilgrim.* Graham's interest in politics marched second in his view of himself and in the public's view of him. Sometimes it ran a close second, other times a distant one, but rarely any farther back than that. Boosters often tried to deny this plain fact. They pretended that Graham spent all of his waking time in soul-winning ministry. Debunkers went to the other extreme and often tried to pretend the opposite, that Graham's main occupation in life was back-room wheeling and dealing. The truth lay exactly where Graham said it did. He repeatedly acknowledged that he loved to follow state, national, and international politics. If he had not been a preacher, he admitted, he would have run for office.[16] But he was a preacher, and he did not run for office. Evangelism was his vocation, politics his avocation. Still, the avocation always loomed large, and it therefore merits a place in any serious study of Graham's place in modern history.

The book's third part focuses on culture, the trickiest category to measure. Charting exactly where Graham's influence took root, grew, and then stopped requires a delicate touch. By many measures, Graham's influence reached far beyond the pulpit and the presidential golf course. To cite one of countless examples, in 1950 NBC (unsuccessfully) offered Graham one million dollars a year to host a national television talk show.[17] The network had its financial finger on the pulse of the culture.

Andrew Finstuen's study of Graham's face-to-face presentations and Q&A exchanges in mainline seminaries and secular universities opens the book's first part. Finstuen challenges conventional academic dismissals of Graham as anti-intellectual. Drawing on rarely (or never) consulted archival materials, he argues that Graham manifested a different model of intellectual ability, which he dubs "intellectual virtue." This notion, stemming from Aristotle's notion of practical wisdom, emphasizes the role of humility, courage, and honesty in Graham's approach to his academic conversation partners. Graham, uniquely among evangelists, spoke in literally dozens of non-evangelical institutions. In those settings, audiences sometimes proved politely skeptical at best, or openly hostile at worst, especially at the beginning. Yet like Teddy Roosevelt's famous "Man in the Arena,"

Graham courageously strode into the ring, undeterred. More often than not he emerged with the moral victory of having won audiences with his spirit if not his ideas.

Graham also displayed curiosity—not the curiosity of the intellectual antiseptically analyzing issues from afar, but the curiosity of a man profoundly engaged in the world around him. Beyond that he displayed a desire for mutual understanding. He rarely, if ever, challenged mainline/liberal or secular assumptions, nor did he offer to change his own. But he did suggest places where mainline Protestants and evangelicals might work together for the good of the church and the larger society. Graham's thinking, Finstuen concludes, unfolded as a pilgrimage, "marked by increasing wisdom about what he had to say, and what he had to learn."

The crusade meetings rested on two foundations, Michael Hamilton argues in his contribution, and both of them require a close look to appreciate fully. The first was a nuanced set of theological premises undergirding Graham's forceful preaching style. Many observers, including sympathetic ones, found Graham's theology thin at best. Yet Hamilton sees more. He discerns serious theology—not necessarily academic, but serious—expressed in vernacular language. He shows, for example, that in Graham's preaching, apocalyptic threats always marched arm in arm with promises of millennial hope. Everything hinged on whether the nation proved feckless or faithful in its obedience to Scripture. The other foundation was the deeply ritualized structure of the crusade meetings. Visitors got what they expected: a spectacle. The spectacle atmosphere consisted of "banners, flowers, a massed choir of thousands of voices, bright lights, popular singers and bands, symphony orchestras, celebrity guest speakers, local and national politicians, concession stands, television cameras, wandering reporters, special services for children." If it all felt like pageantry, it really was pageantry, and that sense fueled the crusades' success.

In her chapter, Edith Blumhofer explores the strangely underexamined contributions of George Beverly Shea and Cliff Barrows to Graham's ministry. For many participants, the vocalizing of Canadian crooner Shea, and the choir directing (and general cheer leading) of Barrows may have been the best-remembered and most-loved parts of the crusade meetings. Though Graham himself had no musical talent (the "malady of no melody," Shea said), he astutely understood the role music played. Old favorites predominated, yet the meetings increasingly featured classical, country, folk, rock, Latino, and African American musical genres as well. Blumhofer documents the remarkable racial and ethnic diversity of the guest artists—a point rarely noted in the standard biographies. In the beginning, she shows, Graham, Shea, and Barrows occupied roughly equal places of prominence. That equality soon gave way to a clear hierarchy. Still, Shea's resonant baritone and reverential if not ponderous style soon earned him billing as America's "beloved gospel singer." The inexhaustibly energetic Barrows ran every other aspect of the crusade meetings, including the selection and direction of the often-massive choirs. Together, Shea and Barrows produced the "signature" sound of the Billy Graham crusades.

In the final chapter of the Religion section, biographer William Martin grapples with the challenge of tracking and interpreting Graham's farflung international ministry. In 1946, just months after the evangelist entered the itinerant circuit for Youth for Christ, he took his preaching and organizational skills overseas. Tracking Graham's international travels, region by region, Martin allows that some endeavors proved more successful than others. But no one can doubt the historical significance of his outdoor meeting in Seoul in 1973, and of his call for the elimination of nuclear weapons in Moscow in 1982. Martin also tracks Graham's hand in creating a series of world conferences among evangelicals, such as the landmark First International Congress on World Evangelization in Lausanne in 1974. In the end, Martin argues, Graham's legacy lay in two areas. The first was his pioneering efforts to apply cutting-edge communications technology to evangelism. The second was his pivotal role in galvanizing world evangelicalism into a coherent movement. The latter ran alongside the mainline ecumenical groups such the World Council of Churches, and in the long run may have proved one of his most influential achievements.

Billy Graham: American Pilgrim's second part, "Politics," starts with David King's examination of Graham's continually growing attention to the challenges of global poverty, particularly through his work with World Vision International. The international scope of Graham's vision started early, in the late 1940s and the 1950s, with his fear—shared by millions of others at home and abroad—of the menace of global communism. In time, however, his focus shifted to hunger, healthcare, economic scarcity, and disaster relief. In the early decades of his ministry, Graham seemed more aware of poverty abroad than at home, but that awareness balanced out over time. By the final years, Graham had come to register a sturdily progressive stand on numerous issues, including the dangers of spiraling militarism on both sides of the Atlantic. In later years, Graham also increasingly warned Americans about the dangers of affluence and the smugness that prosperity fostered. In the course of a very long time on the public stage, his moral and ethical commitments traveled a very long distance.

All but the most ardent supporters understood that Graham's avocation lay in politics. Yet Curtis Evans widens the usual notion of politics as electoral events to a more expansive framing of politics as *polis*: the corporate identity of the nation. Graham sought to bring not only individuals, but also the entire nation, to Christ. This emphasis, Evans argues, "enlarged his vision [so] that it incorporated a universal call to personal and social change." Still, tensions remained. Graham's emphasis on the conversion of individuals as the only sure path to the conversion of the nation "had little to say to those who did not undergo it." More troubling, Graham seemed never to grapple with the plain fact that the most evangelical part of the nation, the South, was also the part that most stoutly resisted the civil rights acts of the 1960s and other means of legal redress of injustice. Evans's empathetic yet critical analysis draws attention to the paradoxical breadth and narrowness of Graham's vision.

In his revisionist chapter on race, Darren Dochuk moves in a different direction. He challenges the older dichotomies that portrayed Graham either as a supporter or a resister to the civil rights struggle. Instead, he argues that Graham's view of race must be calibrated to specific contexts. Dochuk points to Graham's embrace of free market economics as a key that would help unlock the iron cage of racial discrimination. For Graham, the Southwest in general, and the Houston region ("Baghdad on the Bayou") in particular, served as Exhibit A. Graham found in Houston's white and black business elites a swashbuckling style, fueled by federal funding, political leverage, and "gushing crude." They displayed exceptional philanthropic generosity, along with eagerness to throw their financial support behind his evangelistic causes. For Graham, as well as Houston business supporters and many white and black clergy, conversion of the heart, coupled with federal civil rights legislation and economic opportunity, offered the best opportunity for enduring racial progress.

Elesha Coffman's analysis of Graham's relation to the media opens the book's final section, "Culture." Graham, Coffman argues, sought not only to evangelize a nation but also to create a religious movement that would provide an enduring instrument for that purpose. For both aims, Graham needed the support of the media, and especially the secular press corps. His challenge, Coffman quips, was to figure out how to be a "George

Whitefield in an Elmer Gantry world." Graham proved acutely aware that the media possessed the power to torpedo his ministry if they successfully linked him with the fictional Gantry and real-life reprobates like him. At the same time, they also possessed the power to catalyze his ministry if they successfully linked him with his venerable eighteenth-century predecessor, Whitefield. And with few exceptions, they did. One reason was Graham's refusal to see himself as a victim of a hostile press corps. More important, Graham knew that journalists could verify his authenticity by reporting the honesty of his methods and the sincerity of his aims. And here, too, they did. Most important, at least for understanding Graham's place in the larger story of American religious history, the press could document how his work formed the "center of gravity" of evangelical Protestantism. Graham and the press together defined the evangelical tradition's boundaries.

The paradoxes that marked Graham's career grow even sharper in Seth Dowland's treatment of Graham and gender. As Dowland puts it, the preacher "subtly changed what it meant to be a 'real man' for millions of American evangelicals." In many ways Graham projected conventional images of masculinity. Movie star handsome, he knew perfectly well that women found him attractive. He kept himself athletically fit and trim. In his first visit to US troops overseas, in Korea in 1952, he revealed admiration for the rugged courage of the soldiers he visited. The list goes on. But in many other ways Graham carefully avoided the Hollywood image of a promiscuous male. He made clear, both by his words and his actions, that he had maintained absolute fidelity to his wife. In his talk to a peace conference in Moscow in 1982, he showed that true courage consisted not in swaggering militarism but in the moral strength to resist it. And most revealing was how he combined theological certitude with evolving progressivism on social issues.

Graham's wife of nearly sixty-four years, Ruth Bell Graham, described her life as "an odd kind of cross to bear." Anne Blue Wills's examination of Ruth Graham's heart, mind, and work explores some of that oddness, bringing to light the contours of her understudied life. In this chapter, Wills analyzes the "officially unofficial" public-private dynamics of their marriage, focusing on the "unique space where public and private work and family matters collide and collude." Though Ruth Graham never shirked the faithful accessory role, over time the balance shifted toward greater equality in their public roles. But then, seemingly ironically, it shifted back again. Turning to the larger cultural landscape, Wills shows how Ruth Graham's struggles to navigate the stormy waters that both divided and connected her private and the public roles represented the struggles that countless other clergy wives faced. Wills also unpacks Ruth Graham's acuteness as a lay theologian. Speaking plainly to modern audiences, she shared her "hard-won insights" about the appropriate human response to God's saving presence in Jesus Christ. Through it all, Ruth Graham presented herself as a "woman who saw God in the most ordinary places." Indeed, Billy Graham admitted—or boasted? —that some of his "best thoughts" came from her.

Marshall Frady's *Billy Graham: A Parable of American Righteousness*, published in 1979, proved to be one of the most influential biographies ever written about the evangelist. Steven Miller concludes the Culture section with an examination of Frady's "strangely angry yet perceptive" (as Anne Wills said elsewhere[18]) treatment of Graham. Frady, who prided himself on being an ex-evangelical post–civil rights Southerner, saw his fellow Southerner Graham as a holdover from the revival soaked pre–civil rights era. In Frady's mind, the preacher perpetuated the shallow un-self-critical outlook so characteristic of the white evangelical South. Graham served as "the apotheosis of the American Innocence itself," incapable of grasping the region's deep ironies and dark secrets. At the same time, Frady freely acknowledged Graham's unparalleled charisma and impeccable personal integrity. This influential biography offers Miller a venue for peeling back the multiple layers of Graham's image. It is not surprising, Miller concludes, that Graham has emerged as "America's most complicated innocent."

In the volume's Afterword, Margaret Bendroth measures the long shadow Graham cast over the religious landscape. Predictably, she finds that his public persona was "always more subtle and oblique than his strident platform rhetoric and vivid media profile seemed to imply." Like most evangelists before him, Graham's overriding goal was to win converts to Christ. But how Graham pursued that goal was another matter. Evangelicals, Bendroth urges, wanted more than an evangelist. They wanted a prophet, "someone with an intuitive grasp of the 'signs of the times.'" Graham not only produced the goods but also remained "culturally nimble enough" to stay on the stage for more than six decades. Still, Bendroth allows that figuring out where his legacy will fall is not easy. The next Billy Graham will not be a white American, but, like Graham, a person of hope, hard work, and moral integrity. That person will have to negotiate evangelicals'—or at least mainstream evangelicals'—growing distaste for confrontation, their desire for "the freedom of going off the grid, completely wireless." Where Graham's shadow will fall in this new world cannot be known, but that generation "will still be living in a world he made possible."

In the Epilogue, journalist Ken Garfield looks back, around, and ahead. What will endure? Surely the quest to touch and heal "broken souls." And the quest to "build up the church universal one altar call at a time." But the legacy will prove elusive. Graham came along at "precisely the right moment, after World War II, when American Christendom was searching for a symbol of assurance and hope." The high visibility of Graham's son Franklin, who became president of the BGEA in 2001, complicates the picture. Garfield concludes with the sobering suggestion that Americans may be "too suspicious of celebrity" of any kind to give their devotion again to any one person.

IV: *The Measure of the Man*

Billy Graham: American Pilgrim seeks to enrich our understanding of the relation between Graham and other parts of (mostly) American history. The authors pose new questions and provide fresh answers for old ones. In one way or another, all of the writers find themselves addressing the signs of change and paradox that marked Graham's career from beginning to end. But this book, like all books that are focused on a single titanic figure, runs the risk of claiming too much. So let it be said as forthrightly as possible that Graham never spoke for everyone. No one questioned his personal probity, and for a religious celebrity, that is saying a lot. Yet probably a majority of African Americans, "ethnic" minorities, Jews, fundamentalists, Catholics, mainline liberals, and secular-minded folk, among others, found him irrelevant at best or destructive at worst. He did not speak for all white evangelicals either. Many found him theologically shallow or status hungry, or both.

Nonetheless, there can be little doubt that millions of people admired him decade after decade. Moreover, the number who viewed him favorably steadily grew as the years slipped by and Graham became more irenic and inclusive. At least four reasons for his influence present themselves. First, the persistence of his appeal through wars, depressions, and technological revolutions betokened an enduring current of aspiration in Heartland America that he touched and helped to satisfy. Second, he offered a pole star of decency, a model of self-restraint in the face of extraordinary opportunities for personal enrichment, sexual conquest, and the abuse of power. Whatever their own behavior, Americans admired Graham for his. Third, Graham made it possible for believers to be Christian, American, and modern all at the same time. Pundits saw conflicts and contradictions, but Graham did not, and neither did the moms and pops who routinely tucked a ten spot into their letters of appreciation. And finally, for evangelical and non-evangelical Christians alike, he offered the promise of a second chance. If Graham served as a "public vehicle for private pain,"[19] as the historian Heather Vacek put it, he also served as a physician of the soul, showing Americans a way through to the other side.

Will there be another Billy Graham? Probably not. That answer might seem indefensibly dogmatic, not least because historians have never been good at predicting anything. But it is hard to imagine any scenario in which another Graham might arise. For one thing, another person with Graham's unique blend of looks, voice, style, stamina, charisma, integrity, sincerity, savviness, common sense, and, well, *presence* seems unlikely any time soon. More important, Graham rose at a particular time and place in American history, and addressed the concerns of that time and place in the idioms of the age. But history kept moving. By the early years of the twenty-first century, a third of Americans under the age of thirty no longer knew who Graham was, let alone why he was so important.[20]

Even so, if in some ways Graham's ministry has come and gone, his influence lingers. *Billy Graham: American Pilgrim* aims to help college and seminary students, as well as thoughtful readers everywhere, understand how a very average farm kid from the South became one of the most memorable and compelling Christian leaders of the twentieth century.

Notes

1. See Grant Wacker, *America's Pastor: Billy Graham and the Shaping of a Nation* (Cambridge, MA: Harvard University Press, 2014), 266–274, for a description of the Billy Graham Center Archives' (BGCA) collection of the letters—their extent, provenance, physical characteristics, and substantive content.

   The letters I examined are largely from "Counseling Letters" (letters sent to Graham that his assistants considered for the "My Answer" column), in Box 28, Folders 1, 2, 6, 7; Box 29, Folders 1–3; Box 30, Folder 6; Box 31, Folder 6; Box 33, Folders 3–8, all in Group I.C, Collection 575, BGCA. Other letters are from "Appreciation Notes, 1948–1950," Folder 1, Box 3, Collection 74, BGCA;

and "My Conversion Story" questionnaires, Folders 4–6, Box 20, Collection 19, BGCA. I estimate that these collections contain more—possibly far more—than five thousand letters. I read approximately five hundred, and took careful notes on 164. (It is a time-consuming process because of the difficulty of deciphering handwriting, even on carefully scribed ones.)

2. The BGCA prohibits copying or any use of the letters that might reveal the identity of their authors. For that reason, as well as my sense of an ethical obligation not to identify or quote letters that writers obviously intended for Graham or his staff—and not outside researchers—I have summarized the thrust of the letters rather than quote actual ones in the collection.

3. For documentation of most of the factual data and direct quotations in Part I of this essay, see Grant Wacker, "Billy Graham's America," *Church History: Studies in Christianity and Culture* 78, no. 3 (September 2009), 490–95; and Wacker, *America's Pastor*, 20–28. For passages in this essay that are not documented in "Billy Graham's America" or in *America's Pastor*, I have added endnotes here, as needed. See also the data about Graham's stature and influence in Grant Wacker, "Billy Graham, Christian Manliness, and the Marketing of the Evangelical Subculture," in *Religion and the Marketplace in the United States*, ed. Jan Stievermann, Philip Goff, and Detlef Junker (New York: Oxford University Press, 2015), 79–101; and Grant Wacker, "Rising in the West: Billy Graham's 1949 Los Angeles Revival," in *Turning Points in the History of American Evangelicalism*, ed. Heath W. Carter and Laura Porter (Grand Rapids, MI: Eerdmans, 2017), 226–246.

4. Graham's relationships with Kennedy and Carter were friendly but not extensive or conspicuously warm.

5. Martin E. Marty, featured speaker, "Worlds of Billy Graham Conference," Wheaton College (IL), September 28, 2013.

6. Bob Dylan, "Bob Dylan: The Uncut Interview," with Robert Love, *AARP: The Magazine*, February/March, 2015, http://www.aarp.org/entertainment/style-trends/info-2015/bob-dylan-aarp-the-magazine-full-interview.4.html.

7. In a phone conversation between Nixon and Graham one year later (February 1973), Graham briefly spoke of "two kinds of Jews"—authentic and inauthentic. When a tape of the conversation surfaced in 2009, it received differing interpretations, ranging from claims that it provided evidence of continuing anti-Semitism to the exact opposite. Interpreted however, the conversation received relatively little attention in the media and likely did not change anyone's mind about whether Graham was or was not fundamentally anti-Semitic. See my discussion in *America's Pastor*, 197–198.

8. George F. Will did not apply the "most embarrassing export" words explicitly to Graham, but the context makes clear that he had Graham in mind. Will applied the "substitutes for intelligence . . ." criticism to "some of today's clergy, on the left and the right," which included Graham.

9. For a summary of texts by and about Graham, with comments about the scope and usefulness of particular items, see Wacker, *America's Pastor*, 319–321. To the best of my knowledge, no one has yet written a full-scale bibliographical/historiographical article on the topic.

10. Billy Graham, *Just As I Am: The Autobiography of Billy Graham*, rev. ed. (New York: HarperOne, 2007), 63, 425–426, and Wacker, *America's Pastor*, 122–123.

11. Graham quoted in J. Martin Bailey, "Billy Graham in Moscow: The Media Missed the Story," *Christianity and Crisis*, June 7, 1982, 155, 173.

12. Billy Graham, "Religion, Morality, and Politics," address at the John F. Kennedy School of Government, Harvard University, April 20, 1982, quoted in "Billy Graham: Advocate for Human Rights in America," in *Billy Graham: Footprints of Conscience* (Minneapolis: World Wide Publications [BGEA], 1991), 9.

13. Elesha Coffman, "Book Shelfies as Autobiographies and Aspiration," *Religion in American History*, blog, December 19, 2013, http://usreligion.blogspot.com/2013/12/book-shelfies-as-autobiography-and.html.

14. For journalists' shifting attitudes toward Graham, see Wacker, *America's Pastor*, chap. 3; for Jews, 192–198; for Franklin Graham, 287–289. See also the chapter by Elesha Coffman and the Epilogue by Ken Garfield in this volume.

15. David Brooks, *The Road to Character* (New York: Random House, 2015), 69.

16. Graham, *Just As I Am*, 410–411, 413–414, 744–745.

17. William Martin, *A Prophet with Honor: The Billy Graham Story* (New York: William Morrow, 1991), 153.

18. Anne Blue Wills, "Billy Graham, Man of God, 1949–1954," paper presented at the American Society of Church History Winter Meeting, San Diego, CA, January 8, 2010.

19. Heather Vacek, Duke/UNC American Religion Colloquium, Chapel Hill, NC, November 18, 2008.

20. Under thirty: see data cited in Wacker, "Billy Graham's America," 511.

PART ONE

Religion

I

Professor Graham

BILLY GRAHAM'S MISSIONS TO COLLEGES AND UNIVERSITIES

Andrew Finstuen

FROM 1950 UNTIL the 1990s, Billy Graham visited colleges and universities as often as he could. He went to these institutions of higher learning with his evangelistic message of sin and salvation, but much more than evangelistic effort took place. Graham went to universities out of curiosity and in search of open, mutual understanding between his evangelism and his largely non-evangelical audiences. Facing these audiences, whether at Yale, Harvard, Stanford, or any number of state and private institutions across America and Europe, required courage and humility. Especially in the early days, he walked into auditoriums and chapels as an anti-intellectual target. He usually walked out with applause and invitations for future visits. Throughout his five decades of missions to colleges and universities, Graham operated as a centrist, evangelical bridge to institutions of higher learning, and he embodied habits of intellectual virtue.

Graham's behavior in these settings recalled attributes outlined by Aristotle in his classic *Nicomachean Ethics*. For Aristotle, moral and intellectual virtue was expressed in habits of thought, but just as importantly in habits of action. Graham was, of course, more a man of action than a man of thought. But his action, especially how he frequented universities, exemplified notions of intellectual virtue stretching from Aristotle's idea of practical wisdom, understanding, and good sense to the contemporary scholarly emphasis on humility, courage, and honesty.[1]

From this angle of vision, Graham's education and subsequent ministry unfolded as an intellectual pilgrimage marked by an increasing wisdom about what he had to say and what he had to learn. He began that journey after he left the strident, fundamentalist context of Bob Jones College and enrolled at Florida Bible Institute (FBI). Though FBI qualified him to pursue a preaching career, Graham decided for more education and Wheaton College. After Wheaton, Graham served a small church in the suburbs of Chicago before joining Youth for Christ (YFC) in 1944 as an evangelist. While with YFC, Graham considered still further education. In 1948, Charles Templeton, a friend and fellow YFC evangelist, urged Graham to enroll with him at Princeton Theological Seminary. Templeton had grown skeptical of YFC's work and thought he sensed similar reservations in Graham. Graham countered Templeton by suggesting they attend the University of Oxford. In the end, Templeton left for Princeton and Graham left YFC for his own evangelistic ministry.

During the next year, however, they stayed in touch, and their conversations turned on Templeton's critical study of the Bible and theology. In 1949, just prior to Graham's storied Los Angeles crusade, Templeton's comments shook Graham's faith. Unnerved and in search of answers, he hiked alone into the San Bernardino Mountains of California. After prayer and anguished contemplation, he emerged from the mountains with faithful certitude in the truth of the Bible and the way of Jesus Christ.[2]

With a new sense of conviction, Graham launched his career free from agonizing intellectual questions about the veracity of the Christian faith, but it was a career firmly tied to the importance of ideas and education. If the mature Graham had a résumé, it would show a clear interest in the life of the mind. Under "Employment," "evangelist" would be joined by "president, Northwestern Schools (1947–1952)." Under "Book Publications," he could list more than thirty titles. Under "Academic Activities and Interests," Graham could list his service as a trustee to both Gordon Conwell Theological Seminary (1955–1972) and Fuller Theological Seminary (1958–). He could note his cofounding of *Christianity Today* (1956), a periodical he hoped would "give theological respectability to evangelicals";[3] or highlight his involvement in two unsuccessful efforts to establish a university inspired by his work: Crusade University in 1959 and Billy Graham University in 1967. Finally, under "Lectures," Graham could chronicle dozens of visits—often multiple visits—to premier institutions such as Harvard, the University of California at Berkeley, Dartmouth, the University of Chicago, Princeton, Oxford, and Cambridge.[4]

This record of intellectual and university engagement has been absent from most treatments of Graham. It was certainly absent in the historian Richard Hofstadter's Pulitzer-prize-winning *Anti-Intellectualism in American Life* (1962), where he called Graham a key "exhibit" of anti-intellectualism.[5] For Hofstadter, Graham's evangelical anti-intellectualism emerged from an eighteenth- and nineteenth-century heritage of equality, antinomianism, and common sense philosophy. Graham had been schooled in this legacy, and such a curriculum differed from secular Enlightenment-inspired truth claims. That difference led Graham to argue, in so many words, that the Bible, not the library or universities, contained truth. Graham's evangelistic method and Hofstadter's criticism of it explain why many scholars rank Graham as a primary figure in the annals of anti-intellectualism. The prevalence of such views regarding the supposed anti-intellectualism of evangelicals led the sociologist Peter Berger to observe in 2007 that the dominant understanding of evangelicals among academics in America was "cartoonish" at best.[6]

The picture of Graham at dozens of university lecterns—including Graham at Harvard Law School in 1962, the year of Hofstadter's publication—tells a very different story about the evangelist's relationship to the life of the mind. In his memoir, *Just As I Am*, he recalled that opportunities to speak at colleges and universities "touched me most deeply." He did not elaborate on how they touched him specifically. Still, he offered that from his earliest speaking tour on campuses in 1950, which included stops at MIT, Brown, Harvard, Yale, Amherst, Vassar, Wellesley, and the University of Massachusetts, he discovered that "my appetite for more opportunities to speak in university settings had been sharpened." His readiness to address college students correlated to his recollection that they were spiritually hungry and "open to the Gospel."[7]

Graham's visits to colleges and universities joined an escalation of religious programming on campuses in the mid-twentieth century. The evangelical InterVarsity Christian Fellowship organized in America in 1941.The California businessman Bill Bright founded Campus Crusade for Christ in 1951. Bright's tract on the *Four Spiritual Laws* became the most recognizable evangelical literature among college students. That era also saw the development of the less strictly evangelical "Religious Emphasis Weeks." The likes of Paul Tillich, Reinhold Niebuhr, Martin Luther King Jr. and other post–World War II Christian leaders keynoted such events at institutions big and small, religiously affiliated and not. The Catholic television personality Bishop Fulton Sheen addressed the Harvard Law

School Forum in 1966 under the title "God and the Intellectual." Outside Christianity, Malcolm X stirred audiences in the early 1960s with his provocative intellect and devotion to the Nation of Islam at places like Harvard, the University of Wisconsin, Madison, Columbia, Berkeley, and Yale.[8]

Graham visited as many or more universities and a wider range of institutions than these other midcentury religious figures. To be sure, Martin Luther King Jr.'s and Malcolm X's dark skin and racial advocacy narrowed their opportunities in postwar America. King and Malcolm X, however, may have been less controversial on certain campuses than Graham. The Harvard Law School Forum and the Institute of Politics at Harvard's Kennedy School of Government, for example, often featured left-leaning preachers. Graham was the lone conservative preacher in the 1960s. Not until the 1980s did another conservative preacher, this time the fundamentalist Jerry Falwell, appear at the forum and the institute.[9]

At these Harvard venues and at other universities, Graham's presentations differed from his crusade appearances in two ways. First, he claimed he did not preach, but rather gave a "lecture." Second, with few exceptions, he issued no invitations for audience members to come forward and accept Christ. Instead, he often followed his "lectures" with a question and answer period with students and faculty members.

Still, these "lectures" sounded a lot like preaching. Apart from increased references to academic disciplines and intellectuals, these lecture-sermons adhered to his usual three-part structure: he highlighted the dissatisfaction of individuals and the dysfunction of society, he diagnosed these problems of individual and social life in the context of sin, and he proclaimed Jesus Christ as the answer to the meaninglessness of the age and the way out of the human mess of sin. This method underscored his insistence that he was an evangelist. As he once put it, "The Bible has been my Harvard and Yale."[10]

His interest in university dialogue became more ambitious in 1954, and he accepted an invitation to Union Theological Seminary in New York City. Union was a particularly bold move. Home to the theologians Reinhold Niebuhr and Paul Tillich, it was a bastion of neo-orthodox and liberal Protestantism. In the social hall there, he addressed a standing-room-only crowd of faculty and students and answered questions in a session following his talk. According to the professor of social ethics John Bennett, Graham, then just thirty-six years old, "received one of the greatest ovations given in recent years." Bennett, writing of the experience in *Union Seminary Quarterly Review*, asked, "How could this be?" He answered rather cynically, speculating that Graham "knows where to say what," adding that his audience was "very much relieved to find that he [Graham] was better than they had expected, or not as bad as they had feared."[11]

Bennett and his fellow liberal colleagues and students found Graham "not so bad," partly because Graham had distanced himself from his fundamentalist past. In the talk, he questioned the legitimacy of the 1950s religious revival, and he called for a "reemphasis on 'sin' in our preaching." He also raised doubts about biblical literalism and embraced ideas about church cooperation and social ministry. On biblical literalism, he confessed, "we can't understand certain parts of it [the Bible]." But there was no mistaking Jesus's unifying ministry. Graham warned that until "the intolerance to the extreme right" and "to the extreme left" abated, and until "we can gather at the cross of Christ as a common denominator, I'm afraid we'll never win the world, and we'll never make our total impact on society." He pressed the social message of Christianity further, declaring "I have no use for a fundamentalism that will take 'Ye must be born again' in one hand . . . and refuse to enter into the social problems of our day with the other hand." Even if he knew where to say what, he entered the premier liberal Protestant seminary and engaged them in a spirit of ecumenism and social ministry. His openness to aspects of Union's values raised the possibility of, at best, some common cause for conservatives and liberals and, at worst, a détente between them.[12]

Graham continued to confront skeptical audiences, first at Oxford and Cambridge in 1955 and then at Yale in 1957. At Cambridge, for example, he faced a "barrage of questions" from "academic doubters," according to the *Manchester Guardian*. The paper noted that Mr. Graham's "directness and shrewd tactics" held them at bay, and that despite Graham's smile he wryly commented, "any fool can ask a question that ten men can't answer." The *Guardian*, in a nod to Graham, concluded that "the point went home."[13]

In the early days of his San Francisco crusade of 1958, one of Graham's toughest crowds met him at St. Mark's Episcopal Church in Berkeley, California. Five hundred seminarians from six local schools (now known as the Graduate Theological Union) insisted on a private session with the evangelist, "because the seminaries do not want to be identified officially with the crusade"; moreover, organizers thought a closed session would "encourage sharp questions and blunt answers in the theological discussion." Newspaper reports confirmed the "no-holds-barred" conversation, with Graham admitting he could not answer many of the questions lobbed at him. Still, he outlined his approach to evangelism, stressing that it had to appeal to "the whole man, his intellect, emotions, and will." But, he continued, in the end, evangelism stood squarely upon the message of sin and the answer of Christ, a proclamation that transcended logic, emotionalism, and misguided worship of the Bible itself.[14]

Following the volley of skeptical questions at St. Mark's, he addressed students and faculty at San Francisco State, UC Berkeley, and Stanford. Despite initial controversy about his visit at San Francisco State and the UC Berkeley proviso that Graham could speak but, in telling language, not "'perform,'" each campus received Graham without much resistance or criticism. Between the three campuses, he spoke to over ten thousand students and faculty. All of them heard a variation on the same theme: humans created the immense problems of the world, but humans alone could not solve those same problems. At Stanford he expressed this idea sharply: "Neither scientists nor college degrees can save the world. . . . Some of our finest brains and intellects are being given to the creation of the weapons of war instead of to the weapons of peace. We don't need more Ph.D.'s but more Christ."[15]

In a 1962 tour of North Carolina colleges, Graham took a different tack and called for more education, not less. In a world threatened by communist ideology, education played a definitive role in the "struggle for the minds of men."[16] At Wake Forest, his last stop on the North Carolina tour, he argued for greater educational efforts, not as a function of anticommunist classroom warfare but as a "valid instrument of the church." He called it an "important part of the commission of Christ who said 'Go ye into all the world and preach the Gospel.'"[17] "The gospel," he continued, involved three areas: "humanitarianism, education, and evangelism."[18]

For the North Carolina journalist Virtie Stroup, such comments indicated a changed Billy Graham. In his round of university talks, Stroup reported, Graham's "down-to-earth" biblical interpretations remained, but he also drew upon a tip sheet that he carried in his Bible. It contained "'name-famous theologians' statements to supplement his own." Stroup thought this practice reflected Graham's meetings with and study of theologians, "even the difficult ones," and his desire for "mental gymnastics." For Stroup, this increasingly informed and mentally fit Graham answered reporters' questions with fewer ready and certain answers, more often saying, "I don't think a preacher should get into that," or "I don't know."[19]

Later that spring, Graham dropped his tip sheet and joined Harvard's James Luther Adams, Krister Stendahl, and Richard Niebuhr (son of H. Richard and nephew to Reinhold), for a discussion at the law school on "Evangelism and the Intellectual."[20] He began his remarks by distinguishing himself from such company: "I am not a professor; I am not an intellectual . . . and I am not a theologian." But he reminded his audience that a university "is a place to have disagreement."[21] Graham's opening statement was a savvy tactical move and an appeal to the high ideal of honesty and charity in university life.

Following his preface, and at breakneck speed, Graham outlined his view of the challenges facing America and the world. He opened with the tension between "communism and freedom," which he referred to as the problem of our age. From there he commented upon decolonization; the age of fear; the age of confused morals; the "American sex revolution;" the age of escapisms, including alcohol and drugs; the world of lost people; and the no exit attitude of the existentialists. Along the way, and to make his point about these crises, he cited the *Harvard Business Review*, famed public intellectual Walter Lippmann, novelist Ernest Hemingway, psychoanalyst Carl Jung, a few lesser-known professors of mathematics and sociology, playwright Eugene O'Neal, and existentialist philosopher Jean-Paul Sartre. Next, he quoted distinguished figures like Harvard president Dr. Nathan Pusey and Princeton Theological Seminary president John Mackay, who had voiced their concerns about the human search for meaning.[22]

For Graham, these expressions of the problems of the age—of any age really— were familiar to the Bible. They pointed to an "old word," and, he said, the "Bible calls it sin." In his view, sin turned humans every which way but toward God, and the result was the emptiness, restlessness, and lack of fulfillment that psychologists, sociologists, philosophers, and novelists pointed to in America. If the Bible had a word for these challenges, it also spoke of the answer to them in the life and death of Jesus Christ. Pilgrims on this way traveled by faith, not by intellect. Waiting for human answers and, as he put it, the "perfect intellectual panacea" promised no ultimate peace. God was no anti-intellectual, however. "God" said Graham "has given us minds and reason" to be used on the journey, but for Graham the journey would never lead anywhere without faith.[23]

The Harvard address echoed themes from prior "lectures" and foreshadowed those to come. Taking time out from his Chicago crusade that same year, Graham spoke at the University of Chicago. Unlike the sprawling Harvard address, Graham narrowed his focus to psychology. He insisted that it offered a partial diagnosis of the human condition and no answer for it. He argued that psychologists viewed the problem of humanity as a function of "a constitutional weakness running through humanity." But, he said, the "Bible calls it sin," and the cure for it "is possible only by an inner change in man."[24]

The renowned Swiss theologian Karl Barth gave Chicagoans a similar diagnosis. On his first and only visit to the United States, Barth delivered a series of lectures that overlapped with Graham's Chicago crusade. In fact, the day Graham spoke on campus, he breakfasted with Barth. A few weeks later, while Graham crusaded, Barth argued that "[p]roblems do not change—the problem is still man's existence in this world."[25] If both Barth and Graham agreed that "man" was a problem unto himself, Barth told the press that he and Graham approached the problem differently. Barth recounted his frank challenge of Graham during their breakfast, where he told the evangelist, "You point a pistol at a man's breast. I prefer a more inviting approach."[26] Still, Barth affirmed Graham, if not his method, and he publicly endorsed the crusade, as he had two years earlier during Graham's campaign in Switzerland. In the end, Barth praised Graham's simple, clear communication of an "evangelical theology" that "seeks to bring about a change in man." And though he admitted that "mass evangelism is not for me," he nevertheless noted that "the gospel can be preached in a football stadium."[27]

Graham received similar respect, even if it was staid, from several intellectuals of the era. As early as 1955, the historian Donald Meyer published an article about Graham in the leftist *New Republic*. Like Barth, he saw in Graham's message a critique of human egotism and a sharp articulation of human limitation and the tragedies of existence.[28]

These themes consumed postwar secular and Christian intellectual culture. They certainly consumed Reinhold Niebuhr. With such ideas in mind, Niebuhr alternately praised and criticized Graham in nine articles between 1955 and 1958—about one every four months. For his part, Graham spoke publically of his debt to and interest in Niebuhr at least six times, the last coming in 2005, some thirty-four years after Niebuhr's death.[29] Graham ultimately frustrated Niebuhr, but they remained linked by their shared cultural authority as interpreters of American Protestantism in the postwar era.

As one measure of that shared status, they received an invitation to appear at a Princeton forum on "Evangelism in Our Time." Graham attended, but Niebuhr did not. The forum met in December 1956 and gathered distinguished leaders of midcentury transatlantic Protestantism such as John Stott, pastor of All Soul's Church, London; John Mackay, president of Princeton Theological Seminary; Paul Lehmann, then at Harvard Divinity School; Theodore Gill, managing editor of *Christian Century*; James Jones, of Union Seminary in Richmond, Virginia; and Sidney Lovett, chaplain of Yale University.[30] Graham's inclusion among this group demonstrated his reach within left-leaning Protestant intellectual circles. Others from the Protestant left and center-left not in attendance at the forum but who expressed qualified support of Graham at key junctures in his career (even if they could also be critical) included E. G. Homrighausen, professor at Princeton Theological Seminary; Henry Pitney Van Dusen, president of Union Theological Seminary; John C. Bennett, professor at Union Theological Seminary; Krister Stendahl, professor and later dean of Harvard Divinity School; Paul Tillich, of Union Theological Seminary, Harvard Divinity School, and the University of Chicago Divinity School; Harvey Cox, of Harvard Divinity School; Will D. Campbell; and the European theologians Emil Brunner and Helmut Thielicke.[31]

In a letter to Graham in 1963, Thielicke, like Barth, expressed a view of Graham that many of his colleagues held. He wrote that he begrudgingly attended a crusade service in Los Angeles that same year. The experience changed his initial skepticism of Graham. He asked in his letter, "What is lacking in me and in my theological colleagues in the pulpit and at the university lectern, that makes Billy Graham so necessary?" After hearing Graham, he realized, "that you, my dear Dr. Graham, are passing out Biblical bread and not intellectual delicacies and refined propaganda. I wish to thank you for that." Thielicke's praise for Graham's clarity, as Barth's had been the year before, prefigured Grant Wacker's judgment that Graham "aimed to be simple but not simplistic."[32] The estimations of Barth and Thielicke suggest Graham's embodiment of the virtue of lucid communication.

Graham passed out still more "biblical bread" at university lecterns during his 1963–1964 mission to universities. The idea had been several years in the making. He first announced the idea of a targeted college campaign during his 1962 visits to the North Carolina schools. Within weeks of that declaration, he received three hundred invitations from American colleges and universities. He chose a few smaller colleges in the South, as well as the University of Michigan, Princeton, Wellesley, Harvard, and MIT.[33] Graham met with tens of thousands of students on these campuses and found that young people hungered for both the cross and the library. In these settings, he maintained his view that Christ was the answer to both their personal searching and the social problems of the day. On the whole, students received him warmly, with the exception of some Harvard undergraduates. Still, his visit to Harvard included a two-hour question and answer period on theology, poverty, and race relations. These unscripted moments were rare in Graham's career and indicated courage to undergo scrutiny by an audience far less amenable than his usual constituency.[34]

After mid-sixties stops at the Air Force Academy, University of Houston, and Oxford, Graham joined Campus Crusade efforts at Berkeley and UCLA in 1967. Initially, a small group of Berkeley students greeted him with warmth of another kind, brandishing a sign that read, "Go to Hell Billy." A much larger crowd of three to five thousand Berkeleyites, described as a mixture of "barefoot hippies, peace demonstrators, white-haired women clutching Bibles, and rows and rows of young believers,"[35] listened to Graham without incident. Six thousand or more heard him at UCLA. His theme on both campuses was again the search for meaning. Current educational practices, he told the throng of Bruins, failed searching students because they neglected education of the soul. And the consequences, he said, were grave. With customary exaggeration, Graham announced that every 1.5 hours a college student committed suicide, and he maintained that this crisis of meaning and purpose dwarfed the crisis of Vietnam. It also trumped escapism through sex or LSD. With all of this in mind, he urged students to "try a Christ trip."[36]

These Californians had definitely been on a Graham trip. According to the journalist Bill Ross of the *Oakland Tribune*, a thirteen-year veteran of Graham reporting, the evangelist's visits almost always concluded with him winning "the respect and admiration of the dubious, suspicious and hostile." Ross had seen it happen over and over, noting that "newsmen, ministers, students and others set traps with barbed questions," only to witness Graham diffuse the hostilities. After a session with faculty at Berkeley, for example, one professor noted, "His sense of humility and sincerity disarms you and then he follows it up by employing a sense of humor."[37]

From late 1967 through 1973, Graham had limited and strained contact with universities. During all but one of these years, he evangelized overseas. When he was stateside, he visited a few schools, two of which, Belmont Abby College (North Carolina) and Jacksonville University (Florida), awarded him honorary degrees. Despite these honors, Graham's campus appearances grew more controversial owing to his inconsistent position on Vietnam—sometimes hawkish, sometimes neutral—and his unflagging support of Nixon during the Watergate investigations.

The Vietnam concerns flared up at Graham's May 1970 Knoxville, Tennessee, crusade at Neyland Stadium on the University of Tennessee campus. Students and citizens were reeling from President Nixon's late April announcement about the invasion of Cambodia and the May 4 shooting deaths of four students at Kent State University in Ohio. Graham added to the charged atmosphere by bringing Nixon to address his crusade audience. That day, Tennesseans young and old protested within and outside of the stadium.[38]

Cool receptions on campuses continued into the early 1970s, most notably at Kansas State in 1974. There to deliver the prestigious Landon Lecture, he filled the arena only to half capacity. He delivered a typical address focused on the moral and spiritual crisis facing America and prescribed a "Divine answer to the national dilemma." His audience expressed a deeper ambivalence about his talk. The surest sign of his embattled situation was the criticism from ministers of Methodist, Nazarene, Presbyterian, and Southern Baptist denominations. The most critical of these came from the KSU Baptist campus minister, who said Graham had "failed to address himself to some of the crying needs and some of the critical moral and ethical issues which are a part of our society and part of our national government at this point." The half-filled seats and his half-way reception signaled Graham's diminished cultural authority both on and off campuses.[39]

He met resistance from within the evangelical fold again in 1980 at his alma mater, Wheaton College. His scheduled appearance at the dedication of his namesake library and graduate school, the Billy Graham Center, concerned faculty. Some of them worried the center would stamp Wheaton as a Bible school for, as one faculty member put it, "Bible thumpers," rather than a rigorous liberal arts college.[40] Graham's remarks echoed this tension, and he split his emphasis between his respect for education and his evangelistic concern. He praised the center as a hub for research and graduate study but warned, "God forbid" that conferences at the center "become simply intellectual exercises and social gatherings" rather than a strategy center for "spiritual warfare."[41]

Graham sought out spiritual peace, not warfare, for individuals and the international community during his second and longest university mission, in 1982. He traveled to eight New England Universities—Northeastern University, the University of Massachusetts at Amherst, Yale, MIT, Harvard, Dartmouth, Boston University, and Boston College—under the pledge for "peace in a nuclear age." This campaign theme restored some of the authority he had lost in the early seventies among students.

The promise of a peacenik Graham brought masses of students to each of his eight university stops. At Yale, they asked about his embrace of a firm antinuclear position. Graham called his stance a "pilgrimage." He spoke of visiting Auschwitz, where he realized that "a nuclear holocaust" threatened the world. Prior to that experience, Graham admitted that he had not spoken out "very forcefully" about nuclear weapons, and he decided to "take a stand with those who say 'we must do something about the arms race.'" Accordingly, Graham endorsed "Ground Zero Week," the antinuclear advocacy group Ground Zero's awareness campaign, and pressed for what he called "Salt X," the destruction of all nuclear and bio-chemical weapons.[42]

Graham's antinuclear position did not overshadow his core message of sin and salvation. Students at all campuses, especially from Northeastern and UMASS Amherst, noticed this emphasis and complained that he talked too little about the nuclear issue and too much about Christianity.[43]

Graham never promised that he would offer more or less than a twinned message of peace in a nuclear age and peace with God. At Harvard, as he had done in 1962, he emphasized his role as an evangelist called to spread the gospel. But in the twenty years since his Harvard Law School Forum visit, Graham had grown more intellectually humble and charitable. He opened, as he often did, with a self-deprecating joke. Coming to Harvard, he said, made him feel "a little like the man in my part of the country who entered a mule in the Kentucky Derby." Onlookers cackled that he couldn't possibly expect to win the race. The man replied, "No, but look at the company he'd be in." Amid the laughter, Graham reinforced the point: "And that's the way I feel." He felt that way because he had no pretension "to know all of the answers," nor had he "always seen many of the complexities that are involved in the subject that I am assigned tonight." But, he observed, "I am still learning. I'm on a pilgrimage. The more I learn the less dogmatic I become about some of them. My stance, as you know, is that of a Christian who takes the Bible seriously." Graham's feeling of infe-riority and his overt Christian perspective did not stop him from search-ing out common ground with his Harvard audience. The problem was not a difference in perspective, but "that we fail to see what each other's assumptions are, and often we do not seriously examine them."[44]

Graham's preface was masterful, honed by years of practice and engage-ment with suspicious campus audiences. It displayed an intellectually mature Graham, one who blended a conviction about what he valued most highly with humility to acknowledge when that conviction had been naive and unyielding. In that moment, he simultaneously put the discussion on his terms and their terms. He was an evangelist riding a mule in a Harvard race, but they were an audience ostensibly trained to welcome all comers to the race.

Graham interrupted his university tour for a literal pilgrimage to Russia. He suspended his campus visits to attend a Soviet-sponsored peace conference, the "World Conference of Religious Workers." His decision met with concerns from all angles. President Ronald Reagan urged Graham to stay home. Others from both the political left and right thought the Soviet propaganda machine would swallow Graham. Back home, Graham endured accusations of being "soft" on communism from both parties. Their common charge came from Graham's unwillingness to criticize his Communist hosts and from his euphemistic portrayals of religious freedom within the Soviet Union.[45] Between Graham's gaffes and his gumption to travel to Moscow was a man who had little to gain from the trip, as nearly everyone reminded him both before and after he left. Yet he modeled exactly what he had said to students: peace in a nuclear age required a willingness to engage in mutual understanding and peace with God.

Graham's pilgrimage language, his antinuclear crusade, his Soviet trip, and his increasing call for evangelical social responsibility inspired headlines chronicling a "changed" or "new" Billy Graham. The *Boston Globe* journalist James L. Franklin noted these changes but also insisted that the evangelist, in many ways, had not changed at all. What Franklin termed Graham's "faults" had stayed constant: "the tendency to drop the names of great men he has prayed with and dined with, to ingratiate himself with his audience, to see a private relationship with God as the solution to every human problem."[46]

Franklin was correct about Graham's tendency to drop names. The evangelist often cherry-picked references to intellectuals and ideas, which sounded trite and invited dismissive analyses like the one Franklin offered.[47] Franklin's other concerns, however, said more about the journalist's negative predisposition toward Graham and his message. First, Graham was plain likable—nearly everyone who ever met him came away convinced of Graham's sincerity and charisma—and he deployed his likability with the skill of a social genius.[48] Second, while he may have won people over with his personality, he was more interested in winning them to Christ. At Harvard in 1982, and at every campus before and after it, he pushed for individual decisions for Christ because his evangelical theology of history held that sinful individuals and sinful "isms" could never correct the sinful workings of society.

He returned to Harvard in 1999 as the picture of continuity and change. At the Kennedy School he reiterated the mystery of human destiny and the weakness of secular responses to answer for it. For him, the twenty-first century could not evade the threefold dilemma of human life: the problems of evil, suffering, and death. These problems had no ultimate scientific or technological answers. They could be only answered spiritually.[49] Later, at Harvard's Memorial Chapel, this firm message joined his increasing openness to peoples and traditions different from his own life and ministry. From the pulpit, he prefaced his sermon by acknowledging the openly gay but celibate Harvard chaplain, Peter Gomes, as his friend and fellow brother in Christ.[50]

Graham's connection to Gomes represents how his decades of university visits brought him together with scholars and students of various intellectual, religious, and irreligious persuasions. In these settings, he came as one concerned about ideas and with an evangelical vision of humanity and history. "Of all the ideas which shape the destinies of men," Graham preached in his "Christian Philosophy of Education" sermon in 1959, "the religious concept is basic." Religion meant "neither sectarianism nor secular dogma but the broad need for man to understand his existence and relationship to his Maker." This sermon, his visits to places like Union Theological Seminary and Berkeley, his late 1990s support of Gomes—these all testified to his increasingly centrist evangelical vision of American life.

Graham's centrist impulse and evangelical interpretation of humanity and history also connected him conceptually to a particular set of twentieth-century intellectuals: Walter Lippmann, Reinhold Niebuhr, C. S. Lewis, Hannah Arendt, Philip Rieff, Christopher Lasch, and Allan Bloom. With the possible exception of Bloom and Lewis, not one of these thinkers would have recognized any or much affinity with Graham. Graham may not have either. Still, they, like Graham, worried about a Western culture forgetful of the wisdom and virtue of the past and consumed by a too optimistic devotion to purely secular ideas of individual and social progress. For Lippmann in the 1920s, it was the fear of the void left by what he understood to be discredited Christianity, and he called for a humanistic ethos that looked very much like the "high religion" that he admired even as he criticized it. For Niebuhr, from the 1930s through the 1950s, it was the fear that Americans would pledge faith to what he called "other schemes of meaning," none of which could restrain immoral man or provide for a truly moral society. Lewis echoed Niebuhr's themes for an even broader audience. Arendt's critical stance toward Christianity, though she shared with it a grim view of human capacity for evil, was not enough to make her a friend of modernity, which she addressed, like Lippmann, as a source of alienation and emptiness. For Rieff in the 1960s, although he was also no friend of Christianity, it was the fear that "psychological man" had replaced "religious man" in postwar society, and that an ethic of entitlement rather than sacrifice prevailed. For Lasch in the 1970s and 1980s, it was not just "psychological man" but "narcissistic man" that had prevailed in America, along with a devotion to progress as an article of faith. For Bloom, also in the 1980s, it was the fear that universities and colleges had ceased educating the soul in habits of virtue. More recently, Daniel Rodgers, in his *Age of Fracture* (2011), contends that the splitting apart of America has accelerated in the past thirty years, and he concludes that the nation exists in near complete disaggregation.[51]

For Lippmann, Niebuhr, Lewis, Arendt, Rieff, Lasch, Bloom, and Rodgers, ideas and traditions mattered, providing context and direction to place and person. For them, ideas shaped how people talk, vote, eat, marry, work—in short, how they live. Graham knew this, too. His missions to colleges and universities were in fact a contest of ideas. At these universities, he articulated an evangelical theology of history and humanity, which held that sinful individuals and sinful "isms"—Marxism, Freudianism, existentialism, humanism, idealism, and so on—could not save humanity or history. But for Graham, universities prescribed just such manmade solutions for human well-being and the common good. For him, these secondary truths left students and societies groping for stable sources of meaning and purpose as they cycled through the latest psychological, social, philosophical, or political panacea.

This made Graham neither an intellectual nor an anti-intellectual nor a paradox of anti-intellectual intellectualism. Rather, Graham was an undaunted intellectual pilgrim who established and served institutions of higher learning, founded the gold-standard periodical for evangelical thought, and journeyed to college campuses with a serious message about history and humanity. He did it all with native powers of social, emotional, and cognitive intelligence—a rare and potent combination that increased through the years. He almost never "lost" a college audience, whether they were predisposed to him or not. He made it look easy to, as Grant Wacker has written, "step into the ring anytime, anyplace." Few public figures have shown such steely resolve in the face of skeptical, even hostile, audiences.

Less known for his intellect and sometimes targeted as a simpleton, Graham often displayed a sharp wit and quick intelligence when he spoke off the cuff or during question and answer periods. His exceptional combination of skills and activities contributed to the most impressive and lasting intersection of evangelicalism and the life of the mind in American history.[52]

Graham's success may indeed have been a function of John Bennett's reaction in 1954. Graham knew where to say what. But he also knew how to say it and why he said it. He was an evangelist who "lectured" that secular ideas about life failed where a way of life in Jesus Christ succeeded. He took that message to a broad range of universities, and he delivered it by practicing the core intellectual virtues of courage, honesty, and humility. It took courage to risk looking the fool in front of academic audiences, honesty to cultivate mutual understanding with them, and humility to return to them for more.

Notes

1. Aristotle, *Nichomachean Ethics*, trans. Martin Ostwald (New York: Macmillan), 146–173; Jason Baehr, *The Inquiring Mind: On Intellectual Virtues and Virtue Epistemology* (New York: Oxford University Press, 2011), 4–5, chap. 2. Baehr directs the Intellectual Virtues and Education Project at Loyola Marymount University.

2. William Martin, *A Prophet with Honor: The Billy Graham Story* (New York: William Morrow, 1991), 111–112.

3. Martin, *Prophet with Honor*, 211; Mark Toulouse, "*Christianity Today* and American Public Life: A Case Study," *Journal of Church and State* 35, no. 2 (1993): 241.

4. These features of Graham's career led the historian Mark Noll to conclude that Graham was an evangelical "imprimatur for serious intellectual labor." See *The Scandal of the Evangelical Mind* (Grand Rapids, MI: Wm. B. Eerdmans, 1994), 214.

5. Billy Graham, "Evangelism and the Intellectual" (presentation at Harvard Law School Forum, Cambridge, MA, March 26, 1962); Richard Hofstadter, *Anti-intellectualism in American Life* (New York: Vintage Books, 1962), 15.

6. Hofstadter, *Anti-intellectualism in American Life*, 44–51; William G. McLoughlin, *Revivals, Awakenings, and Reform* (Chicago: University of Chicago Press, 1978), 187–191; Others within the evangelical movement, like Francis Schaefer, regarded Graham as anti-intellectual. See Patrick Allitt, *Religion in America since 1945: A History* (New York: Columbia University Press, 2003), 157. For an extremely negative view, see Christopher Hitchens, "The God Squad," *The Nation*, April 15, 2002, http://www.thenation.com/issue/april-15-2002; On Berger, see, John Seel, "The Opening of the Evangelical Mind: An Interview with Dr. Timothy Shah," *Comment*, May 16, 2008, http://www.cardus.ca/comment/article/38/the-opening-of-the-evangelical-mind-an-interview-with-dr-timothy-shah/.

7. Billy Graham, *Just As I Am: The Autobiography of Billy Graham* (New York: HarperCollins, 1997), 165.

8. For a selection of Malcolm X's speeches, see http://malcolmxfiles.blogspot.com/p/malcolm-x-speeches_9918.html.

9. See Harvard Law School Forum's archive of events at https://orgs.law.harvard.edu/hlsforum/events/; see Harvard's Institute of Politics archive of events at http://iop.harvard.edu/forum/past?f[o]=im_field_s_tr_sitewidetags%3A180.

10. "Billy Graham—The Man Everyone Knows," *The Florence Times—The Tri Cities Daily*, June 13, 1965, http://news.google.com/newspapers?nid=1842&dat=1965 0613&id=2CcsAAAAIBAJ&sjid=vscEAAAAIBAJ&pg=2648,6030299.

11. John Bennett, "Billy Graham at Union," *Union Seminary Quarterly Review*, May 1954, 9–14.

12. Billy Graham, "Lecture by Evangelist Billy Graham," unpublished manuscript, special collections, Emmaus Bible College, Dubuque, Iowa, 4, 7, 9.

13. *The Guardian* quotations appear in "Graham's Reception is Remarkable," *Ashville Citizen*, November 20, 1955, Collection 360, Reel 8, Billy Graham Center Archives (hereafter BGCA).

14. "Graham Addresses Future Pastors at Seminary," *San Rafael Independent Journal*, April 30, 1958, Reel 8, Collection 360, BGCA; Nate Hale, "Graham Meets 500 Seminary Students," *San Francisco Chronicle*, May 1, 1958, Collection 360, Reel 8, BGCA.

15. "Graham Chides Church Failings," May 19, 1958, Reel 8, Collection 360, BGCA; 1,050 Hear Billy Graham Talk at S.F. State College," *San Francisco Examiner*, May 21, 1958, Reel 8, Collection 360, BGCA; "Billy Graham Addresses 7,500 at U.C.," *San Francisco Examiner*, May 24, 1958, Reel 8, Collection 360, BGCA.

16. "Graham Says Emphasis to Shift to Colleges," *Baptist Standard*, March 28, 1962, Reel 28, Collection 360, BGCA; see also, "College Campus is 'Crucial' Area," *Greensboro Record*, March 15, 1962, Reel 28, Collection 360, BGCA.

17. "Graham Wants to Read New Novel," *Winston-Salem Journal*, March 22, 1962, Reel 28, Collection 360, BGCA.

18. Joe Hawley, "Graham Tells Students to Commit Themselves," March 25, 1962, Reel 28, Collection 360, BGCA.

19. "Virtie Stroup, "A Changed Billy Graham Is Evident from Talks," *Winston-Salem Journal and Sentinel*, March 25, 1962, Reel 28, Collection 360, BGCA.

20. Harold John Ockenga also participated.

21. Billy Graham, "Evangelism and the Intellectual," (lecture at the Harvard Law School Forum, Cambridge, MA, March 26, 1962).

22. Ibid.

23. Ibid.

24. "Sin Creates Its Own Hell Graham Tells U. of C. Group," undated, Collection 360, Reel 28, BGCA.

25. "Theologian Talks on Billy Graham," May 15, 1962, Reel 28, Collection 360, BGCA.

26. Adon Taft, "Billy: Bibles, Barth," *Boston Herald*, undated, Reel 28, Collection 360, BGCA; "Theologian Talks on Billy Graham," May 15, 1962, Reel 28, Collection 360, BGCA.

27. "Clergyman Servants, Not Lords, Says Barth," April 20, 1962, Reel 28, Collection 360, BGCA. See also, Grant Wacker, *America's Pastor: Billy Graham and the Shaping of a Nation* (Cambridge, MA: Harvard University Press, 2014), 55.

28. Donald Meyer, "Billy Graham—and Success," *New Republic*, August 22, 1955, 8–10.

29. Martin, *Prophet with Honor*, 228, 229; John Pollock, *Billy Graham: Evangelist to the World* (San Francisco, Harper & Row, 1979), 157; Paul Hendrickson, "Billy Graham: Preacher's Progress," *Washington Post*, April 28, 1986, B1; Graham, *Just As I Am*, 135; "The Words of a Preacher: Billy Graham on His Life, the Pope's Death and Politics in Religion," *New York Times*, June 12, 2005, 1.34.

30. Billy Graham, "Four Great Crises," *Hour of Decision* radio program (Minneapolis: Billy Graham Evangelistic Association, 1957), Box 2, Folder 8, Collection 191, BGCA. Kenneth Henke, archivist at Princeton Theological Seminary, confirmed this meeting and its attendees. The collection regarding this event is closed.

31. Andrew Finstuen, "The Prophet and the Evangelist: The Public 'Conversation' of Reinhold Niebuhr and Billy Graham," *Books & Culture*, July/August 2006, 8–9, 37; Andrew Finstuen, *Original Sin and Everyday Protestants*, chap. 2; Frye Gaillard, "Billy Graham Took Hard Road to Social Activism," *Charlotte Observer*, April 25, 1982, Reel 38, Collection 360, BGCA.

32. L. David Cowie, "Apostolic Preaching in Los Angeles," *Christianity Today*, October 25, 1963, 42–43; Wacker, *America's Pastor*, 62.

33. "College Campus is 'Crucial' Area," *Greensboro Record*, March 15, 1962, Reel 28, Collection 360, BGCA; "Graham Says Emphasis to Shift to Colleges," *Baptist Standard*, March 28, 1962, Reel 28, Collection 360, BGCA; Graham, *Just As I Am*, 422.

34. Eugene Gauger, "Billy Graham's Message Unaltered," *Toledo Blade*, February 15, 1964, Reel 29, Collection 360, BGCA; Donald E. Graham, "Billy Graham Discusses College Students, Race," *Harvard Crimson*, February 17, 1964, http://www.thecrimson.com/article/1964/2/17/billy-graham-discusses-college-students-race/0; Donald E. Graham, "Billy Graham," *Harvard Crimson*, February 20, 1964, http://www.thecrimson.com/article/1964/2/20/billy-graham-pwhy-have-you-come/0.

35. Sara Davidson, "Billy Graham Hands Berkeley a Challenge," January 28, 1967, Reel 31, Collection 360, BGCA.

36. Anne Morgenthaler, " 'Try Christ,' Graham Urges Bruins," January 21, 1967, Reel 31, Collection 360, BGCA; "9,000 Hear Billy Graham Speak at Greek Theater,"

January 28, 1967, Reel 31, Collection 360, BGCA; "Graham: Why Not Christ?" January 30, 1967, Reel 31, Collection 360, BGCA.

37. Bill Ross, "Crusade of Evangelist Graham at U.C. a Success," *Oakland Tribune*, January 29, 1967, Reel 31, Collection 360, BGCA.

38. John Shearer, "Anti-war Protests, Graham's Crusade, Nixon's Visit to Knox All in May 1970," *Knoxville News Sentinel*, May 7, 2010, http://www.knoxnews.com/news/local-news/a-month-to-remember.

39. "Feelings Mixed on Graham Lecture," March 4, 1974, Reel 35, Collection 360, BGCA; see also "Students, Faculty, Guests Dig Disciple," *The Mercury*, March 4, 1974, Reel 35, Collection 360, BGCA; Bill Colvin, "Sidestepping Evangelist Avoids Political Topics," *The Mercury*, March 4, 1974, Reel 35, Collection 360, BGCA.

40. David Smothers, "Billy Graham to Dedicate Center Named for Him," *The Telegraph*, September 11, 1980, http://news.google.com/newspapers? nid=2209&dat=19800911&id=26ArAAAAIBAJ&sjid=b_wFAAAAIBAJ&pg=7145,2258552.

41. "Billy Graham's Dedication Message," BGCA, CN 003 V1, http://www2.wheaton.edu/bgc/archives/BGCdedication.htm.

42. Martin, *Prophet with Honor*, 500–501; "Graham Sees Need for SALT 10 Treaty," April 16, 1982, Reel 38, Collection 360, BGCA.

43. Frye Gaillard, "Billy Graham Opens His Crusade for Disarmament," April 16, 1982, Reel 38, Collection 360, BGCA; "Ivy League Warms to Billy Graham, His New Mission," Reel 38, Collection 360, BGCA; Dudley Clendinen, "Evangelism vs. 'the Bomb,'" *New York Times*, April 16, 1982, Reel 38, Collection 360, BGCA.

44. Billy Graham, "Religion, Morality, and Politics," V 660, Collection 113, BGCA.

45. James M. Johnston, "Reagan Plea Won't Halt Graham USSR Trip," *Milwaukee Journal Sentinel*, April 24, 1982, Collection 360, BGCA; David Aikman, *Billy Graham: His Life and Influence* (Nashville, TN: Thomas Nelson, 2007) 159–166.

46. "Graham's New Message," Reel 38, Collection 360, BGCA; "Evangelism: A New Style," Reel 38, Collection 360, BGCA; James L. Franklin, "Billy Graham is Changing with the Times," *Boston Globe*, June 8, 1982, Reel 38, Collection 360, BGCA.

47. For example, at Oxford University in 1980, Graham cited Solzhenitsyn's *One Day in the Life of Ivan Denisovich* but he stumbled at "Denisovich," and moved on without pronouncing it. This gaffe elicited derisive chuckles. See T3485, Collection 26, BGCA. Decades earlier, during his "Evangelism and the Intellectual" address at Harvard, he pronounced Kierkegaard correctly but invited sarcasm from the *Harvard Crimson* for citing both the melancholy Dane's *Sickness unto Death* and the *Reader's Digest* in the same talk. J. Michael Crichton, "Graham Seeks Peace in Spiritual Revolution," *Harvard Crimson*, March 27, 1962, Reel 28, Collection 360, BGCA; "Personal Comtm't," March 27, 1962, Reel 28, Collection 360, BGCA.

48. Wacker, *America's Pastor*, 296.

49. Billy Graham, "Is God Relevant for the 21st Century" (lecture presented at the Kennedy School's Institute of Politics, Harvard University, Cambridge, MA,

September 27, 1999), Collection 265, BGCA; Billy Graham, "Christian Philosophy of Education," *Hour of Decision* radio program (Minneapolis: The Billy Graham Evangelistic Association, 1959), Box 2, Folder 6, Collection 191, BGCA.

50. http://www.huffingtonpost.com/michael-g-long/peter-gomes-and-billy-graham-a-holy-love_b_2211828.html

51. See, for example, Walter Lippmann, *A Preface to Morals* (New Brunswick, NJ: Transaction, 1982); Reinhold Niebuhr, *Faith and History* (New York: Charles Scribner's Sons, 1951); C. S. Lewis, *The Screwtape Letters* (New York: HarperOne, 2001); Hannah Arendt, *The Human Condition* (Chicago: University of Chicago Press, 1958); Philip Rieff, *The Triumph of the Therapeutic: Uses of Faith after Freud* (New York: Harper & Row, 1966); Christopher Lasch, *The True and Only Heaven: Progress and Its Critics* (New York: W. W. Norton, 1991); Allan Bloom, *The Closing of the American Mind* (New York: Simon & Schuster, 1987); Daniel Rodgers, *The Age of Fracture* (Cambridge, MA: Harvard University Press, 2011). Useful surveys of the intellectual climate that Graham tapped into, even if he did so with less depth, include Richard H. Pells, *The Liberal Mind in a Conservative Age: American Intellectuals in the 1940s and 1950s* (Middletown, CT: Wesleyan University Press, 1985); George Cotkin, *Existential America* (Baltimore, MD: Johns Hopkins University Press, 2003); Mark Grief, *The Age of the Crisis of Man: Thought and Fiction in America, 1933–1973* (Princeton, NJ: Princeton University Press, 2015).

52. Mark Noll, *The Scandal of the Evangelical Mind* (Grand Rapids, MI: W.B. Eerdmans), 214.

2

From Desire to Decision

THE EVANGELISTIC PREACHING OF BILLY GRAHAM

Michael S. Hamilton

Deciding for Christ

In the fall of 1958, Billy Graham returned to his hometown, Charlotte, North Carolina, for a five-week crusade. He was just thirty-nine years old, but he already had ten years' experience preaching around the world to the largest crowds ever to hear an evangelist. By the time of the Charlotte crusade, he knew exactly what to do at the end of his half-hour sermon. With the organ softly playing the hymn "Just As I Am," he closed with these words:

> I'm going to ask all of you in this building to get up out of your seat right now. ... And say tonight, "I want Christ. ... I want him to fill my life. I want him to help solve my problems and forgive my sins and lift my burdens. I want him to come in and be closer than a brother. I want him to come in and help me and forgive me and cleanse me. ..." I'm going to ask you to come right now. ... Now you come, quickly.[1]

Nearly a half-century later, an eighty-seven-year-old Graham was in Baltimore where he gave one of his last public sermons. With the piano softly playing "Just As I Am," he ended by saying,

I'm going to ask you to do something that we've seen thousands of
people do in different parts of the world. I'm going to ask you to say,
"I do want my life to change. I want to be certain that if I die I'll go
to heaven." I'm going to ask you to come and make this decision.
Make certain that you know Christ as your Lord and Savior. You may
want to rededicate your life. You come.[2]

Thus, Billy Graham concluded his sermons with more or less the same
words for more than sixty years. He invited his listeners to get out of their
seats and come forward to show that they had made a decision for Christ.

And come forward they did. From the very beginning of his preaching, people responded to his invitation in far greater numbers than
anyone expected. The very first time he ever gave an invitation he was
a "boy preacher" in a little storefront church. Nearly a third of the one
hundred people there came forward.[3] A few years later Graham was one
of several staff evangelists for Youth for Christ. Fellow evangelist Chuck
Templeton noted that night after night, Graham "got more results than
anybody." Everyone in Youth for Christ thought that Templeton was the
better preacher, but when he and Graham preached on consecutive nights
in the same circumstances, Graham won the bigger response. "I would
get seventeen," Templeton recalled, and "he would get twenty-three, or
I would get two hundred and he would get three hundred."[4]

This is the puzzle of Billy Graham's preaching. Why did so many
people in so many times and places get out of their seats and come forward? Not even the biographer William Martin was able to figure it out.
"The reasons," he concluded, "defy facile explanation."[5] No one, including Graham's wife, ever rated him a great preacher. Critics often ridiculed
his exaggerations—"seventy-five percent of all movies are immoral"—and
his oversimplifications—the rise of the Soviet Union was "masterminded
by Satan himself."[6] After Graham's 1950 crusade in Portland, Oregon,
Christian Century magazine struggled to understand how such "imma-
ture" homiletics could prove so compelling to an audience.[7] And nearly
everyone, including Graham himself, observed that his sermons had an
unmistakable sameness to them. Yet, at the end of every sermon, people
streamed forward anyway. Why?

Graham's sermons over time suggest a pattern. Though the destina-
tion was a decision, the road was desire. Consider the first two paragraphs
of this essay. Notice that in both those invitations Graham gave his listeners a script for a dialogue they should initiate with God. Notice especially

how every sentence of the dialogue began with the words, "I want." People may not have known exactly why they came to the crusade, but Graham did. They came hoping for help with some kind of problem in their lives. The purpose of his sermon was to get them see that they wanted help and wanted change. His method was to awaken desires that his listeners brought with them to the crusades, either by rousing slumbering desires or sharpening desires already astir. Having awakened desire, he would then channel it toward the only thing that would satisfy it—a decision to begin a new life in Christ.

This formula was nothing new. It had been discovered two centuries earlier by one of America's greatest theologians, Jonathan Edwards. This essay begins with a look back at what Edwards learned about the role of desire in bringing people to Christian faith and how that helps us understand Graham's preaching. It then discusses two dimensions of the context in which Graham's sermons took place—the evangelist's legendary humility and sincerity, and the crusade as a special religious ritual. The essay then concludes with the climax of the crusade ritual—the sermon—and looks at exactly how it led individuals to focus on their personal needs and how it awakened and intensified their desire for change in their lives.

Awakening Desire

Back in the 1740s, the Puritan theologian Jonathan Edwards was trying to understand the revivals of religion that had happened under his own preaching and under that of the evangelist George Whitefield. After much experience and thoughtful analysis, the sharply analytic Edwards concluded that emotions—in those years called "the affections"—lie at the heart of true religion. The emotions, he wrote, are "the spring of men's motion and actions" in all matters, worldly and religious. The emotions motivate our actions by awakening and uniting our understanding and our will. One of the most important emotions is desire, and Edwards cited numerous Bible passages to demonstrate that the desire to know and live for God is the foundation of true Christian faith. He therefore reasoned that all religious practices—preaching, singing, worship, and sacramental rituals—ought to appeal to the emotions, especially the emotion of desire.[8]

In recent years, evangelical writers have given new attention to the role of desire in Christian life. The philosopher James K. A. Smith's 2009 book *Desiring the Kingdom* tries to move the focus of Christian education away from a preoccupation with the mind and toward inclusion of the heart.

"We are essentially and ultimately desiring animals," Smith argues. What we desire defines who we are and "what we worship." Writing a couple of decades before Smith, the Baptist preacher John Piper rose to popularity with a book called *Desiring God*. The book borrowed heavily from Edwards to say that people come to Christ not through thoughts or ideas but through their desires, which he described as the things people crave. Piper argued that evangelism should not persuade people to make decisions for Christ; it should lead them to desire Christ.[9]

Piper likely had Billy Graham in mind when he criticized evangelism that aimed at decisions. After all, *decision* was Graham's well-known tagline. Graham's sermons urged listeners to make a decision. He named his magazine *Decision*. His radio program was called *Hour of Decision*. He often described his own conversion as a simple decision, free of emotion.

But Graham had good reasons for emphasizing decision. When he was starting out as an evangelist in the 1940s, mass revivalism had endured two decades of hard times. In the 1920s the decline of the bigger-than-life Billy Sunday and the advent of the fictional but all-too-believable Elmer Gantry had made many Americans skeptical about evangelists. So in November 1948, during a crusade in Modesto, California, Graham called his team together and asked them to come up with a list of the ways evangelists damaged their own reputations. They immediately thought of the obvious personal sins that might bring down any religious leader—financial irregularity and sexual impurity—but they also thought carefully about problems particular to mass evangelism. One was inflating success, so they chose to call those who came forward at the end of the sermon *inquirers* rather than *converts*. They also determined to keep careful counts of attendance and inquirers, rely on outside counts whenever possible, and report only conservative estimates to the press. Another problem was the perception that people came forward solely because the evangelist had whipped them into an emotional frenzy. So Graham and his team resolved to limit emotionalism in their services. To put further distance between what they were doing and the taint of emotional manipulation, they adopted the term *decision* to describe the commitment people were making when they gave their lives to Christ. A decision did not exclude emotion, but it did emphasize that coming forward was a calm, rational, and considered choice.[10]

Despite downplaying emotion, Graham continued to be hit with the charge that he was manipulating people's feelings to get them out of their seats. Whenever a Graham crusade arrived in a new city, the newspapers asked local ministers to comment. In the mid-1950s ministers frequently criticized Graham for using mass psychology and religious emotionalism. Graham became so sensitive about this that he often mentioned it when he met with the press. In 1954 he promised that there would be no "mouth-foaming hysterical emotionalism" at his upcoming three-month crusade in London. At the end of one sermon in Manchester, England, in 1961 he abruptly stopped and said, "I have been criticized for emotional appeal, for choirs singing softly and for artificially urging people to come forward. Tonight the choir will not sing. I will just say, 'Come forward.'" And they did—twelve hundred people, much to the surprise of skeptical onlookers.[11]

Despite his disclaimers, Graham actually had mixed feelings about emotional appeals. He knew that the main obstacle an evangelist faces is complacency, and that there is no better solvent for complacency than strong emotion. His ambivalence about emotion was never on better display than in a sermon he gave at the 1965 Houston crusade. He told the Bible story of the Philippian jailer who was so terrified by an earthquake that he threw himself at the feet of Paul and Silas, asking what he must do to be saved. Graham acknowledged that this was an emotion-driven conversion, and he praised it. The church, he said, needs more emotion:

> I know that in this type of evangelistic services one of the accusations . . . is, "It's too emotional," and we have leaned over backwards not to have any emotion. . . . But I believe we have made a mistake. I believe we need to feel our faith in Christ.

He then praised the emotional conversions of John Newton and Martin Luther, both occasioned by intense fear in the middle of a major thunderstorm.

But as Graham continued his sermon he was soon urging his listeners to *ignore* their emotions:

> As you go through this world with all its storms and its trials. . . . keep your eyes on the Bible, keep your eyes on Christ, and you won't go wrong. Don't you follow your feelings. You follow Christ.[12]

By the end of the sermon, however, he finally found his way back to a more balanced position. He said that belief in Christ requires commitment, and

[c]ommitment involves the mind, the emotions and the will—the whole man is involved when you come to Jesus Christ. . . . My mind says he must be the Son of God. My emotions watch him on the cross dying and suffering and bleeding . . . and I say . . . I could follow a man like that. But I'm not really saved, I'm not going to heaven until my will makes the final decision.[13]

Late in life Graham revised his own conversion narrative along similar lines. For most of his adulthood he described his conversion like this:

I didn't have any tears, I didn't have any emotion, I didn't hear any thunder, there was no lightning . . . I didn't feel all worked up. But right there, I made my decision for Christ. It was as simple as that.[14]

But in his 1997 autobiography he described it more holistically:

Intellectually, I accepted Christ to the extent that I acknowledged what I knew about Him to be true. That was mental assent. Emotionally, I felt that I wanted to love Him in return for His loving me. But the final issue was whether I would turn myself over to His rule in my life. . . . That was the moment I made my real commitment to Jesus Christ. . . . I simply felt at peace.[15]

Graham was never enough of a systematic thinker to articulate exactly how he understood the role of emotion in Christian faith, but his functional model of conversion involved a person's understanding, emotion, and will all working in concert. His framework of how one comes to faith was, in fact, not so different from that of Jonathan Edwards.[16]

Crusade Context: The Evangelist's Character

Graham knew that before those in his audience would make a decision for Christ they had to desire a new life in Christ, and this meant he had to engage their emotions. He also knew that some emotions were trustworthy and some were not. Why should people trust the emotional response they felt when listening to his sermons? Jonathan Edwards asked this same question. He was fully aware that there were both "false affections" and "holy affections." How do we tell the difference? Gracious and holy affections, observed Edwards, "are broken hearted affections." Godly desires "are humble desires." Reliable indicators of holy emotion are "lowliness of mind" and "lowliness of behavior." It is out of a humble heart, said Edwards, "that all truly holy affections do flow."[17]

This is where Billy Graham's legendary humility and sincerity, as the context for his tone of authority when preaching, help explain his impact on listeners. Graham was as famous as anyone on the planet, but in the clamorous world of celebrities and would-be celebrities, his genuineness and humility set him apart. At the last crusade of Graham's career, in New York in 2005, a twenty-three-year-old man explained to a reporter that "Billy Graham has lasted so long because he seems to be true. He's a soft-spoken man. In days when everything is so loud and biased, he talks to people in a loving way."[18] Graham's humility made him trustworthy, and when audiences trusted the man, they trusted the words he said and the emotions they felt. This trust fused the inquirer's reason and emotion. Any emotion sparked by the preaching of a man this humble and this sincere was surely a holy emotion pointing toward God.

Crusade Context: A Special Religious Ritual

Graham rode to fame on the back of mass meetings. He was a featured speaker at youth rallies in the middle and late 1940s that drew as many as 65,000 people. Soon he began organizing his own large meetings, coming to national attention in 1949 through an eight-week crusade in Los Angeles that drew 350,000 people and saw 3,000 answer the evangelist's invitation to come forward. Outside critics, certain that Graham's early crusades were the death rattle of the old revivalism, were appalled at the spectacle. "Seduction," complained the British journalist Alistair Cooke. "A show," dismissed the British novelist J. B. Priestley. The "engineering of mass consent" carped the American historian William McLoughlin. The liberal *Christian Century* editorialized that Graham would "set back Protestant Christianity a half century."[19]

But spectacle was precisely the point. Each Graham crusade originated with an invitation from hundreds of churches in a local area. A ceremonial oversight committee of prominent and wealthy notables was appointed. A team from Graham's organization moved to the city up to two years in advance to set up local work committees. These committees recruited thousands of volunteers, set up thousands of prayer groups, and distributed hundreds of thousands of packets of promotional materials and hundreds of thousands more personal invitations. Many thousands more volunteers were organized into counseling groups, evangelistic training programs, and special ministry teams. Each of these steps was accompanied by steady publicity in newspapers, magazines, radio, television, billboards, and, later, the Internet. After months of preparation, when the crusade finally opened, people streamed to the stadium in buses, trains, and cars from throughout the region. The several days of the crusade were conducted in a festival atmosphere—banners, flowers, a massed choir of thousands of voices, bright lights, popular singers and bands, symphony orchestras, celebrity guest speakers, local and national politicians, concession stands, television cameras, wandering reporters, special services for children. "It's like a sporting event," said a Graham staffer. "You can buy a hot dog, and you don't have to wear a coat and tie."[20]

Scholars of comparative religion have found that all religions need special rituals that give the believers a sense that they are changed. Regular rituals are those that a person repeats daily, weekly, monthly, or annually. In Christianity, communion is an example of a regular ritual. In contrast to this, a person usually undergoes a given special ritual only once in a lifetime. Baptism is a common special ritual in Christianity. Special rituals are stimulating events with high levels of sensory pageantry. They are often rites of passage that single out an individual or a small group of individuals, whose ritual is attended by an audience of those who have gone, or will go, through it themselves. Special rituals are costly to participate in, whether the cost is physical, economic, or psychological. A person comes out of a special ritual with a new self-understanding that shapes their identity from that day forward.[21]

Compared to other world religions, evangelicalism is relatively barren of ritual. It is not unusual for people to convert from evangelicalism to other forms of Christianity because of this barrenness. This is why Thomas Howard, a member of one of evangelicalism's most prominent families, famously converted to Catholicism in the 1980s. In evangelicalism, he explained, worship is little more than a "meeting" where people are "sitting in pews and listening to words."[22] But a Billy Graham crusade was a grand exception. Its pageantry and spectacle contrasted sharply with normal evangelical worship and heightened the expectation that something momentous was about to happen.

Critics often pointed out—and the Graham organization acknowledged—that most people who attended the crusades were churchgoing Christians. Only about 4 percent of every audience were *inquirers*—those who came forward to register a decision for Christ. Among the inquirers, only one-third were certain that they were *not* Christians before they came forward. Only half of all inquirers were making what they considered to be a first-time decision for Christ. The other half came forward to renew their faith in Christ and recommit to a Christian life.[23]

But understanding a crusade as a special ritual diminishes the significance of these distinctions. A person passing from the realm of nonbelief to belief needs the ritual participation of believers. A person passing from the realm of the unchurched to the churched needs churchgoers present to affirm the reality and meaning of the transition taking place. And since the goal of a special ritual is to effect a dramatic and long-lasting change in one's life, it is not terribly important if the change is a first-time dedication or a rededication. For most people, a Graham crusade came to their city only once or twice in their lifetimes. This heightened the significance of any given crusade for any given person. What better occasion to turn one's life in a new direction?

Crusade Climax: The Sermon

Special religious rituals do more than give someone a sense of personal change. They also promote an image of what the universe is like, how it works, and how everyone fits into it. In evangelical terms, a special ritual conveys an image of one's relationship to God and the consequences for one's life.[24] This image is conveyed in the climax of the crusade ritual: Billy Graham's sermon.

Some things about Graham's sermons changed over time. As he moved into middle age, he no longer preached in the loud rapid-fire style that gave him the nickname "God's machine gun."[25] He stopped painting vivid word pictures of sinners standing before the judgment throne: "All those things that you covered up and hid as secret . . . are going to be brought to life . . . and you'll stand there with perspiration dripping down your cheeks and with your eyes rolling in fear."[26] He also quit doing dramatic re-enactments of Bible stories, like this one described by a Boston reporter in 1950:

> [Graham] prowls like a panther across the rostrum. . . . He becomes a haughty and sneering Roman, his head flies back arrogantly and his voice is harsh and gruff. He becomes a penitent sinner; his head bows, his eyes roll up in supplication, his voice cracks and quavers. He becomes an avenging angel; his arms rise high above his head

and his long fingers snap out like talons. His voice deepens and rolls sonorously—the voice of doom.[27]

In his early years Graham imitated Billy Sunday and countless other revivalists in the way they characterized whatever city they happened to be in as a sink-pit of corruption. Graham greeted Angelinos in 1949 by telling them that their city "is known around the world because of its sin, crime and immorality. . . . Demon power is felt as you walk down the streets." In 1950 he told Bostonians that Satan had the upper hand in their city, but if they joined together with Graham "the Devil can be run out of Boston."[28] Over the next few years, however, he dropped the condemnations, instead greeting his host cities with positive encouragement and praise that, given his hyperbolic style, often crossed over into flattery. In 1965 he told Houston, "The eyes of the world are on Texas as never before in your history" because of "your glorious history, fabulous wealth, and booming industry." Therefore you "have great responsibility to the world." A "spiritual awakening in Texas could have a profound impact not only on the nation but throughout the world."[29]

Americans have always been fond of thinking that their nation is exceptional. Graham believed the Puritan version of this idea, which holds that God has specially chosen America to bring Christianity, democracy, and freedom to the rest of the world. His early preaching, therefore, often had strong nationalistic tones. In some of his sermons he seemed to reduce the gospel to little more than a servant of national purposes. An early example is "America's Hope," which was published in his first book, *Calling Youth to Christ*. The sermon's prologue declared that "millions throughout the world are looking to America today for leadership, materially, economically, socially, and spiritually. The eyes of the world are on America!" It concluded by saying, "To safeguard our democracy and preserve the true American way of life, we need, we must have, a revival of genuine old-fashioned Christianity." But as Graham traveled and preached around the world he became noticeably less nationalistic and parochial. The problem of American-themed sermons for an evangelist with international aspirations showed up immediately. When he published a British edition of the book, he realized just how inappropriate the sermon was. So he retitled it "The Nation's Hope," eliminated nearly all the prologue, and in the conclusion changed "the true American way of life" to "the better way of life." He continued for many years to preach sermons featuring America as God's chosen nation, but only to American audiences. And even these gradually declined, so that by the 1980s the nationalistic themes appeared only on rare occasions.[30]

Graham's early preaching often reflected the dispensational premillennialism he had learned from his mother.[31] This was the view that biblical prophecy testifies that God has an undisclosed but definite timetable for the return of Christ and the final judgment and destruction. A key feature of the timetable is that natural disasters and social chaos will accelerate as Christ's return draws near. But as time went on, Graham amalgamated his dispensationalism with the older tradition of the Puritan jeremiad, where God blesses a nation for obedience or punishes it for disobedience. In dispensationalism, judgment and destruction are inevitable; in the jeremiad, punishment and destruction are contingent on the faithfulness of the nation.[32]

From the 1940s through the 1960s, Graham's sermons often portrayed the world situation in dualistic terms. Atheistic communism sought to crush "Christendom" and its leading nation, the United States. Communism, he told Los Angeles, is "a religion that is inspired, directed and motivated by the Devil himself who has declared war against Almighty God. Do you know that . . . communists are more rampant in Los Angeles than any other city in America?"[33] Occasionally, communism featured in his sermon titles: "Christianism vs. Communism." "The Soviet Threat to Life." "Why Communism is Gaining."[34] But when his favorite president, Richard Nixon, initiated détente with the Soviet Union in 1969, and when Graham started getting opportunities to preach in communist countries eight years later, the anticommunist rhetoric virtually disappeared from his sermons.

In one sense these changes as he matured were superficial, because the core of his sermons remained constant throughout the years. Rather than preaching a classic three-point sermon, he typically preached a one-point sermon. Rather than developing his biblical text, he used it merely to introduce a theme. His operative text, whether stated or not, was always John 3:16: "For God so loved the world that he gave his only begotten Son, that whosoever believeth in him should not perish, but have everlasting life." A sympathetic commentator summed it up this way: "No matter what his text, Graham basically preaches one sermon, which might be entitled 'Come unto Christ.' "[35]

Graham framed his typical sermon with a description of how the world is in crisis: War! Crime! Rebellion of the young! Flagrant immorality! Political paralysis! Economic collapse! Religious decline! Graham's style was always hyperbolic: "There is at this moment an unprecedented moral decline!"[36] His hyperbole allowed him to tap into the myths cherished by his audience. Since the time of Puritans, Americans, like people in other times and places, have been fond of diagnosing present-day troubles as evidence of decline from a golden age.

Graham leveraged this myth again and again. A classic example is his first sermon ever in Boston, preached on New Year's Eve in 1950. He told Bostonians that, without a doubt, "1950 will go down in history as one of the most momentous in the world." America was in its most desperate "fight for survival" ever. . . . "alone and isolated . . . faced by the most powerful enemy the nation has ever known." American prospects were worse than during "the bleak, cold days at Valley Forge, or the darkest days of the Civil War, or that black December Sunday in 1941" when Japan bombed Pearl Harbor. Graham lamented that the days were long gone when America had the Christian character to see it through such a crisis. Spiritual giants like Jonathan Edwards, George Whitefield, Francis Asbury, and Charles Finney no longer walked the land.[37]

What then, he asked, could save America? In every culture and every historical period, the way to arrest a decline from a mythical golden age is always the same: rededication to the values and restoration of the practices that were present in the golden age. This was exactly Graham's timeless prescription. Only "spiritual awakening and revival" can "stay the judgment hand of God." No need to wait for Christ's return for all to be made right. "Whoever you are," he concluded, "you can know the peace of God today. And you, as a part of America, can say yes to Jesus Christ at this moment."[38]

The Personal Is Paramount

Though Graham talked much of global and social threats, the personal was always paramount. One of the most fascinating and important elements of his sermons is how he would seamlessly blend national or global crisis together with personal crisis. In his younger years he only occasionally preached about the biblical hell of eternal torment, and by his later years he had eliminated this entirely. But throughout his career he threatened his audiences with a this-worldly hell of moral, political, economic, and social chaos. Then he would blend the hell of social crisis with the hell of personal crisis so thoroughly that they became indistinguishable:

There are storms in the world today: Storms of unbelief, materialism, secularism, moral degeneracy and international difficulties. And there are storms in your own life: storms of temptation, confusion and difficulty. By neglecting church, by neglecting daily Bible reading and prayer ... you have broken away from the moral moorings and are out in a storm. ... A stormy conscience says, "Stop before it is too late!" Our international problems reflect these personal problems. There will be no peace in the world until individuals have peace in their hearts. ... As long as there is one man who hates, one man who has prejudices, one false society anywhere in the world, we are in danger of a world explosion that could wipe us into oblivion.[39]

In other words, Graham preached not only about a society plagued by addiction, but my addiction. Not only youth rebellion, but my rebellion. Not only family breakdown, but the conflict in my family. Not only rampant sexual immorality, but my lust and adultery. Not only widespread homelessness, but my loneliness and estrangement. Not only the emptying of the churches, but my denial of God.[40]

The sermons were a blend in another way. Just as Graham mixed social and personal crisis, he also mixed appeals to non-Christians and Christians. His crusade teams kept careful statistics about why inquirers came forward, always distinguishing between first-time decisions for Christ and three categories of rededication to Christ. But in Graham's sermons every one of these distinctions melted away.

This pattern was intentional, because Graham aimed for the heart as well as the head. In 1983, speaking to an international conference of evangelists, he explained the basic principles of his preaching. Regardless of the audience, he assumed that no one's true needs could be totally met by social improvement or material affluence. Everyone has a fear of death, everyone feels guilty, everyone is subject to loneliness, and everyone experiences emptiness in life without Christ. Trying to fill these needs with counterfeits—money, sex, power—was doomed to fail. But Christ—and only Christ—could meet the needs of every person.[41]

To get to the heart, Graham needed a listener to have an open heart, and this is where music came in. Cliff Barrows would enlist the audience as participants by getting them to sing. Then, immediately before Graham's sermon, George Beverly Shea would sing a solo. As Edith Blumhofer notes in her chapter in this volume, Shea's heartfelt, understated singing style emphasized lyrics that engaged the mind and pathos that engaged the heart. This worked on two levels. For those in the audience who were committed Christians, it moved them to feelings of sympathy and compassion for those who had not yet given their lives to Christ. For potential inquirers, it softened their hearts, opening them to the message.

Then came the climax of the entire crusade—the sermon. The blended character of Graham's sermons worked like a radio scanner. The sermon ranged back and forth across Graham's list of social anxieties and his list of human needs. When a listener with an open heart heard *her* fear or need she locked in and paid attention. Having raised her awareness of need the sermon then sharpened her desire for change and persuaded her that the road to change began with a decision for Christ. A 1968 study found that virtually all who came forward at the Chicago crusade six years earlier said they did so because they desired change in their lives. Their combined list of the specific changes they desired correlated to Graham's assumptions about universal human needs. A few said they wanted to go to heaven and be saved from hell, but far more often they mentioned changes that would impact them in this life. Some desired a better relationship with God and empowerment to live a more Christian life. Some wanted to reverse personal disintegration. Some desired a stronger sense of purpose and direction. Some wanted a better sense of worth and meaning in their lives. Some desired more harmonious marriages, family lives, and other personal relationships—in short, to love and be loved. Some wanted freedom from guilt, bitterness, or loneliness. Above all else they desired immediate change—and apparently, most of them found it. Two-thirds of those surveyed reported behavior or attitude changes lasting throughout the six years following their crusade decision.[42]

The view of the universe in a Billy Graham sermon, therefore, was that every society and every individual has desperate needs; these needs are bound together; change is possible; and it begins with a personal decision to accept and follow Christ. In Graham's 1983 address to evangelists he quoted the nineteenth-century British preacher Charles Spurgeon's advice: "Take your text and make a beeline for the Cross."[43] This is exactly what Graham was doing when he told his audiences again and again and again: "Christ is the answer to *every* problem."

This message was simultaneously empowering and enfeebling. It convinced people that their personal demons need not prevail. By putting faith in Christ and walking with Christ, anyone could transform bad choices, bad relationships, and bad circumstances into good ones. Beyond that,

Graham's message taught that the individual was not helpless in the face of international threats, economic crisis, or social chaos. If social change begins with individual change, then anyone can immediately do something to make the world better by commencing a life of faith in Christ.

But in giving individuals the conviction that conversion was a way to do something about social problems, Graham's message inevitably exaggerated the impact of individual conversion on social conditions. Graham's defenders are quick to assert historical examples of widespread evangelical conversion leading to social change—the rise of British antislavery sentiment in the early nineteenth century, for example, is often cited. Graham's critics, however, argue history is not on his side. In most cases the belief that social problems are nothing more than the sum total of individual sins has reinforced evangelical complacency about social conditions and put them on the sidelines of social reform.

None of Graham's contemporaries understood this better than the theologian Reinhold Niebuhr. Niebuhr spent his whole career trying to understand societal sin and explain in Christian terms how it could only be addressed by society as a whole. For two decades Niebuhr subjected Graham to a running critique about this, and Graham's legacy on the question is still debated by scholars.[44]

The mixed nature of Graham's legacy is nowhere clearer than on the question of race relations and civil rights. Graham was personally progressive on race relations, and he often channeled his personal positions into bold public statements and actions. At the same time, most of his main American audience—white, born-again, evangelical Protestants—passively resisted reformers' efforts to bring about racial equality through direct protest, legislation, and judicial decisions. Graham sometimes challenged this resistance, but at other times he reinforced it. And he never wavered in his insistence that only individual change could produce social change. Little wonder that among Graham's constituency, supporters of civil rights were, in the words of the historian David Swartz, a "moral minority."[45] (For more on Graham and politics, see Curtis Evans's chapter, "A Politics of Conversion.")

Conclusion

Ultimately, why did people stream forward at the end of Graham's sermons? The answer has defied easy explanation because there is no secret; there is no single decisive element. It was, rather, the whole package that brought people out of their seats to give their lives to Christ. Most of the audiences were churchgoers who had already made their decisions for Christ. The potential inquirers came for any number of reasons—maybe a churchgoing friend invited them, maybe they wanted to reconnect to Christianity, maybe they wanted to see the famous evangelist, or maybe they were just curious. In many cases they could not say exactly why they came. But they came expectantly. The buildup to the crusade, the festivity and pageantry and music of the event itself, the milling crowds, and the platform filled with celebrities all generated anticipation—something special was going to happen.

Crusades were often held in sporting venues, but the crusade transformed the venue into a sacred space. Unlike a sports contest, there was no competition, no winners and losers, no beer vendors, no cursing, no cocky young men strutting and spitting, no dancing young women in skimpy outfits. Admission was free. A crusade audience was a broader cross-section of the population than a sporting event—more women, more older people, more children, more social classes. The very wholesomeness of the crusade created a temporary sanctuary from many of the world's troubles and offered a glimpse of one version of what individual peace and social harmony might look like.

The crusade audience watched not a competition, but rather a string of politicians, sports heroes, well-known entertainers, and other celebrities take the stage and tell how Jesus Christ had changed their lives, while the churchgoers in the audience murmured and nodded in assent. This helped make giving one's life to Christ plausible. The audience also heard a massed choir of ordinary people and famous musicians sing songs about Jesus, songs designed for gentle emotional appeal. By the time George Beverly Shea finished his solo and sat down, the potential inquirers were prepared in heart and mind, anticipating something momentous.

Then Graham, usually wearing a simple suit, stepped alone to the microphone. Once past his earliest years, he delivered his opening greetings in such a simple and unaffected style that it proved his reputation for genuineness and sincerity. He gave no sign of cleverness or subtlety, no hint of preening or basking in attention. All the markers of holy affections that Jonathan Edwards had identified and that Graham exhibited in conversations with reporters and interviews on television—lowliness of mind, lowliness of behavior, humbleness of heart—were now in view on the crusade platform. Potential inquirers could see it for themselves.

Then came the sermon. The confident authority of the evangelist provided an arresting counterpoint to his personal humility. Might this man with a godly character be speaking a message from God? When he appealed to the universal myth of decline from a former golden age and combined it with national myths cherished by his audience, listeners understood that Graham's view of God in the world encompassed their own view of the world. Graham did not challenge his audience to throw out their old worldview; he merely asked them to enlarge it. When he then mixed images of national decline and crisis with images of personal failure and crisis, the open-hearted listener who trusted Graham heard a message that seemed personal. As one person who came forward at the 1962 Chicago crusade commented six years later, Billy Graham "was speaking directly to me. ... He knew what I was thinking and what my problem was."[46] Social scientists call this confirmation bias, while others would call it a word from God.

All of this engaged the listener's emotions and heightened a desire for change. The possibility of change—real, long-lasting change—seemed at hand. At this crucial moment, Graham then pointed the way to change. It began, he told them, when they said, "I want Christ in my life." When this made rational and emotional sense to someone—when they desired to have Christ in their life—then they made their decision. In that instant the listener became an inquirer, stood up, and started walking forward. It was psychologically significant, perhaps even costly. Thousands of people were watching, including friends or family. There were no histrionics. Audience members typically sat quietly, perhaps praying, sometimes singing softly to themselves. Graham himself did no pleading or weeping, typically standing in silence, head bowed, for several long minutes. Inquirers typically came forward in orderly fashion, with none of noisy displays that so often accompanied Pentecostal worship.

However, even though inquirers remained calm, they reported the decision to go forward as a deeply emotional moment.[47] And, more often than not, the personal change they hoped for seemed really to have taken place. The crusade and its pageantry and the testimonies of the famous and the gently emotional music and the affirming audience and the humble man who spoke with the authority of a messenger of God—they all came together and formed a powerful memory marker of the special ritual through which the inquirer had passed.

Sometimes the memory landmark matured into a family legacy. In 1996, at the final crusade Graham did in his hometown of Charlotte, the journalist Ken Garfield interviewed Nellie Roth, a mother of four. Years earlier her own mother, at that time pregnant with Nellie, came forward at a crusade. Because of that decision Nellie was raised in a Christian home and was now raising her own children in a Christian home. So Nellie went to the Charlotte stadium forty-four years later. She took in the sights and sounds, listened to the testimonies, remembered the familiar songs, and drank in the sermon. Then, with tears in her eyes, she sat and watched hundreds of people make the same pilgrimage her mother had made, testifying to their desire and their decision for a new life in Christ.[48]

Notes

1. Billy Graham, "The Great Judgment," sermon preached at Charlotte, NC, Oct. 19, 1958, online at http://youtube.com/HuTA8PbVA5s.

2. "Billy Graham Preaching at Camden Yards in Baltimore, MD, July 7, 2006," online at http://youtube.com/crWAkXtiMJc.

3. William Martin, *A Prophet with Honor: The Billy Graham Story* (New York: William Morrow, 1991), 75.

4. Charles B. Templeton, Interview with William Martin, Dec. 2, 1987, quoted in Martin, *Prophet with Honor*, 110.

5. Martin, *Prophet with Honor*, 75.

6. Ibid., 77, 163.

7. John Pollock, *Billy Graham: The Authorized Biography* (New York: McGraw-Hill, 1966), 92.

8. Jonathan Edwards, *A Treatise Concerning Religious Affections* (Grand Rapids, MI: Christian Classics Ethereal Library, [1746]), 13–16, quotation on 13, online at http://www.ccel.org/ccel/edwards/affections.pdf; Paul Lewis, "'The Springs of Motion:' Jonathan Edwards on Emotions, Character and Agency," *Journal of Religious Ethics* 22 (1994): 281–284.

9. James K. A. Smith, *Desiring the Kingdom: Worship, Worldview, and Cultural Formation* (Grand Rapids, MI: Baker Academic, 2009), 50–51; John Piper, *Desiring God: Meditations of a Christian Hedonist* (Portland, OR: Multnomah, 1986), 53–54, 219–220.

10. Pollock, *Billy Graham*, 48–50; Martin, *Prophet with Honor*, 106–108.

11. Andrew Finstuen, *Original Sin and Everyday Protestants: The Theology of Reinhold Niebuhr, Billy Graham, and Paul Tillich in an Age of Anxiety* (Chapel Hill: University of North Carolina Press, 2009), 132; "Billy Graham Promises 'No Emotionalism,'" *Chicago Tribune*, February 26, 1954): Part 1, p. 10; Pollock, *Billy Graham*, 232–233.

12. An edited print version of this 1965 sermon is Billy Graham's "Saved or Lost?" in *20 Centuries of Great Preaching: An Encyclopedia of Preaching*, Vol. 12, *Marshall*

to King, edited by Clyde E. Fant Jr. and William M. Pinson Jr. (Waco, TX: Word Books, 1971), 303–311, quotations on 307 and 308. An abridged recording of the same sermon is Billy Graham, "Do You Believe?," online at http://billygraham. org/audio/do-you-believe/.

13. Graham, "Saved or Lost," 310–311.

14. Graham sermons given in Washington, DC, May 3, 1986, and in Columbia, SC, April 29, 1987, quoted in Martin, *Prophet with Honor,* 64.

15. Billy Graham, *Just As I Am: The Autobiography of Billy Graham* (San Francisco: HarperCollins, 1997), 30.

16. Historians have recently begun studying the emotional history of American evangelicalism. John Corrigan notes that the Boston clergy were equally ambivalent about the role of emotion in the revivals of the 1850s; see Corrigan, *Business of the Heart: Religion and Emotion in the Nineteenth Century* (Berkeley: University of California Press, 2002), 104–105. Corrigan also sees a direct line between the emotion-based preaching of Jonathan Edwards and that of Billy Graham; see Corrigan, *Emptiness: Feeling Christian in America* (Chicago: University of Chicago Press, 2015), 146. Todd M. Brenneman finds that in the generation after Graham, popular evangelical writers appealed to emotional sentimentality by romanticizing the tropes of the fatherhood of God as father, the infancy of human beings, and nostalgia for home and family; see Brenneman, *Homespun Gospel: The Triumph of Sentimentality in Contemporary American Evangelicalism* (New York: Oxford University Press, 2014), 1–11.

17. Edwards, *Religious Affections,* 28, 186, 200–201.

18. Andy Newman, "Graham Ends Crusade in City Urging Repentance and Hope," *New York Times,* June 27, 2005, http://nytimes.com/1lyPsI5y.

19. Cooke and Priestley are quoted in Stanley High, *Billy Graham: The Personal Story of the Man, His Message, and His Mission* (New York: McGraw-Hill, 1956), 51; William McLoughlin, *Modern Revivalism: Charles Grandison Finney to Billy Graham* (New York: Ronald Press, 1959), chap. 9; "Fundamentalist Revival" (unsigned editorial), *Christian Century* 74, no. 25 (June 19, 1957), quotation on 749.

20. Martin, *Prophet with Honor,* 24–31, 221; quotation is from Sarah Lyall, "Billy Graham, Not Joel, Takes Long Island," *New York Times,* September 21, 1990, http://nytimes.com/1xV23HP.

21. Robert N. McCauley, "The Importance of Being 'Ernest,'" in *Creating Consilience: Integrating the Sciences and the Humanities,* ed. Edward G. Slingerland and Mark Collard (New York: Oxford University Press, 2012), 266–281.

22. Thomas Howard, *Evangelical Is Not Enough* (Nashville, TN: Thomas Nelson, 1984), quotations on 37, 54, and 60.

23. Robert O. Ferm, with Caroline M. Whiting, *Billy Graham: Do the Conversions Last?* (Minneapolis: World Wide Publications, 1988), 21, 28–29, 83–85.

24. David I. Kertzer, *Ritual, Politics, and Power* (New Haven, CT: Yale University Press, 1988), 40.

25. Martin, *Prophet with Honor*, 29.

26. Billy Graham, "Judgment," sermon given in Los Angeles in 1949, print version in Billy Graham, *Revival in Our Time: The Story of the Billy Graham Evangelistic Campaigns* (Wheaton, IL: Van Kampen, 1950), 138; audio version online at http://billygraham.org/audio/judgment-2/.

27. Billy Graham, "Prodigal Son," sermon given in Boston as reported by *Boston Daily Globe*, January 10, 1950, quoted in Martin, *Prophet with Honor*, 127.

28. Billy Graham, "We Need Revival," sermon preached in Los Angeles in 1949, print version in Graham, *Revival in Our Time*, 52, 55; Garth M. Rosell, *The Surprising Work of God: Harold John Ockenga, Billy Graham, and the Rebirth of Evangelicalism* (Grand Rapids, MI: Baker Academic), 37.

29. Graham, "Do You Believe?," introduction to sermon, audio version only.

30. Billy Graham, "America's Hope," sermon given during his Youth for Christ days in the mid-1940s, print version in Graham, *Calling Youth to Christ* (Grand Rapids, MI: Zondervan, 1947), 11, 29; compare Billy Graham, "The Nation's Hope," in Graham, *Calling Youth to Christ* (London: Marshall, Morgan and Scott, n.d.), 7, 21.

31. Graham, *Just As I Am*, 25.

32. See, for example, Billy Graham's sermon "Whither Bound?," print version in Billy Graham, *America's Hour of Decision* (Wheaton, IL: Van Kampen, 1951), 139–148; an audio version entitled "Whitherbound" is online at http://billygraham.org/audio/whitherbound/.

33. Graham, "We Need Revival!," print version in Graham, *Revival in Our Time*, 55.

34. These sermon titles and recordings can be found by searching "communism" at http://billygraham.org/tv-and-radio/radio/audio-archives/.

35. Fant and Pinson, *20 Centuries of Great Preaching*, 295.

36. Graham, "America's Hope," 19.

37. Graham, "Whither Bound?" quotations on 139–140; see also 145–146.

38. Ibid., 148; concluding quotation is in the audio version only.

39. Billy Graham, "Faith," sermon preached on *Hour of Decision* radio program in 1956, print version in Fant and Pinson, *20 Centuries of Great Preaching*, 332.

40. For another discussion of this pattern, see Fant and Pinson, *20 Centuries of Great Preaching*, 301.

41. Billy Graham, "Ministry: We Set Forth the Truth Plainly," *Preaching* (July 1985), online at http://www.preaching.com/sermons/11566810/, originally published as "The Evangelist and His Preaching: We Set Forth the Truth Plainly," in *The Work of an Evangelist*, ed. J. D. Douglas (Minneapolis: World Wide Publications, 1984).

42. Lee Morris, "Projecting Pastoral Care in Revival Preaching: Billy Graham," *Pastoral Psychology* 19 (June 1968): 33–41.

43. Graham, "Ministry."

44. Andrew S. Finstuen, "The Prophet and the Evangelist," *Books and Culture: A Christian Review*, July 1, 2006, online at www.booksandculture.com/articles/2006/julaug/3.8.html.

45. For a thorough and carefully nuanced discussion of Graham and civil rights, see Wacker, *America's Pastor: Billy Graham and the Shaping of a Nation* (Cambridge MA: Harvard University Press, 2014), 120–136; for Wacker's reflections on Graham's record on civil rights as it intersected the "give your life to Christ" approach to social problems, see pp. 132–133. On the passive conservatism of evangelicals, see David R. Swartz, *Moral Minority: The Evangelical Left in an Age of Conservatism* (Philadelphia: University of Pennsylvania Press, 2012), esp. 2–4. For recent scholarship critical of Graham's record on race relations, see Michael G. Long, *Billy Graham and the Beloved Community: America's Evangelist and the Dream of Martin Luther King, Jr.* (New York: Palgrave Macmillan, 2006); and the chapters by Gary Dorrien and Rufus Burrow in Michael G. Long, ed. *The Legacy of Billy Graham: Critical Reflections on America's Great Evangelist* (Louisville, KY: Westminster John Knox Press, 2008), 144–177.

46. Quoted in Morris, "Projecting Pastoral Care," 35.

47. Ferm with Whiting, *Billy Graham: Do the Conversions Last?*, 59.

48. Ken Garfield, "The Crusade—Graham Homecoming: Crowd Drawn to Stadium to Witness Part of History," *Charlotte Observer*, September 27, 1996, 1A.

3

Singing to Save

MUSIC IN THE BILLY GRAHAM CRUSADES

Edith L. Blumhofer

IN APRIL 1951, a mere sixteen months after *Life* magazine noticed "a new evangelist aris[ing]," a reporter for the *Hammond Times* pointed out that Billy Graham was not arising alone: "Music plays a big part in the Graham services—so big, in fact, that such co-workers as Cliff Barrows, the song leader, and singer Beverly Shea have become as well-known to congregations as Graham."[1] The crusade advertising posters that volunteers plastered on the sides of buses, stretched over streets, or mounted on billboards often featured three smiling faces, and already some observers were suggesting that people attended the crusades as much for the music as for the sermons.[2] In 1957 an astute *New York Times* reporter pointed to gospel singing as "an integral part" of Graham's operation and suggested that in the recent mammoth New York crusade, "many persons attending the Graham rallies in [Madison Square] Garden were moved more by Mr. Shea's rendering of 'How Great Thou Art' than by the preaching of the evangelist."[3] Reporters uniformly applauded Barrows and Shea for their own talents as well as for the team spirit that combined music, message, and invitation in a seamless whole. Even critics at the *Christian Century* commended the men's ability to "ally method to message": "The boys in the Graham team know their business. They're in evangelism. What's your line?"[4] Graham preached to elicit decisions; Barrows and Shea sang to save.[5]

By the time Graham entered the revival circuit in the 1940s, music had a venerable tradition in evangelism. In the 1870s, Dwight L. Moody and Ira Sankey perfected a marriage of gospel singing and gospel preaching, and their successors generally followed their example, relying heavily on the vast repertoire of gospel hymns Sankey had popularized. When Billy Graham began his crusades, he knew exactly what music and which musicians he wanted. He preferred "the old hymns of revival, consecration, and salvation," and he asked George Beverly Shea and Cliff Barrows to join him for his first citywide revival in the Charlotte Armory in 1947.[6] Both men remained with Graham through the final crusade in 2005 and beyond. The staying power of this platform team-of-three made them crusade legends, and understanding Graham crusades requires reckoning with Shea and Barrows and the principles and purposes that guided crusade music from beginning to end.

If the consistency of the team-of-three suggests that it is easy to identify a "signature" crusade sound, the diversity of crusade musical guest artists reveals another function of crusade music. Barrows and Shea anchored the familiar crusade sound, but crusade platforms and programs also functioned as a mirror of the musical and ethnic variety that *was* America. From the first, the list of guest artists included a variety of genres and a remarkable racial and ethnic mix. Barrows and Shea never changed their guiding principles, nor did they alter their own performance styles, but they abetted change in the Christian musical culture by recognizing, featuring, and celebrating the artistry of people with strikingly different sounds from their own. Crusade music also influenced the content of Christian song by recovering neglected hymns, reinvigorating a handful of gospel hymns at a time when gospel hymns were falling from favor, and giving visibility to emerging Christian artists. And for several decades music functioned prominently in pre-crusade advertising. Pre-crusade concerts, generally featuring George Beverly Shea and pianist Tedd Smith, attracted thousands to events complete in themselves but pregnant with anticipation of great moments to come.

The Team

One might say that Billy Graham had everything and nothing to do with crusade music—everything because he grasped its importance and entrusted it to Barrows and Shea, and nothing because his lack of musical ability forced him to leave it to others. George Beverly Shea once quipped that Billy Graham suffered from "the malady of no melody."[7] But unlike his most immediate predecessor, Billy Sunday, Graham did not begrudge time for music. He often said that he knew of no better evangelistic tool than a gospel song well sung—and when the last crusade was over, he still insisted that he knew no singer he would rather hear than George Beverly Shea and no better song leader than Cliff Barrows.[8] The "threefold cord" (Eccl. 4:12) that bound these men was broken only by the deaths of George Beverly Shea in 2013 and Cliff Barrows in 2016.

Shea partnered with Graham first. In 1943, during Graham's brief stint as a Chicago-area pastor, he enlisted Shea for a live late-night financially struggling radio broadcast called *Songs in the Night*. Shea was a radio personality with a growing public, first on the Moody Radio Network and then on ABC Radio, and Graham knew that Shea could command a listener base. Graham was right: Shea attracted both a late-Sunday-night congregation to Graham's Village Baptist Church and a broadcast following, and within a few weeks, *Songs in the Night* paid its way. Graham's fame came later. When he and Shea first collaborated, Shea had the larger public, and his name appeared first on the advertising. A decade older than Graham, Shea had already adopted the principles that guided his approach to music in evangelistic work.

The son of the Canadian Wesleyan Methodist pastor-evangelist Adam Shea and his wife, Maude Whitney Shea, George Beverly Shea spent his early years in rural Winchester, Ontario. Both of his parents had musical abilities, and making music together was part of the family's daily routine. Wesleyan hymns and camp meeting gospel favorites were among Shea's earliest memories, and in old age he still recalled his deep emotional childhood response to hymns. He sang his first solos at an Ontario camp meeting in 1926; the next year he "came forward" at a revival during the singing of "Just As I Am," and soon he decided to devote himself to the "musical side of God's great work of evangelism."[9] How he would accomplish that remained unclear, but he began to hone his skills during a year at Annesley College, a small holiness institute in Ottawa, and another year at the Wesleyans' Houghton College in upstate New York. Voice lessons, recitals, and choral performance opportunities expanded his musical world. In 1929 he moved with his family to Jersey City, where his father had taken a pastorate. Shea worked at an insurance company in lower Manhattan and enrolled in private voice lessons. Opportunities came his way—occasional solos on Christian radio broadcasts and in area churches and summer engagements at the evangelist Percy Crawford's Pinebrook Bible Conference in Pennsylvania—as well as distractions in the form of secular music. One Sunday morning during the weeks that

George Beverly Shea pondered his future in music, his mother placed a poem by Rhea F. Miller on the family piano, where she knew her son would see it. He found it early on a Sunday morning, composed a tune on the spot, and a few hours later he sang it as a solo in his father's church. Its lyrics became his life's theme song and a featured number at every Graham crusade: "I'd rather have Jesus than anything this world affords today." Shea resolved anew to devote his voice to Christian song, and he never looked back.

In 1938 Shea and his Canadian bride, Erma Scharfe, moved to Chicago, where Shea took a job at WMBI, the radio station associated with Moody Bible Institute. Shea's varied duties included auditioning musicians, singing solos, and hosting a daily hymn broadcast called *Hymns from the Chapel*. He occasionally returned to New York to sing in the Word of Life youth rallies conducted by his friend Jack Wyrtzen, an ex-cavalry bugler turned youth evangelist. Pundits marveled at Wyrtzen's appeal, noting that, "without benefit of college or seminary," he managed to fill Carnegie Hall, Madison Square Garden, and, later, Yankee Stadium's 70,000 seats with modern youth eager for the old-fashioned gospel.[10] In Chicago, Shea communicated his enthusiasm for Wyrtzen's youth work and helped bring into being a vigorous youth movement known as Youth for Christ. In 1944 Shea resigned from Moody Radio to accept an offer from Club Aluminum Corporation to develop and host a new broadcast featuring hymns. Known as Club Time, it went nationwide on ABC and the Armed Forces Network in 1945. Shea's contract required him to sing Sunday mornings and eve-nings in different churches to promote the weekday broadcast. Now billed as "America's beloved gospel singer," his religious world expanded as he sang and worshiped in churches of every denomination.

The principles that shaped Shea's vocation in music evangelism were simple and owed much to his parents' influence: he vowed always to sing a message, to sing from his own heart to the hearts of others, and to know ever more intimately the one of whom he sang. He disliked applause and admitted no ambition to entertain; showmanship simply had no place. Rather, "One feels a great responsibility and dependence on God in the task of preparing the people for the message of God's servant. ... My prayer is always, 'None of self but all of Thee.'"[11] He regarded evangelistic singing as a "sacred vocation" and resolved always to sing with conviction, heart-to-heart, and eye-to-eye. To this end, when he sang to live audiences, he sang from memory and with a purpose he summarized as follows: "to convict sinful hearts, to sing God's message of cheer to the downhearted and God's message of comfort to sorrowing hearts."[12] From the start, people recognized in Shea an unusual ability to use his rich voice to convey deep religious conviction. His "unshowmanlike delivery, sensitive phrasing, and impeccable diction" kept the focus on his message.[13] In 1951 a pamphlet produced by the Billy Graham Evangelistic Association (BGEA) for the upcoming Washington, DC, crusade introduced Shea with the comment, "The Gospel invitation could be extended following his solos, so clearly is the message presented."[14] The lyrics of Shea's first solo at a Graham crusade (Charlotte 1947) aptly summarized what he set out to do all his life: "I will sing the wondrous story of the Christ who died for me." When Shea was inducted into the Gospel Music Hall of Fame in 1978, his citation noted the simplicity of his faith and the "clean-cut nature of his code." "To Bev Shea," it read, "compromise is unthinkable. Every word he sings must tell the story of the Christ who died for me."[15]

Unlike Shea, Cliff Barrows signed onto the Graham team as a relative novice. As one of the evangelist-turned-educator Bob Jones's "preacher boys," though, he had training in and ideas about the things that mattered most to collaborative work with Graham and Shea. Clifford Burton Barrows was born in Ceres, California, on April 6, 1923. His family worshiped in the local Baptist church, and Barrows learned the power of hymns at home and in the congregation—where he began leading singing in the Sunday evening service in his early teens. The Ceres Baptist Church used *Tabernacle Hymns #3*, and Barrows liked to recall that he learned his theology from its pages.[16] Converted in 1934 at age eleven, Barrows realized by 1936 that he wanted a future making music in evangelistic work.[17]

The first graduate of Bob Jones College's sacred music concentration (1944), Barrows had a remarkable command of the gospel hymnody that nurtured fundamentalist piety. The new Youth for Christ movement provided a logical setting in which to develop his enthusiasm for all things evangelistic. Dubbed "Wheel" Barrows by young admirers, Barrows was just twenty-two when a reporter introduced him in *Power Magazine* as "a reasonable facsimile of a guy a maiden might dream about," who had everyone singing two minutes after he took the platform, "even the photographers, because making people sing and like it is Cliff Barrows' specialty!"[18] Barrows told his young admirers, "I got my idea from cheerleaders. I believe if a cheerleader can put all he's got into a cheer, a song leader for the Lord ought to exert himself enough to wake up a congregation to sing with joy and enthusiasm." His early approach? "I just open my mouth and let my hands fly."[19]

Barrows met Billy Graham in Asheville in 1945 when he and his wife, Billie (then on a brief honeymoon), filled in for absent musicians at an evangelistic rally. In 1946 the Barrows accompanied Billy Graham to England for six months of networking and contemplating future evangelistic work.[20] When Graham decided to move on from Youth for Christ, he invited the Barrows to join him. The couple made a deliberate choice to set aside personal ambitions for collaborative work with Graham, and they never looked back.

There was much more to Barrows than the congenial upbeat demeanor audiences loved. Already thoroughly conversant with the repertoire of gospel hymnody, Barrows read widely about the history of music and evangelism, and also sought advice from seasoned song leaders. He admired Billy Sunday's longtime musician Homer Rodeheaver for his ease with people and his ability to get crowds to sing, and he spent productive hours conversing with the older man at Rodeheaver's Winona Lake, Indiana, home.[21] He appropriated to himself two maxims from Charles Alexander, the musician who assisted Reuben A. Torrey and J. Wilbur Chapman in evangelistic work around the world: "Sing to save," and "Sing as if you were preaching, not singing."[22] He studied the stories of hymns and pored over the biographies of their authors.

Graham's mammoth audiences saw in Barrows a man they instinctively trusted. Within five years reporters commented regularly on his already legendary ability with the mass choirs that delighted people around the world, but he was equally passionate about hearty congregational singing. During his time with Youth for Christ, Barrows had observed a trend toward performance rather than participation: programs featured one singer and speaker after another, making audiences spectators. Barrows had regretted the absence of congregational singing, and although congregational singing in massive crusades presented logistical challenges of the first order—selecting songs far in advance, soliciting copyright permissions, printing, shipping, distribution, and more—he considered it worth the effort and made it a feature of every service. Between 1949 and 2005, more than one million people sang in his choirs, and he personally led over 200 million crusade attendees in song. The largest crusade choirs numbered more than 11,000 in Rio de Janeiro (1974) and 10,300 in Anaheim, California (1969).[23] The largest single congregation Barrows led in song gathered in Seoul, Korea, on June 3, 1973—more than one million strong.

The principles that guided Barrows' musical choices in his expanding sphere derived from his experiences at home, church, and Bob Jones University. These principles were honed during his stint with Youth for Christ, his conversations with veteran song leaders and hymn writers, and his vociferous reading about singing and revivals. Because he believed that music had the potential to determine how people listened to or received sermons, he insisted, first, that crusade music have a purpose. "Music is not an end in itself," he insisted. "It is the means to an end."[24] Its primary purpose was to glorify God.[25] Second, crusade music would aim for excellence. As Barrows put it, "if it doesn't sound good to the ear, it will not reach the heart."[26] Third, Barrows wanted music to unite, encourage, and facilitate common affirmations and resolves.[27] For his part, he aspired to be perceived as "natural" rather than "professional," to relate easily to people and draw them into the program.[28]

Although millions around the world knew him best as the host and music director at every Graham crusade, Cliff Barrows filled other strategic roles in the Billy Graham Evangelistic Association. Unlike Shea (who was never a full-time employee of the BGEA), Barrows weighed in on all aspects of crusade scheduling, pre-crusade training, and crusade follow-up.[29] He also took responsibility for the behind-the-scenes logistics that made each crusade run smoothly, from amplification systems to parking and shuttles to accessible seating. He decided who sat on crusade platforms, who spoke, and what was sung. When the strains of "Just As I Am" faded, Barrows—the first to arrive and the last to leave every service—stepped from the platform to thank volunteers and counsel penitents. The vice chair of the BGEA from 1950 to 2000, Barrows was also program director and host of the BGEA's popular radio program, *The Hour of Decision* (1950–2014). When the BGEA ventured into moviemaking, Barrows was deeply involved from the start, and then served from 1965 to 1970 as president of the BGEA's production company, World Wide Pictures. From planning to follow-up to new initiatives, Cliff Barrows had vision and ability that made him Billy Graham's indispensable collaborator.

In his role as crusade music director, Barrows enlisted outstanding accompanists willing to subsume their own considerable talents to the cause of evangelism. They could do anything required—transpose, bridge, compose, arrange—but the point was not to showcase their own artistry but to contribute effectively to the "one thing" the whole team was about. The longest-serving accompanist was the Canadian-born virtuoso pianist and arranger Tedd Smith, who trained at The Royal Conservatory of Music in Toronto but devoted much of his career to Graham's endeavors.[30] On their own time, Smith and other crusade musicians gave recitals, published hymn arrangements, recorded albums, and in other ways remained part of their larger professional world, but they were always on call for crusade-related assignments.

The three men's titles may have differed: Cliff Barrows, music director; George Beverly Shea, soloist; Billy Graham, evangelist. But in evangelistic work their hearts beat as one, and mutual trust deepened as the years passed. They were friends as well as colleagues, and their friendship included their families. Each man had considerable freedom within his crusade role: Barrows selected congregational and choir music, invited platform guests, and led each service until Billy Graham rose to preach; Shea sang solos, one of which often preceded the sermon. Graham found that Shea's singing prepared his heart to preach, while others noticed that it also quieted the audience and disposed them to listen. Shea often chose his solos as he rose to sing, basing his selection on his sense of the flow of a service. Graham supported Barrows's and Shea's choices, solicited their advice, sometimes requested particular songs, and regularly commended their music-making. He depended absolutely on Barrows and Shea, and both men generally appeared where Graham was scheduled to speak— at prayer breakfasts, state legislatures, the White House, denominational gatherings, or voluntary association rallies.

Diversity

Guest artists participated in Graham crusade music from the beginning, and over the years they made crusade platforms and musical sounds mirror what was familiar to wide swaths of the American population. Several factors entered into Barrows's decision to invite a guest artist. It was a given that every featured artist had a "testimony" (a singer without a vibrant witness was automatically disqualified), but beyond that, Barrows was attentive to region; he thought about demographics and local tastes.

Attention to region came, over time, to mean attention to ethnic diversity as well. Already in the 1960s, southwestern crusades often featured Latino recording artists—who performed at least partly in Spanish—as well as American Indian musicians. Hawaiian crusades brought an opportunity to showcase local talent like Mark and Diane Yasuhara, a husband-wife team known as The Hawaiians. Evie Tornquist Karlsson was a favorite in Minnesota, where Scandinavian Americans came out in large numbers.

California crusades might feature Samoan musicians like the Katinas and the Laulu Sisters. The Inuk singer Susan Aglukark delighted crowds in the Northwest; the Palermo Brothers (Louis and Phil) made much of their Italian roots as they sang their way into people's hearts. The Korean sopranos Kim Wickes, Sung Sook Lee, and Young Mi Kim used their highly trained voices to sing simple hymns in American cities with expanding Asian populations. As the one responsible for platform guests, Barrows made it a point to include a wide variety of ethnic groups. Their roles included testimony and prayer as well as song.

At the height of the civil rights movement, reporters who made it their business to notice the racial mix—or lack thereof—in crusade audiences often failed to comment on the platform, where African Americans regularly took the podium, often several in the same service. The incomparable blues, jazz, and gospel vocalist and actress Ethel Waters quietly joined the choir for the 1957 New York Crusade, but when Barrows learned she was there, she stepped up to sing "His Eye Is on the Sparrow," backed by the mass choir. The crowds already knew her for that song: from January 1950 through June 1951, she had sung it eight times weekly in the award-winning Broadway play *Member of the Wedding* (which hit the big screen in 1952), and audiences thrilled to hear her render her signature song alongside the mass choir. She remained a crusade favorite until her death in 1977.[31]

Barrows first brought the lyric soprano Myrtle Hall, a recently discovered talent, to the platform during a 1966 crusade in her hometown of Greenville, South Carolina. And the list of award-winning and beloved black crusade artists goes on: Leontyne Price, Willa Mae Dorsey, Joy Simpson, and Kathleen Battle, vocalists whose operatic training gave them singular styles; the "Queen of Gospel," contralto Mahalia Jackson; Johnny Ray Watson; the acclaimed gospel and jazz musician Joe Bias; the Danniebelles; ten-time Grammy Award winner CeCe Winans; Delores "Mom" Winans; singer/songwriter Larnelle Harris; Babbie Mason; Andraé Crouch; Archie Dennis; Jimi Mamou; Deniece Williams; the Montreal Jubilation Gospel Choir; the Prestonians; and Nashville's Born Again Church Choir. The black singer-songwriter Nicole C. Mullen, whose eclectic blend of soul, R&B, hip-hop, and funk made her a youth crusade favorite in the 1990s, told the Cincinnati *Enquirer*, "I've been around the Graham association for several years, and I've found them to be very much wanting all the races there. . . . That's always been part of their goal and their mission, so I am honored to be a part of it. This is part of the solution, not part of the problem.'[32] Not all black Americans concurred with Mullins, of course, but many did.

Musical guests also brought a remarkable mix of musical genres. From the brilliant classical styles of Greg Buchanan, Christopher Parkening, Jerome Hines, Ben Heppner, and Sung Sook Lee; to the pop-inspired sounds of Pat Boone and Ray Hildebrand; to the country music of Johnny Cash and Randy Travis; to the rich contralto of Mahalia Jackson, the Christian rock of dc Talk, the western flavor of Redd Harper, Roy Rogers, and Dale Evans; to the praise-and-worship-attuned stylings of Fernando Ortega, Michael W. Smith, and Amy Grant—Graham crusades relied on an array of musical idioms to do the "one thing" that every crusade set out to do. For each service, every platform guest was literally recruited to be a member of the team.

Guest artists had their own publics, and both sides benefited from guest appearances. A Graham crusade delivered a mammoth live audience, and guest artists drew their publics to Graham's message.[33] Many also donated their time. the BGEA offered only token honoraria, but there were other compensations—witness, audience exposure, brisk recording sales. Many artists drew audiences Graham could not easily access on his own. Guest artists, strategically chosen, made it more likely that certain demographics would come under Graham's preaching. By celebrating the Christian witness of popular musical stars, the Graham team in effect endorsed the authenticity of their witness, vastly increased their audiences, and celebrated new sounds in Christian music.

The limits to the embrace of musical genres were tested in the 1990s when worries about a generational disconnect between the aging team of three and American youth led some advisors to suggest a new format for the youth nights that had been part of every crusade for decades.[34] Graham, Barrows, and Shea were in their seventies and eighties, and youth nights seemed to have declining appeal. Crusades offered a predictable package: on youth nights Barrows generally added younger singers with a contemporary sound to the pre-sermon program, but the boilerplate service format remained essentially the same. Could that format be fundamentally altered without jeopardizing the whole enterprise? The question came down to music.

Advocates for a new musical sound—like pianist Tedd Smith and crusade director Rick Marshall—proposed to devote the first half of youth night programs to a concert featuring the sounds of the most popular contemporary Christian artists, and then to assign the band leader to introduce

Graham. The idea excluded Barrows and Shea and reimagined the stage setup. There would be no platform filled with participants, dignitaries, and sponsoring pastors; no choir; no "Just As I Am;" no organ or piano; even Graham would not appear until the concert ended, and he would dress casually. George Beverly Shea's soothing tones would be replaced by very loud music, and the decorum of a typical crusade service would yield to the lighting, sounds, and behaviors associated with rock concerts. Even the pulpit would be different—a Plexiglas stand would replace Graham's customary wooden podium. Some of Graham's closest associates implored him to resist. Like many conservative Protestants, they deemed Christian rock, rap, or R&B inappropriate and even "unchristian." Featuring it even in its Christian dress seemed to them like selling out to the contemporary culture. Barrows had full charge of the programming, but he recognized the explosive potential of the suggestion and referred the matter to Graham.

Graham recalled his own start in Youth for Christ, with its motto "Geared to the times and anchored to the Rock" and its innovative programming to attract crowds. Fifty years later, program components might be different, but the goal was the same: to do what it took to attract youth to hear the gospel. And Ruth Bell Graham weighed in with the observation that the proposed change had the potential to give her husband a bigger pond in which to fish. So a decision came from the top down: youth nights would follow a new format. Graham's choice had many detractors both inside and outside his immediate circle, but Barrows put it into action and saw an immediate gratifying response.

Beginning in 1994, youth nights opened with a concert by one or more performers an Ohio paper labeled "the monsters of Christian music." Tedd Smith resigned as pianist to produce the concerts. The first occurred on June 11, 1994, when over 60,000 young people crowded the Cleveland Stadium to hear Michael W. Smith and Toby Mac, a founding member of dc Talk, the wildly popular hip-hop, rap, and pop rock trio known for its energetic performance style. The billing also featured the Cleveland Cavalier three-point shoot-out champ Mark Price. Once the concert was underway, teens jammed the area in front of the stage and danced and shouted to the music. An hour into the event, a golf cart brought Billy Graham across the field to the stage to be introduced as someone the performers trusted. He preached a shorter-than-usual sermon. At its end, some 6,000 teenagers came forward, a response so unexpected that counselors were in short supply.[35]

In October 1994, at an Atlanta youth night billed as *Jammin' for Jesus*, the Georgia Dome echoed to the sounds of dc Talk while a light show flashed sixty feet above the stage. Nine trucks had hauled in the equipment required to produce the concert, but the 78,000 under-twenty-ones in attendance seemed to justify the effort. Reflecting on the evening a few years later, Graham mused, "Admittedly, it wasn't really my kind of music, nor was it what we have ordinarily featured in our meetings during most of our ministry. But times change. As long as the essential message of the gospel is not obscured or compromised, we must use every legitimate method we can."[36] As Shea put it, on youth nights he, Barrows, and the choir "stepped aside" to allow others to present the gospel in a different idiom. In time, youth programming came to be known as Concerts for the NeXt Generation. They featured music as a bridge between generations: even if young audiences did not fully grasp Graham's message, he was confident that they understood the music and that it reinforced his words.[37] Cliff Barrows, meanwhile, met with the performers before each concert to review the program line by line. He wanted no surprises. Personally, the team of three may not have related easily to the new format, but their warm interest in the young performers eager to share their testimonies in the contemporary musical idiom won the older men the appreciation of a new generation of Christian artists.

When 102-year-old George Beverly Shea received a Recording Academy Lifetime Achievement Award in 2011, his tribute was jointly written by two of the biggest names in contemporary Christian music—Michael W. Smith and Amy Grant. Grant recalled, "Sitting backstage with Bev before a crusade gave perspective to the task at hand. The 'job' before us wasn't just to entertain the crowd, but to provide a vehicle to allow Dr. Graham to do what he was called to do, and no one did that better than George Beverly Shea." Michael W. Smith summarized the general feeling when he said of Shea, "He has been a source of inspiration to millions, and especially to me."[38]

Not surprisingly, the Gospel Music Hall of Fame welcomed Shea in 1978 and Barrows in 1988. But in 1999, the Gospel Music Association honored Billy Graham by making him the only nonmusician ever inducted into the Gospel Music Hall of Fame. The association honored Graham for the platform his crusades provided GMA artists whose styles covered the range of gospel music idioms. Crusades gave extraordinary visibility not only to individuals and groups, but also to the musical genres they promoted. They had benefitted GMA musicians in immeasurable ways.

The music of the Graham crusades influenced what American Christians sang in a number of ways. First, the crusades gave a fresh sound to selected gospel hymns, and recordings by crusade musicians kept them in the public eye at a time when many Protestant congregations were beginning to replace gospel hymns with a more contemporary idiom. Second, crusades popularized neglected hymns. Third, crusade musicians arranged, composed, published, and popularized new music, much of which gained enduring popularity. Fourth, crusade follow-up surveys regularly showed that people who participated in crusade music breathed new life into local church musical practice.

First of all, crusade choir and solo numbers revived favorite songs of prior generations. People often requested old-time hymns, and some became virtual theme songs of specific crusades. During the twelve weeks of the 1954 London crusade, for example, capacity crowds sang Fanny Crosby's "Blessed Assurance" every night. People learned it, liked it, purchased recordings, and brought it to their churches. New attention to this old hymn made it one of several Crosby songs to enjoy a boost in popularity thanks to the crusades, and popular artists' recordings of crusade favorites brought the songs to wider audiences. After 1954, "Blessed Assurance" appeared in a wider range of hymnals, and recordings by popular artists from Elvis Presley to Aretha Franklin to a rousing, rocking rendition by Manhattan's Riverside Church Choir both contributed to and confirmed the expanding reach of this nineteenth-century holiness favorite. Recordings by crusade musicians, meanwhile, made the crusade sound widely available long after crusades ended. In 1951 Shea signed an exclusive recording contract with RCA-Victor. He had already cut a record with Decca and recorded several times for Alfred B. Smith's Singspiration Series.[39] Shea's contract with RCA Victor gave him visibility in the secular market that few other contemporary Christian singers then enjoyed. All told, Shea recorded over seventy albums.

Second, the crusades went beyond the familiar to transform little-known hymns into popular favorites. For example, Fanny Crosby wrote "To God Be the Glory" in 1875, but hymnal editors neglected it when they compiled the era's most influential hymnals; it appeared only in a few obscure collections. Cliff Barrows came upon the hymn during the 1954 London crusade, used it there, and then introduced it in the United States, where it quickly gained favor. Millions sang it in crusades, and media did the rest: a century-old forgotten hymn found a receptive public and made its way into standard hymnals.

Perhaps the most influential hymn associated with the crusades was "How Great Thou Art." Composed in Swedish by Carl Boberg in the late nineteenth century, the hymn was translated into English by Swedish immigrants for their own denominational collections. The text also migrated separately from Sweden to Germany to Russia to England, where in 1954 Shea and Barrows obtained copies of a version translated and expanded by the Englishman Stuart K. Hine. Shea first sang "How Great Thou Art" in the Toronto crusade in 1955, using an arrangement Barrows and crusade instrumentalists prepared for solo and choir. As he sang, he made two small alterations to the text, substituting "worlds" for "works" and "rolling" for "mighty":

> *O Lord, my God, when I in awesome wonder*
> *Consider all the worlds thy hands have made,*
> *I see the stars, I hear the rolling thunder,*
> *Thy power throughout the universe displayed.*[40]

Two years later, Shea and the choir opened the 1957 New York Madison Square Garden crusade with "How Great Thou Art," and there, as well as via Graham's broadcast, the *Hour of Decision*, the little-known hymn came into its own. Whenever Shea and the choir sang it, requests poured in for a repeat. In 1957 Shea sang the hymn ninety-nine times during the sixteen weeks of the Madison Square Garden crusade where attendance approached two million and occasional televised services drew in millions more.[41] The song was soon picked up by denominational hymnals (after Vatican II, it found its way into Catholic hymnals, too), and it was used in movies and on television; since 1957, three presidents have named it their favorite hymn.[42] The National Endowment for the Arts and the Recording Association of America ranked Shea's recording of "How Great Thou Art" number 204 among the top 365 recordings of the twentieth century. Elvis Presley recorded it for RCA Victor in 1967 on an album with the same name, using Shea's slightly altered text (which by then had become the standard American text). His renderings of the song won him his first Grammy the same year—and his third Grammy in 1974. (In 1968 the album *How Great Thou Art* was certified Gold; it reached three times Platinum in 2010.)

Third, Barrows's and Shea's frequent references to their use of "old-time hymns" tended to obscure the relatively recent—and even contemporary—origins of many of crusade favorites. From 1947, crusade musicians made generous use of twentieth-century compositions by people like Alfred Ackley, George Bennard, Oswald J. Smith, John Peterson, Jack Hayford, Redd Harper, Stuart Hamblen, the Gaithers, and many more

Finally, post-crusade surveys suggest that church members involved in Graham crusades brought new enthusiasm to local churches. The thrilling experience of participating in a mass choir made people eager to explore how music could become more effective in local worship settings.[43] One choir member put it this way: "I'm sure those listening . . . at the crusade were inspired, but not so much as the vocalists themselves. . . . Those of us who did it got the most out of it."[44] Pastors tended to feel encouraged by the ways crusade participation—counseling, ushering, singing—quickened their members' attentiveness to worship and outreach.[45]

Music had a prominent place in publicizing crusades well in advance of the advertising that saturated communities as Graham's arrival approached. This publicity featured George Beverly Shea and one of the crusade accompanists, generally Tedd Smith, in a program interspersing Shea's solos with keyboard hymn arrangements. These were musical evenings, not worship services, in neutral spaces seating 3,000–5,000, and they drew capacity crowds to churches or civic auditoriums across the United States and Canada.[46] In scheduling musical evenings, Shea made sure that they would build into a future crusade. "There should be a definite purpose and planning," he insisted, "beyond contacting people and entertaining them for the evening."[47] The sacred concerts offered a more intimate opportunity for the public to enjoy two leading crusade musicians. Especially in the years before televised services became commonplace—when crusades had more local character—they contributed to grass-roots momentum for the massive undertaking to come.

If music helped publicize a crusade, the media gave crusade music staying power long after Graham's team moved on. George Beverly Shea's albums sold briskly and made his familiar voice available in homes and via broadcast media. Tedd Smith and other crusade accompanists published hymn arrangements that enabled church musicians to mimic the crusade musical style. Occasional recordings featured mass crusade choirs directed by Barrows. In such ways, crusade music wove its way into the popular religious culture. Much of it had been familiar before, but when renewed and performed by crusade musicians, it lived on with new power for another generation. At the same time, Barrows, Shea, and Graham chose to celebrate and disseminate the contemporary sounds of young Christian artists around the world. By any measure, the crusade musical legacy is wrapped up in Barrows and Shea. For sixty years they stepped up to create and sustain the familiar—and iconic—sounds of Graham crusades, but they also knew when to step aside to feature the artistry of another generation. In the end, they lost nothing by yielding the stage; rather, they gained the esteem of a new generation of Christian artists and created space for testing the evangelistic potential of contemporary Christian music.

Conclusion

During Graham's first London crusade (1954), the *British Weekly* ventured: "George Beverly Shea deserves his reputation as a gospel singer . . . Barrows led the choir in the Lord's Prayer. It was magnificently sung and worth everything that has so far been done—except Graham, and maybe even including him." A few weeks later, the *Church of England Newspaper* used the same adjective for the overall music of the London Crusade: "magnificent."[48] Over the decades, most journalists concurred. Already in 1952, a writer for the *Baptist Messenger* recognized that music ably set the stage for Graham's effectiveness.[49] It also influenced responses to the message. Commenting on "Just As I Am," Walter Floyd mused in 1954 that of all the crusade components, its simple rendering did "the greatest good to the greatest number."[50]

Barrows and Shea adhered lifelong to the principles that guided their choices before they became a team. In their hands, the crusade musical sound, appreciated by millions in its own right, had as its primary purpose partnering with Graham in eliciting decisions. Their simplest goal was also their highest ambition: sing to save.

Notes

1. "New Evangelist Arises," *Life* Magazine, November 21 1949, 97; Billy Graham, "Evangelistic Crusade with Song," *Hammond Times*, April 1951, p. 4, Scrapbook 379(6), Collection 360, BGEA Scrapbooks, Billy Graham Center Archives (hereafter BGCA); see also Jan Kaye, "William Franklin Graham: God's Angry Messenger," *Pageant*, July 1951, 78.
2. For example, *Life of Faith*, 3/11/54, 151.
3. George Dugan, "Graham Outdrew Past Evangelists: Almost 2,000,000 Said to Have Heard Preacher . . . Singing Moved Audiences," *New York Times*, 3 September 1957, 52.

4. Cecil Northcott, "Billy Graham in Britain," *Christian Century*, June 2, 1954, 669–670.

5. The men made frequent references to doing "one thing," as in "Everything in our planning was channeled toward but one thing—the invitation to unconverted men and women to accept Christ as personal Savior." George Beverly Shea, "God Was There," *Youth for Christ Magazine*, January 1950, 16.

6. Billy Graham, "Second Thoughts on Evangelism," June 1955, Scrapbook (412)39, p. 5, Collection 360, BGEA Scrapbooks, BGCA.

7. Quoted in Margalit Fox, "George Beverly Shea Dies at 104," *New York Times*, April 17, 2013, B19.

8. Quoted in George Beverly Shea, "What Are You Singing?" *Christian Life*, October 1952, 85.

9. "Bev Shea Writes from Canada," *Houghton Star*, May 11, 1928, 4.

10. Frank S. Mead, "Advance," *Presbyterian Life* October 14, 1950, 12.

11. Shea, "What Are You Singing?," 85.

12. Shea, "What Are You Singing?," 86; during the 1954 London crusade, Shea sang 266 times, delivering his repertoire of 125 hymns from memory. Beverly Shea, "Subway Songs," *Moody Monthly*, October 1954, 43.

13. Margalit Fox summarized these characteristics in her superb *New York Times* obituary for Shea, April 2013, B19.

14. Brochure, Billy Graham Evangelistic Association, Scrapbook 381(8), Collection 360, BGEA Scrapbooks, BGCA.

15. Gospel Music Hall of Fame, Inductees Archive, http://www.gmahalloffame.org/speaker-lineup/george-beverly-shea/.

16. Tape 70, Collection 26, Audiotapes, BGCA.

17. W. Lyndel Vaught, interviewer, "Cliff Barrows: An In-Tune Encourager," *Church Musician*, April–June 1992, Folder 4, Box 11, Collection 622, Papers of Cliff Barrows, BGCA.

18. "Music by "Wheel" Barrows," *Power Magazine*, April 1946, 1–3, 6, Folder 4, Box 11, Collection 622, Papers of Cliff Barrows, BGCA.

19. Ibid., 2.

20. James Collier and Russell Busby, interview with Cliff Barrows, April 1982, Folder 1, Box 1, Collection 622, Papers of Cliff Barrows, BGCA.

21. "Cliff Barrows: An In-Tune Encourager," 70.

22. Dorothy C. Haskins, "Young Man with a Trombone," *Gospel Gleaners*, May 28, 1950, Folder 4, Box 11, Collection 622, Papers of Cliff Barrows, BGCA.

23. American Television Archive, Interview with Cliff Barrows, Part I, http://www.emmytvlegends.org/interviews/people/cliff-barrows.

24. "An In-Tune Encourager," 72.

25. Cliff Barrows, "Soul Harmony," Address at the School of Evangelism, The Cove, Asheville, NC, 1977. Tape 394, Collection 527, Records of BGEA: North American Ministries, BGCA.

26. Cliff Barrows on the effectiveness of music in crusades, Tape 70, Collection 26, Audiotapes, BGCA.

27. Barrows, "Soul Harmony."

28. "An In-Tune Encourager," 72.

29. Like most crusade musicians, Shea had a contractual relationship with the Billy Graham Evangelistic Association. He received a stipend in relation to specific schedule dates of musical ministry for crusade events, rallies, schools of evangelism, and other public events organized and created through the Billy Graham Evangelistic Association. He kept his schedule open to Graham, but he never moved to the headquarters, had an office and staff support, or fully relinquished his recording career (which provided another revenue stream). The arrangement gave him a degree of independence to do studio and concert work, but his friendship and commitment to Graham and Barrows and his devotion to music evangelism meant that he prioritized crusades and activities related to Graham's work.

30. Tedd Smith interview with Robert Ferm, 1976, Folder 23, Box 10, Collection 141, Oral History Project, BGCA.

31. Ethel Waters, *To Me It's Wonderful* (San Francisco: Harper & Row, 1972); Waters, *His Eye Is on the Sparrow* (Garden City, NY: Doubleday, 1951).

32. Larry Nager, "Graham Draws Big Names," *Cincinnati Inquirer*, http://www2.cincinnati.com/billygraham/music.html; Janelle Gelfand, "Faith Fuels Stardom," *Cincinnati Inquirer*, 26 October 2003.

33. For example, in Las Vegas in 1978, Cliff Barrows scheduled Johnny Cash with the hope that Cash's name would attract people from the Strip. Cliff Barrows to Johnny Cash, September 26, 1977, Folder 5, Box 11, Collection 622, Papers of Cliff Barrows, BGCA.

34. Billy Graham, *Just As I Am: The Autobiography of Billy Graham* (San Francisco: HarperCollins, 1997), 648–649.

35. Tammi Reed Ledbetter, "Will Mass Evangelism Efforts Continue to Reach Teenagers?" *The Christian Post*, November 27, 2002, http://www.christianpost.com/news/will-mass-evangelism-efforts-continue-to-reach-teenagers-8608/ Toby Mac gave Graham a typical introduction to 71,800 youth at Nashville's Adelphia Coliseum in 2000: "We'd like to introduce a friend of ours. . . . He's a listener, and he listens to teens. He's our hero and a great man of faith." Sarah Aldridge and Gregory Rumberg, "Gotta Serve Somebody," *Today's Christian Music*, August 24, 2000, http://www.todayschristianmusic.com/artists/various/features/gotta-serve-somebody/.

36. Graham, *Just As I Am*, 648.

37. Graham, *Just As I Am*, 648.

38. Recording Academy, Lifetime Achievement Award: George Beverly Shea, http://www.grammy.com/news/lifetime-achievement-award-george-beverly-shea.

39. "Shea Records for RCA," *Christian Life*, May 1951, 38.

40. Matt Schudel, "George Beverly Shea, Gospel Singer Who Preceded Billy Graham Sermons, Dies at 104," *Washington Post*, April 17, 2013, http://www.washingtonpost.com/local/obituaries/george-beverly-shea-gospel-singer-who-preceded-billy-graham-sermons-dies-at-104/2013/04/17/4388e9a2-a77b-11e2-a8e2-5b98cb59187f_story.html.

41. George Beverly Shea with Fred Bauer, *Then Sings My Soul* (Old Tappan, NJ: Fleming H. Revell Co., 1968), 141–145.

42. Edward Spann, *Presidential Praise: Our Presidents and Their Hymns* (Macon, GA: Mercer University Press, 2008).

43. Already in 1955, Hawaii Baptist pastor Frank T. Woodward noticed that participation in Barrows's mass choir made his musicians sing with "greater zeal, love, and purpose." *Hawaii Baptist*, April 1956, 8. See also CN 19, Papers of Robert O. Ferm, Box 11, Folder 8.

44. Lynda Hollenbeck, "The View from the Crusade Choir," *Benton (AR) Courier*, October 4, 1989.

45. Interviews by Robert and Lois Ferm as well as post-crusade survey responses indicate increased levels of congregational participation by people involved in Graham crusades. See especially CN141, Oral History Interviews, BGCA.

46. Collection 19, Robert O. Ferm Papers, Box 2 includes representative arrangements and programs for these concerts.

47. Robert Ferm to Victor Nelson, March 12, 1964, Folder 4, Box 2, Collection 19, Robert O. Ferm Papers, BGCA.

48. Morag Allerdice, "What It Looked Like at Harringay," *British Weekly*, March 4, 1954, Scrapbook 387(14), 9, Collection 360, BGEA Scrapbooks, BGCA; "80,000 People Pack Harringay in First Week," *Church of England Newspaper*, March 12 1954, 5.

49. W. P. Durnal, "Man and Message of the Hour," *Baptist Messenger*, April 1952, 8.

50. Walter Floyd, "The Harringay Hymn," *The Christian*, May 28, 1954, p. 5, 40, in Scrapbook 393(20).

4

God's Ambassador to the World

William Martin

BIOGRAPHERS AND OTHER chroniclers of Billy Graham's long career have called him "America's greatest evangelist," "America's pastor," "a parable of American righteousness," "a shaper of the Republican South," "the preacher [to American] presidents," and "the quintessential American." All of these are plausible descriptions, but as those of us who have given attention to Graham's long career know, his impact on the United States will not be the only part of his legacy. It is possible that it may not be the most lasting part. Graham held more than two hundred preaching missions of varied length in more than eighty countries and reached virtually every country in the world through various electronic media. In the process, he developed reputation, influence, and authority that enabled him to play a dominant role in creating a worldwide evangelical movement. In this chapter, I will briefly describe representative and, in my judgment, the most important evangelistic efforts on each of the continents other than North America where he proclaimed the Christian gospel in a substantial way. In addition, I will give a brief account of major international conferences that he and his BGEA associates organized, joining Christians from almost every nation into a world in ecumenical concord. The organization is roughly chronological and geographical, with appropriate flexibility on both dimensions.

The First Missionary Journey

Graham's first international evangelistic effort came in the spring of 1946, when he and a small band of coworkers in the vibrant Youth for Christ

(YFC) movement embarked on a forty-six-day tour of England and the European Continent. Though they had done little planning, they used techniques that had worked at home to organize rallies that attracted an aggregate audience estimated at more than 100,000 people. Then, working with receptive local clergy and American military personnel, they helped set up YFC organizations in numerous cities in Great Britain and on the Continent. Encouraged by that initial success, Graham returned to England in the fall to begin a six-month stay, during which he spoke at 360 gatherings, including extended campaigns in Birmingham, Manchester, and London.

After leaving his position with YFC in 1948 to devote the rest of his life to a ministry of evangelism, Graham rapidly rose to national prominence in the United States with successful campaigns in Los Angeles, Boston, and other leadings cities across the nation. A 1952 effort in Washington, DC, drew wide positive attention from members of Congress and strengthened an already developing friendship with Dwight Eisenhower, who would soon become president. These enhanced Graham's symbolic stature as a key spokesman for Protestant Christianity. During the 1952 Christmas season, he visited troops in Korea as a guest of the Pentagon, paralleling a visit from Francis Cardinal Spellman, the nation's leading Roman Catholic prelate.[1]

After preaching to GIs from makeshift platforms set up on hillsides or airstrips, visiting orphanages for children who had lost their families in the war, and stopping at hospitals where wounded soldiers were being treated, Graham reflected, "These experiences changed my life. I could never be quite the same again. . . . I felt sadder, older. I felt as though I had gone in a boy and come out a man."[2]

Graham had also been deeply impressed by the dedication he saw among Korean Christians who gathered for 5:00 a.m. prayer meetings and stood or sat on straw mats in subfreezing weather to hear him preach. When Korean pastors grasped his hands in gratitude for his visit, he felt humbled and ashamed: "These men had suffered persecution for Christ—their families had been killed because of their testimony for Christ—their homes were gone, they had nothing of worldly possessions—and here they were, coming to listen to me preach the Gospel and thanking me for it. They were preaching to me, but they did not know it."[3]

Majoring in anthropology at Wheaton College had introduced Graham to the valuable truth that no culture has a monopoly on righteousness or, for that matter, on evil. These seasons of fieldwork were driving that truth home in ways that would shape the rest of his long ministry.

The United Kingdom and Western Europe
Harringay, 1954

Graham's career included a range of impressive mountain peaks, but no crusade looms higher in the mythos and memory of his organization than the twelve-week 1954 London crusade,* better known in BGEA circles simply as "Harringay," after the drab arena used mainly for boxing matches and gambling and located in a section of London no more likely than Nazareth to produce a good thing.

The invitation had come from Britain's Evangelical Alliance. The British Council of Churches, representing the great majority of British Christians, chose not to sign on, viewing his theology as decades out of date and his preaching as high-pressure salesmanship unsuitable for a British audience.[4] Determined not to fail, Graham and his team unleashed a triple-powered formula for success: prayer, publicity, and political patronage. While more than 18,000 people organized to pray for the crusade's success months before it began, Graham's public relations operatives launched a promotional blitz so dazzling that both the Publicity Club and the Advertising Club of London named it the top advertising effort of the year.[5] On the political front, President Eisenhower heartily endorsed the campaign, and Secretary of State John Foster Dulles and US ambassador to Great Britain Winthrop Aldrich used their influence behind the scenes to help.

Advance materials that criticized socialism, which many British regarded as an attack on the British Labour government, created a storm of criticism from media and politicians, but by backtracking, apologizing, and meeting personally with his harshest critics, Graham managed to weather it and launch the most remarkable religious revival in modern British history.

---

* In the later years of his ministry, in part to avoid offending Muslims and others uncomfortable with warlike imagery, Graham called his preaching campaigns "missions" or "festivals," or gave them individual titles such as "ProChrist 93." Because "crusade" was the operative appellation for so long, I am retaining it in this chapter.

The crusade ran from March 1 to May 22, packing the 12,000-seat arena for all but two or three services. Attendance was helped by the introduction of a technique called Operation Andrew, named for the apostle who invited his brother Peter to meet Jesus (John 1:40–42). To attract the unconverted, churches offered free tickets and transportation to members who brought an unchurched friend with them. From Harringay onward, Operation Andrew was a standard part of crusade operations.[6]

A second innovation was even more far-reaching—using telephone lines to relay Graham's message to theaters, rented halls, and churches. This worked so well that by the final weeks of the crusade, the services were being transmitted to 430 venues in 175 different cities and towns in England, Ireland, Scotland, and Wales.[7] As the unprecedented success of the crusade continued, elite resistance to Graham ebbed, leading to invitations to meet in posh settings with British social, political, and religious leaders, including Prime Minister Winston Churchill, who welcomed him to 10 Downing Street. He spoke to capacity crowds at Oxford, Cambridge, and large gatherings at the University of London, Imperial College in Kensington, and the London School of Economics. He addressed a crowd of 12,000 in Trafalgar Square, 40,000 in Hyde Park, and, on the final day of the crusade, 185,000 in Wembley Stadium—beating the attendance record set during the 1948 Summer Olympics. Total attendance for the crusade, including the relay services, exceeded two million.[8]

For decades, numerous key British church leaders, most of them evangelical, would trace their conversion or their decision to enter the ministry to the Harringay Crusade.[9] But no individual experienced a greater impact than Graham himself. By touching London, he touched the entire British Empire and transformed into a true world figure.

In 1955 Graham returned to London for a weeklong stint in Wembley stadium and a six-week stay in Glasgow, where a Good Friday service broadcast by BBC radio and television reached a larger audience than any program in the history of British television other than the Queen's coronation. And he continued to cultivate high connections everywhere he went. Princess Margaret and the Queen Mother entertained him at Clarence House, and he preached to the Queen and other members of the royal family in the chapel at Windsor Great Park on the Sunday following the London crusade. Thus began a long friendship with the highest social stratum in Anglo-American society.[10]

After both the Harringay and Glasgow crusades, Graham made a whirlwind tour of cities on the Continent, usually holding only one service in each. Despite limited advance planning, crowds were larger than expected—304,000 overall, with the best turnouts in Amsterdam (40,000), Stockholm (65,000), and Berlin, where an astonishing 80,000 filled the great stadium where the 1936 Olympics had been held.[11]

Earls Court, 1964

Graham returned yet again to London in 1964 for a month-long effort in the Earls Court exhibition center. By this time, a Billy Graham crusade was a well-oiled operation, and Graham himself a well-known quantity. That familiarity bred contentment but not excitement, reflected in a comment in the *Daily Mail*: "We've grown accustomed to his faith."[12]

Despite the lukewarm response, the crusade was certainly no failure. Though it lasted only a third as long, average attendance was higher than at Harringay, as was the total number of inquirers, and it marked the first use of closed-circuit television to send the evangelist's visage as well as his voice to sites far from London.[13] While not the public sensation he had been a decade earlier, Graham was hosted on separate occasions by the American ambassador, the Lord Mayor of London, Princess Margaret, and the Queen herself in Buckingham Palace.[14] But a disappointing report published by the Evangelical Alliance and based on a survey of eighty-five British churches that had supported the crusade concluded that lasting impact on the unchurched was modest.

Graham returned to England several times over the following decades, most notably in the 1984 Mission England campaign, during which he spent up to a week in six different cities (not including London) over most of three months, and a 1985 effort linking fifty-one venues by satellite from Sheffield.[15]

Although he never attempted a formal crusade in Ireland, Graham did make a visit in May 1972, in part to explore the possibilities, but also in the hope of finding some way to ease the tensions that had riven Catholics and Protestants for generations. On his first full day, a Sunday, in Belfast, he displayed his confidence in personal diplomacy by joining the colorful and controversial street preacher Arthur Blessitt as he dragged a large cross (with a wheel) through areas of the city infamous for enmity and violence between Catholics and Protestants. For two and a half hours, they distributed tracts, talked with individuals, did a bit of preaching, and prayed for a revival that might bring peace between warring Christian factions. Graham acknowledged some anxiety, not eased by Blessitt's admission that they could easily be shot in the back by members of the fiercely anti-Protestant Irish Republican Army (IRA). The outing proceeded without trouble, though not without the evangelist's gaining a tangible sense of the atmosphere during "the Troubles."[16]

In the days that ensued, Graham met with hundreds of political, religious, and social leaders in groups of varied sizes, spoke at the Queen's University in Belfast, and appeared on Ulster TV and the BBC. Once again, theologians, journalists, and professors criticized his theology as shallow, his political understandings uninformed, and his confidence in the transforming power of revival naive, but they could not help being impressed by his humility, sincerity, and unshakable confidence in the power of faith to transform the lives of individuals and the culture of nations.[17]

Graham received a warmer reception in the southern, Catholic-dominated Republic of Ireland, where priests and nuns not only attended and praised his addresses, but also played recordings of them in convents and rectories—evidence they did not regard the most famous Protestant in the world as an enemy of Catholics. The visit to the two Irelands did not bring peace, but it did underscore Graham's commitment to efforts to increase understanding among separated people.[18]

India, 1956, 1972, 1977

Having proved himself in spiritual warfare in England and on the Continent, Graham decided it was time to wield the sword of the Spirit in the Far East. Jack Dain, an Anglican priest he had met during the Wembley crusade and who had served as a missionary in India for many years, organized a month-long tour of the parts of the subcontinent where Christianity had at least a modest foothold. Dain was excited at the prospect, but not overconfident. Graham had his own doubts, but was bolstered by the opinion of President Eisenhower and Secretary Dulles that, by authoritative preaching of the Christian message, he could serve as a counterbalance to recent efforts by the Soviet Union to bring an officially "nonaligned" India under the umbrella of atheistic communism. Graham liked the idea of having a dual role of soul winner and semi-official representative of American foreign policy, and he relished the opportunity to visit a quite different culture.[19]

Unrelated political turmoil forced cancellation of public services in Bombay (now Mumbai), but attendance in Madras topped 100,000 over three days. An early high point came at Kottayam, in the heart of India's

Christian population in the far south of the country. Though the population of the city was only 50,000, 5,000 worshipers gathered at 4:00 a.m. to pray for the evangelist and the crusade. They surely felt their prayers had been answered that evening when Graham took the platform to address a crowd of 75,000, the largest gathering of Christians ever seen in the region.[20] An even larger crowd, estimated at over 100,000, greeted him at Palamcottah a few days later.[21]

The excitement of revival did not cause Graham to forget his role as a diplomat without portfolio, nor were India's political leaders unaware of his ties to the highest levels of the American government. The head of India's ruling Congress Party met his plane at the airport in Bombay and ambassadors and staff members from various embassies were seated in places of honor at crusade services. Near the end of the tour, he received, with the aid of efforts by Secretary Dulles and US ambassador John Sherman Cooper, a coveted but awkward meeting with Prime Minister Jawaharlal Nehru.[22]

Although Graham had been careful to compliment and refrain from public criticism of Indian culture and Hindu religion, a book by an evangelical journalist who had accompanied the team on the tour quoted passages from Graham's diary and letters home that spoke of the "powers of darkness and heathenism" manifested in the spectacle of priests laying offerings before phallic sculptures in a Benares temple. The author added to the offense by observing that "a majority of the economic problems now suffered in India could be wiped out overnight if they would eat their cows instead of worshiping them." Such statements drew heavy fire from the Indian government and the religious community, both of which felt deeply aggrieved that Graham's apparent warmth toward Indian culture masked a typically Western attitude of superiority and condescension. Graham apologized, insisted he had "learned a lesson," and vowed, "It will never happen again."[23]

Sixteen years later, in 1972, Graham made a second visit to India, this time to the strife-torn region of Nagaland, a predominantly Christian state in the northeast of India whose fight for independence from the Hindu-dominated New Delhi government had led to decades of guerrilla action against national troops, making the region so dangerous that Westerners seldom received permission to enter. Permission was eventually granted, but the peace was not perfect. A few days before the first service in the capital city of Kohima, guerrillas attacked an army convoy, killing several soldiers. After the meeting got underway, a man attending a morning

Bible class died from a guerrilla's bullet and several more deaths occurred during a resulting skirmish. The authorities did not deem these sufficient reason to cancel the event, in part because 100,000 people had come from all over the region and were causing less trouble than they might if their long-held hopes were dashed by state authorities.

More than 4,000 made decisions for Christ during the three-day campaign. Christianity will always be a minority religion in India, but the evangelical version is the largest and most vibrant component of that minority in Nagaland. One minister deeply involved in the effort said, "In Nagaland, we never call it the Billy Graham Crusade. To this day, we call it the Kohima Miracle."[24]

Before returning to the United States, Graham met with Prime Minister Indira Gandhi in New Delhi to ask her, at President Nixon's request, what qualities she wanted in the person the president would soon appoint to be the US ambassador to India. "She told me," Graham recalled, " 'I want one who has the ear of the President, who knows economics, and who knows something about India.' So I went right over to the embassy and said that straight to the president, and he appointed [Daniel Patrick] Moynihan." When he returned to Washington, Graham met with Moynihan and shared his insights about India, including information he had received from Christians in Gandhi's cabinet. Moynihan was grateful for the information, Graham said. "He thought I had had him appointed. We got down on our knees and prayed together about his going to India."[25]

A third campaign, styled a Good News Festival, occurred in December 1977, two weeks after India had suffered a devastating cyclone. Sharing the preaching with his Indian associate Akbar Haqq, Graham preached to large crowds in Calcutta and Hyderabad, then packed Madras's Jawaharlal Nehru Stadium, named for the prime minister who had received Graham so coolly two decades earlier.[26]

Australia and New Zealand, 1959, 1968–1969, 1979

After his first visit to India in early 1956, Graham spent almost all of the next three years holding crusades in in the United States. With the exception of a three-week tour in the Caribbean to begin 1958, he did not venture abroad again until 1959, when he spent four months in Australia and New Zealand. The initial invitation had come from the

Anglican archbishop of Sydney, joined by most other Anglican leaders and other prominent Protestant churchmen as well.[27] In a number of ways, the tour, which included eight cities in Australia and three in New Zealand, with landline relays to more than four hundred communities, was reminiscent of Harringay. Attendance outstripped expectations and final services set attendance records in the largest venues, including the Melbourne stadium that had hosted the 1956 Olympics.[28] Television had come to the region only two years earlier, and Billy Graham was its first national attraction, dominating its schedule for nearly three months and, in the words of one observer, attracting "the closest to national adulation of an overseas figure, other than the Queen, that Australia has ever seen." Attendance for all services in both countries exceeded three million, and countless others heard the sermons on television. Known inquirers numbered almost 150,000, three quarters of whom claimed to be making first-time decisions.[29] An Anglican bishop reckoned the crusade to be "the biggest thing that ever happened in the church history of Australia." As in the aftermath of Harringay, significant numbers of young men entered seminary. A quarter-century later, Jack Dain, who transferred from India to Sydney, claimed, "The Anglican Church in Sydney is totally Evangelical."[30]

Encore visits to Australia and New Zealand in 1968 and 1969 produced a mix of responses. Sydney once again shone brightest. A high number of clergy and other church leaders who traced their spiritual rebirth to the 1959 crusade took the lead in this effort, which attracted an aggregate audience of more than 500,000 over eight days. More than 70 percent of inquirers said they were making a first-time decision, implying a net gain for the supporting churches, not just revival among existing members. The reception in Melbourne, Adelaide, and Auckland was cooler, even hostile at times, but less because of Graham's theology than because of his perceived closeness to President Nixon and presumed approval of US policy in Vietnam. The closing service in Melbourne, however, drew 85,000 and an unusually large number of youthful inquirers. A three-week campaign in 1979, limited to Sydney, drew a total of 491,000—a good showing, but only 10,000 more than the eight-day event had drawn a decade earlier. As J. Edwin Orr, one of evangelical Christianity's foremost scholars of revival, observed in 1986 about Graham's visits, "They were the greatest crusades Australia has ever seen, but Australia is still far from revived."[31]

Africa, 1960, 1973

In 1960, Graham made an eight-week tour of sixteen cities in ten countries in Africa.[32] Not all those new stars in his crown were equally bright.
North and South Rhodesia and Nigeria provided nearly two-thirds of the
aggregate audience of 570,000 and half of the 35,000 souls who answered
Graham's invitation over thirty-one services.[33] Public response to the evangelist also varied more pointedly than in campaigns in other countries. The
invitation to visit Liberia had come from President William V. S. Tubman.
Vice-President William R. Tolbert chaired the crusade, and Graham was
made a Grand Commander of the Humane Order of African Redemption,
Liberia's second-highest civil honor. Despite such high-level backing, the
five days of meetings drew fewer than 13,000 people. Crowds in Ghana
were also unimpressive, despite a warm reception from President Kwame
Nkrumah.

More predictable opposition came from other religionists. In Islam-
dominated northern Nigeria, Muslims sharply attacked his claims for the
deity of Christ and resented his criticisms of Islam in his sermons. He
had to abandon plans to preach in Sudan after Muslims there complained
that services would disrupt proper observance of Ramadan.[34] Elsewhere,
he was confronted though not really threatened by practitioners of indigenous native religions—animism, shamanism, juju, idolatry, and the
like—whose beliefs and practices were less familiar to him and for which
he had little response other than to tell them, "God loves you, and Jesus
died on the cross for you," and to make clear that becoming a Christian
meant repudiating their idols and other aspects of tribal religion. [35]

Inevitably and repeatedly, Graham had to deal with the issue that was
roiling his own country as much as some of the countries in Africa: race.
Wherever he preached, he emphasized that Jesus was not a white man,
not a European; that he was born near Africa and taken there for safety
as an infant; and that an African helped carry his cross. White and black
Christians took counselor training together and sat mingled in the services in Kenya and elsewhere.[36] His insistence that blacks be admitted to
services in Northern and Southern Rhodesia (now Zambia and Zimbabwe)
resulted in the first integrated public meetings ever conducted in either
country.[37] He declined to carry the crusade to South Africa after being told
blacks would not be permitted to attend its meetings, and he pointedly
criticized that country's policy of apartheid. "I don't see how the South

African approach can possibly work," he said. "Race barriers will ultimately have to end."[38]

Acknowledging the failures of segregation in America and the past unjust
treatment of Native Americans, he said, "to keep the races in total separa-
tion is a policy that won't work and is immoral and unchristian."[39]Though
such statements indicated he had come to understand the importance
of altering social structures, he angered black nationalists in some areas
by repeating the assertion that the changes needed in both America and
South Africa would come only through widespread religious revival and
changing individual hearts.

The tour concluded with visits to Addis Ababa, Ethiopia, where
Graham was received by the patriarch of the Ethiopian Orthodox Church
and Emperor Haile Selassie, a longtime friend of evangelical missions,
and to Cairo, where he spoke to a crowd of 10,000, apparently the first
such gathering in Egyptian history.[40]

Graham stopped briefly in both Jordan and Israel before returning to
the United States. In Jordan he denied having worked to assist Israel in
any significant way, and in Israel he readily accepted Prime Minister David
Ben Gurion's request that he preach only at explicitly Christian gatherings and not mention Jesus when speaking to Jewish audiences. [41] At a
press conference in the King David Hotel, he announced that he had no
intention of proselytizing anyone. In fact, he said, "I must be grateful to
you for proselytizing me. For Jesus Christ was a Jew, all the apostles were
Jews, and the whole early church was Jewish." Graham also used the time
in Israel to visit with and form long-standing friendships with the Israeli
political giants Abba Eban and Golda Meir. A few years later, Ms. Meir presented him with one of his most treasured possessions, a Bible inscribed,
"To a great teacher in all the important matters to humanity and a true
friend of Israel."[42]

Though certainly not a failure, the African campaign apparently convinced Graham that the task of evangelizing Africa should be left to others.
The only other visit to the vast continent in his capacity as an evangelist
was in 1973, when he consented to participate in the Congress of Mission
and Evangelism in South Africa. In addition, he agreed to hold a rally in
Kings Park Rugby Stadium in Durban, the site of the conference, and also
at the Wanderers Cricket Ground in Johannesburg a week later. As a pre-
condition for both appearances, Graham insisted that it would be open to
all races, with no segregated seating.[43]

The Durban event drew 45,000 for the first major public interracial gathering in the country's history. As he tried to absorb the sight of blacks and whites sitting together without apparent discomfort, a Zulu Christian said, "Even if Billy Graham doesn't stand up to preach, this has been enough of a testimony."[44] When Graham did stand up to preach, he stressed that "Christianity is not a white man's religion. Christ belongs to the whole world. His gospel is for everyone, whoever you are." [45]Even though he did not use the word "apartheid," the implication was not missed. The next day, the Durban newspaper headline proclaimed, "Apartheid Doomed." In Johannesburg a week later, Graham spoke to a thoroughly integrated crowd of 60,000 at a service carried over the state-run radio network, leading a popular magazine to characterize the two services as "knockout blows" against apartheid. The nefarious system still had plenty of corrosive life left in it, but these giant demonstrations of belief that God is "no respecter of persons" surely left a significant mark.[46]

South America, 1962, 1974

Graham added another continent to his life list in 1962 by making two forays into seven South American countries. As had become his custom, the preacher met with the president beforehand. President John F. Kennedy, a Roman Catholic, asked Graham if he expected to run into trouble with Catholics, who might resent his intrusion into their territory and the implication that they were not acceptably Christian. It was a relevant question, and reception was indeed mixed.[47] In Baranquilla, Colombia, Catholic clergy pressured the mayor into denying Graham permission to speak at the city's largest baseball stadium. In Maracaibo, Venezuela, protesters tore down crusade placards, posted anti-Graham leaflets in their place, and assailed a government building where Graham was speaking, firing guns into the air and holding signs that read "Yankee No," "Down with Kennedy," and "Castro Si." Those sentiments indicated the opposition was primarily political, and anti-American rather than anti-Protestant, and Graham was able to preach without problems to a crowd of 4,000 at a baseball park.[48] Response in Cali, Colombia, and Caracas, Venezuela, was friendlier, but in Paraguay the Catholic archbishop explicitly warned parishioners not to attend Graham's meeting. Whatever the impact of such opposition, crowds were modest in both Paraguay and neighboring Uruguay. Larger crowds greeted the evangelist in Chile, Argentina, and Brazil, giving him and Protestant Christianity exposure in the media. A veteran missionary credited Graham's visits with stimulating a surge of evangelistic efforts. That said, instead of listing every city in which Graham held a service, BGEA records compress these five weeks into a single line, "Tour-South America." Histories of Graham's ministry are scarcely more informative, although one of the iconic photographs in Graham publications and other media is that of a 225,000-person crowd packing Maracana Stadium in Rio de Janeiro in 1974.[49] At the direction of the president of Brazil, himself an evangelical, the largest television station in Rio made that service available to over 100 million people.[50]

East Asia
Tokyo, 1967

In 1967 Graham took on a daunting challenge by agreeing to hold a crusade in Tokyo, where only 16,000 of the city's 11 million attended any Christian church on Sunday, and that tiny minority was riven by sectarian strife, competition, and jealousy among leaders. As elsewhere, however, competing factions came together and the campaign packed a 15,000-seat indoor arena for ten days, providing encouragement and some lasting growth in the city's churches. Graham himself was sufficiently encouraged that he established a branch office of BGEA in Tokyo, to provide a staging base for efforts in the Far East.[51]

China, 1971

Following the example of Presidents Eisenhower and Lyndon Johnson, Richard Nixon made good use of Graham as an informal—and quite willing—envoy in situations where his reputation and contacts could plausibly make him more effective than a member of the diplomatic corps. "We thought highly of his abilities in that regard," Nixon's chief of staff H. R. Haldeman acknowledged. "He had contact at a very personal level with people of enormous diplomatic importance. He was astute in those situations, in the sense of his being a keen observer of people. People tend to confide in him more than they would to other people. He draws out their inner feelings. That can be enormously important diplomatically."[52]

Those skills proved especially valuable in 1971, when Graham aided Nixon's efforts to forge better relations with the People's Republic of China, an initiative eventually regarded as one of Nixon's most notable achievements. Though he had once called the PRC "the most dangerous enemy of freedom in the world," Graham trusted Nixon's intentions and assembled a group of more than thirty wary conservative leaders for a detailed briefing on the situation from the national security adviser, Henry Kissinger, hoping they could tamp down anxiety in their circles of influ-ence.[53] Shortly after that, he visited with Generalissimo and Madame Chiang Kai-shek in Taipei, stressing to them that the United States would not abandon the Republic of China and would honor its long-standing commitment to defend the small and vulnerable country. According to briefing papers in the National Archives, Nixon asked Graham to extend his warmest personal greetings to the Chiangs, acknowledge the personal anxiety he realized they must be experiencing, and assure them that "no secret deals have been struck or will be struck" that permit "improvements in relations with Peking at the expense of the vital interests of our allies in Asia, especially the Republic of China." The White House obviously regarded Graham as a crucial interlocutor—"the one person from this country that [the Chiangs] will listen to and would like to meet with."[54] The personal ties between Graham and the Chiangs were indeed binding. When the Generalissimo died in 1975, Graham presided over a memorial service for him at the National Cathedral in Washington, and Madame Chiang returned the favor by serving as honorary chairman of a successful five-day crusade in Taipei later in the year.[55]

Korea, 1952, 1974

When Graham visited American troops in Korea in 1952, he was deeply impressed by the intense dedication he found in the rapidly growing Christian church. When he returned in 1974, he witnessed the fruit of that dedication in unforgettable fashion. By that time, 10 percent of the population claimed to be Christian, and their number was growing at a rate four times that of the population. It helped greatly that the govern-ment, oppressive in many respects, viewed Christianity as an effective counterforce to communism and gave it favored treatment. "Anything that promotes anticommunism," one prominent Korean leader explained, "the Korean government favors."[56]

As evidence of that assertion, Graham and the sponsoring committee were given permission to use the People's Plaza, a mile-long former air-strip on Yeouido Island that was usually restricted to military parades and state-sponsored events. In addition, the Army Corps of Engineers built a platform large enough to hold a 10,000-member choir and installed powerful arc lights and a superb sound system.

Both Graham and his hosts had voiced some apprehensions about holding the event at such a vast venue, fearing that even a good crowd would seem tiny and insignificant. They need not have worried. Hours before the first service began, 300,000 people were already in place. By the time Cliff Barrows led the first hymn, the congregation had swelled to half a million. At the closing service on Sunday afternoon, a densely packed ribbon of people stretched half a mile to either side of the platform, comprising an estimated 1,200,000 souls, one of the largest public religious gatherings in history. In five days, Graham had preached to an aggregate audience of more than three million. On the last day, as a helicopter lifted him above the plaza and skimmed along the sea of white handkerchiefs waving beneath him, Graham said the only thing that made sense to him: "This is the work of God. There is no other explanation."[57]

Dr. Han Kyung Chik, a Presbyterian pastor who headed the committee that had invited Graham, reckoned that "with the Billy Graham crusade, the Korean church came of age." As had happened in so many places before, churches and parachurch agencies that had been competitors, and not always friendly ones, came together in a cooperative spirit that lasted beyond the crusade and enabled them to be effective collaborators in future ventures. Over the next three years, Presbyterians, Baptists, and charismatic churches exploded in growth, establishing hundreds of new churches. A Korean-only crusade on the same plaza in 1977 drew more than a million each night. By the end of the twentieth century, almost 30 percent of Koreans professed to be Christians, and South Korea is now a major producer of foreign missionaries.[58]

Communist Nations
Behind the Iron Curtain, 1977–1992

One of most fascinating and controversial segments of Graham's ministry comprised the years 1977–1992, when he managed to penetrate the former Soviet Union and its satellite countries behind the Iron Curtain. After having been described in America as "Communism's Public Enemy Number One" and blasted in the Communist press as a warmongering, hypocritical demagogue serving as an agent of US foreign policy, he obtained unprecedented privileges for his own ministry and played a significant role in extending religious freedom to others in many of those countries.

The first crack in the curtain came in 1977, with the aid of Alexander Haraszti, a physician and Baptist minister who had left Hungary during the 1956 Hungarian Revolution and moved to Atlanta, but had maintained extensive contacts in his native country.[59] After years of cultivating ties among evangelical leaders and appropriate bureaucrats in the Hungarian government, Dr. Haraszti obtained official permission for Graham to preach in several small evangelical churches and to make a few remarks at the closing services at a Baptist youth camp in the mountains near the Danube. He informed a hesitant Graham that no demands would be made and no promises given, but that if he proved to be a good guest and reported on the degree of religious freedom he did see rather than on its limits, he could expect return visits to follow. Publicity for Graham's appearances was meager, but churches were allowed to sell tapes and transcripts of his sermons. Estimates of the size of the audience for his "closing remarks" at the youth camp ranged between 15,000 and 30,000, many of whom had traveled hundreds of miles to hear the man whose name was not even on the program. In interviews with Western reporters, Graham spoke positively of the extent of religious liberty he had seen in Hungary. In return, the bureaucrat in charge of the State Office for Religious Affairs assured him that his ministry to the socialist countries of Eastern Europe was just beginning.

That prediction proved correct. In 1978, Graham took a ten-day tour of Poland, with good cooperation from the state and from both Protestant and Catholic churches. A visit to Auschwitz had a profound effect on him, stiffening his growing resolve to work for peace and reconciliation.[60] A few months later, when the World Council of Churches began to call for approval of the new Strategic Arms Limitation Talks (SALT II), Graham added his voice to the chorus and soon began to call for "SALT 10," a leapfrogging over incremental gains to "the bilateral, verifiable eradication of all nuclear, biochemical and laser weapons used for mass destruction."[61] In 1982 Graham received and accepted—despite stiff objection from high levels in the US government, especially in the State Department, and also from his wife Ruth—an invitation to participate in the World Conference of Religious Workers for Saving the Sacred Gift of Life from Nuclear Catastrophe, sponsored by the Russian Orthodox Church. The early sessions of the conference, held at an International Trade Center in Moscow, confirmed suspicions that it was to be a propaganda barrage against the

United States and other Western powers. After listening to anti-US dia-
tribes for a bit, Graham, sitting on the platform and visible to all, removed
his headphones as a signal that he would not listen to further attacks on
his country. After other prominent American churchmen expressed their
displeasure, the attacks abruptly ceased.

When Graham's turn come to speak the next day, he spoke bluntly,
comparing the United States and Russia to small boys playing with lighted
matches in a room knee-deep with gasoline, both knowing that if either
dropped just one match, mutual destruction was certain. He also noted
that the monies spent on weaponry robbed millions of the necessities
of life, causing "a hidden holocaust of unimaginable proportions in our
world." He then called on all nations to recognize and respect the right of
religious belief and practice of all people and renewed the call for SALT
10, "to remove this deadly blight from our midst and save the sacred gift
of life from nuclear catastrophe." His address received three minutes of
sustained applause and Cossack-style foot stamping.[62]

Unfortunately, those minutes of triumph were soon eclipsed by
repeated encounters with reporters in Moscow and after his return to the
United States, in which Graham ineptly expressed appreciation for the
gracious hospitality—"caviar at almost every meal"—and religious freedom he had been accorded while in Russia, giving an impression that
ordinary Soviet citizens enjoyed those same benefits. Such sentiments
met with dismay from religious people in Russia and anger and disdain
from staunch friends and usual critics in the United States. Astonished,
Graham claimed his words had been distorted, acknowledged that he
realized the Soviets were using his statements for propaganda purposes,
but insisted that his propaganda, the gospel of Christ, was stronger than
theirs. In general, American media and religious leaders did not buy it.

Much as Graham and his colleagues hoped, however, his behavior at
the Moscow conference convinced Soviet authorities that he was no apparent threat to public order or political stability. Later that year, he obtained
permission to visit the German Democratic Republic (East Germany) and
Czechoslovakia. Neither visit was a great success with either church or
government leaders, but they kept doors open. Then, in 1984, he was able
to speak more than fifty times in churches and other religious settings
in four USSR cities, including Moscow and Leningrad, something no
Westerner had ever been allowed to do. While in Moscow, Graham met
with Boris Ponomarev, a high-ranking member of the Central Committee
of the Communist Party and the Politburo. In a long and reportedly warm

conversation, Graham acknowledged deep differences between the United States and the USSR, but expressed his conviction that the countries must learn to coexist in peace. He stressed that religious people, whether Orthodox, Protestant, Jew, or Muslim, were not a threat to the Soviet order, and that repressing them was a significant barrier to detente between the two world powers, given the high value Americans place on freedom of religion. He specifically recommended lifting regulations and administrative measures that discriminate against believers, allowing Bibles and other religious materials to be freely published, and permitting freer operation of seminaries and other institutions for training religious leaders.

Without question, Graham's own opportunities to proclaim the Christian gospel expanded beyond what he had ever dreamed possible, even when circumstances were less than ideal. In Romania in 1985, for example, the repressive Ceausescu government forbade the use of loudspeakers to address huge overflow crowds outside churches in Timosoara and Bucharest.[63] A return visit to Hungary not long after that went more smoothly. A crowd of more than 20,000 gathered in front of the Roman Catholic cathedral in Pecs not only heard him but were able to see him on a twelve-by-eight-meter Diamond Vision screen brought in from Great Britain. In Budapest, he spoke to 14,500 people in a state-owned sports arena.[64] A third visit, in 1989, marked a fitting culmination of Alexander Haraszti's dreams. In marked contrast to his tightly circumscribed first visit, Graham's appearance was widely advertised and given prominent attention in state-owned media. At the final service, Dr. Haraszti stood at Graham's side on the platform, translating the evangelist's sermon for the estimated 110,000 people who packed Hungary's largest stadium. At the invitation, 27,000 people came forward, the largest response Graham had ever seen in his long ministry. A week later, the service was aired on the state television network. And shortly after that, the State Office for Religious Affairs was abolished and the government announced it was removing all barriers to the free development of churches in Hungary.[65]

Other efforts followed, including an event in 1990, a year after the Berlin Wall came down, when Graham preached in front of the Reichstag, next to the Brandenburg Gate, to more than 10,000 people who stood in freezing rain for the first ecumenical gathering of East and West Germans in more than thirty years.

For Graham, however, "Something beyond all expectations" would soon come to pass. In 1959, while traveling (officially) as a tourist, he had knelt in Red Square and prayed that he might live long enough to see revival come to Russia. As late as 1986, after all the progress he had seen, Dr. Haraszti had said, "We don't expect that Billy Graham will ever be able to preach in public in Moscow." But in 1992, with the support of 150 churches in the city and 3,000 more from elsewhere in Russia, Graham preached in the huge indoor Olympic Stadium, smashing the venue's previous attendance record of 38,000 on each of three nights. At the final meeting on Sunday, 50,000 people jammed into the arena and 20,000 others watched on a large screen outside as Graham told "the old, old story." The famed Russian Army Chorus sang "The Battle Hymn of the Republic," bringing the audience to its feet for the refrain, "Glory, glory hallelujah / His truth is marching on."[66]

China, 1988

In 1988, Graham fulfilled a long-standing dream of his and Ruth's—to preach the gospel in China, where Ruth had spent her childhood in a Presbyterian medical mission run by her parents, and to urge the Chinese Communist government to allow Christians to worship and evangelize freely. The trip had full approval from both the US and Chinese governments, and the Graham team was extensively prepped by former president Richard Nixon, a study group from the State Department, a China expert from Johns Hopkins, the noted China consultant Sidney Rittenberg, and the former Chinese ambassador to the United States Zhang Wenjin. Zhang was also the head of the Chinese People's Association for Friendship with Foreign Countries, which had played a major role in arranging the invitation.[67]

Following the template that had worked well behind the Iron Curtain, the Grahams had three goals for the mission: (1) assure the Chinese government that Christians were model citizens, (2) assure Chinese Christians that the rest of the Christian world was aware of them and their difficulties, and (3) emphasize the importance of peace.

In contrast to the low-key, almost clandestine nature of Graham's first visits to Eastern Europe in 1977, this seventeen-day tour of five cities was a major public event that included a banquet hosted by Ambassador Zhang in the Great Hall of the People, a luncheon for political and religious leaders at the US Embassy, and an hour-long visit with Premier Li Ping during which the premier acknowledged a gap between official guarantees of religious freedom and actual practice. He conceded that China needed "moral power" and "spiritual forces" to undergird its efforts at modernization.

The unannounced visit with the premier was featured on Chinese television, radio, and in newspapers throughout the country. Appearances in the other cities on the itinerary met with similar excitement and media attention.[68] Christians are likely to remain a tiny minority in China, but Rittenberg commended Graham for representing Christianity to Chinese leaders as "a powerful moral force to support the Chinese people in their mighty, backbreaking efforts to escape from poverty, both moral and material," and providing valuable suggestions as to "how they might better shape and administer the policy on religious freedom." In this manner, Rittenberg said, "Mr. Graham is opening the big door for the advance of Christianity in China. In doing so, he will promote the opening of all the little doors."[69]

North Korea, 1992, 1994

North Korea—officially the Democratic People's Republic of Korea (DPRK)—was a different story. Professing Christians numbered fewer than 2 percent of the population, and that estimate may have been high. The officially atheistic Communist regime opposed almost all religious expression, and the capital city of Pyongyang had only two Christian church buildings, one Protestant and one Catholic. Despite this regime of repression, the Korean (Protestant) Christian Federation and the Korean Catholics Association somehow managed to get government approval to invite Billy Graham to visit their country, with the understanding that his appearances would be quite limited, as indeed they were. With the approval of President George H. W. Bush and Secretary of State James A. Baker III, he accepted and made the visit in April 1992. He preached at both of the Pyongyang's churches and spoke to about 400 students at Kim Il Sung University, giving them the basics of Christian faith and some idea of the role it had played in American history.[70]

The high point of the April 1992 trip was a long and well-publicized visit with Kim Il Sung, the DPRK's elderly leader, to which state television gave extensive coverage, describing their conversation as "warm and cordial." President Kim expressed hope that "a new spring will come in the relation between our two countries." Two years later, Graham received and accepted another invitation. In most respects, the second visit was a replay of the first, but the three-hour visit with the president went beyond customary politesse as Graham sought to explore the possibilities of that "new spring," bringing word from President Bill Clinton that the United States would be open to a warmer relationship once North Korea agreed to allow international teams to inspect its nuclear weapons facilities. This agitated Kim, who said the two presidents needed to establish a personal relationship before talking about their problems. Steven Linton, a Korean expert who accompanied Graham on the trip, described the scene as "two old men bantering," with Graham trying to assure Kim that Clinton was a young man "doing the best he can, under the circumstances." In effect, Linton discerned, this was "a polite way for one old man to tell another old man that they were dealing with young men, and that young men can sometimes be brash," but that Clinton's intentions were sincere and honorable. A few weeks later, Kim agreed to let international inspectors visits the nuclear sites. Linton thought it quite plausible that Graham's informal diplomacy played a role in this concession by "[providing] a motive for allowing the inspections that didn't hurt Kim Il Sung's pride. It made it more a favor that he was bestowing than a concession that had been wrung out of him."[71]

Franklin Graham has since made several trips to the DPRK, and his Samaritan's Purse organization has provided more than $10 million in dental, medical, and other aid to that country. In a conversation with Fox News's Greta Van Susteren, he recalled the warmth of his father's friendship with Kim Il Sung and, while acknowledging the repressive nature of Kim's regime, felt that "if he had lived, we would be in a much better relationship between the United States and the DRPK."[72]

To the Uttermost Parts of the Earth: Billy Graham as a Media Innovator

Though he was best known for record-breaking appearances at major venues around the world, Graham was always ready to extend his reach to the multitudes who could not hear him in person by creative use of media. As noted, more than a million people were able to hear the 1954 Harringay crusade in London via landline telephone relays to theaters, churches, and rented halls throughout much of the United Kingdom. The Earls Court crusade ten years later featured an upgrade from audio lines to closed circuit television. The next major step came in 1970, when crusade services in Dortmund, Germany, were relayed to Eidophor big-screen television projectors in thirty-nine venues in ten nations in Europe. Although dubbed Europe 70, the services were also sent from Monte Carlo by the missionary-run Trans-World Radio to Africa and the Middle East, as well as to all of Eastern and Western Europe.[73]

Closed-circuit transmission gave way to satellites in 1985, when meetings from Sheffield, England, were beamed all over Great Britain. The capstone of this ever-evolving process was named Mission World, signifying an attempt to preach the gospel "to the whole creation." The first phase, in 1989, extended services in London to more than 30 countries in Africa. The 1990 second phase, Mission World Asia, proclaimed the gospel, translated into 45 languages, from Hong Kong to more than 70,000 satellite and video crusades in 30 countries in Asia and the Pacific. Two years later, in November 1991, crusade services originating in Buenos Aires reached an estimated 65 million people in 20 countries of South America, Central America, and Spanish-speaking countries in the Caribbean. The European segment, ProChrist 93, featured services originating in Essen, Germany, translated simultaneously into 44 languages, and transmitted via satellite to more than a thousand venues in 56 countries and territories in 16 time zones. This brought the number of countries reached through Mission World to 141, involving at least 95 different time zones.

The culmination of Mission World came when culturally adapted programs were molded around sermons Billy Graham preached in Hiram Bithorn Stadium in San Juan, Puerto Rico, on March 16–18, 1995. After translation into 116 different languages, the sermons bounced off 30 separate satellites to 3,000 downlink sites in 185 countries in all 29 time zones, to be viewed at appropriate hours. In addition, the programs were aired over national television networks in 117 countries and seen in the United States over several cable television systems and in national syndication. BGEA estimated that more than a billion people heard at least one of the programs. With the possible exception of the Olympics, this project, dubbed Global Mission, may well have been the most technologically complex example of worldwide communication ever attempted. David Barrett, coauthor of the *World Christian Encyclopedia* and widely regarded as a top authority on world missions, predicted that future students of world missions would view this initiative "as one of the most significant events in the worldwide spread of Christianity."[74]

Ecumenical Conferences

Ever since Acts 2:41 recorded that, in response to Peter's sermon on the day of Pentecost, "there were added that day about three thousand souls," evangelists have kept track of the size of their crowds and the number who responded to the invitation they extended. By that measure alone, Billy Graham has been the most successful evangelist in Christian history, with little chance his records will ever be broken. But those numbers can obscure contributions that are more far-reaching and longer lasting. Foremost among these has been Graham's role as an ecumenical leader. His early practice of insisting that his crusades have the backing of a majority of denominations in a locale resulted in what has been called "project ecumenism." The experience of working with people from different denominations in preparation for crusades led to warmer feelings and altered stereotypes that made theological differences seem less important and future cooperation more likely.

Graham's more enduring ecumenical achievement, however, was his leadership in the formation of a worldwide evangelical movement that has taken its place alongside Roman Catholicism and "mainline" Protestantism. Absolutely crucial to that development, particularly outside the United States, were a set of landmark conferences in Berlin, Lausanne, and Amsterdam.

Berlin

The Protestant ecumenical movement is often traced to the 1910 World Missionary Conference in Edinburgh, when the Methodist layman John R. Mott, general secretary of the World Student Christian Federation, called on all Protestant denominations to subordinate their theological differences and work together for "The Evangelization of the World in This Generation." Two world wars, the Great Depression, and the growing influence of "modernist" biblical criticism and theology seriously undercut the rationale for that enterprise and eroded confidence that it could be achieved.[75] When the World Council of Churches was founded in 1948 at a conference in Amsterdam, its mission was seen not as rescuing lost souls from eternal punishment in hell, but as transforming sinful structures in efforts to repair the physical, social, and psychological damages caused by World War II. In subsequent major conferences, particularly those in Evanston, Illinois, in 1954 and New Delhi in 1961, the Council explicitly distinguished its mission from "the old form of evangelism" represented by Billy Graham. Although Graham attended all three of these meetings as an observer and declared himself "thrilled at the whole process of seeing world churchmen sitting down together, praying together, discussing together," he felt the Council had taken the wrong road and set about to think of ways to gather evangelicals together to recapture Mott's vision of worldwide evangelism.[76]

After conferring extensively with other leading evangelicals, Graham decided to convene, under the auspices of *Christianity Today*, which he had founded in 1956, the World Congress on Evangelism, to be held in Berlin in 1966. Its purpose would be to define biblical evangelism, expound its relevance to the modern world, vigorously stress the urgency of proclaiming the gospel throughout the world, and summon the church to give priority to that task.[77] Eventually, an impressive and diverse group of 1,200 theologians and experienced evangelists met for ten days in October in the ultramodern *Kongresshalle* near the Berlin Wall. In a keynote address, Graham sharply criticized the ecumenical advocates of universalism, which he charged with having taken the heart out of the missionary movement. Just prior to the opening of the Berlin congress, the World Council of Churches had sponsored a conference in Geneva that called for "a revolutionary change in social and political structures," and even sanctioned the use of necessary violence. More pointedly, it specifically singled out Graham and others of the "evangelistic type" as "traitors to Christ's cause" because of their reluctance to criticize unjust social structures.

Graham hit this one head-on, repeating his conviction that "if the Church went back to its main task of proclaiming the Gospel and getting people converted to Christ, it would have a far greater impact on the social, moral, and psychological needs of men than it could achieve through any other thing it could possibly do." To accomplish that goal would require the churches to put aside minor differences and work in a spirit of cooperative unity, as people from many denominations worked together in his crusades for the purpose of evangelizing.[78]

The Berlin congress attracted wide attention in the United States and elsewhere, as the *New York Times* and other major papers gave it daily coverage. A reporter for the Religious News Service compared the gathering to the Second Vatican Council and Graham to Pope John XXIII, "holding together forces that would unquestionably have exploded in all directions save for his presence." Though perhaps hyperbolic, that description reflected the fact that hundreds of people who knew little about each other had found a unity in their enthusiasm for evangelism that more than offset their differences over doctrine and polity. Moreover, representatives from traditional evangelical denominations were amazed to find that representatives from denominations associated with World and National

Councils of Churches still retained a strong commitment to evangelism. *Christianity Today* editor Carl F. H. Henry agreed that the congress "shaped a mood in which Evangelicals sensed their larger need of each other and of mutual encouragement and enrichment," and Western delegates seemed particularly surprised by what one observer called "the dynamic surge of evangelistic emphasis coming from the newer churches of Latin America, Africa, and Asia."[79] One of the more consequential effects of the conferences resulted from Graham's inviting Pentecostal luminary Oral Roberts to attend the congress. Roberts was hesitant, as were some of Graham's associates, but Graham's large spirit and Roberts's desire to be accepted resulted in a strong friendship between the two men and proved to be important in bringing Pentecostals and evangelicals under the same rapidly enlarging ecumenical tent.[80] The Berlin congress proved to be a crucial event for evangelical Christianity, establishing it as an international movement capable of accomplishing more than its constituents had ever imagined.

Lausanne

As successful as it was, the Berlin gathering had been predominantly Western in composition. In the years that followed, the BGEA financed and helped organize regional follow-up conferences in Asia, Latin, America, Africa, Europe, and the United States. The success of these gatherings led to the desire for another world congress, this one to give more attention to specific strategies for implementing the dream of "the evangelization of the world in this generation." After extensive consultation with leaders he had long known and respected, Graham persuaded the BGEA board to assume responsibility for financing the event, and in August 1974, 2,400 evangelical leaders from 150 countries gathered for ten days in Lausanne, Switzerland, for the International Congress on World Evangelization. Noting that it had been "[b]rought together largely through the efforts of the Rev. Billy Graham," *Time* magazine called it "possibly the widest-ranging meeting of Christians ever held," and said it "served notice of the vigor of conservative, resolutely biblical, fervently mission-minded Christianity. [81]

In his keynote address, Graham reiterated his conviction that the decline of confidence in evangelism among liberal churches could be traced to a loss of confidence in the truth and authority of the Bible and a preoccupation with social and political problems, but he also acknowledged the need for greater attention to valid social concerns and warned against identifying the Christian gospel with any particular program or culture.

In addition to deepening the sense among evangelicals that they belonged to an increasingly unified, worldwide movement, the Lausanne congress moved beyond the Berlin gathering in several significant ways.

First, it gave high-profile visibility to the concept of "unreached peoples." Originally articulated at the Fuller Theological Seminary School of World Mission by recognized missiology experts Donald McGavran and Ralph Winter, the term refers to "people groups" having "no indigenous community of believing Christians with adequate numbers and resources to evangelize [their] people group without outside (cross-cultural) assistance." Prior to the conference, the Fuller School had collaborated with World Vision to produce a handbook of "Unreached Peoples," providing detailed information about the nearly two billion people in the world who fit this definition. Later versions of this publication, now known as the *World Christian Encyclopedia* and available online as the World Christian Database, are regarded as essential reference sources for world missions.

In his presentation to the assembly, Winter delineated three types of evangelism, code-named E1 (evangelizing "near neighbors," people sharing the same culture), E2 (evangelizing people with moderate cultural differences, as when US missionaries evangelize in Scandinavia or South America), and E3 (evangelizing people of radically different cultures). While acknowledging that E3 evangelism is the most difficult, he stressed its importance in creating a critical mass that could then conduct E1 and E2 evangelism, both of which are more likely to succeed because fewer cultural barriers stand between them and their targets.

These closely related concepts have dominated evangelical understanding of missions since the Lausanne congress. Don Hoke, a Japan missionary and longtime Graham associate who served as executive director of the congress, explained, "[T]hose concepts were an in-house thing at Fuller. It would have taken years to get them out to the church. By giving Ralph that platform, [Lausanne] gave him worldwide visibility in one night. The press picked it up, mission leaders picked it up, and the whole thing has gone forward since then."[82]

Understanding missionaries' often ethnocentric reactions to unfamiliar cultures, speakers noted the need for greater cultural sensitivity and flexibility. This could include observing anything from noting dress codes and rules for interaction between the sexes to accepting polygamy—there is, after all, a biblical precedent—and not trying to discourage former Muslims from meeting on Fridays and praying five times a day.

Lausanne also gave explicit attention to the responsibility of Christians to address issues of social justice, noting particularly the tendency of evangelicals to identify with political and economic conservatism and, in the words of one speaker, to condemn "all the sins that well-behaved middle-class-people condemn, but say nothing about exploitation, intrigue, and dirty political maneuvering done by great multinational corporations around the world."[83] The tension between "otherworldly evangelism," concerned only with saving souls for eternity, and efforts to give serious attention to hunger, poverty, racism, injustice, and authoritarian governments was directly addressed in a landmark document emanating from the congress and known as the Lausanne Covenant. Hammered out by a committee led by the evangelical intellectual giant John Stott, the Covenant affirmed the primacy of evangelism but made clear that "the results of evangelism include . . . responsible service in the world. . . . We affirm that evangelism and socio-political involvement are both part of our Christian duty. . . . Faith without works is dead."

In the years that followed, evangelicals who had been brought together by Lausanne joined to form regional research centers, seminaries, extension programs, and in Asia alone at least two hundred agencies that trained and sent missionaries to neighboring nations. The *International Bulletin of Missionary Research* asserted that the Lausanne Covenant "may now be the broadest umbrella in the world under which professing Christians can be gathered to pray and strategize for the salvation of their cities."[84]

The "Lausanne Movement" that followed the 1974 congress has organized numerous smaller conferences focusing on specific major topics or regions and two global gatherings, Lausanne II in Manila in 1989 and Lausanne III in Cape Town in 2010, the latter attended by 4,000 Christian leaders from 198 countries.[85]

Amsterdam

The third landmark ecumenical initiative culminated in three International Conferences for Itinerant Evangelists, held in Amsterdam in 1983, 1986, and 2000. These conferences sprang from a longtime dream of Graham's to find an efficient way to share the simple, practical knowledge he felt would help men and women go about the task that had occupied his life, helping people answer the question, "What must I do to be saved?"

They were not designed for prominent church leaders, or even primarily for missionaries engaged in E2 and E3 evangelism among unreached or unfamiliar peoples, but for everyday, mostly unknown preachers engaged in itinerant E1 evangelism—traveling from place to place, preaching to their "near neighbors," as Graham himself had done for most of his life.

Attendees—4,000 in 1983, 9,600 in 1986, and 10,700 in 2000, all chosen from much larger pools of applicants—came from almost every country in the world. As the number of countries in the world rose, each conference could plausibly claim to include representatives of more countries than any event, religious or secular, in the history of the world. At the 1986 conference, which I attended, the average age of the 9,600 attendees was thirty-one. There were more Baptists than from any other single denomination, but Pentecostals outnumbered Baptists and 500 delegates were women—two years after the Southern Baptist Convention ruled that women should not serve as pastors or in other roles requiring ordination.

At that conference, similar in format to the others, the agenda featured dozens of plenary addresses by evangelical luminaries, including Graham himself, delivered in English and translated simultaneously into fifteen languages. More than a hundred workshops on such practical topics as "Finding and Securing New Sources of Financial Aid," "Preparation and Delivery of an Evangelistic Message," "Counselor Training," "Follow-Up Methods," and "The Evangelist's Family Life" were broken into multiple language and regional groups. As at Pentecost, all heard in their own tongue.

In the years following these mammoth gatherings, numerous smaller regional conferences organized along the same lines have conveyed similar training to tens of thousands of additional evangelists from all over the world.

These conferences likely provide the true answer to the oft-asked question, "Who will be the next Billy Graham?" It will not be a single towering figure, but the thousands of men and women trained by BGEA to carry on his kind of ministry, not in great stadiums or via synchronous-orbit satellite, but in the highways and byways of the world, largely unknown outside their modest spheres. Like Billy Graham, they, too, serve as ambassadors—ambassadors for God and perhaps even, unofficially but with little sense of conflict, for their countries.

Notes

1. "Two Visits to Korea," *Time*, January 5, 1953, 34.

2. Billy Graham, *I Saw Your Sons at War: The Korean Diary of Billy Graham* (Minneapolis: Billy Graham Evangelistic Association, 1953), 34, 55. The United Press also reported that Graham was truly shaken by scenes of battle and the wounds of soldiers (December 27, 1952).

3. Ibid., 24, 38, 44, 54; AP, December 15, 1952.

4. Limited support, even among evangelicals: Robert O. Ferm, oral history, 1978, Folder 37, Box 3, Collection 141, BGCA; Frank Colquhoun, *The Harringay Story: The Official Story of the Billy Graham Greater London Crusade, 1954* (London: Hodder & Stoughton, 1955), 18; "His theology is fifty years behind contemporary scholarship." *Reynolds' News*, May 22, 1955.

5. Gerald Beavan, interview, March 1988. BGEA shared one of the awards with Craven-A Cigarettes. Colquhoun, *Harringay Story*, 44.

6. Stephen Olford, interview, April 21, 1988; Robert O. Ferm, manuscript for article on the history of Operation Andrew, Collection 19 (Ferm Papers), Box 11, Folder 3 (February–March, 1965), BGCA.

7. Herbert Lockyer Jr., "The Relay Meetings," *Moody Monthly*, October 1954; "Graham London Crusade Is Breaking All Records," *United Evangelical Action*, 1954, 148; Colquhoun, *Harringay Story*, 130–132.

8. Giant rallies: "34,586 Decisions," *Time*, May 31, 1954, 58–59; Cornwell, *A Time for Remembering: The Story of Ruth Bell Graham* (New York: Harper & Row, 1986), 108; John Pollock, *Billy Graham: The Authorized Biography*, (New York: McGraw Hill, 1966), 129–130; Charles T. Cook, "Memorable Climax to London Crusade," *The Christian*, May 28, 1954. Harringay statistics: "Assess Permanent Results of the Graham London Campaign," *Christian Century*, March 2, 1955, 262; "Billy's Britain," *Time*, March 22, 1954, 67; also, Colquhoun, *Harringay Story*, passim.

9. Ordained evangelicals in 1956: *Charlotte Observer*, November 13, 1956, citing British religious journals; John Pollock, "England Four Years after Graham," *Christianity Today*, April 28, 1958, 10–12.

10. Wembley crusade and meeting the royal family: Pollock, *Authorized Biography*, 151–154; George Burnham, *Mission Accomplished* (Westwood, NJ: Fleming H. Revell, 1955), 101–103.

11. Pollock, *Authorized Biography*, 136–137; Beavan, interview; "Billy Graham's Story: New Crusade in Europe," *U.S. News & World Report*, August 27, 1954, 83. Estimates of the numbers of East Germans were possible because most had come across the border in buses; European Tour: "Billy Graham's Story," 86; "Graham London Crusade Is Breaking All Records," *United Evangelical Action*, August 1, 1954.

12. "We've grown accustomed to his faith": Vincent Mulchrone, London *Daily Mail*, quoted in Mitchell, *London Crusade*, 13.

13. Earls Court statistics: BGEA crusade statistics.

14. Curtis Mitchell, *The Billy Graham London Crusade* (Minneapolis: World Wide Publications, 1966), 73; John Pollock, *Crusade '66: Britain Hears Billy Graham* (London: Hodder & Stoughton, 1966), 81–82.

15. BGEA crusade statistics.

16. BG and Blessitt tour Belfast: Graham Lacey, oral history, 1974, Collection141, Box 11, Folder 27, BGCA. John Pollock, drawing on Lacey's account, tells much the same story in *Evangelist to the World*, 93–95.

17. "Billy Graham: From Birmingham to Belfast," *Christianity Today*, June 9, 1972; John Pollock, *Billy Graham: Evangelist to the World* (New York: Harper & Row, 1979), 91–92.

18. Pollock, *Evangelist to the World*, 95–96, 98–102; *Charlotte Observer*, June 8, 1972; Brian Kingsmore, interview, July 7, 1986.

19. Telegram from Eisenhower, Dulles's advice: From a letter from Billy to Ruth Graham, quoted in "The Sweep of God in India—Billy Graham's Diary," *Christian Life*, July 1956, 14–19. In Collection 74, MF Reel 1, from Box 299, (Pre-presidential Papers of Richard Nixon, National Archives and Record Service).

20. George Burnham, *To the Far Corners: With Billy Graham in Asia* (Westwood, NJ: Fleming H. Revell, 1956); Dain, oral history and interview.

21. Burnham, *To the Far Corners*, 53–54.

22. Meeting with Nehru: Ibid., 61–63; Noel Houston, "Billy Graham," *Holiday* February 1958, 138.

23. Indian resentment of Burnham's book: "Billy Graham Answers His Critics," Letter to the Editor, Madras *Sunday Standard*, February 24, 1957. Also, Pollock, *Authorized Biography*, 165.

24. Pollock, *Evangelist to the World*, 3–26; Robert Cunville, oral history, Collection 141, Box 3, Folder 9, BGCA; Pollock, *Evangelist to the World*, 9.

25. BG, interview, March 5, 1989. Graham's account is supported by internal memos between WH aides David Parker and Bruce Kehrli. Parker to Kehrli, December 20, 1972, and Kehrli to Parker, December 22, 1972, Folder "CF FO 2/CO-66–FO 2/CO-99," CF Box 30, WHSF, NPM.

26. Augustine Asir, "Taking the Gospel to Chennai, India," *Decision*, January 5, 2010. <https://billygraham.org/decision-magazine/january-2010/taking-the-gospel -to-chennai-india/>.

27. Stewart Barton Babbage and Ian Siggens, *Light Beneath the Cross* (New York: Doubleday, 1960), 20–22.

28. Melbourne venues and attendance figures: Ibid., 32; Pollock, *Authorized Biography*, 190–196.

29. Ibid., 96.

30. The Reverend A. Jack Dain, interview, July 14, 1986.

31. Sydney crusade: Dain interview; "Australia Crusade Begins," *Christianity Today*, April 12, 1968, 42–43; "The Cross over Sydney," *Christianity Today*, May 24, 1968, 43–44. New Zealand and Melbourne: *Christian Century*, May 29, 1968, April 2, 1969; *Christianity Today*, March 28, 1969, 41; April 11, 1969, 45; John Pollock,

Crusades: 20 Years with Billy Graham (Minneapolis: World Wide Publications, 1969), 290–297. "Australia far from revived": J. Edwin Orr, interview, July 14, 1986.

32. Most of the citations in the material about the Africa tour are to press releases prepared by Tom McMahan and syndicated in American newspapers. The Graham-sanctioned book *Safari for Souls* (Columbia, SC: State-Record, 1960) was in large measure compiled from these releases. Also, Collection 19 (Ferm Papers), Box 5, Folder 50, Africa 1960, BGCA.

33. BGEA crusade statistics.

34. Islamic opposition: "Moslems vs. Billy," *Time*, February 15, 1960, 86; "Graham Wins Friends but Alienates Moslem," *Christian Century*, February 17, 1960, 180–181; "New Attitude," *Christian Century*, February 24, 1960, 214; UPI, February 4, 1960.

35. McMahan, *Safari for Souls*, 14–16.

36. "All over Africa . . . Christ Belongs to All Races," UPI, March 30, 1960; "Safari for Souls," *Time*, February 1, 1960; 37; Christianity associated with colonialism: McMahan, "Safari" press release, Jos, Nigeria.

37. First integrated meetings in Rhodesia: "Billy Graham's World," *Newsweek*, March 28, 1960, 86; McMahan, *Safari for Souls*, 54, 57.

38. "I don't see how the South African approach can possibly work": Unidentified clipping from press conference at Victoria Falls, in Collection 360, MF Reel 14, BGCA.

39. AP, in Charlotte *News*, April 4, 1960; also, stories in *Charlotte Observer*, March 30, 1960, and April 1, 1960. McMahan, "Safari" press release.

40. McMahan, "Safari" press release.

41. Hussein welcomes Graham: Roy Gustafson, oral history, 1976, Collection 141, Box 4, Folder 12, BGCA.

42. BG in Israel: McMahan, *Safari for Souls*, 88–92; "Mission's End," *Time*, March 28, 1960, 63–64; Graham, interview, February 26, 1987; Gustafson, oral history. BG did not meet with Ben-Gurion, who was in New York at the time.

43. BG accepts invitation to preach in South Africa: Pollock, *Evangelist to the World*, 28–31.

44. Ibid., 33.

45. Film, *South Africa*, World Wide Pictures, 1973.

46. Pollock, *Evangelist to the World*, 36.

47. Kennedy and Graham: BG, interview, March 26, 1987. The incident is recounted in several newspaper articles, including a story by Eustaquio Ramientos Jr., "Billy Graham a Great American," Quezon City, Philippines, *Examiner-News Weekly*, March 1963, Collection 360, MF Reel 50, BGCA.

48. BG in Venezuela: AP stories in *Charlotte Observer*, January 23, 24, 25, and February 2, 1962; Sandra Hill, story in Charlotte *News*, January 30, 1962; Norman Mydske (a BGEA operative who specialized in Latin American ministry), interview, November 25, 1987; Russ Busby (BGEA photographer), interview, April 30, 1986.

49. Russ Busby, *Billy Graham: God's Ambassador*, Time-Life Books, 1999, 106f.

50. Pollock, *Evangelist to the World*, 294f.

51. The Tokyo crusade: Don Hoke, interview, March 6, 1989; Ken McVety, interview, July 18, 1986; Pollock, *Crusades*, 255–261; "The Graham Crusade," *Christian Century*, February 21, 1968, 240–242.

52. White House valued BG's diplomatic skills: H. R. Haldeman, interview, August 14, 1989.

53. Kissinger briefs BG's conservative friends: HRH to BG, July 17, 1971, Folder "China 1/1/71," Box 17, EX CO 34; Folder "HRH Chronological," Box 197, HRH Files WHSF, NPM; HRH to Kissinger, August 3, 1971, Folder "HRH Chronological," Box 197, HRH Files, WHSF, NPM. The briefing occurred on August 10, 1971.

54. Graham to visit Chiangs on Nixon's behalf: HRH to HAK, November 11, 1971, Folder "Kissinger, November 1971," Box 86 (Alpha names files, A-X Oct–Dec 1971, Kehrli 10/71–Klein 11/71), HRH Files, WHSF, NPM; Talking Points for BG's conversation with Chiangs: HRH to BG, November 22, 1971, Folder "HRH Chronological Nov. 1971, A–L," Box 197, HRH Files, WHSF, NPM.

55. Taipei and Hong Kong crusades: "Harvest Time on Taiwan," *Christianity Today*, November 21, 1975, 51–52; "Happiness in Hong Kong," *Christianity Today*, December 5, 1975, 51; Charlotte *News*, April 11, 1975; Henry Holley, oral history, January 9, 1976, Collection 141, Box 4, Folder 29, BGCA.

56. Growth of Korean Christianity: Billy Kim, interview, July 17, 1986.

57. Korean Crusade description: Pollock, *Evangelist to the World*, 54–57; Kim, Abdul-Haqq, Holley, interviews; Holley, oral history.

58. "Yoido Full Gospel Church," *Wikipedia*, http://en.wikipedia.org/wiki/Yoido_Full_Gospel_Church.

59. Unless otherwise noted, information on Alexander Haraszti's role in the Eastern European campaigns is drawn from a five-hour interview with Haraszti on July 16, 1986; Haraszti's oral histories in the Billy Graham Center Archives: Collection 141, Box 45, Folder 1, May 21, 1979; Collection 141, Box 45, Folder 2, December 26, 1979; Collection 141, Box 45, Folders 3–4, June 30, 1982. Many of the descriptions of these events are also based on these materials. The 1982 Russia visit also draws on interviews with John Akers, a key member of Graham's inner circle and a close and valuable adviser on international matters.

60. Graham at Auschwitz: Edward Plowman, "Billy Graham in Poland," *Christianity Today*, 1978, 54, 57.

61. SALT 10: Billy Graham, *Approaching Hoofbeats: The Four Horsemen of the Apocalypse* (Waco, TX: Word Books, 1983), 146.

62. 1982 Moscow conference: See William Martin, *A Prophet with Honor: The Billy Graham Story* (New York: William Morrow, 1991), 498–518.

63. Romania tour: Edward Plowman, "Fanning the Flames of Revival in Romania," *Christianity Today*, November 8, 1985, 59–61; Edward Plowman interview, February 10, 1987; Haraszti interview, July 16, 1986.
64. 1985 Hungary tour: Edward Plowman, "Relations Improve between Church and State in Hungary," *Christianity Today*, November 22, 1985, 64–66; Plowman, interview.
65. 1989 Hungary visit: Ed Plowman and John Akers, *Billy Graham in Budapest* (Minneapolis: World Wide Publications, 1989), 18; *Billy Graham in Hungary*, BG syndicated television program, January 1990.
66. "Something Beyond All Expectation," *Decision* (January 1993), 7–13.
67. Grahams discuss China trip: Interviews, February 26, 27, 1987, and March 5, 1989.
68. BG received by Li Peng: Richard N. Ostling, "And Then There Was Billy," *Time*, November 14, 1988, 41; Edward Plowman, *Billy Graham in China* (Minneapolis: Billy Graham Evangelistic Association, 1988), 10, 26.
69. Rittenberg assesses BG visit: Plowman, *Billy Graham in China*, 47.
70. Korean visit: BGEA press release, March 27, 1992.
71. BG and Kim Il Sung: "Kim Il Sung, Up Close and Personal," *New Yorker*, March 1994, 33.
72. "Rare Footage of Rev. Billy Graham in North Korea Uncovered," Fox News, December 27, 2011, http://video.foxnews.com/v/1348279977001/rare-footage-of-rev-billy-graham-in-north-korea-uncovered/?#sp=show-clips.
73. Billy Graham Evangelistic Association, "BGEA History, http://billygraham.org/news/media-resources/electronic-press-kit/bgea-history/.
74. Mission World: Bob Williams, interviews, February 28, 1990, June 12, 1987, June 9, 1986; "Soft Sell and Satellites Deliver Biggest Audience," *Christianity Today*, August 18, 1989, 48–49; BGEA press release 90–16. Richard S. Greene, "Gospel Message Goes to Millions in Asia," *Decision*, February 1991, 11; Richard S. Greene, "Mission World Asia Continues—Thirty Countries, Bringing the Gospel," *Decision*, April 1991, 28–29. Mission World, Latin America: Richard S. Greene, "In Buenos Aires: A Cause for Celebration," *Decision*, February 1992, 7–10; ProChrist 93, BGEA press releases 93–2, 93–96, and 93–97; David Neff, "Personal Evangelism on a Mass Scale," *Christianity Today*, March 8, 1993, 64, 66; World Television Series, BGEA publicity materials.
75. Mott's story is well known. For one carefully researched and well-documented account, see Arthur E. Johnston, *World Evangelism and the Word of God* (Minneapolis: Bethany Fellowship, 1974).
76. BG thrilled with World Council meetings: BG, interview, February 27, 1987.
77. Purposes of the congress: Stanley Mooneyham, "Do It Again, Lord," unidentified clipping, March 4, 1966, Collection 83–108, MF Reel 10 (Clippings, England 1/66–6/66), BGCA.

78. BG's opening address: Graham, "Why Berlin?," *Christianity Today*, November 11, 1966, 5–6; "The Heart of a Revolution," *The Christian and Christianity Today*, 1, 12, 20, 22.

79. "The World Congress," *Christianity Today*, November 25, 1966, 34; Dave Foster, "Flags of 100 Nations Fly in Berlin," *The Christian and Christianity Today*, November 4, 1966, 1; Pollock, *Crusades*, 234.

80. BG introduces Oral Roberts: From Oral Roberts, "We Have Been Conquered by Love," *Abundant Life*, February 1967, 23, quoted in Harrell, *Oral Roberts*, 203.

81. "A Challenge from Evangelicals," *Time*, August 5, 1974, 48. The chief religion writer for *Time* was Richard Ostling, a former *CT* staffer. Leighton Ford's 1986 Fuller Lectures, *A Vision Pursued: The Lausanne Movement 1974–1986* (photocopy for private distribution). and subsequent conversation have been quite valuable in providing an overview and perspective on the Lausanne Movement, which he has served as a principal leader.

82. El, E2, E3: Ralph D. Winter, "The Highest Priority: Cross-Cultural Evangelism," in *Let the Earth Hear His Voice*, official reference volume of the International Congress on World Evangelism, ed. J. D. Douglas (Minneapolis: World Wide Publications, 1975), 213–241. Ford and Hoke assessments of El, E2, E3: Ford, *Vision*, 13; Hoke interview. Winter agreed that the Lausanne meeting gave great visibility to his and McGavran's ideas. Interview, February 6, 1991.

83. Samuel Escobar's address, "Evangelism and Man's Search for Freedom, Justice and Fulfillment," in Douglas, *Let the Earth*, 304, 324, 326.

84. Lausanne Covenant "the broadest umbrella": Hoke, interview; *International Bulletin of Mission Research*, October 1984.

85. Lausanne Movement, "All Gatherings," http://www.lausanne.org/all-gatherings.

PART TWO

Politics

5

Preaching Good News to the Poor

BILLY GRAHAM AND EVANGELICAL HUMANITARIANISM

David P. King

IN 1950, FRESH from a meteoric rise into the national spotlight after his Los Angeles crusade, Billy Graham publicly announced he was canceling his order for a new Chevrolet. Instead, he would give all the money to American missionary Bob Pierce and his new organization World Vision to support evangelistic and relief efforts among Korean War orphans.[1]

More than fifty years later, at his last major public crusade in New York in 2005, a reporter asked the famous evangelist what he considered the world's most pressing problem. Graham did not hesitate with his answer: global poverty. Only a few years removed from September 11, Graham deliberately distanced himself from other American evangelicals forecasting a clash of civilizations between Christianity and Islam and labeled the chief conflict instead as one of "hunger and starvation and poverty."[2] He went on to highlight not only the efforts of evangelists, missionaries, and faith-based relief agencies, but also large-scale efforts such as the United Nations' Millennium Development Goals.

Graham always remained first and foremost an evangelist, but he also served as a political strategist, cultural critic, *and* global humanitarian. He constantly preached the necessity of applying one's faith to the world's most pressing problems, and this message remained remarkably consistent for over fifty years. The two examples mentioned above serve as relative bookends to Graham's active career and illustrate a continued commitment to an evangelical humanitarianism. While his positions often defied simple binaries, Graham was often unclear on how best to articulate the subtle shifts that shaped his social ethic. As he was with many other subjects, Graham was more of a doer than a thinker. His social ethic was often formed in response to the issue in front of him.

It would be overly simplistic to say Graham's social ethic followed a trajectory from evangelism to humanitarianism. He did not simply give up one approach and embrace another. It was more complex and rarely systematic. His humanitarianism surfaced around particular issues and always alongside his primary evangelistic impulse. Most often these particular issues were international rather than domestic. Global poverty, world hunger, and oppressive political regimes abroad stood out to Graham in ways urban poverty and racism at home rarely did. Graham came to notice structural injustices in the United States only after his many experiences abroad. The international reframed the domestic for Graham.

Debates over evangelism versus social action were polarizing for evangelicals at the height of Graham's popularity, and they were ones Graham could not avoid. He often succeeded by staying just ahead of the evangelical majority. He spoke their language: stories of personal transformation over structural injustice; both praise for America's good work and threats of God's judgment for falling short. Throughout his career, Graham illustrated that evangelicals had a social ethic, and it was often in flux. Reconsidering social issues did not predicate only one particular means to address the ends of alleviating poverty or the embrace of a single political party. Yet, through the intersections of social issues at home and abroad, Graham sought to preach good news to the poor. What he meant by such a phrase evolved over the course of his career.

Graham's role in race relations, Vietnam, and presidential politics have rightly drawn scholars' attention, but his encounters with poverty—global and domestic—offer another window into his social concern. Constant exposure to ever-widening contexts led him to use his public platform to speak out on certain issues: advocating US foreign aid to fight the early Cold War, lending support for a time to the War on Poverty at home, and later publicizing the United Nations' efforts to eliminate global hunger amid war and disease. Other times, Graham preached Christian compassion but avoided divisive social and economic issues. He defined these as outside an evangelist's scope. Some critics believed Graham too naïve; others felt he was too calculating—avoiding controversial topics in order to broaden his popular appeal. Along with these attacks from critics, debates within American evangelicalism as well as his broader international experience and exposure to the global church led Graham to alter his social message even as his own rhetoric in turn shaped how many American Christians related their faith to social concerns. He always reminded audiences that winning people to Christ was his priority, but he also stated that "Christians, above all others, should be concerned with . . . social injustices."[3]

Both Graham's willingness and hesitancy to engage social issues made him a lightning rod praised by supporters and assailed by critics. While rarely a prophet, he was not simply the priest of American civil religion. Graham always admitted that his own social ethic remained a work in progress, and on issues like poverty his positions evolved over the course of his ministry. Most often subtle, but sometimes dramatic, Graham's humanitarian impulses moved from meeting needs through individualized charity to addressing a call for corporate responsibility and social justice.

American Evangelicals Debate a Social Ethic

Within the postwar American evangelicalism from which Graham emerged, the relationship between *evangelism* and *social action* served as a clear boundary marker for the movement. Graham would later persuade Carl F. H. Henry, the preeminent evangelical theologian of his generation, to serve as founding editor of the evangelical flagship magazine *Christianity Today*. First, however, Henry made a name for himself by articulating a new social outlook for evangelicals with his 1947 manifesto *The Uneasy Conscience of Modern Fundamentalism*. Henry believed the social gospel emerged from and perpetuated a liberal theology that abandoned the necessity of biblical supernaturalism and individual salvation, yet he feared that fundamentalists' reprisals "against the Social Gospel" had led to a "revolt against the Christian social imperative."[4] By ignoring a social ethic and retreating into isolationism and sectarianism, he worried that fundamentalists were forfeiting their right to be heard as agents of the gospel. Yet he was equally concerned that mainline and ecumenical Christians sacrificed spiritual aims for political ones. Henry instead called for a third way—a coalition of "neo-evangelicals" whose willingness to engage social issues distinguished them from fundamentalists on one side, and whose commitment to prioritize evangelism set them apart from mainline Christians on the other. As a number of neo-evangelicals latched onto Henry's vision, he served as the theological architect for the new movement. On this issue, like most others, Graham followed Henry's vision and toed the party line for postwar American evangelicals. Social concern played a role (even if often undefined), but his hope for larger social change rested in changing the hearts of individuals. But if Henry was the theological architect, Graham remained the evangelist who put the vision into practice.

Graham built this evangelical social ethic into his preaching. To address the world's most pressing problems, he depicted the world, the nation, and individuals at a moment of crisis in need of a personal relationship with Jesus as the answer. Over time, Graham's sermon illustrations changed, but the form largely stayed the same. Through the 1950s he repeatedly referenced juvenile delinquency, disease, poverty, illiteracy, and communism. In the 1960s he added race, sex, overpopulation, and youthful rebellion to the list. In the 1970s it was self-absorption and the "me generation." By the 1980s AIDS, abortion, and nuclear disarmament had captured his attention. Despite the diversity of issues, underneath every social problem was a moral and religious one. The solution was the spiritual conversion of individuals. (See also Curtis Evans's chapter, "A Politics of Conversion.")

Graham Goes Global

Graham became an international evangelist during his earliest days with Youth for Christ. Preaching throughout Europe in the aftermath of World War II and touring the political hotspots of Asia soon thereafter, Graham quickly began to develop a global vision, even if that vision was often cast though an American lens. Graham and his associates always combed the local newspapers for sermon illustrations from the specific contexts where he preached, but from the crusade platform, Graham's illustrations pointed to universal over parochial themes. His critics chastised him for depicting social issues as overly abstract, but Graham countered that he sacrificed specificity because these problems were universal in scope.

Graham's budding internationalism was most evident in his rabid defense of America's efforts in fighting the Cold War. For Graham and many Americans, the Cold War was a spiritual war, pitting a Christian America against a godless communism. As an evangelistic crusader in a spiritual battle, Graham felt he played an important role, and he preached, "The greatest and most effective weapon against Communism today is to be a born again Christian." In the 1950s Graham saw communism making inroads among Americans, and through his domestic crusades he cautioned audiences to see it for what it was, an "anti-Christian religion competing with Christianity for American souls."[5] Yet Graham realized that communism was a global threat, thrusting his attention into international concerns. He knew the front lines of the Cold War were not at home, and he did his part for God and country by spending months every year outside the United States. Many years during the 1950s, he conducted as many, or more, crusades overseas as he did at home.[6]

Graham counted conversions in the thousands as victories for both Christianity and the Cold War, but his international experiences also confronted him with humanitarian need like he had never before seen. In 1952, Bob Pierce, Graham's fellow Youth for Christ evangelist and founder of evangelical missionary agency World Vision, took him on a tour of war-torn Korea, where he visited orphanages, field hospitals, and flattened churches. (For another account of Graham's experience with the Korean War, see Seth Dowland's chapter, "Billy Graham's New Evangelical Manhood.") What had been only a mental picture for Graham when he pledged his initial financial support to World Vision in 1950, he now saw with his own eyes. Deeply moved by the sacrifice of Korean pastors, Graham testified, "These men had suffered persecution for Christ—their families had been killed . . . their homes were gone . . . and here they were, coming to listen to me preach the Gospel." Graham concluded, "I came to the Orient a boy, but I'm going home a man."[7] At home, he would retell these stories of Christian martyrdom and suffering as illustrations of the deep faith of the Korean church, and as a reproach against what Graham deemed the comparative unwillingness of American Christians to make similar sacrifices. Thus, his international encounters began to shape his views of Christianity back home.

A few years later, in 1956, Graham made a return tour to Asia. The abject poverty he witnessed again overwhelmed him. Walking the streets of Bombay one afternoon, he emptied his pockets of rupees to every beggar he encountered, only to be mobbed by requests for alms and forced to be rescued by his missionary hosts. Graham sometimes lauded the poverty and suffering of Asian Christians as a badge of honor and a lesson to the comforts of cultural Christianity in America, but by the time he returned from India, he had new eyes for the magnitude of global poverty and his inability to eliminate it simply through personal compassion.[8] Graham still preached individual conversion as the only proven mechanism for larger social change, but as a sustainable solution, personal conversion was only the first step in a larger process.

Graham's newfound awareness accompanied a surge of evangelical interest in compassion ministries overseas. Graham followed suit in calling for a new generation of missionaries, lauding the efforts of the indigenous church, while highlighting the work of newly formed evangelical relief organizations like the National Association of Evangelicals' (NAE) World Relief Commission, the Everett Swanson Evangelical Association (later renamed Compassion International), and World Vision.[9] Emerging from within this neo-evangelical movement, these mission agencies also ascribed to Henry's social ethic. They highlighted both their evangelistic efforts and their compassion ministries caring for orphans and widows. As the hands and feet of evangelical compassion abroad, Graham promoted the work of these agencies as exemplars in his crusades.

With the caveat that spiritual conversion always came first and served to motivate Christian compassion, Graham also acknowledged the biblical mandate to care for the world's poor. With a myriad of global issues marking the beginning of most Graham sermons, poverty was almost always on the list. Asking his audience how to resolve these pressing issues led Graham to the sermon's crisis, but he rarely relieved the tension by offering concrete solutions to these social problems. How individual Christians should work to address and alleviate global poverty was left unclear. Graham refused to offer solutions. He never pretended to be an expert in social policy, yet he was keen to mark boundary lines. He avoided the structural categories favored by the leading mainline voices that many evangelicals saw as a slippery slope sacrificing the need for individual conversion, but Graham was also keen to note that if born-again Christians were confronted with an immediate need and refused to respond out of compassion, God would not be pleased.

Graham sometimes expanded on the biblical mandate for individual Christians and offered a humanitarian role for America in the world. By the mid-fifties, he lobbied for the expansion of US foreign aid increasing the delivery of surplus goods and technical support to developing nations. "The world of angry, hungry men are looking to us for answers," Graham claimed, "They have asked for bread, and we've given them a stone."[10] At one level, this was political pragmatism. Graham saw foreign aid as a tool to win the Cold War and squelch revolutions in a new postcolonial world. He cautioned, "They (the world's poor) are soon going to run over us unless we are willing to share the surpluses that God has endowed us with."[11] He feared the United States was losing ground to the Soviet Union for the support of non-aligned third world nations. As both a political and spiritual battlefield, Graham acknowledged that the "godless religion" of the communists was outgaining Christian America in the number of converts to their cause.

But Graham's call for increased aid was more than political and humanitarian; it also served as a spiritual indictment of Christian America. Graham acknowledged, "Too long have the privileged few exploited and ignored the underprivileged millions of the world."[12] Contrasting the greed at home with abject poverty abroad, Graham preached, "We in America cannot go on driving Cadillacs and getting richer, while the rest of the world drives oxcarts and gets poorer. One of the biggest sins of America is selfish refusal to share its wealth with the world's poor."[13]

Graham's firsthand experience abroad did not always map onto his experience at home. During the 1950s and early 1960s, Graham overlooked and even dismissed the rural and urban poverty in America. While he preached that "three-fifths of the world lives in squalor, misery, and hunger," he countered that "the substandard conditions of people in Appalachia would make them wealthy in comparison to millions in India, Africa and Asia."[14] He was more concerned with what America's newfound postwar prosperity was doing to individuals and the nation. While he preached it was the *love* of money and not money itself that served as the root of all evil, Graham was clear that affluence presented a strong distraction from the spiritual life of individuals. He avoided chastising the rich and powerful for their wealth per se, but he often cautioned that the materially rich often faced additional temptations that could lead to spiritual bankruptcy.[15] The contrast Graham provoked was clear. If the biggest global threat was poverty, America's greatest threat was affluence.

Akin to social policy, Graham avoided making specific recommendations on how much accumulated wealth it took to make one rich or how much someone should give away to avoid the threat of materialism. In addressing affluence at a national level, however, Graham was more direct. While he continued to praise America as a chosen nation, in typical jeremiad fashion Graham worried that too much prosperity would lead it astray from its divine purpose. In a 1964 sermon to an annual NAE gathering, he claimed, "If I wanted to destroy a nation I would give it too much and would have it on its knees miserable greedy and sick." Comparing contemporary America to the conditions that led to the downfall of the Roman Empire, Graham saw increasing violence, cruelty, hypocrisy, and indifference as "symptomatic of a people which has too much."[16] Graham admonished Americans not to put their trust in worldly things. If global poverty served as a major social issue to which American Christians must respond, Graham also cautioned that America's own abundance led its citizens astray from spiritual concerns. Graham believed the needs of the global poor were both material and spiritual. For Americans, he saw the danger as primarily spiritual. If American Christians would not share their abundance with the rest of the world, America would lose not only its role as global leader, but also its soul.

Debating the Role of Social Concern in Graham's Gospel

Graham continued to highlight the world's most pressing problems even as he held fast to the priority of evangelism. That layered commitment led to continued evangelical support, but it also provoked heavier criticism from mainline Christian voices. In the late 1950s, the nation's leading public theologian, Reinhold Niebuhr, criticized Graham for his "pietistic individualism" that ignored any definition of sin as a collective or social category.[17] The critiques stung Graham because he respected Niebuhr's work. In a *Saturday Evening Post* article published right before Graham's record-setting 1957 Madison Square Garden crusade, he credited Niebuhr for helping him "to apply Christianity to the social problems we face . . . and to comprehend what those problems are."[18] In 1960 Graham admitted to the *Christian Century*, the leading mainline periodical, in its popular "How My Mind Has Changed" series, that his "belief in the social implications of the gospel has deepened and broadened," and he expressed disappointment that he was often accused of having no social concern. Yet Graham was clear that he still refused categories such as structural sin, and he reiterated that "international problems are only reflections of individual problems, . . . social sins are merely a large-scale projection of individual sins."[19] Graham held firm to his conviction "that you cannot change the world "with all its lusts and hatred and greed, until you change men's hearts."[20] Jesus' command to preach good news to the poor was decidedly evangelistic. Overseas, Graham saw these twin themes together— evangelizing often went hand in hand with healthcare, education, and poverty amelioration. At home, he saw less evidence of and made less effort to intertwine evangelism with efforts to battle institutional poverty or racism.

The continued conflict over the relationship of evangelism and social concern took up an inordinate amount of evangelical energy in the 1960s, and as the public face of a renewed evangelicalism, Graham considered this an issue he must address directly. Concerned that ecumenical groups like the World Council of Churches were diluting the gospel by focusing more on changing political structures than saving souls, Graham responded by convening the World Congress on Evangelism in Berlin in 1966. The congress was a "breakthrough" for evangelical unity and media exposure, but social issues remained on the periphery behind the priority of evangelism.[21] Graham's opening address set the tone:

> Evangelism is the only revolutionary force that can change our world. . . . If the church went back to its main task of . . . getting people converted to Christ, it would have a far greater impact on the social, moral, and psychological needs of men than any other thing it could possibly do.[22]

The Berlin congress acknowledged social suffering but said little about how to address it. Many evangelicals, however, began to realize they could no longer ignore these social issues and remain relevant.[23] The Fuller Seminary missiologist C. Peter Wagner spoke for many evangelicals in claiming, "Too often we have rushed by the hungry ones to get to the lost ones."[24] Evangelical leaders had clarity on what they were not. They would not forego evangelism for the sake of social outreach as they accused the mainline, nor would they bury their heads in the sand and wait for Christ's second coming as they accused the fundamentalists. Evangelicals were less clear, however, about how best to put their social ethic into practice.

If uncertainty frustrated other evangelicals' ability to act, Graham seemed to have no problem holding these tensions together. As Graham wrote in 1965, "This sounds like a paradox, but it is not. We as Christians have two responsibilities. One, to proclaim the Gospel of Jesus Christ as the only answer to man's deepest needs. Two, to apply as best we can the principles of Christianity to the social conditions around us."[25] At the same time, Graham began to ratchet up the language of crisis in his sermons. If poverty and disease illustrated pressing problems in the 1950s, then by the 1960s, poverty had joined issues like race, overpopulation, and sexual license not as problems, but rather as revolutions perched to tear apart the world if they were not addressed.[26]

Graham continued to address humanitarian crises—especially international ones—much as he had in the previous decade, but he also peppered his evangelistic language with an expanded vocabulary of social concerns. In encouraging help for victims of a major Indian famine the same year that he delivered his 1966 Berlin address, Graham reminded Christians that "the hungry and the diseased are on the mind and heart of Christ. There is a social aspect of the Gospel that many people ignore."[27] In reflecting on Christian history, he followed other neo-evangelicals' rediscovery of the social conscience of nineteenth-century evangelicals and their efforts in education, temperance, and abolition.[28] He even went on record affirming the social gospel that had often served for fundamentalists and evangelicals as the theological flashpoint when Christian missions went awry—sacrificing personal evangelism in order to change social structures. In addressing the World Council of Churches in 1967, Graham stated, "There is no doubt that the Social Gospel has directed its energies toward the relief of many of the problems of suffering humanity. I am for it! I believe it is Biblical."[29]

Graham's Turn to Domestic Poverty

Yet if Graham highlighted poverty abroad and expanded his own language to encourage Christian social engagement, he often continued to overlook human need at home. For him, America still represented abundance in contrast to the widespread poverty he encountered overseas. At first, as President John F. Kennedy introduced the issue of "poverty in the midst of plenty" and President Lyndon B. Johnson subsequently institutionalized it through his War on Poverty, Graham proved largely uninterested.[30] For starters, Graham was disappointed in the program's lack of attention to moral and spiritual questions. He felt the Great Society was too idealistic and too prone to rely on the resources of big government over the need for change in the human heart.[31] What would be the role of churches and individual Christians in these government programs? Graham grew increasingly irritated with what he saw as the politicizing of the gospel. Particularly irritating for Graham were fellow ministers who spoke outside their field of expertise. Spiritual concerns were the realm of the clergy; politics and economics were not. Referencing the mainline church's penchant for making political statements, Graham lamented:

When most major Protestant denominations have their annual councils, assemblies, or conventions, they make pronouncements on matters having to do with disarmament, federal aid to education, birth control, the United Nations, and any number of social and political issues. Very rarely are any resolutions passed that have to do with the redemptive witness of the Gospel.[32]

While admitting that he had spoken out for increased humanitarian assistance to fight the Cold War and alleviate poverty abroad, Graham saw this as his individual opinion and continued to claim that church bodies should not endorse political positions. To reiterate his disdain of political preachers, Graham would recount a conversation with the former Secretary of State John Foster Dulles. After his 1956 Asian tour, Graham returned to make a few policy suggestions to the secretary of state, only to have Dulles respond by letting Graham know that he might be an effective preacher, but he had no knowledge of the complexity of global markets and foreign aid.[33] Graham followed his conversation with Dulles with another account of a more recent conversation with a US president, who told him "he was sick and tired of hearing preachers give advice on international affairs when they did not have the facts straight."[34] With the irony of his own close relationship to power apparently lost on Graham, Graham seconded the president's perspective. In the turbulent 1960s, Graham grew even less patient. Going as far as calling them false prophets, he criticized liberal clergy for making political statements on issues like Vietnam or civil rights, and he chastised them for advocating "social service without also providing a solid spiritual basis for it."[35] Graham was perfecting a penchant for taking both sides of an issue. He criticized liberal theologians and politicians for believing legislation and social programs would solve injustice even while encouraging Americans to take "a stand on the moral, social, and spiritual issues of our day." His words sometimes hinted that everyone—rich or poor—should be content with their situation, even as he also claimed Christians cannot remain content with the present social order "as long as any person goes to be hungry at night."[36]

Yet by 1965, Graham was making his own political statements in the response to the riots in Watts, California, and subsequent urban cities. These race riots on American soil took Graham by surprise. Labeling them "a dress rehearsal for revolution," Graham pleaded with Congress to drop "all other legislation and devise new laws to deal with riots and violence."[37] He first described "sinister forces set on overthrowing the American government" as the primary cause for the violence. But after touring Los Angeles by helicopter with the city's mayor in the wake of the riots, he admitted the poverty and social conditions of urban ghettoes might also be part of the problem.[38] His mainline critics at the *Christian Century* had fun with Graham for making this discovery for the first time: "With words more hysteric than prophetic, Mr. Graham issued dire warnings like a man who knows something is dreadfully wrong but who hasn't the slightest idea what caused it."[39] The *Century* was right that Graham offered few concrete suggestions for change, but addressing domestic poverty as an alarming social issue was a new step for Graham. Long a proponent of foreign aid, Graham even suggested to President Johnson to take some of the money the United States gives away abroad and invest it at home.[40] The following year, Graham's talking points on domestic poverty were more polished. At the 1966 National Prayer Breakfast, he preached, "If we love the poor and underprivileged we will want to destroy the slums and ghettoes that have no place in an affluent America."[41] Graham may have overlooked domestic poverty before, but he could do so no longer.

By 1967 Graham even named himself a "convert" to the War on Poverty. With a looming battle in Congress for the reauthorization of War on Poverty programs, President Johnson coveted his support, but Graham was still reticent to give it. Presidential persuasion, along with Graham's searching of the Scriptures, seemed to change his mind. That year, Graham recounted how he reread the Bible with poverty in mind and found over one hundred passages indicating Christians' moral responsibility to help those in need. He began to sprinkle these verses into crusade sermons, while also lending his official support to Johnson. With Graham's endorsement, Sargent Shriver, head of the Office of Economic Opportunity, took him and a film crew to Avery County, North Carolina, to observe a federally funded irrigation project. Alongside Shriver, Graham appeared in the film *Beyond These Hills*, which was shown throughout the South to rally support for the poverty program. In the film, Graham recounted his newfound biblical discovery, and he admitted that he now also saw there were thousands in genuine need in the United States. Anticipating objections, Graham acknowledged that the church had done much of this work for generations, but with the present need so great, people of faith needed government's help. Graham made sure to position his support as assistance for the working poor and not a handout. He maintained the biblical injunction that those "unwilling to work shall not eat," but he defended that the federal programs he observed in North Carolina demonstrated how the poor were not lazy but rather taking personal responsibility.[42] While still holding fast to the American dream that hard work would lead to a better life, Graham acknowledged that the world was changing. America was not the same land of opportunity for everyone, and he realized that some needed extra help.[43]

Graham's position put him at odds with a good portion of his conservative constituents: donors, southern politicians, and populist evangelicals. But now Graham was all in. Speaking before Congress, Graham claimed, "I've been before different congressional committees on 17 occasions. But I tell you today that I have never testified for anything like I do for this poverty program. I was critical of it when it started. Now I'm a convert. It's not a giveaway program."[44] If Congress didn't reauthorize funding, Graham said, America would "pay for it spiritually, morally and in every phase of society."[45]

Graham in the Midst of Evangelicals' Evolving Social Concern

Graham's support of the War on Poverty stood out within his social ethic for his clear shift of position: his newfound domestic focus, support of government assistance, and direct lobbying efforts. At the same time, a new generation sought to prick the social conscience of evangelicals during the 1960s. In 1969 Graham appeared at the US Congress on Evangelism in Minneapolis alongside Oregon senator Mark Hatfield, the black evangelist and firebrand Tom Skinner, and his brother-in-law Leighton Ford. If the Berlin congress had sidestepped social issues, evangelicals in Minneapolis promised social action would be a primary focus, and speakers addressed Vietnam, revolution, race, and poverty. *Christianity Today* reported that "perhaps no evangelical conclave . . . has responded more positively to the call for Christians to help right the wrongs in the social order."[46] But not all were supportive. In *Christianity Today*'s next issue, Graham's father-in-law and the magazine's executive editor, L. Nelson Bell, expressed his fear that evangelicals were veering off course to chase a new social gospel.[47]

If Graham saw himself somewhere in between this theological and generational divide, a growing group of "young evangelicals" did not.[48] Yes, Graham had come to support the War on Poverty, but by the early 1970s, as the program lost its public face, he conveniently backed away. His own cozy relationship with Nixon led younger evangelicals like Sojourners' founder Jim Wallis to see Graham as a purveyor of the status quo and more a backslider than a convert on social issues. In 1971 Wallis would write in his *Post-American* journal, "Our leading evangelist plays golf with the corporate elite, opens his pulpit to the President's politics, presides over nation-worship ceremonies, and thinks the poor should kill their own rats."[49] Wallis's reference to rat killing was a response to a remark Graham made during a celebration in his adopted hometown of Charlotte. Designated as "Billy Graham Day" and with President Nixon by his side, Graham remarked, "We had rats when I was a boy, and we got rid of them ourselves. We didn't have the Federal government to come in and do it for us."[50] Graham had acknowledged the need for federal government support and the reality of entrenched structural inequities after observing the urban riots and poverty programs of the 1960s, yet at other times he dismissed those same concerns. Such a quotation might represent his continued penchant for giving audiences what they wanted to hear, a throwaway line to a home crowd. Critics, however, pounced and claimed such comments demonstrated that establishment evangelicals feared misguided social and structural change and had little experience with entrenched poverty. Such an example demonstrates that the evolution of Graham's social ethic was never crystal clear. He often succeeded in building his popularity precisely as he was able to maintain a careful balance—speaking to multiple audiences even as his views changed. Sometimes he pushed just ahead of fellow American evangelicals' popular opinion; other times, he fell back into a familiar evangelistic vernacular.

On top of appearing to backtrack on poverty issues, Graham was also attacked by young evangelicals and mainliners for his unwavering support of America idealism and US involvement in Vietnam. Headlining a 1970 "Honor America Day" extravagance in Washington, DC, designed to unite a divided country, Graham praised America as the greatest nation in history because of its willingness to open its doors to the persecuted, for its generosity in sharing its wealth and faith with the rest of the world, and its honesty to acknowledge and work to solve her social problems.[51] Again, young evangelicals like Wallis did not recognize the America that Graham described. Instead, he saw an American empire drunk on wealth, power, and pride. Wallis warned that Graham's priestly civil religion squelched any prophetic voice. Graham's response was that God called him "to be a New Testament evangelist, not an Old Testament prophet."[52] His critics refused the distinction.

By 1974, however, with the unrelenting pressure of Watergate, Graham finally began to distance himself from the White House. While acknowledging Nixon's sins to *Christianity Today*, Graham also defended himself against attacks that he dismissed social issues. In the same article he claimed, "We have to identify with the changing of structures in society and try to do our part."[53] He even admitted his support for most of the recent Chicago Declaration of Evangelical Social Concern, the manifesto of younger evangelicals calling for economic justice, peacemaking, racial reconciliation, and gender equality.[54]

Graham continued to preach the priority of evangelism, but a dichotomy between saving souls and feeding bodies no longer made sense to many American or global evangelicals. In July 1974, Billy Graham convened the International Congress on World Evangelization in Lausanne, Switzerland. Gathering 2,700 evangelicals from 150 countries, this "Lausanne Congress" was truly a global one. The congress's stated purpose was still to reinvigorate the goal of world evangelization, but Graham realized that clarifying the relationship between evangelism and social concern was also key for evangelical unity and continued growth.

In his opening address, just a few months removed from Nixon's resignation, Graham articulated a newfound humility, admitting it was wrong to "identify the Gospel with any one particular political program or culture. This has been my own danger." He added, "When I go to preach the gospel, I go as an ambassador for the kingdom of God, not America."[55] But several other speakers, most notably the Latin American theologians Samuel Escobar and René Padilla, went much further, denouncing American evangelicalism as "a cultural Christianity" while arguing that social concern was at the heart of the gospel.[56]

The resulting Lausanne Covenant represented an unprecedented evangelical statement on the need for Christians to resist poverty, hunger, and injustice. The section on social concern was by far the Covenant's longest, but it left open the question of how exactly to explain the relationship of social action and evangelism.[57] John Stott, a leading British evangelical and chief architect of the Covenant, interpreted the two as equal partners, but there was room for all to see whatever they wished to see.

After the congress, voices sought to lead the Lausanne movement in two directions. Church growth experts promoted strategies for winning souls, while other evangelicals planted the seeds for social justice.[58] Speaking in Mexico City in 1975 at the continuation committee charged with implementing the Lausanne movement's next steps, Graham affirmed evangelicals' greater social engagement but worried that social concerns would become a distraction from the greater goal of world evangelization. Stott disagreed, and he felt that he must stick up for the global evangelical voices not present in Mexico City. If Lausanne was focused strictly on evangelism and social issues were relegated to specialized agencies supplementary to the main agenda as Graham had framed it, then Stott felt global evangelicalism would continue to splinter and lose relevance. In a heated moment, Stott threatened to withdraw from the movement if Graham took social concern off the table.[59] Graham relented, and Stott proceeded with a compromise statement. Yet Graham and the majority of American evangelicals he represented still won, since the Lausanne Movement prioritized evangelism and church growth. At the same time, Graham began losing interest in the movement. While the Billy Graham Evangelistic Association (BGEA) had been the largest funder and promoter of Lausanne, Graham's institutional and financial support dwindled. He did empower his brother-in-law Leighton Ford to be a major leader within Lausanne, but Graham's efforts shifted else- where. He invested money instead in corollary initiatives such as train- ing international evangelists. Lausanne demonstrated that, as a global movement, evangelicalism could no longer ignore its social responsibili- ties. Stott became the leader of efforts to unite global evangelicals around evangelism, education, and social issues. While not ignoring these issues, Graham became even clearer that his primary focus and particular gift was crusade-style evangelism.

Graham as Global Humanitarian

After Watergate, Vietnam, and evangelicalism's own growing divisions, Graham was less eager to engage politically or socially divisive issues. He focused on evangelism, but he did not give up humanitarian concern. The issue that most resonated with Graham and fellow evangelicals in the mid-1970s was world hunger.[60] With famine spreading through Africa, relief agencies and media outlets beamed images of malnourished chil- dren as the face of an immediate problem. Like Graham's initial plea to meet global need in the 1950s, world hunger rallied evangelicals with little hesitation. They could provide emergency aid without abandoning evangelism or becoming entangled in debates about structural change. They could funnel support through mission and parachurch agencies without turning to government programs. Enthusiastic support led to the proliferation of evangelical relief and development organizations like World Vision, as well as new agencies such as Samaritan's Purse, led by Billy's son Franklin.[61] Graham touted these organizations, and the BGEA even created one of its own. In 1973 the World Emergency Fund collected contributions from Graham supporters to assist those struck by famine or other natural disasters.

By the 1980s it appeared that Graham was experiencing another conversion, and his continual encounter with global poverty was one major factor. He reminded audiences that he remained an evangelist: "My basic commitment as a Christian has not changed. . . . But I've come to see in deeper ways some of the implications of my faith and of the message I've been proclaiming."[62] Referencing the Good Samaritan, Graham admitted the need for something more than charity:

> From the very beginning I felt that if I came upon a person who had been beaten and robbed and left for dead that I'd do my best to help. . . . But I never thought of it in terms of corporate responsibility. I had no real idea that millions of people throughout the world lived on the knife-edge of starvation and that the teachings of [the Bible] demanded that I have a response toward them.[63]

While Graham had invested heavily in defining evangelicalism through past conflicts over the relationship of evangelism and social concern, he now acknowledged "the debate which existed in the church between 'the liberals' who supposedly minister 'to the body' and 'the evangelicals' who supposedly minster 'to the soul' is about over."[64] He was even more certain this division made little sense in his experience overseas. Graham was ready to move beyond these binaries to meet individual needs as well as change social structures. In his 1983 popular interpretation of Revelation, *Approaching Hoofbeats*, Graham identified the Four Horsemen of the Apocalypse as false religion, war, famine, and death. But rather than apocalyptic prediction, Graham offered statistics and analysis of infant mortality and economic disparities between nations. While he had long acknowledged global poverty and the need for American Christians to help, the methods he was willing to consider were changing. He now recommended structural readjustment and debt forgiveness to eliminate the inequities between rich and poor nations, along with individual compassion and spiritual conversion. He also admonished Americans to embrace a simpler lifestyle, accepting lower standards of living for the sake of others.[65]

Graham increasingly incorporated these views into his crusade sermons and public speeches. Addressing Harvard students in 1982 at the John F. Kennedy School of Government, Graham remarked, "As a Christian,

I believe that God has a special concern for the poor of the world, and public policy should in some way reflect that concern."[66] Graham's evolving
views also led him to become an advocate for nuclear disarmament. As
one of the most outspoken cold warriors in the 1950s and 1960s, Graham's
about-face on this issue drew significant attention. While he sought to
persuade audiences for disarmament through political pragmatism and
ethical compulsion, he also connected his work for peace to his newfound
biblical base for global humanitarianism. Quoting a familiar line from
President Eisenhower, he repeated, "Every gun that is made, every warship
launched, every rocket fired signifies—in a final sense—a theft from those
who hunger and are not fed, those who are cold and are not clothed."[67]

In engaging these social issues, Graham played with a new public persona. If he had often presented himself before as unwavering, an evangelical stalwart, now he was willing to talk about himself as "a man who
is still in progress."[68] He more readily admitted when he did not have all
the answers and felt more comfortable acknowledging uncertainty over
dogmatism. The public noticed Graham's change as well, and the majority liked what they saw. The secular media offered headlines highlighting
Graham's "conversion," "mellowing," or "political education."[69] While his
fiercest mainline and young evangelical critics did not dismiss his past,
most appreciated Graham's new statements and offered him a second
chance.[70] Even his evangelical base reading the pages of *Christianity Today*
listened with admiration to Graham's growing social conscience.[71] A few
evangelicals questioned this new Graham, but he ultimately lost very few
supporters. Past champions gave him the benefit of the doubt, while he
forced former critics to reconsider.

Graham retained the penchant for speaking in ways that appealed to
the broadest constituencies while alienating as few as possible, but now it
was clear that he was speaking in a different tone. It still remained clear
that he had not abandoned the priority of evangelism, but he was enlarging
his gospel. He traced his pilgrimage partly to wisdom that comes with age
over youthful certainty, but he also admitted past mistakes. He repented
for aligning the gospel too closely to his own nation's interests, as he now
envisioned himself more as an international evangelist than American
apologist. Having been personally hurt by his association with Nixon and
Watergate, Graham cautioned fellow evangelicals enamored with the rise
of the Religious Right to avoid repeating his mistakes.[72] Yet fear of evangelicals' political retrenchment at home took a backseat to Graham's international encounters. Time and again, he narrated how his own pilgrimage

of discovering the gospel's insistence on meeting social needs turned on his experience amid the global church and poverty overseas. New conversation partners and global experiences gave Graham a broader perspective that refused to be confined to the categories that defined American evangelicals in the past.[73]

Graham always saw himself as an evangelist, but that never excluded him from engaging the political and social issues of his day. With his humanitarian impulses evolving over the course of his ministry, he presents an intriguing study of a public figure willing to admit mistakes and change his mind. Graham's evolving humanitarianism also offers a lens into the emergence and developing prominence of postwar evangelicalism. First, Graham's engagement in debates over the relationship of evangelism and social concern demonstrated their prominence in shaping the contested boundaries of a postwar American evangelicalism. Second, through a focus on global poverty, Graham demonstrated how important American evangelicals' global outlook was in shaping their own self-identity as well as their international engagement. Third, Graham's humanitarianism highlighted evangelical debates over the relationships with government, the role of federal funding to religious agencies, and the size of government programs.

Yet Graham's embrace of a global humanitarianism also offers insight into the development of a contemporary evangelicalism. While the influence of crusade evangelism may have slipped in today's American evangelicalism, an interest in meeting social needs internationally is growing across the evangelical spectrum. Graham's humanitarianism may ultimately serve as his closest link to contemporary evangelicalism.[74] AIDS, sex trafficking, and global poverty are now the subjects of evangelical mission. Twentieth-century evangelicalism often defined itself in diametric opposition to modernism's social gospel, but by the early twenty-first century, a new message of humanitarian concern had come to shape the direction of an influential strand of American evangelicalism. Graham's own career illustrates that process.

Notes

1. "World Vision United States," World Vision United States Archives, Federal Way, Washington (WVUS Archives).
2. Billy Graham's son, Franklin Graham, was one prominent voice predicting a clash of civilizations. See Ken Garfield, "Graham Stands by Comments on

Islam," *Charlotte Observer*, November 19, 2001, 9A; Laurie Goodstein, "Spirit Willing, One More Trip Down Mountain for Graham," *New York Times*, June 12, 2005, http://www.nytimes.com/2005/06/12/national/12graham.html.

3. Billy Graham, *Peace with God* (Garden City, NY: Doubleday, 1953), 190.

4. Carl F. H. Henry, *The Uneasy Conscience of Modern Fundamentalism* (1947), in *Two Reformers of Fundamentalism, Harold John Ockenga and Carl F.H. Henry*, ed. Joel A. Carpenter (New York: Garland, 1988), 32.

5. Billy Graham, "Satan's Religion," *American Mercury*, August 1954, 42; Graham, "Our World in Chaos: The Cause and Cure," *American Mercury*, July 1956, 21. Both quoted in Thomas Aiello, "Constructing 'Godless Communism': Religion, Politics, and Popular Culture, 1954–1960," *Americana: The Journal of American Popular Culture* 4, no. 1 (Spring 2005), http://www.americanpopularculture. com/journal/articles/spring_2005/aiello.htm.

6. For example, from 1954 through 1956, Graham conducted twenty overseas campaigns but only six domestic ones. Andrew S Finstuen, *Original Sin and Everyday Protestants: The Theology of Reinhold Niebuhr, Billy Graham, and Paul Tillich in an Age of Anxiety* (Chapel Hill: University of North Carolina Press, 2009), 134.

7. "Stirred Graham Stirs Orient," *Youth for Christ*, February 1953

8. William Martin, *A Prophet with Honor: The Billy Graham Story* (New York: William Morrow, 1991), 192.

9. Graham served as chairman for the first Board of Reference for World Vision (founded 1950), and he often introduced his friend Pierce at crusades while highlighting his work in Korea and Vietnam. Everett Swanson began his ministry after traveling to Korea in 1952, and a few years later he endorsed the same child sponsorship model as World Vision. World Relief was the original evangelical relief agency, initially formed as the War Relief Commission by the National Association of Evangelicals (NAE) to distribute aid to war-torn Europe. The NAE renamed it World Relief in 1950.

10. Billy Graham, "Sleeping through a World Revolution," Mar. 25, 1962, Tape 637, Collection 191, Records of the *Hour of Decision* Radio Program, Billy Graham Center Archives, Wheaton, Illinois (hereafter cited as *Hour of Decision* Records).

11. Billy Graham, "A Look at 1956," January 1, 1956, Tape 312, Collection 191 (*Hour of Decision* Records).

12. Billy Graham, *The Seven Deadly Sins* (London: Marshall, Morgan & Scott, 1956), 78–79.

13. Graham, *Seven Deadly Sins*, 78–79.

14. "Graham's Fight on World Poverty," *New York Times*, May 25, 1964, 38.

15. Graham's reference to the "love of money" is from 1 Timothy 6:10. In contrast, Graham often relied on Jesus's parable of the rich man and Lazarus from Luke 16:19–31 in his preaching about spiritual and material wealth. For example, see Graham, "Too Rich and Too Poor," October 1, 1969, Anaheim, CA, Sermon 888,

Folder 50, Box 1, Collection 265, Records of the BGEA Montreat Office: Billy Graham Papers, BGCA(hereafter cited as Graham Sermon Records).

16. Billy Graham, "National Association of Broadcasters Address," April 8, 1964, Chicago, Sermon 224, Folder 111, Box 25, Collection 265 (Graham Sermon Records).

17. Finstuen, *Original Sin and Everyday Protestants*, 60.

18. Billy Graham, "Theologians Don't Seem to Understand," *Saturday Evening Post*, April 13, 1957, Quoted in Martin, *Prophet with Honor*, 228.

19. Billy Graham, "What Ten Years Have Taught Me," *Christian Century* 77, no. 7 (February 17, 1960): 188–189.

20. Graham, "Theologians Don't Seem to Understand," 228.

21. "The World Congress: Springboard for Evangelical Renewal." *Christianity Today*, November 25, 1966, 34–35.

22. Billy Graham, "Opening Greetings," and "Why the Berlin Congress," in *One Race, One Gospel, One Task: World Congress on Evangelism, Berlin, 1966*, ed. W. Stanley Mooneyham and Carl F. H Henry (Minneapolis: World Wide Publications, 1967), 8, 22.

23. Carl Henry, *Evangelicals at the Brink of Crisis, Significance of the World Congress on Evangelism* (Waco, TX: Word Books, 1967). While the Congress made little official space for addressing the relationship of evangelism and social concern, evangelical commentary after the Congress regretted that more attention was not paid to this topic.

24. C. Peter Wagner, "Evangelism and Social Action in Latin America," *Christianity Today*, January 7, 1965, 10–12.

25. Billy Graham, *World Aflame* (Garden City, NY: Doubleday, 1965), 187.

26. For examples of Graham's focus on the language of "revolution," see Graham, "Crisis," June 19, 1966, London, Folder 16, Box 9, Collection 265 (Graham Sermon Records); Graham, "(The) Unchanging Message in a Revolutionary World," April 28, 1968, Sydney, Folder 10, Box 15, Collection 265 (Graham Sermon Records).

27. Joan Kerns, "Famine Stalks India," *Christianity Today*, April 1, 1966, 52–54.

28. Johns Hopkins historian Timothy Smith popularized a return to the social conscience of nineteenth-century evangelicals to expand the evangelical historiography prior to the fundamentalist-modernist controversy of the 1920s, and a number of evangelicals (Graham, Henry, and a younger generation of evangelicals) found this a helpful resource in articulating their social concern). See Timothy Smith, *Revivalism and Social Reform* (Nashville: Abingdon Press, 1957).

29. Martin, *Prophet with Honor*, 343.

30. "Poverty amidst Plenty," *Christianity Today*, January 17, 1964, 28.

31. Michael G. Long, *Billy Graham and the Beloved Community* (New York: Palgrave Macmillan, 2006), 163.

32. Graham, *World Aflame*, 180.

33. In the 1960s, Graham repeated his conversation with Dulles to illustrate his own naiveté in international political contexts. By the 1980s he was repeating the same story for a different purpose. Leaving out how Dulles corrected him, Graham used his suggestions to Dulles as an example of how he had promoted the need for foreign aid for decades. Graham, *Approaching Hoofbeats: The Four Horsemen of the Apocalypse* (Waco, TX: Word Books, 1983), 171.

34. Graham, *World Aflame*, 182.

35. Ibid., 180. "False Prophets in the Church," *Christianity Today*, January 19, 1968, 3. Also see Martin, *Prophet with Honor*, 343.

36. Graham, *World Aflame*, 184–188.

37. "Graham Predicts Worse Violence," *New York Times*, August 16, 1965.

38. "Get Tough Policy Urged by Graham," *Atlanta Journal and Constitution*, August 15, 1965, 2; Referenced in Long, *Billy Graham and the Beloved Community*, 163.

39. "Be Specific, Mr. Graham," *Christian Century*, September 1, 1965, 1053; referenced in Nancy Gibbs and Michael Duffy, *The Preacher and the Presidents: Billy Graham in the White House* (New York: Center Street, 2007), 142.

40. "Graham Predicts Worse Violence," *New York Times*, August 16, 1965; "Graham Asks LBJ FBI Bare Race Agitators," *Atlanta Journal*, July 19, 1966; "Graham and King as Ghetto-Mates," *Christian Century*, August 10, 1966, 976–977, referenced in Gibbs and Duffy, *Preacher and the Presidents*, 144.

41. Billy Graham, "Our God Is Marching On" (Minneapolis: BGEA, 1966), 7.

42. The biblical reference is 2 Thessalonians 3:10.

43. *Beyond These Hills*, MP 953, produced by the Office of Economic Opportunity, 1967, LBJ Library video MP953, https://www.youtube.com/watch?v=Qolw12mYZuM.

44. Nan Robertson, "House Hearing: Its Ritual and Reality," *New York Times*, August 21, 1967, 1. Gibbs and Duffy, *Preacher and the Presidents*, 144.

45. Martin, *Prophet with Honor*, 343.

46. "U.S. Congress on Evangelism: A Turning Point?," *Christianity Today*, October 10, 1969, 32.

47. L. Nelson Bell, "Beware!," *Christianity Today*, October 24, 1969, 24–25.

48. Both "young" and "establishment" evangelicals were terms popularized by Richard Quebedeaux. "Young evangelicals" soon became a category used in the early 1970s to distinguish these new voices eager to solve social problems and recalibrate the direction of American evangelicalism from "establishment evangelicals." If Jim Wallis, Ron Sider, and Mark Hatfield fit the young evangelical category, Quebedeaux identified Graham, Carl Henry, and Harold Ockenga as the leading "establishment evangelicals." Richard Quebedeaux, *The Young Evangelicals* (New York: Harper & Row, 1974), 50–51.

49. Jim Wallis, "The Movemental Church," *The Post-American*, Winter 1972, 2.

50. Robert B. Semple, "President and Graham Switch Roles in 'Day' for Evangelist," *New York Times*, October 16, 1971, 27; William Alberts, "Minister Slams Graham on Race, Poverty Issues," *Boston Globe*, April 25, 1972, 8.

51. Billy Graham, "The Unfinished Dream," Honor America Day, Washington, DC, July 4, 1970, Folder 148, Box 18, Collection 285 (Billy Graham Sermon Records). He would often repeat this same message. For example, see Graham, "Freedom," October 10, 1977, Atlantic City, NJ, Folder 71, Box 22, Collection 265 (Billy Graham Sermon Records).

52. Jim Wallis, "The Issue of 1972," *The Post-American*, Fall 1972, 2; "Graham Calls Ministry Evangelistic, Not Political," *Dallas Morning News*, January 4, 1973.

53. Billy Graham, "Watergate," *Christianity Today*, January 4, 1974, 9–19.

54. Ronald J. Sider, *The Chicago Declaration* (Carol Stream, IL: Creation House, 1974); Brantley W Gasaway, *Progressive Evangelicals and the Pursuit of Social Justice* (Chapel Hill: University of North Carolina Press, 2014).

55. Graham, "Why Lausanne?," in *Let the Earth Hear His Voice: Official Reference Volume, Papers and Responses, International Congress on World Evangelization*, ed. J. D. Douglas (Minneapolis: World Wide Publications, 1975), 22–36.

56. Samuel Escobar, "Evangelism and Man's Search for Freedom, Justice, and Fulfillment," in Douglas, *Let the Earth Hear His Voice*, 304–305; and René C. Padilla, "Evangelism and the World," in Douglas, *Let the Earth Hear His Voice*, 125–126, 139–140. Padilla went on to say that such a "fierce pragmatism" was found not in Scripture but "in the political sphere [that] has produced Watergate."

57. Douglas, *Let the Earth Hear His Voice*, 4–5.

58. Robert Hunt and Samuel Escobar differentiate three trajectories within the Lausanne Movement: post-imperial (European evangelicals like John Stott), managerial (American evangelicals of the church growth school, like McGavran and Dayton), and critical (Global South evangelicals such as Padilla and Escobar). Robert Hunt, "The History of the Lausanne Movement, 1974–2010," *International Bulletin of Missionary Research* 35, no. 2 (April 2011): 83–84; Samuel Escobar, "A Movement Divided: Three Approaches to World Evangelization Stand in Tension with One Another," *Transformation* 8 (October 1, 1991): 7–13.

59. Alister Chapman, *Godly Ambition: John Stott and the Evangelical Movement* (New York: Oxford University Press, 2012), 141–143; Brian Stanley, *The Global Diffusion of Evangelicalism: The Age of Billy Graham and John Stott* (Downers Grove, IL: IVP Academic, 2013), 175–177.

60. Robert Booth Fowler, *A New Engagement: Evangelical Political Thought, 1966–1976* (Grand Rapids, MI: Eerdmans, 1982), 182–183.

61. Evangelical relief and development agencies grew from an income of $21.8 million in 1969–1970 to $190 million in 1981–1982 (a ninefold increase, far exceeding the growth of traditional evangelical mission agencies). Overall evangelical giving to Third World poverty grew over the decade from $147.7 million to $622 million. Linda Diane Smith, "An Awakening of Conscience: The Changing Response of American Evangelicals toward World Poverty" (PhD diss., Washington University, 1987), 95, 104–108, 312–316 (ft. 104).

62. Graham, *Approaching Hoofbeats*, 144–145.

63. "The Political Education of Billy Graham," *Washington Post*, April 14, 1986.

64. Graham, *Approaching Hoofbeats*, 198.

65. Graham, *Approaching Hoofbeats*, 152.

66. "Political Education of Billy Graham," *Washington Post*, April 14, 1986.

67. Graham, *Approaching Hoofbeats*, 170. Graham and Eisenhower are alluding to Jesus's words in Matthew 25: 31–46.

68. Graham, *Approaching Hoofbeats*, 144.

69. Frye Gaillard, "The Conversion of Billy Graham: How the Presidents' Preacher Learned to Start Worrying and Loathe the Bomb," *The Progressive*, August 1982, 26–30; Galliard, "Righteousness Reconsidered: The Mellowing of Billy Graham," *Tar Heel*, August 1981, 20–27; The Political Education of Billy Graham," *Washington Post*, April 14, 1986.

70. James A. Nash, "The Bomb, Rev. Billy, and the Second Coming," *Christianity and Crisis*, May 30 1983, 215–217; "A Change of Heart: Billy Graham on the Nuclear Arms Race," *Sojourners*, August 1979, 12–14.

71. Billy Graham, interviewed by Bruce Buursma, "Concerns of the Evangelist," *Christianity Today*, April 5, 1985, 22–24.

72. Marguerite Michaels, "Billy Graham: America is Not God's Only Kingdom," *Parade*, February 1, 1981, 6.

73. Graham repeated this message of pilgrimage often: "As I've traveled around through India and Africa and Latin America and all those places for all these years, it can't help but be a heavy pressure. ... For a person who hasn't been there and touched those people and seen those people, it is really difficult to explain ... [but] as I traveled and studied the Bible more, I changed." "Political Education of Billy Graham," *Washington Post*, April 14, 1986.

74. For further reading on evangelicals' growing international engagement, see Robert Wuthnow, *Boundless Faith: The Global Outreach of American Churches* (Berkeley: University of California Press, 2009). For a more popular perspective, see Nicholas D. Kristof, "Following God Abroad," *New York Times*, May 21, 2002.

6

A Politics of Conversion

BILLY GRAHAM'S POLITICAL AND SOCIAL VISION

Curtis J. Evans

IN A 1957 sermon on the "Four Great Crises" facing the nation, Billy Graham thundered that America needed a spiritual awakening and that the country was not in "great need" of economic prosperity or new organizations. The four crises were communism, race, juvenile delinquency, and moral deterioration.[1] When Graham delivered this message, the nation was still experiencing a postwar economic boom, but even when economic struggles were evident throughout the nation, Graham indicated his priority for the American people: not bigger paychecks or better working conditions, but spiritual revival.[2] This division between work life and spiritual life made it seem that Graham was pitting civic problems against spiritual problems. Often, he treated them as if they were in distinct realms, and he claimed that Americans were so preoccupied with material and economic matters that they had forgotten spiritual realities.

Yet Graham's call for spiritual solutions to the nation's problems was an expression of his demand for a different kind of politics, a politics of conversion. He repeatedly called for and envisioned a massive spiritual awakening of converted and revived Christians whose personal lives and collective influence would provide the necessary moral fiber to sustain the nation. For Graham, this spiritual revival would have a profound impact on the economic and political fortunes of the nation and was an essential ingredient to national prosperity. His politics of conversion contained a note of hope that collective Christian action and national revival could prevent the judgment of God upon the nation and help it maintain its position as a beacon of democracy and spiritual hope.

Billy Graham was a representative figure, the embodiment and evangelist of a certain kind of Christianity, which held that revived Christians were significant and integral to the nation's moral health and international standing. At a crucial moment when some Christians were worried about their place in the nation, Graham urged these Christians to become more politically active. He also made a moral claim about the essential and salutary influence that Christians could and should play in helping to realize this social and political vision of a nation responsible to God.[3] Developing a deeper understanding of Graham's politics of conversion is crucial in clarifying his political and social vision and why he believed so strongly in the potential of individual (converted) leaders to have a significant impact on the nation's standing in the world and in the eyes of a judging God.

Christianity was foundational to Graham's vision of American history. However, this was not simply any version of Christianity. Graham was not pleased with the practice of Christianity in the United States, not even the much vaunted post–World War II religious boom. He was among those critics who found it to be shallow and superficial. Graham's sermons from the late 1940s through the early 1960s indicate and invoke a sense of crisis about impending national destruction and hordes of communists about to batter America's moral and spiritual fortresses. He preached a scathing critique of what he saw as the weak and ineffectual Christianity of churchgoing America. For Graham, high levels of church attendance were not an indication of spiritual vitality. He called for Christians to be revived and awakened. Graham's continuous emphasis on individual and collective awakening was the key to his vision for national health. Only the truly converted could bring about a politics of enduring value.

From the late 1940s onward, Graham regularly preached to a large public and was heard by millions on the radio. At the same time, these years, especially the 1950s to the early 1970s, were the years when Graham was most actively involved in political issues (mostly behind the scenes) and engaged in building friendships with American presidents. He preached and spoke in different contexts, but his most consistent and regular voice to the nation in his early career (as he was becoming the face of American revivalism) came across on his weekly radio broadcast, *Hour of Decision*, which began airing in 1950. The program reported news of crusades, broken and repentant lives dedicated to Christ, and the travels of the Graham team. It featured moving songs by soloist George Beverly Shea and a choir, and ended with Graham's urgent and powerful message.

A note of urgency was woven into the very style of these radio programs. They began with the intonation, "So for you and the nation, this is the hour of decision!" Graham's opening of his message with commentary on and interpretation of world events meant that millions of Americans heard the reflections and theological and biblical analyses of current events through the eyes of this respected southern evangelist. Graham was introduced from the late 1940s until well into the 1960s as a "man with God's message for these crisis days." The "crisis" was not simply about the problems facing the nation, especially the threat of nuclear annihilation, but the internal crisis of the individual, whether he or she would make a decision that had eternal implications: to decide for Christ and his kingdom.

Graham simply could not avoid politics, given how he constantly grappled with portraying a common vision for the American nation. We know about Graham's detailed advice on "secular" issues and public policy concerns to a number of presidents, but we also know Graham explicitly and regularly invoked political and social themes in his radio messages and sermons, advising Christians to play a crucial role in leading and sustaining the nation as a Christian republic.

In that context, what view of the world did he paint? And what political and social vision did he cast? Because he was not a systematic thinker, Graham's political and social vision, though consistent, has to be pieced together from various sources and contexts. I make use of Graham's broadcasts for much of my analysis of Graham's early career, though I also draw upon his many sermons in other contexts and some of his writings in response to significant social, political, and cultural changes. Regarding his political and social vision, I make reference to and draw upon Graham's explicit statements about how the nation should be run, what leaders he admired, and how he responded to pieces of legislation to address major social problems.

My primary concern is to get at Graham's underlying theological vision, his anthropology (his doctrine of the human person), and his more general sense of how the nation should exist in terms of its obligation to the laws of God, which Graham believed were clearly articulated (in the Old and New Testament of the Christian Scriptures) for individuals and nations. I am particularly interested in Graham as a transitional figure whose revivalistic Christianity articulated major grievances against the nation and a critique of what he saw as a secular reading of American history, a claim that would become the dominant rhetoric of the Christian Right in the 1980s. I attend especially to the Cold War years of the 1950s and place much emphasis on Graham's preaching and sermons into the late 1960s.

The Personal

In any discussion of Graham's political and social vision, it is absolutely essential to note his prior and unvarying emphasis on personal conversion to Jesus Christ as one's Lord and Savior. Everything else hinged on this decision. Graham called upon all to undergo a personal transformation, a singular dramatic conversion experience under his preaching (though many made a rededication to faith at his crusades, and Graham often urged Christians to revive their initial commitment). For him, salvation by acceptance of Jesus was the necessary key to personal peace and a life of contentment. It made one fit for service to one's neighbors, family, and the larger society. This emphasis on a singular conversion experience constrained Graham's political and social vision, in that it had little to say to those who did not undergo it or who did not share his views about personal and social transformation. But this emphasis also enlarged his vision, in that it incorporated a universal call to personal and social change that ideally transcended race, class, or social status. Graham repeatedly proclaimed the individual's need for a radically new life in order to participate in a larger community, with the church functioning as the primary community for believers. Even so, Graham's individualist notion of personal change often left out any explicit mention of the necessity of church or a more organic notion of believers as incorporated into a broader community. While Graham did cooperate closely with local churches, much of his preaching emphasized conversion within individual believers' hearts. One finds very little language of a corporate conception of the church in such messages, with the exception of specific messages on the nature of the church.

Graham's crisis preaching, especially in the 1950s, and his often bleak portrait of the accomplishments of human intelligence and efforts at social betterment all aimed at the regeneration of individual sinners into converted Christians. This singular and sharp focus on the conversion of individuals shaped the contours of Graham's social and political vision by minimizing or rarely mentioning social and political structures beyond individual persons. Many of his sermons placed a heavy emphasis on the power of exemplary leaders to change the nation and alter the course of history. Examples included not simply biblical figures and heroes (an expected set of figures, given Graham's high regard for Scripture), but also historical and political figures such as George Washington, Abraham Lincoln, and Douglas MacArthur. For Graham, their Bible reading habits and their reliance on God at crucial moments in their lives were the kinds of personal practices that made them great men and leaders.[4] In other words, personal piety was often the cardinal virtue that explained their greatness in Graham's eyes, and he extended this vision of the power of individual piety by multiplying its effects through projected mass conversions.

I am not suggesting that this was always a straightforward matter in terms of how Graham believed his vision could be realized in practice. Yet there are instances in his preaching when he used language suggesting that simply practicing some virtue, such as neighborly love, would presumably address a massive social evil, such as racism and segregation. Graham's emphasis on the necessity of a personal conversion experience required a skeptical view about human nature and human motives. It thus critiqued the mixed motives of any human efforts at social betterment or attempts at rectifying long-standing social injustices. In practice, however, Graham often valorized the efforts of Christians simply because, in his estimation, they were converted. Graham agreed with Carl Henry, a prominent evangelical theologian, who argued that individual conversion was the indispensable means of social and political reform. In other words, the latter could not be genuine or lasting without the former (true conversion). From this notion of conversion, it followed that the saved necessarily promoted social justice with greater clarity and grace than the unsaved or unregenerate. This clarifies Graham's many statements that spiritual solutions were necessary to solve political problems, as well as his recurring remarks that true social reform was the effect of individual conversions.[5]

The Political

Even with the importance of Graham's style of preaching and his focus on personal conversion, there must still be a healthy critical analysis of religious figures like Graham who stated or intimated that their work was nonpolitical or spiritual.[6] I put forth a broader notion of politics as being in more places than traditionally acknowledged, and as relating to the organization of social life, especially in matters of law, resources, and power, in addition to the familiar spaces of public life such as state and federal government offices.[7] Graham's references to John Wesley's preaching and missionary campaign is one notable example of his particular reading of history, which combined an exhortation to Christians of what was possible for the truly converted and revived believer. Though suspicious of labor unions, Graham asserted that Wesley's evangelical revivals of the eighteenth century fostered and nurtured a widespread social conscience that resulted in an incipient labor movement concerned with the welfare and working conditions of laborers. He also tied the emergence of religious liberty and toleration to the preaching and ministry of the great evangelical revivalists such as George Whitefield and Francis Asbury.[8] For Graham, this reading of history served as a corrective to what he saw as secular and insufficient accounts of the rise of religious liberty and the labor movement. It also served as a relatively recent example of what spiritually awakened Christians can and ought to accomplish. Graham was responding to specific criticisms that his message lacked a social ethic, but he was also making a broader generalization about the social effects of Christianity.

Graham's preaching performed two basic functions, especially during the height of fears generated during the Cold War. First, at the beginning of nearly all his radio broadcasts and in many of his sermons and writings, Graham surveyed world events and portrayed human attempts to bring about a peaceful and enduring system of government as one long grasping at futility. Few evangelists spoke with such a rapid pace and certainty as did Graham, who rattled off what one world leader said or did only to find things ending in more wars, broken treaties, or blasted hopes. This unremittingly bleak assessment of the impotence of human intelligence and action demonstrated that no political or social system could succeed apart from it being grounded in divine revelation and obedience to that revelation. By lowering or devaluing the "works" of unconverted humans, Graham sought to heighten the potential contributions of revived Christians.

Second, though revival messages were obviously intended to bring about individual conversions, Graham's preaching seemed unique for a revivalist in that he did not focus solely on the personal as sufficient to induce conversion (though he did touch on a host of personal issues in his many messages and writings). While Graham had been reared in a tradition where churches as social institutions or organized bodies should not make pronouncements on political or social issues, it is quite notable that he employed the "first use" of the law in the sphere of world events rather than in the realm of the personal, unless specific notice was made to human sinfulness or personal problems.[9] This notion of the first use of the law has a long history in the Calvinist or Reformed tradition, going back to the works of John Calvin and other Protestant reformers of the sixteenth century. Protestant reformers argued that one purpose of the law is to bring about a sense of human impotence, noting that humans discover that they are unable to obey the law of God and thus feel a consequent sense of futility and frustration. This is seen as the first stage in a process that should eventuate in repentance and acceptance of grace through Christ. In this interpretative tradition, which would have been taught among southern Presbyterians, emphasis is placed on a personal or psychological struggle within the individual as he or she reaches the limits of struggle in trying to live a moral life by adhering to the moral law.

Graham, however, could not take for granted that sole or primary attention to individual salvation would produce the kind of revived Christianity that he envisioned. Painting a scenario of imminent national destruction, especially during the Cold War, did indeed involve a use of fear, but Graham did so with a keen sense of inviting Christians to forestall disaster by recommitting themselves to the faith and engaging in areas where presumably the unconverted had tried and failed.[10] Revived Christians were therefore crucial to the fate of the nation. Graham's politics of conversion should therefore be regarded as a hopeful vision of spiritually awakened Christians who could transform the nation. He aimed to temper his frightening visions by trying to infuse Christians with hope that their religious practice was integral to the health of the nation. While judgment was imminent, Graham believed that Christians had a vital part to play in determining the nation's fate. This particular preaching style was a prescriptive call for Christian involvement and a rhetorical performance or demonstration of what Christians had done to make America a nation under God.

Because Graham tried to adhere to what he regarded as an unvarying standard to judge the nation and assess its moral progress or regress and the health of its politics, he offered assessments of social and political events that put him at odds with any straightforward valorization of America as a chosen nation. At times, he asserted that America was not exceptional, that she was beholden to a moral law, adherence to which could ensure the fortunes of the nation's future. Graham had always grounded his public pronouncements in a narrative of faithfulness to or departure from divine law and biblical prescriptions. He interpreted international and national events for his listeners and readers by and through this framework. This vision and critique of political life and national destiny served as a consistent guide behind his statements on changing political and social realities, such as the growth of communism, juvenile delinquency, divorce, and crime. Over time, Graham's growing alarm at the "sexual revolution" (an expression he was already using in the late 1950s), the "rights revolution" of the Supreme Court (which conservatives decried as soft on criminals and prejudicial toward minorities and special interest groups), crime in urban centers, the negative implications of technological advances, and the specter of a rapidly growing communist threat to Western democracies all led him increasingly toward a conservative position that had as one of its central aims the restoration of Judeo-Christian values to preserve the nation from moral decline.[11] After the Cold War years and amid the dramatic social changes of the 1960s, Graham published a response to a range of social issues facing America in his book *World Aflame* (1965). In it he warned that his generation was "now on the verge of seeing a democracy gone wild."[12] Only revived Christianity could save the nation and return it to the "moral and spiritual principles that made the West great."[13]

These cultural changes and growing critiques of the nation by liberals because of racism, women's issues, and the Vietnam War increasingly put Graham into a defensive posture about the nation. While criticizing America as having deviated from its roots and for its failure to adhere to a divine mandate of righteousness, Graham also tended to strike out verbally against those he deemed too critical of the nation, especially if he felt that they were singling out America as being uniquely racist or imperialistic.

Graham's view of social transformation was always caught between his belief that the ultimate resolution to perennial political and social problems would take place only in the future at the return of Jesus and his very active involvement, usually behind the scenes, in trying to get certain policies implemented. There are plenty of instances of his claim that only the return of Jesus would solve human problems. In a 1955 sermon titled "Christ is Coming," Graham stated, "Christ is the hope of the world. There is no possibility that the nations of the world will solve the basic problems of human nature until Christ comes again."[14] This vision of social change did not express much hope in human effort, given that it gave little confidence in humanity's ability to make basic progress in dealing with the problems of "human nature." However, Graham was not a passive observer of the world scene, despite his sometimes dour view of the world. He was deeply enmeshed in the details of social and political issues, giving very specific and detailed advice to presidents on issues ranging from civil rights to the Vietnam War. Graham was certainly not apolitical, and he regularly urged Christians to make their voices heard and their votes count. It appears, however, that Graham tended to postpone the solution to particular problems to the future when he disagreed with proposals that he regarded as unduly optimistic or that challenged his view of the good society.[15] Even so, at other times he offered a vision that not only transcended a narrowly nationalist vision of the American nation, but that also seemed a bit more sanguine about humans' capacity to make substantive and enduring changes in their political systems, however flawed such attempts might be.

When Graham published *World Aflame* in 1965, the political landscape seemed particularly tumultuous. President Lyndon B. Johnson had been elected the previous year. Congress had passed the Civil Rights Act, which banned discrimination in public accommodations, strengthened federal power to protect voting rights, and prohibited discrimination by employers and unions, among other provisions. Massive efforts were underway to register poor black voters in the South. Early in the year Johnson began to escalate the bombing campaign of North Vietnam, leading to protests and public demonstrations against the war.[16] Surveying these developments, Graham expressed deep fears and worries about what was going on. He wrote, "The whole world is filled with riots, demonstrations, threats, wars, and with a rebellion against authority that threatens civilization itself."[17] Graham offered his book as an examination of the causes of these "raging fires," and to address these issues he proposed a "Biblical answer to world conflagration."[18] In examining the causes of these upheavals, Graham rejected what he saw as the leading explanations, which were mainly economic, diplomatic, educational, and sociological. He did not believe that monetary inequity was the cause for such dissensions, or that a redistribution of wealth would solve such problems. He quickly dismissed a failure of diplomacy as the cause of such violence and disarray. He minimized the work of the United Nations in a few sentences, ending a paragraph on this dour note: "The diplomat ignores the evidence that international diplomacy is a record of broken dreams, broken promises, and broken treaties."[19] Nor did Graham think more education would help. A bad environment was also quickly dispensed with as the primary cause of a world aflame. Graham argued, without producing any evidence, that affluent suburbs were likely to produce "greater social problems" than urban slums and poor rural areas. For him, this was sufficient to falsify sociological arguments that a "bad environment" was behind social problems.[20]

Graham's quick dismissal of complex explanations of social issues and his scant treatment of them were primarily prefatory matter to what he really wanted to say. Few readers would get the sense that he gave serious consideration to these ideas. What is striking is how Graham tended to lump all of these approaches to social and political problems under the label "worldly philosophies," as though they were self-contained and had no overlap with solutions he culled from a "biblical philosophy of man and of history."[21] This had the advantage of presenting Graham as a fearless leader who would not compromise his convictions by trying to harmonize his Christian view of social and political problems with "modern philosophy." Yet this tendency to demarcate between a Christian or biblical view of the world and worldly philosophies invariably meant a simplification of the latter and a rather narrow understanding of what one could draw from Scripture and the Christian tradition.

Even with Graham's grim diagnosis of world affairs, his social and political vision was ultimately optimistic. Yet it was always tempered with a conception of social transformation as discontinuous and in the future. In other words, this new society would not grow out of present developments, and it would be inaugurated by a radical in breaking of the divine into history. Graham wrote,

> Ultimately, the Bible looks into the future to foresee a new world in which peace and righteousness prevail. There is to be world peace. There is to be a new social order. There is to be a new age. There is to be a completely new man in whom will be no false pride, hate, lust, greed, or prejudice. This will be the climax of human history. This will be unlike anything the world has ever known. The Kingdom of God will triumph.[22]

This hopeful vision, which postponed any substantive change, allowed him to paint a bleak vision of the present without giving any clear sense of how such a future could grow out of or be related to the present.

Graham railed against legislation and social engineering, proposing instead that the church's primary mission was the changing of the hearts of humans by calling to them to repent and accept Jesus as Lord and Savior. Graham pitted lobbying, passing laws, and making resolutions against preaching a regenerating message of personal transformation. Here again was evident his tendency to make radically distinctive categories as if they had no overlap. While Graham could confidently state that if the entire "human race should suddenly turn to Christ, we would have immediately the possibility of a new Christian order," he left out what actual work would remain to be done if this occurred.[23] One way Graham put this was to say that we "backslide as individuals before we begin to decay as a nation."[24] In a radio address in 1958, he argued that the "greatest contribution you can make to the nation is to give your life and your heart to Jesus Christ."[25] Graham argued that military armaments, taxes, and consumer goods were not the true index of a nation's greatness, but that the nation's foundation and security rested on the virtue and Christian faith of its citizens. That in fact individuals rather than political parties or governments were to blame for the nation's decline. While Graham clearly had much to say about corruption in government and the necessity of moral leadership, these messages to inspire collective revivals enunciated his ultimate vision of what constituted good politics and social transformation. Essentially, Graham settled for churches speaking out on difficult moral issues and preachers and evangelists making their views known as individual Christians, but not as spokespersons for the church as a corporate body.

To the extent that Graham did have a *vision* for social and political transformation that went beyond calls for piecemeal change or tinkering with a broken system in the present, it was about the future. As Graham wrote, "The fabulous future we Christians are looking for will not be the natural development of history. It will not come by political structuring. It will not be the result of education or science alone. It will come in the establishment of the Kingdom of God by God's direct intervention!"[26] In practical terms, this meant hostility to any "social gospel" and deep skepticism about various proposals to radically alter the social and political structures of the nation. Graham's political and social vision for much of his public life was thus about the future. It held out little hope for *significant* developments in the present.

Politics at Home

In reflecting on the passage of the Civil Rights Act of 1964, Graham quoted Senator Hubert Humphrey as reputedly saying to him, "Billy, legislation alone can't do it. It must ultimately come from the heart." The words sound remarkably similar to Graham's own words, words that he had been uttering for over a decade or more. Graham argued that the "only possible solution" to the race problem was a "vital person experience with Jesus Christ on the part of both races"[27] But Graham and other evangelists already had remarkably free rein to preach their message of salvation in Christ, to the South and the rest of the nation. Given that a significant proportion of the evangelical South professed Jesus as Lord and Savior, Graham had a glaring problem: Why did he not reflect publicly on the seeming incongruity of his claims about a vital personal relationship with Jesus leading to the elimination of racial prejudice and structural racial oppression? After all, surely Graham was aware of the fact that many of the staunchest opponents of civil rights legislation were Christians who adhered to the revivalist form of Christian faith that he professed. And certainly Graham was aware that legislation was passed precisely because individuals who professed Jesus had not voluntarily agreed to end segrega- tion, nor was there any evidence that many of them felt that this was one of the central demands of their faith.

What then gave Graham confidence that this conversion experi- ence would have the profound "social implications" that he expected? Furthermore, it was always a curious claim for Graham to say that leg- islation alone could not solve political problems, or that these problems required a spiritual solution, when Graham himself often noted that "law- lessness" was a symptom of a lost world. Why this selective devaluation of the efficacy of law? Graham could often write or talk about laws as the expression of deeper values, respect for which indicated a concurrence between individual moral conscience and the highest values of a society. So it is puzzling that Graham would so often speak of laws enacted to address social injustices as being inherently ineffective or lacking in efficacy.

Why this worry about the efficacy of laws? Was it merely a tactical response to legislation with which he and others disagreed? That is part of the answer because the frequency of the claim that laws could not change hearts increased precisely when laws were being proposed that would pro- foundly alter the relationship that white southern evangelicals in particu- lar would have with state and local customs. These laws would gradually diminish their privileged status in society. But Graham's individualism, his preference for and deep convictions about transforming human hearts, and his belief that personal human relations grounded in love and respect, meant that for him changed environments imposed by legal and politi- cal solutions would not erase bitterness from human hearts. Therefore, he felt that they would only deal with externals and never really affect or change the inner person. For Graham, voluntary change from within was thus crucial for social transformation, because all human relations had a personal and local dimension.

The fierce resistance of white southerners to Supreme Court decisions and even acts of the national Congress proved to Graham that unless something within changed, no law could ultimately compel persons to change, especially if some were willing to fight or even die for their deeply held convictions. Yet the very fierceness of white southerners' reaction to some decisions, such as *Brown v. Board of Education*, which Graham did not object to in principle, demonstrated the limitations of his focus on changing hearts. Many southerners professed Christian faith, but it appeared their hearts weren't changed on these particular matters. Unlike Graham, Martin Luther King Jr. and others felt it was immoral to expect blacks or other minorities to suffer under unjust laws that remained on the books, and that were felt in the lives of real people, until whites experienced a change of heart, which presumably would lead to the passage of just laws that reflected such underlying beliefs. Hearts were simply too slow. This emphasis on internal change also implicitly held faith in local communities to address their own problems with justice and compassion, a faith that the very history of the South, with its call for states' rights on issues such as lynching and segregation, called into serious question. Graham's personalist solution to social problems was thus stuck on the horns of an unresolved dilemma.

Politics Abroad

Graham evolved in his views. His experience with Richard Nixon and the debacle of the Watergate crisis, which led to Nixon eventually resigning his office in disgrace, was one factor in his rethinking his views about politics.[28] Then, too, Graham's many international travels were a source of ever broadening views of the world and church communities beyond the United States. (See David King's and William Martin's chapters in this volume.) He came to offer a more nuanced view of social change in history and began reframing some of his older ideas. In a speech titled "The Christian Faith and Peace in a Nuclear Age," which Graham delivered in 1982 in the Soviet Union, he appeared more tempered in his assessment of contemporary efforts to address the proliferation of nuclear weapons and the possibility of a worldwide nuclear war. The speech was widely criticized by some conservatives, who felt Graham was duped by the Soviet Union simply by speaking behind its Iron Curtain.[29]

More generally, Graham offered a more hopeful view of human efforts at social and political betterment. Graham began as he usually did at such gatherings, introducing himself as a disciple and follower of Jesus Christ and a man who grounded his plans and proposals in the Bible. The young southern boy who once preached to fish in a local pond to improve his speaking skills was now a world-renowned evangelist who had preached to more people than any other living person. Here was Graham on a stage addressing one of the most pressing issues of his day. As he had done in so many of his talks, he proposed what he called a "spiritual solution" to the problem of nuclear proliferation, denying the efficacy of a merely political solution. Graham stated that "the possibility of nuclear war is primarily a moral and spiritual issue that must concern us all. I furthermore am convinced that political answers alone will not suffice, but that it is now time for us to urge the world to turn to spiritual solutions as well."[30] Graham elaborated on this point by saying that human hearts needed to be changed, and that spiritual revival would be the most effective way to produce permanent change. He affirmed the sacredness of all human life, emphasizing that humanity was created in God's image, that there was a possibility of all having a personal relationship with God, and that humans were the object of God's love.

At one point in his talk, Graham returned to his consistent claim that only at the return of Jesus would problems such as war be resolved. For a moment, it appeared that he had little to say about present or contemporary efforts to address nuclear war. Regarding the distant future, Graham said, "Only then will the spiritual problem of the human race be fully solved. Both the Bible and the Christian creeds teach that there will be universal judgment. Christ will come again . . . then the Kingdom of God will be established, and God will intervene to make all things new. That is our great hope for the future."[31] Yet Graham also indicated that there was an "already" element of the coming Kingdom that Christians often overlooked, that the Kingdom of God "is not only a future hope but a present reality." Christians therefore must work with all those who strive to bring about peace in the world (presumably non-Christians as well). Graham said that he was hopeful in spite of the temptation to be pessimistic because God is sovereign Lord of history. There was always the possibility of people turning to God, and thus being enabled by divine power to grapple with and begin to solve some of the many problems in the world.

Graham's message had a different tone overall than the early *Hour of Decision* broadcasts and many of his earlier reflections on world events.

There was a broader vision of the church and recognition of Christians participating in a larger body of Christ. Graham counseled his fellow Christians: "Our purpose is to rise above narrow national interests and give all humanity a spiritual vision of the way to peace."[32] He urged world leaders to repent, commit themselves to peace and justice, and find ways to implement specific policies that would lead to peace. Always attuned to personal relations, Graham told leaders to get to know each other. He closed his talk with a call that the peoples of the world pray and seek God.

Although Graham often responded to critics who claimed his messages were too negative, he left himself open to the charge that his political and social vision was unduly pessimistic about efforts at social reform. Critics also felt that he placed so much emphasis on individual conversion that he tended to simplify complex issues by reducing them to personal relations. As a person with some roots in Presbyterianism, it would seem Graham would have been aware of Reformed thought on common grace and cooperative work for the common good with those who did not share his understanding of the conversion experience. This consistent emphasis on individual conversion and its alleged beneficent effects for the social order sometimes implied that Graham and his evangelical compatriots, as one critic put it, left the common good and social reform in the hands of "benevolent individuals."[33] What about continued struggles with sin within persons and the temptation to hubris, self-righteousness, greed, and avarice among the converted? Graham acknowledged that even some of those converted at his crusades continued to wrestle with hatred, racism, and various other sins. What then made him believe in the singular efficacy and social effects of the conversion experience?

Graham's individualizing tendencies shrank the circle of those who could participate in his social and political vision and radically circumscribed the object of his critique. In other words, he rarely mentioned social institutions and structures that made even the determined efforts of the most noble persons limited in what they could accomplish. Nevertheless, Graham's consistent call for a transformed heart, his clear and urgent preaching that sought to get to the root causes of problems, and his skepticism about any grand or utopian schemes for social transformation made his message appealing and convincing to many Christians. Graham's religious vision and his reading of the nation's history were a catalyst in the emergence of a political coalition that emphasized family values, patriotism, and fighting crime, which gained great support across the nation by the late 1960s. His politics of conversion often incorporated specific criticisms of the nation that became central to the emerging New Christian Right's strong opposition, especially in the South, to the cultural and social agenda of leftist liberalism.[34]

Graham's regular talks about sin and corruption and his pronouncements of judgment on social vices permitted distance from a simplistic valorization of any nation, though at times he succumbed to fusing national and religious ends, especially when he once starkly proclaimed that one could not possibly contribute to the American way of life unless one knew Jesus as one's Lord and Savior.[35] But this latter statement was not representative of Graham's overarching political and social vision. Though modest about what could be accomplished in history, Graham did help a number of Christians wrestle with the complex task of trying to forge a better nation. He urged Christians to be a "conscience to the country" and to engage in the difficult work of exemplifying a political and social reality that would speak of a God who had redeemed them and who continued to offer the gift of salvation to all who would receive it.[36] This was his consistent vision for the nation and for individuals.

Notes

1. Collection 191, T391f, Billy Graham Center Archives (hereafter BGCA).
2. On postwar economic growth, see James T. Patterson, *Grand Expectations: The United States, 1945–1974* (New York: Oxford University Press, 1996), 59–60, 79–80, 311–315. This theme of the necessity of *spiritual* revival is reiterated in many of Graham's sermons in the 1950s and 1960s. For a sample, see Collection 191, T54j, T60j, T67j, T69j, and T85j, BGCA.
3. For more on Graham's role in urging Christians to become more politically involved, see Steven Miller, *Billy Graham and the Rise of the Republican South* (Philadelphia: University of Pennsylvania Press, 2009), and Daniel K. Williams, *God's Own Party: The Making of the Christian Right* (New York: Oxford University Press, 2011).
4. Collection 191, T436g, T448f, BGCA.
5. For more on this point, see Curtis J. Evans, "White Evangelical Protestant Responses to the Civil Rights Movement," *Harvard Theological Review* 102, no. 1 (April 2009): 254–257.
6. See Miller, *Billy Graham*, 10–11.
7. For this broader understanding of politics, see Jason C. Bivins, *The Fracture of Good Order: Christian Antiliberalism and the Challenge to American Politics* (Chapel Hill: University of North Carolina Press, 2003), 2, 154–157.
8. Collection 191, T183j, BGCA.

9. I have addressed the use of the moral law in the Reformed tradition in a very different context, though there is a vast literature on this topic. See Curtis J. Evans, "The Role of the Moral Law in Thomas Shepard's Doctrine of the Sabbath," *Westminster Theological Journal* 63, no. 2 (Fall 2001): 305–325.

10. On the sense of dread, anxiety, and fear during the Cold War years and Graham's crisis preaching gaining a foothold, see Stephen J. Whitfield, *The Culture of the Cold War*, 2nd ed. (Baltimore: Johns Hopkins University Press, 1996), 78.

11. For more on these cultural shifts, see Mary C. Brennan, *Turning Right in the Sixties: The Conservative Capture of the GOP* (Chapel Hill: University of North Carolina Press, 1995); William C. Berman, *America's Right Turn: From Nixon to Clinton* 2nd ed. (Baltimore: Johns Hopkins University Press, 2001); and Michael W. Flamm, *Law and Order: Street Crime, Civil Unrest, and the Crisis of Liberalism in the 1960s* (New York: Columbia University Press, 2005).

12. Billy Graham, *World Aflame* (Garden City, NY: Doubleday, 1965), 15.

13. Ibid., 17.

14. Collection 191, T264f, BGCA.

15. For more on this, see Evans, "White Evangelical Protestant Responses," 259–261.

16. See Terry H. Anderson, *The Movement and the Sixties: Protest in America from Greensboro to Wounded Knee* (New York: Oxford University Press, 1995).

17. Graham, *World Aflame*, xiii.

18. Ibid., xvii.

19. Ibid., xiv.

20. Ibid., xiv-xv.

21. Ibid., xv.

22. Ibid., xvi.

23. Ibid., 178.

24. See his radio message, "America at the Crossroads" (1958) in *Jerry Falwell and the Rise of the Religious Right: A Brief History with Documents*, ed. Matthew Avery Sutton (Boston: Bedford/St. Martin's: 2013), 38.

25. Sutton, *Jerry Falwell*.

26. Ibid., 191.

27. Ibid., 7. For a critical assessment of Graham's response to Martin Luther King Jr.'s vision of the "beloved community," and how King, compared to Graham, sought to address the problem of race, see Michael G. Long, *Billy Graham and the Beloved Community* (New York: Palgrave MacMillan, 2006).

28. For more on Graham and Nixon, see Miller, *Billy Graham and the Rise of the Republican South*, chap. 7. Miller sees more continuity than other scholars in Graham's attempt to exert his influence in the political sphere after the Watergate experience. He brilliantly demonstrates the difficulties and tensions in Graham steadfastly holding to his interpretation of Watergate as a "crisis of individual hearts" and an example of personal sin, rather than addressing it as in part an expression of structural flaws in the political system (184).

29. On the controversy surrounding this talk, see Grant Wacker, *America's Pastor: Billy Graham and the Shaping of a Nation* (Cambridge, MA: Harvard University Press, 2014), 239–242.

30. Folder 1, Collection 390, BGCA.

31. Ibid.

32. Ibid.

33. See Evans, "White Evangelical Protestant Responses," 267.

34. For more on Graham as helping to "construct the political and religious culture that made the Christian Right possible," see Miller, *Billy Graham*, 202.

35. Collection 191, T67j, BGCA.

36. Folder 1, Collection 390, BGCA.

7

"Heavenly Houston"

BILLY GRAHAM AND CORPORATE CIVIL RIGHTS IN SUNBELT EVANGELICALISM'S "GOLDEN BUCKLE"

Darren Dochuk

We very seldom have a stadium filled this early in a crusade, but you people in Houston and Texas do things bigger and better than any place else we've been.[1]
—BILLY GRAHAM, 1965

FROM THE MOMENT he burst onto the national scene to the apex of his influence, Billy Graham was scrutinized for his stand on race. Famously, during the 1957 New York City crusade, he stepped into an intense politicking that would follow him through the next two-and-a-half decades. Aware of growing momentum for race reform, and wanting to convey a message of support, Graham positioned the black preacher Howard Jones alongside other dignitaries on his sprawling stage. "In New York," Jones recalls, "Billy once and for all made it clear that his ministry would not be a slave to the culture's segregationist ways. He was serious about integrating the crowds at his Madison Square Garden crusade . . . and he looked to me for counsel on boosting minority turnout." Graham asked, "Howard, what can we do to get more blacks to the meetings?" Jones replied, "If they're not coming to you, you have to go to where they are. . . . Billy, you need to go to Harlem." Billy accepted the advice, Jones asserts, went to Harlem (several times), and charged forward as a "radical" eager to act out the "countercultural" potentials of Scripture.[2]

Graham faced heavy criticism for his stand. "You should not have a Negro on your team," one irate man inveighed; "You're going to ruin your ministry by adding minorities," echoed another. Meanwhile, the fulminations of the firebrand preachers Carl McIntire and Bob Jones against Graham's theological ecumenism assumed a distinct racial tone. By loosening biblical standards of fellowship, they implied, Graham was threatening to undermine social norms that kept whites and blacks apart. The evangelist shouldered criticism from liberals as well, from men such as Reinhold Niebuhr, who thought that his gestures were token and ignored structural inequalities. Niebuhr wished that Graham would join "a whole-souled effort to give the Negro neighbor his full due as a man and brother." Martin Luther King Jr. appeared on the New York stage, another show of the evangelist's biracial aspirations, yet many on King's team shared Niebuhr's doubt that Graham's soft diplomacy could challenge, let alone dismantle, Jim Crow.[3]

As witnessed in Manhattan, and evidenced throughout his career, Graham's handling of race placed him in a perennially difficult, in-between spot. Seen by allies as a visionary who wanted to map out a fairer society, the preacher was viewed by others as too indecisive and culturally compliant to stand firm on principle, or too beholden to racial norms to find, let alone fight, his way out. According to the journalist Tom McMahan, Graham himself once admitted that he felt trapped in the middle, "like a fellow in the 1860s who put on a blue coat and some grey trousers—and got shot at by both sides."[4]

Considering Graham's own feelings of embattlement, it is no surprise that chroniclers have measured his record on race in similarly divided terms. Southern fundamentalist criticisms of Graham's accommodations have dissipated, allowing evangelical scribes from both sides of the Dixie divide to celebrate his ministry as an emblem of color-blind Christianity. The Niebuhrian critique, however, has enjoyed a longer shelf life. To this day, skeptics continue to stress Graham's ineffectiveness in marshaling God's people for social justice. In their rendering, the radical of Howard Jones's scenario acted quite differently, as—at best—a reluctant pragmatist, whose willingness to "go to Harlem" stood as a sign of a man chasing the winds of change, and who had to travel great distances—physically and philosophically—just to recognize his society's most egregious sin. Fortunately, recent scholarship has carved out a subtler picture that elides the paralyzing question of whether Graham was or was not the civil rights champion Jones claimed him to be, and instead exposes the complexities of a man who was neither radical nor reactionary, but rather middle-of-the-road average among his contemporaries. The historian Steven Miller astutely positions the evangelist "between the segregationist right and the integrationist left," "removed from the fray of both the civil rights era's politics of rage and its politics of protest." Graham, he asserts, "advocated a politics of decency, which invoked evangelical faith, combined with law and order, toward moderate ends." Biographer William Martin echoes Miller when he quips that although Graham was never known to lead the parade for race reform, he did march to the collective beat of those who carried the banners and sounded the notes for change.[5]

"Middle-of-the-road average" hardly makes for compelling history, but in Graham's case it rings true, with some exceptions. When we attend to two other entwined forces in Graham's worldview—economics and geography—we can identify an integrationist stance that was—at key times, and in key settings—more ambitious than this depiction allows. Graham, temperamentally centrist to the core, may not have championed civil rights in the same cutting-edge manner as Niebuhr and King, or lobbied forcefully for federal legislation and Washington's intervention as *the* primary means of reform (though he did support these initiatives), but his blueprint for social change was rigorous just the same. Fashioned out of faith in evangelical entrepreneurialism as a critical mode of social engagement that could make America meritocratic, Graham demonstrated his own steadfast determination and certainty that racial reconciliation could occur through the collective effort of saved, likeminded, empowered individuals, at a fairly rapid pace. In this sense, Graham's confidence in the reconstructive potentials of capitalism at the very least placed him nearer the front of the parade for race reform than at the back.[6]

These forward-looking ambitions are, in turn, best seen through the prisms of place. Landscape matters, the sociologist Robert Wuthnow asserts, for it is in territory-specific contexts that religious ideas, institutions, and idioms "interlace with local . . . traditions" to reinforce particular understandings of economy, ethnicity, and race; shared senses of history; and collective hope for the future. Wuthnow's is a useful prompt for reappraising Graham's pocket-book solutions to America's racial problem as a direct outgrowth of his civic associations in one particularly market-driven region of postwar America: the Sunbelt Southwest. A native of the Deep South, and beholden to its norms, Graham would always be a southern man. During the height of his career, however, amid the country's tensest struggles over civil rights, the evangelist found a more enticing environment west of the Mississippi. There, in a rapidly modernizing region slightly less inhibited by the strictures of Jim Crow, Graham attained a fresh outlet for his social vision.[7]

Indeed, as a brief glimpse at his ties to the Southwest's most dynamic hub illustrates, while the evangelist took the charge to "go to Harlem" to see racial problems firsthand seriously, he was just as eager to go to Sunbelt cities like Houston, where their solutions seemed apparent. Defined by its cosmopolitan outlook, burgeoning ethnic and racial diversity, rabid boosterism, and global potentials, this boomtown served as a perfect test site for an alternative brand of civil rights. Over the course of three decades, during Houston's evolution into a world-class city, Graham shaped a ministry that exhibited parallel aspirations to move America beyond troubling parochialisms into a new dispensation of inclusion and grace.[8]

Texas Ties

Graham's enchantment with Texas began in the 1950s, at a time when the state, like the evangelist, was emerging onto a national stage. During the Cold War era, he often used his time among Texans to sort out his stand on race and civil rights; Texas was, in this sense, his crucible. But it was also an inspiration. Aided by the support of a large constituency of business leaders who were eager to channel their faith in Christ and the potential of unfettered individualism into a mission of progress, Graham's attraction to Texas and its unquenchable drive for the sparkling and new was obvious. Even as media attention at his 1957 New York crusade swirled around debates over race and religion in the Big Apple, Graham found time on his stage to acknowledge Texas as his true trendsetter. "We've been reading a great deal about Texas in the last few days, and we have some Texans on the platform that are on our team. . . . Everything in Texas is big."[9]

Of course, Graham was hardly the only American to marvel at Texas's disproportional power in the 1950s. America as a whole was preoccupied with this state's swashbuckling style, derived as it was from real spectacular gains in economy precipitated by federal funding and gushing crude. Like much of the Southwest, Texas had endured tough times during the 1930s, but compared to neighboring states, it weathered the economic storm with fewer disruptions. A smaller percentage of its population fled for employment in the Far West, leaving workforces intact, and Washington's wartime spending helped stabilize financial prospects. Resting on the Gulf Coast, halfway between the Atlantic and Pacific, Texas was strategic terrain, which is why it received over seven billion dollars in war supply contracts, served as a training site for over 1.5 million soldiers, and housed sixty-five army airfields, thirty-five army camps, and seven naval stations. Ensuring their state's future of massive growth were Texas's powerbrokers, men like Jesse H. Jones, head of the New Deal's Reconstruction Finance Corporation; Sam Rayburn, the Speaker of the House; and Lyndon Johnson, a rising star congressman. Thanks to these Washington insiders, Texas was primed for accelerated and sustained economic expansion.[10]

Texas crude offered another propellant. Texas's "gusher age" crested during the 1930s when huge finds in East Texas confirmed the state's elite standing in global oil and created a new class of independent "wildcat" producers, who despite operating on shoe-string budgets, struck it rich before major companies arrived. As a result of this boom, the state entered the 1950s as an energy-producing juggernaut. By the end of the decade, Texas companies, six thousand total, would produce more than half of the nation's entire oil supply. But volume was not the only measure of "Texas Tea's" ascent. Even as the state enjoyed unmatched success, America ceased to be a net oil-exporter. The rise of Saudi Arabia undermined US hegemony in global petroleum, and at the same time heightened the importance of Texas as America's last hope to be competitive and self-sufficient. Cognizant of this, Texas's wildcatters wore their new cachet with pride, believing that they alone could save the nation. As Lawrence Goodwyn explains, amid Cold War anxieties, they stood as a flickering symbol to all of what was "rare and appealing about America, its economy, and the vibrant social relations of its people."[11]

Billy Graham clearly recognized this, though his wonder at everything Texas was far from abstract. His awe was generated firsthand, through increased exposure to the state's budding economy and leadership. During the first half of the 1950s, he held revivals in each of Texas's fastest-growing cities. The pattern began in 1951 when he traveled to Dallas, Houston, Waco, and San Antonio, then held a month-long crusade in Fort Worth. Besides serving as an introduction to Texas's business elite (aided by his address to the Fort Worth Chamber of Commerce), this sojourn also solidified his ties to its clerical elite. In October, Graham began a routine that he would continue throughout his career: speaking directly to Texas's Southern Baptists, in this case to those gathered at the Texas State Baptist Convention in Houston, in subsequent cases at national Southern Baptist Convention (SBC) meetings (also in Houston). Graham's plea to the 1951 gathering hit the right marks in the way that it affirmed his audience's unwavering belief that societal change came through spiritual regeneration, not government intervention. Indeed, he pulled no punches when touting the Texas Baptist way:

> [T]he average man thanks government, a relief check, a crop reduc-
> tion check, a new deal . . . rather than God, for his daily bread. Millions
> of modern people have been sold on the idea that the problems of sin
> can be cured by government; they have renounced faith in Christ as
> the Savior of [the] human race from the curse of sin and have put their
> faith in government. We are now talking about a new social and eco-
> nomic system instead of a new birth as a means to human salvation.

Graham's jeremiad against secular big government concluded with an entreaty for Baptists to remember the basics of their faith—the totalizing power of personal redemption. "I believe in the social aspects and applica-tion of the gospel," Graham proclaimed, "but I do not believe in any social-ism that takes away the individual responsibility of a man before his God."[12]

Individual freedom and responsibility were exactly what Graham's Texas hosts cherished most, and the evangelist seemed eager to continue honoring those commitments. One of the byproducts of Graham's initial campaign was a closer relationship with SBC luminaries, including Texas executive secretary J. Howard Williams, the man who would do more than anyone else to orchestrate Graham's return visits and place SBC congre-gations in his service. Considering the staggering growth of the SBC in Texas, this gave Graham's ministry a major shot in the arm. In 1952, after a twenty-year span of almost 200 percent growth, Southern Baptists num-bered 1.4 million in Texas, more than twice the total of Southern Baptists living in any other state. Williams was Graham's entry into a whirlwind of activity. So too was grocery-chain-store king Howard E. Butt Jr., whose friendship with Graham was struck at this same time. Even as he ran his family's HEB Food Stores Company and the H. E. Butt Foundation, Butt was also a full-time pulpiteer, leading Graham to deem him one of the nation's "greatest young preachers" and add him to the board of the Billy Graham Evangelistic Association (BGEA).[13]

Another byproduct of Graham's first Texas swing and pleas to protect the values of frontier individualism came via popular media: the filming of *Mr. Texas*, his first major motion picture. Debuting in fall of 1951, aided by Texas donors, *Mr. Texas* combined footage from the Fort Worth gathering and a fifty-day shoot at Hardin Simmons University to create a message perfectly suited to southwesterners. In explaining his film to a Hollywood reporter, Graham said it was a "western with Biblical overtones—about a Texas rancher-turned-oilman who doesn't find true happiness and peace until I convert him." Some surmised that Glenn McCarthy, Texas's "King of the Wildcatters" notorious for his conspicuous consumption, served as inspiration. Graham discounted the rumor, but admitted that his purpose was to expose the McCarthys of Texas to Scripture's teachings on Christian living. Texas's super-rich took notice, in some circumstances internalizing the evangelist's salvation call, and forging lasting ties, all in the name of transforming their society into a reality of their (and Graham's) design.[14]

Baghdad on the Bayou

Boundless in the way they drew him into the heart of Texas's corporate and churchly orbs, Graham's earliest activities were nevertheless particularly critical in linking his ministry to Houston. To be sure, Dallas and Fort Worth would always loom large in his imagination. Through his friendship with Sid Richardson, an oilman who rivaled McCarthy as an all-powerful eccentric, Graham would remain linked to Fort Worth, and thanks to his visits to Dallas he would always consider the city's evangelical community his own. His sense of connection there would lead to his taking membership at First Baptist Dallas, the SBC's flagship congregation led by Reverend W.A. Criswell. Houston, however, quickly became Graham's real Texas abode.[15]

Considering its high profile in a crescent of metropolitan centers that began dotting post–World War II America's southern rim, the city's draw for the evangelist made sense. Thousands of others were drawn there, too. While Los Angeles, site of Graham's breakthrough in 1949, set an early pace for urban growth along the crescent, Houston established its own reputation as a limitless tomorrow-land. When Graham started visiting Houston, it stood second to Los Angeles in population, geographic sprawl, and growth. In 1950 it boasted a population of 596,163 and land area of 160 square miles; in 1960 it contained 938,219 people spread over 321 square miles; in 1970 there were 1,253,479 people spread over 433 square miles. By 1980, Houston would surpass Los Angeles in square mileage and growth, making it the Sunbelt's ultimate boomtown.[16]

But Houston possessed other big features that Graham (and other Americans) found infectious as well. Called "Baghdad on the Bayou" for the prominence of Buffalo Bayou, which cuts across the city's southern half, on whose shores Texas independence was secured, Houston was "Baghdad" in a second sense in that it boasted a powerful merchant class whose vast interests stretched along waterways to international shores beyond. It was Jesse H. Jones who secured this global access when, in the early twentieth century, he lobbied for the construction of a major ship channel from Houston to the Gulf of Mexico. He predicted the waterway would become "the inevitable gateway through which the products of this growing southern and western *empire* can best reach the markets of the world." As illustrated by Jones's ties to Humble Oil Company, oil's corporate presence in Houston further justified its comparison to Baghdad. Since the early twentieth century, when oil was first discovered nearby, Houston had served as the nation's petroleum center. This status was reinforced in the 1950s as Texas crude assumed a larger international role. Alongside its obvious economic importance was its religious vitality, making yet a fourth comparative. Not unlike Baghdad, Islam's crossroads, Houston represented the heart of the Southwest's Bible Belt. Methodists of Jones's ilk, but also Baptists, Presbyterians, and Pentecostals all thrived there, making it a national meeting place for faith as well as finance.[17]

Faith, finance, and family drew Graham to Baghdad on the Bayou during the 1950s. By then, owing to his wife's history, Graham's affinity for the town was already deep. During a cross-country trip in 1922, Dr. L. Nelson Bell and his family had stopped in Houston to visit First Presbyterian Church, a key supporter of their mission in China. While preaching there, Bell implored his affluent hosts to give all they could to support his Tsingkiangpu Hospital. Those heeding the call included Benjamin Clayton, co-owner of the Anderson Clayton Company, the world's largest cotton exporter. Clayton listened to Bell, drew closer as a friend, and then gave. "Nelson Bell has an innate magnetism that has a spell on people," he explained. The Bells' visit to Houston that summer resulted in a $20,000 donation to construct a "Houston Unit" at the Chinese hospital. Clayton, the Bells, and First Presbyterian would give one another much more over the coming years. In 1927, on their first sabbatical, the Bells moved to Houston. During this time Bell assumed an assistant pastorate at First Presbyterian and developed lasting affections for the community. It was this fondness, Houston's press proclaimed years later, that made Graham—Bell's son-in-law—comfortable in the city, and always eager to come back.[18]

The city's expansive Christian business community put him at ease, too. Following in his father-in-law's steps, Graham looked to Houston as a philanthropic wellspring, only with an eye for wider tributaries. In posh neighborhoods scattered throughout the metropolis's rambling grid, the most illustrious of them tucked away on the shores of Buffalo Bayou, lived evangelical laymen of Benjamin Clayton's ilk, men eager to use their extensive wealth to support the evangelist's cause. From Jesse H. Jones to Hugh Roy (H. R.) Cullen, cotton kings to oil czars, Houston had it all; more than other Sunbelt cities, its wealth was concentrated in very powerful hands but also expanded across economic sectors and beyond the city's boundaries.

In the highest ranks were men who prospered from the state's oil age. Few in this realm could match the size of Jones's and Cullen's coffers, or their generosity. The Houston magnates commanded empires by the late 1940s, whose charities funded countless Methodist and Baptist churches, schools, hospitals, and ministries. Cullen and Jones were aware of a third formidable character, one whose presence in Houston was more sporadic but critical just the same, especially where Graham's ministry was concerned. R. G. LeTourneau built equipment for oil drilling, and although his plant was based in East Texas, his primary interests centered on Houston, the origin of his contracts and most cherished church contacts. Throughout the 1950s and 1960s, LeTourneau committed his wealth to a variety of Houston-focused parachurch organizations, including his own. One of the most important recipients of his gifting was Billy Graham and Graham's Houston crusades of 1952 and 1965, on whose executive boards he sat.[19]

As important as these captains of industry were, it was a group of measurably less affluent merchants who secured ties between the preacher and the place and helped make his evangelical entrepreneurialism come alive as a social ethic. Graham's return to Houston in 1952 for a major evangelistic crusade was highly anticipated and planned. Leading it was a legion of clerical and lay advisors. The former included Reverend William Foster of First Presbyterian, the latter Earl C. Hankamer. Hankamer had made a small fortune in East Texas crude before settling in Houston. He quickly became a fixture in the city, offering a blueprint (as his grandson would say) for "sharing . . . material success with others." Hankamer enhanced this reputation by overseeing the crusade, which involved thousands of dollars and workers. Texas had never seen anything like it, and the event left everyone, Graham included, impressed. Writing to Hankamer in the wake of the crusade, Graham expressed gratitude: "Naturally, we have been thinking about you and your wonderful family. . . . We will never be the same after being in Houston."[20]

Graham's correspondence continued as the two men planned a second major undertaking: a sequel to *Mr. Texas*. Wanting to propagate Christ's redemptive powers to a wide audience, Dick Ross, head of World Wide Pictures, and Hankamer produced *Oil Town, U.S.A.*, a story about a wayward wildcatter named Lance Manning who finds Christ in a metropolis where the potentials for good are as great as its immoral excesses. Through Hankamer's ties, Ross gained access to the Petroleum Club of Houston (where Graham was shot preaching to oil barons), permission from Houston's Chamber of Commerce for filming in various locales, and an opulent mansion that could serve as Manning's residence. The mansion was Hankamer's well-appointed French chateau, whose plush lawn lined Buffalo Bayou. The success *Oiltown, U.S.A.* had in inspiring people seemed instant (its three-night preview in Houston in 1953 caused a media storm) and enduring, in Houston and around the world, and Hankamer deserved much of the credit.[21]

Graham's other merchant-allies in this venture were Morris C. Oldham and Carloss Morris. An Ohioan by birth, Oldham relocated to Houston as a moneyless but ambitious entrepreneur who eventually became the region's largest milk retailer. In 1952 his Phenix Dairy Company merged with Foremost Dairy, expanding his profits and capacity to underwrite *Oiltown, U.S.A.* Oldham shared with Hankamer the reputation of being one of the city's leading Baptists; both attended Second Baptist Church and sat on several Baptist boards. Morris was their equal. His mansion, which hosted many dinners for Graham and friends, was around the corner from Hankamer's and Oldham's and was situated on the Buffalo Bayou. Born in Galveston and educated at Rice University, Morris became a lawyer before taking over his father's title company. Alongside Oldham and Hankamer, he labored tirelessly for Graham. In the 1950s he offered legal advice for the filming of *Oiltown, U.S.A.*, and for the next three decades he would help the evangelist negotiate all of the ins and outs and elite networks of his town.[22]

All of these Houstonians saw in their city a bright destiny for their country. Theirs was a confident boosterism that championed their town as a blank slate, a soil on which rags-to-riches men like the fictional Lance Manning could make their lives prosper and count. In Houston they visualized a melting pot of people with big dreams, in which the uprooted and upwardly mobile could remake themselves without the social and economic constraints of home. If unique for the intensity of their convictions, Baghdad on the Bayou's merchants spoke a language of growth that was spoken in other Sunbelt locales. At this time, the discourse of capital as a pathway to the common good also energized booster classes in cities like Atlanta and Phoenix. It drove a new generation of "Chamber Men" (Chamber of Commerce leaders) to build modern metropolises by recruiting northern businesses and professionals, maximizing Washington beneficence, and transforming hinterlands into thriving centers of finance and technology. Pragmatic and profit-seeking to the core, always anxious to trim overhead and protect their bottom line, Houston's Chamber Men, like their cousins elsewhere, were nevertheless earnest in their belief that they could construct a region, an economy, and a social ethic that the nation had never seen manifested in full.[23]

Graham celebrated this truth at his Texas crusades. "Houston's 'boomtown' growth, which has drawn transients from over the U.S.," he admitted, raised challenges. Migrants do not make instant evangelicals, he noted; they have to be prodded out of apathy into communion. Yet once saved, migrants *did* make robust evangelicals. Therein lay Houston's superlative promise. In their master plans, Graham and his Chamber Men friends accentuated the reparative potentials of a pristine capitalism and Christianity uninhibited by old prejudices. Houston, they believed, promised a fresh start for everyone, hence the seed of spiritual repair, and through Graham's soul winning they thought they could move closer to this desired end. As a poster for *Oiltown, U.S.A.* offered: "Why Houston?" "Why not Pittsburgh, or Chicago, or Boston, or Atlanta? Well, the story of Houston is the story of the free enterprise of America . . . the story of the development and use of God-Given natural resources by men who have built a great new empire, and with it, a fabulous central city: Oil Town." Graham and his hosts could not help but be swept up in this narrative.[24]

Corporate Civil Rights

Blinded by exuberance to the full extent of their society's injustice, their narrative nevertheless contained a proactive side where race was concerned. Graham, like his Houston peers, held unwavering certainty in the ability of this new place and its new capitalism to lift people out of their social predicaments. According to their bottom-line rationale, in which individual redemption was considered the true force for progress, what was needed in response to any social challenges, racism included, was not restructuring by a more involved government, but a cost-effective way of sponsoring revival, distilling scriptural truths down to their simplest essences, and setting an example of the Protestant work ethic and Christian charity in motion.

There were a number of reasons why this bootstrap formula for racial uplift had special traction in Texas's Oil Town, and why Graham seemed most comfortable implementing it there. In the first place, Houstonians with whom he associated proved more eager than their counterparts else-where to jettison (at least publicly) their claims to white privilege for the sake of economic growth. Historians have rightly noted Graham's willing-ness to work with some of the Lone Star State's staunchest segregation-ists as evidence of his lingering ambivalence about civil rights. His Dallas connections usually serve as evidence. In associating with First Baptist Dallas, its outspoken pastor W.A. Criswell, and a network of conserva-tive politicos that associated with them, Graham exposed himself to easy and fair criticism. Graham's 1953 Dallas crusade was largely a segregated affair, marking the last time he would implement Jim Crow policy. While the evangelist changed his ways after this scrutinized episode, pledging to make his ministry fully inclusive, many of his Dallas supporters reaf-firmed theirs. Infamously, of course, in the wake of *Brown v. Board of Education* (1954), Criswell lashed out at federal integrationists in defense of state rights. "We don't want to be in church with colored people," he charged. "Ducks live only with other ducks."[25]

His pastor's declarations put Graham in a tenuous spot, forcing him to establish distance from Dallas's right-wing conservatism and make more explicit his creative solutions to racism. Graham was determined to fashion a post-racial conservatism that could capture the quieter majority. And that majority seemed to be present, plentifully, in Houston. Whereas Dallas was earning a reputation as a "City of Hate" for its reactionary populism, Houston approached the 1960s with greater awareness of the nation's and their church's next necessary social progressions. Although hardly free of racial violence, both political and physical, Baghdad on the Bayou contained the seeds of a vibrant evangelical vision of social change. Graham and his ministry seemed to draw special energy from that fact.[26]

This was certainly evident in the messages he regularly delivered to Houstonians. Although his 1965 evangelistic crusade marked the pinnacle of a decade-long itinerary of Houston visits, his many other trips to the city during the 1960s gave him ample opportunity to endorse corporate civil rights to warm audiences of civil-minded corporate types. Graham's four-day tour in 1963 was one such occasion. Joined at the airport by Houston's mayor, Earl Hankamer, Carloss Morris, and other civic leaders, Graham delivered brief but telling public comments upon his arrival. Of Richard Nixon and the prospects of his quiet conservative revolution, Graham offered: "He is my personal friend. I believe he is well qualified to hold any public office. He could be an American Churchill." Of Washington he voiced concern: "Government is becoming bigger and bigger. . . . It will destroy the moral fiber of our nation when our people look to the government to fill their needs." And of civil rights, Graham avowed that Houston and the South held more solutions to race problems than the North, because whites and blacks living there enjoyed bonds of friendship and a shared vision that was rare anywhere else.[27]

In Graham's estimation, the potential of a corporate civil rights movement led by Houston's finest citizens was even more impressive since it was accompanied by an advanced technological wherewithal. Soon after his airport meet-and-greet, Graham and Hankamer journeyed to the construction site of the Astrodome, the world's first roofed stadium. "This," he proclaimed, is "one of the great wonders of the world . . . a magnificent dream coming true before our eyes . . . the boundless imagination of man transformed to reality. To be here is a privilege . . . to see the domed stadium an inspiration." Houston's other wonder of the world—NASA—provoked similar awe in Graham and made him praise the marvels of advanced capitalism as the way past America's social problems. He expressed his wonderment at a speech to Houston's Rotary Club, which followed. After being introduced by Governor John Connally and delivering his praise to alert ears, Graham retreated to his hotel room for an impromptu meeting with his politician friend. Connally took the opportunity to express his concern about President Kennedy's visit the following week to Dallas, a city inflamed with backlash politics.[28]

Graham's short visit in 1963 was followed by several others, during which he articulated Houston's exceptional role in his plans for social reform. The basics of his corporate civil rights changed little over time. Following a long-standing pattern, he continued to speak favorably of federal civil rights legislation, but he also warned against dependency on this action. No act of Congress, he cautioned, "will solve the race problem because the problem lies at [a] much deeper level. It lies in the level of the heart." He conveyed this sentiment to the Layman's Leadership Institute's meeting, held in January 1967 at Houston's posh Shamrock Hilton Hotel. Presided over by Howard Butt, the city's Christian lay leaders heard the evangelist range in his opining from worry about the trials facing America's youth to frustration with the psychological ills that plagued its adults. But above all else, Graham's was an upbeat charge for businessmen to strive for "positive witness" and "compassionate social concern." "Even a casual study of the life of Jesus reveals that He was interested in man's response to the social problem," Graham averred. He pointed at the long line of saints who translated their relationship with Christ into an expansive humanitarianism that sought "to improve living standards" even as the New Testament was proclaimed. "We communicate the Gospel by contagious excitement about Christ," he insisted, highlighting the energy that swirled about Pentecost and the "Selma march," which demonstrated its own "enthusiasm [for] the Person of Christ." Houston's leaders were able to change history as well as "the hearts of men," he concluded; it was time that they act with this same passion.[29]

Of course, there was no broader or brighter platform for this type of exhortation than Graham's major Houston evangelistic crusade of 1965. Night after night in late fall of this year he blended a hope derived from Houston's unique standing as the ultimate modern metropolis with some disquiet about the future it presaged for America. At a preparatory meeting with Houston ministers in October he highlighted the "fantastic" qualities of the place that destined it for spectacular power: its cosmopolitan culture, its architecture, its civic life and leadership in national politics. "Even the American government is now run by Texans!" he chimed. But with the blessings came a special burden. The preaching that those before him needed—that he needed to provide—had to align the fantastic prospects of Houston's good life to designs for social reform. "The man who has experienced the reality of God's love in Christ is called to live a life of responsive love." This responsive love was to be Houston's answer to its challenges—"growing pains," "multiracial" dynamics, gaps between "rich and poor." Once embraced in full, it was also to be Houston's shining example to the nation—this, at least, was Graham's heartfelt plea.[30]

It was also the commission he delivered to his massive audience—forty thousand per night, virtually filling the Astrodome—during late November. In his most stirring sermon, preached on the closing evening, Graham melded his passions for Baghdad on the Bayou into one fervent appeal. Houstonians, like the Apostle Paul during his visit to Athens, needed to be roused by the times and their place in anticipation of the end. "Fashion; fortune; ease; ambition; self-seeking;" "humanizing God and deifying man," making "chrome plated" things "idols," technology "our god:" these traits, witnessed aplenty in Athens, were abundant in Houston as well, Graham declared, demanding counter-action. "Paul was stirred," Graham proclaimed, before asking that his audience be, too. "We Christians should be stirred to action against poverty, illiteracy, disease, racial injustice, the forces of tyranny that seek to destroy . . . the liberties of man."[31]

Of these ills, racial injustice stood out to Graham as especially egregious, warranting an urgent answer. "Athenians were proud," he reminded his listeners, and believed that no one was "superior to them." Transitioning to present-day Houston, he noted that such arrogance still clouded human consciousness. "We have our social snobbery . . . and our racial superiority." Despite the fact that "God says we all come from the same blood," he mused, "racial tension is increasing throughout the world." Graham segued into an extended lamentation, one of the longer ones seen in all of his sermonizing, against the evils of racial sin:

> Being black in some parts of the world, Jewish in other parts, or Oriental in others, or white in some places, imposes intolerable burdens; while those who are accidentally born to the ruling majority enjoy advantages that they have not always earned and of which they seem to have little appreciation. To hate, to discriminate against and to restrict those who look different, who talk different, who have different national backgrounds, or who act differently from the dominant group, is a consistent and universal trait of human nature extending beyond national barriers. Racial prejudice is not limited to the Southern part of the United States or Southern Rhodesia. I've observed it almost everywhere. Where two races live side by side, there exist [sic] prejudice.

Graham then talked solutions. In his estimation, there was only one answer "to the race problem: a vital experience with Christ Jesus on the part of all races." "In Christ," he added, "the middle wall of partition has been broken down. There is no Jew, no Gentile . . . no Oriental, no Negro." Brotherhood was possible in Christ, he insisted, but not "until we come to recognize Him as the Prince of Peace and receive His love in our hearts." Only then would race wars subside.[32]

If wanting to prick the conscience of his listeners, Graham also reassured them that even as God's judgment was upon it, their city was giving direction to a society in desperate need. Houston's corporate leaders, including its oil executives, were seeing to it that "church and industry" worked together to manage abundance in a way that benefited the public sector, and pursuing economic strategies that accounted for Houston's most vulnerable citizens. They were implementing Chamber of Commerce directives to give "social problems" the "same analytical treatment that business uses in solving its own problems." And they were turning "the profit motive" into a blueprint for human betterment. Articulated by a Humble Oil CEO in a corporate journal that Graham found inspiring (and attached to his sermon notes), this charge was accompanied by yet another: "We must do these things not necessarily for ourselves but for the benefit of the total community. We must act on these problems, not only because inaction will result in further violence . . . but because we must reinforce the faith and confidence in the stability and soundness of our private enterprise system." Graham agreed with this imperative for business's revitalized commitment to social justice (and its purest self). Even as he confronted Houstonians with their failings and begged them to do more, he also applauded their eagerness to cast light on injustices where little light could otherwise be found, and to change the system.[33]

It was Graham's gesture to special guests in the stands, a civil rights champion and his wife, that allowed him to illustrate this point. Observing the closing service of the Houston crusade were President and Lady Bird Johnson. Having visited the Johnsons at their ranch earlier in the day and built a close relationship with them over the previous few years, Graham spoke from the heart when he introduced the couple as dear personal friends and the epitome of Houston's promise to America. Lyndon Johnson, Graham reminded his audience, enjoyed "spiritual roots" that ran "deep in Texas' religious history":

> Houston was named for the hero of San Jacinto who labored long and hard for the union of the Republic of Texas and the United States. It was the President's great grandfather who helped Sam Houston find a personal experience with Jesus Christ. The dramatic religious conversion of Sam Houston a century and a half ago not only changed the life of that great Texan, but influences religious life in Texas today. Thus President Johnson was reared in the deep religious faith that has prevailed in this great Southwest country since the beginning.

Graham turned from history to the political present as a way to accentuate Johnson's character. Noting that a "noisy minority" of protestors had stormed Washington the day before to condemn American policies in Vietnam, Graham praised Johnson for holding firm to his convictions, which those in the Astrodome that night also held. "During the past ten days," Graham gestured to the president, "nearly 400,000 people have come to this stadium to protest sin and moral evil—and to affirm their belief in moral integrity and old-fashioned religious convictions." *These protestors*, he charged, were the true majority, as they represented all "creeds and color," came from "various ethnic backgrounds," and as a multitude "marched across this field to commit their personal lifes [*sic*] to Jesus Christ and . . . a higher moral plane." Inspired by a color-blind gospel of help to all, loyal to America regardless of the cost, and wired for constructive change and respect for the past, these Houstonians, Graham reaffirmed, were the people that would help the president extend the legacy of transformation that his forefathers had begun generations before.[34]

Heavenly Houston

As witnessed in 1965, and illustrated through Graham's travels in the years that followed, the evangelist possessed special access to Houston's elites and had reason to believe in their talk about social uplift. Yet the booster spirit that Graham and his friends exhibited at this time was not only multiracial in zeal—it was also multiracial in form. Convinced of Houston's exceptionalism and impressed with a city whose rise seemed at odds with prevailing disruptions of the period, Graham forged ties with South Texans that cut across racial lines. In particular, he carved out influential relationships with nonwhite business and church leaders, whose own entrepreneurial verve caused them to fight for a future of inclusion and universal perspective.

Graham's most substantive connections were with African American pastors and businessmen who bought in to bootstrap capitalism's ideals of race reform. Historians have long contrasted Booker T. Washington and his market-driven plan for social advancement with the more radical W. E. B. DuBois as a way to emphasize philosophical tensions within the twentieth-century African American community. Yet the measuring of black entrepreneurialism on local cultures during the civil rights period is a more recent phenomenon. Shaped by a reading of black entrepreneurship as "myth" (when have African Americans enjoyed a truly "free" market?), scholars, until recently, highlighted those agents who followed DuBois's example into Martin Luther King Jr.'s movement, rather than those in Washington's mode who sought progress by way of economic clout. Yet, in Texas, Graham found a substantial number of black entrepreneurs who preferred Washington's way and who viewed race reform as best achieved through capitalist drive and corporate responsibility. Sharing his optimism that racial reconciliation came through winning souls and empowering individuals, they welcomed Graham to major centers across the Southwest with the same warmth as their white counterparts.[35]

Houston was uniquely generous in this expression because it was a milieu in which black businesses and churches had long flourished. One of the city's other popular monikers spoke to this fact. After World War I, Houston's Chamber of Commerce devised a new marketing slogan— "Heavenly Houston"—to sell the fledgling city as a uniquely welcoming place. The historian Bernadette Pruitt explains that the top-down propaganda truly resonated with black city dwellers: "For civic-minded African Americans, the slogan . . . highlighted the accomplishments of and opportunities for Houston African Americans. Over the next few decades, many copied the phrase when comparing Houston to other southern cities." Indeed, during his sojourn to the city in 1930, one black commentator admitted that "Houston Negroes had the greatest potential of development of any group of Negroes . . . in the South." Another, associated with the National Urban League, agreed, saying that Houston "seemed free of the racial tension that characterized the 'average southern community.'" Clifton Richardson, editor of the black newspaper Houston Informer, helped disseminate these claims through print to urge his peers to build a vibrant economy for the sake of "race pride," their "self-respect," and as an example for other communities.[36]

To be clear, racial bliss was an exaggerated concept when evaluated against the day-to-day difficulties of black communities. Most African Americans living in Houston's Third, Fourth, and Fifth Wards faced undue hardship that belied the "heavenly" features of their town. By midcentury, Houston was suffering from the same disparities as other cities, evidence of which surfaced in both subtle and violent form. Even as Graham's evangelistic services in the 1950s inspired predominantly white audiences to chase progress with abandon, nonwhite Houstonians lived a very different existence. In 1950 the median income for white Anglo males was $2,250, but for African Americans it was $1,050. Sixty-two predominantly white housing tracts were added to Houston's expanding periphery between 1940 and 1950, and twelve thousand homes were built there in 1950 alone, all to fulfill white middle-class suburban dreams. White Houstonians who drove the new freeways linking these tracts to the city, where Graham's meetings were held, they did so without having to contemplate the decaying cityscape outside their windows. A rambling 1950s Houston may not have looked like 1950s Harlem, but under the surface it suffered from equally profound inequities. And by the 1960s, after Graham's many return visits, these inequities were boiling over. Dramatic illustration of this came a few months after Graham spoke at Houston's Layman's Leadership Institute. In mid-May of 1967, Texas Southern University, located in the Third Ward, erupted in confrontation between students and police after false word spread that a "policeman had shot a six-year-old Negro child." The tally, which *Time* magazine reported, was staggering: "488 students were arrested, one student and two policemen were wounded and a rookie cop was dead." Contrary to its Chamber Men's boilerplate, then, Houston was no utopia, and its racial problems were as vexing as the nation's.[37]

Still, compared to other cities, Houston was a noticeably welcoming, multiracial metropolis, if not to the degree that its city fathers wished it to be. Starting in the 1920s and continuing into the postwar years, black business leaders helped guarantee this. As of 1930, Houston's black population, thirteenth largest in the country, "ranked tenth in number of black-owned establishments, seventh in average net sales per store, and third in net sales per capita." Though diminished slightly by postwar trends that benefitted white suburban business, black corporations continued to set high standards. In the 1950s, Houston's black business leaders joined their counterparts in Atlanta in wooing federal contracts to their city, making them cogs in the Sunbelt machine. And even as crises enveloped parts of their town in the 1960s, they continued to endorse government-assisted "capital formation for the Negro Businessman" (coined at Texas Southern University) as the way to inject money into black communities, level economic gaps between haves and have-nots, link corporate initiative to civil rights, and make Houston's black entrepreneurs the face of American progress and virtue on a global scale.[38]

If Baghdad on the Bayou's black financiers supplied the impetus and mechanisms for economic growth, its black pastors provided the moral passion. Clifton Richardson observed their dynamic authority. "The religious or church life of colored Houstonians," he wrote in 1928, "has been given the most prominent place on the racial program. . . . Frankly and candidly, the writer holds to the opinion that 'colored Houston' is top-heavy with churches." The men who shepherded these churches enjoyed a power that trumped that of other black professionals. They wielded it in an effort to command their flocks *and* their town. Antioch Baptist Church's Reverend Jack Yates's labors were characteristic in this regard: in the late nineteenth century, he supervised the paving of streets in the Fourth Ward and the establishment of a park in the Third Ward. Pastor and spiritual counselor, he was also a city planner. Little changed for African American ministers in the twentieth century. By the 1960s, Houston's black clergy, congregated in organizations such as the Houston Baptist Ministerial Alliance, were a formidable force. Besides continuing to monitor brass-tacks conditions in their communities, they also guided ambitious reform movements and pressed hard for change through vigorous civic engagement.[39]

Meanwhile, they continued to build churches of a magnitude rarely seen elsewhere. Few were as eye-catching as St. John Missionary Baptist Church on Dowling Street in the Third Ward. In 1950, the five-thousand-member parish completed a new sanctuary, which featured a "classical revival architectural design with colossal columns, symbolic of the spiritual strength and influence of the church in the community." Three years later it was considered one of the most illustrious African American churches in the country. Proud of its standing, unwilling to pause, it expanded its offerings by establishing a radio ministry, building an educational wing, and hosting key national meetings. One, "the 25th commencement ceremony of the Erma Hughes Business College with Dr. Martin Luther King, Jr. as principal speaker," transpired in 1958. The second came in 1965 when it "hosted the 85th National Baptist Convention of America (NBC)." As advertised, this was "the first religious event to be held at Houston's new Astrodome." Billy Graham's evangelistic crusade that year would be the second. St. John could in truth boast leadership in this national gathering as well, for it was one of the institutions that sponsored it.[40]

St. John was, in this regard, typical among its peer institutions, with the pastors and parishioners who constituted it representative of the way Houston's African American community threw its support behind Graham and the spirit of the 1965 crusade. Though numerically underrepresented, several black businessmen and pastors nevertheless worked alongside white oilmen, lawyers, and clerics on the crusade's Executive Committee, and on a nightly basis served as delegates, platform guests, and program participants. Enabled by a history of forward-looking enterprise in Heavenly Houston, they assumed these tasks with an equally buoyant view of a prosperous future they saw promised to them by Graham's gospel.[41]

Two individuals assumed particularly vital partnerships with Graham. One was Reverend N. C. Crain of St. John Missionary Baptist Church (Gray Avenue), a sister (and competing) church to St. John Missionary

Baptist (Dowling), which was located just around the corner. By the 1950s, Crain oversaw an institution almost as impressive as its rival. Inside his own artful Gothic Revival sanctuary, this one designed by Houston's pre-eminent black architect, Crain promoted revivalism combined with the self-help imperatives of Booker T. Washington. During his forty-year career at St. John, Crain preached this theology in revivals across the South, baptizing some twelve thousand individuals into the fold. But it was in Houston that he exercised power. There he sat on ecclesiastical and political committees, such as the city's Interdenominational Alliance of Colored Churches, and became the inspiration for a rising generation of preachers. This is why he was among the elites who welcomed Graham to Houston for his whirlwind tour in 1963. Along with Earl Hankamer, Carloss Morris, and Houston's mayor, Crain applauded Graham's comments on the virtues of small government, individual initiative, and corporate civil rights as the answer to America's woes. And this is why he was welcomed into Graham's inner circle as a member of the 1965 crusade's Executive Committee and sanctioned the evangelist's applied Christianity as the way to better human relations.[42]

Another collaborator was Reverend E. V. Hill. Native to the area, Hill occupied high-profile positions within the city's ministerial organizations during the early 1960s. Even though he relocated to Los Angeles in the mid-1960s, Hill stayed close to his roots. Throughout the late decade he traveled back there to monitor social developments. At this time his own idea of race reform shifted from a liberal agenda he once endorsed with Martin Luther King Jr. to Graham's philosophy. King's philosophy, he concluded, led to dependency on an enlarged, secular government, while Graham's led to true change. He began speaking on behalf of this new corporate civil rights creed alongside the evangelist, with one of the most dramatic of his performances taking place in Dallas's Cotton Bowl in 1972. To a crowd of youth gathered for Explo '72, the black preacher delivered a doctrine that had long defined Baghdad on the Bayou. "We are not of . . . one race [or] denomination," he exclaimed, but together, as one body united by a shared gospel, "we're going to take this world for Jesus Christ." All its problems—its racial strife, war, poverty—can be solved, he declared, if people stop looking to government for assistance and instead concentrate on saving peoples' souls. "As one who has attempted to better the conditions of men, I am finally convinced that a better world will come with better people. And better people can only come through the power of God. Oh, how I love Jesus!"[43]

Meant for evangelism more than voter mobilization, drained of specifics where free-market economics and partisan platforms were concerned, Hill's proclamations still exuded politics. Indeed, by the time of Hill's sermon, Heavenly Houston had become a place and a moniker with considerable political leverage. Those wielding it included clerics and lay leaders who labored with Graham and Hill; among those benefiting from it was Richard Nixon. Nixon's ambition at this time was to win over a "Black Silent Majority," which he saw centered in the Sunbelt, where—as advisors noted—blacks were more "conservative minded," friendly to free-market capitalism, and "integrated than their northern friends." In 1968 Nixon's team targeted this constituency in hopes of chipping away at the Democratic Party's black voting bloc. Drawing on resources availed to him by black entrepreneurs steeped in Booker T. Washington's teachings, Nixon proclaimed, "I am the only candidate who truly believes that black people, on their own steam and with 'remedial' help from government are going to make it." Even more boldly, he announced that he would generate a "political phenomenon": "the realization by black people . . . that their best hope lies not in the Democratic plantation politics of the past, but in the kinds of programs as I have put forward." If benefitting from the government-aided civil rights platforms of the 1960s, black Americans, in Nixon's view, stood at the threshold of a new era, when empowered individuals could use growth economics as the most direct path to equality.[44]

Nixon's victory in 1968 did not strike the blow at Democratic dominance that he had hoped for, but it did set in motion a four-year project of consolidating GOP gains in the African American community. Through such agencies as the Black Cabinet, Office of Economic Opportunity (OEO), Office of Minority Business Enterprise (OMBE), and Small Business Administration (SBA), the White House aided black corporate lobbies that adhered to the corporate civil rights model. These programs demonstrated their own shortsightedness, such as a privileging of the black middle class over black workers, and rightly faced criticism as a calculated attempt by right-wing Republicans to fracture African American unity. But they clearly appealed to a determined and significant constituency on the rise. Nixon's presidential campaign of 1972 once again tapped into this initiative. Helped along by his "Black Blitz Team," charged with recruiting black leaders to the cause, Nixon received 13 percent of the black vote, a modest but important gain over 1968. Though disappointed by falling short of a desired 20 percent mark, Nixon's team had managed to carve out a movement of a small but disproportionately powerful citizenry.[45]

Graham's black allies played notable roles in the GOP's biracial campaigns. Clerics in Crain's camp did their part by championing a line of thinking associated with the NBC and the denomination's leading spokesmen, Reverend Joseph H. Jackson, who believed that black Christians needed to "go from protest to production" (his words) and endorse policies that equalized the market and facilitated racial betterment through fiscal designs. While Crain's peers preached this message on Sundays, Hill led a brigade of black ministers who used more high-profile and highly charged political occasions to deliver theological justification for Republicans' political plan. In Los Angeles, meanwhile, he used federal programs like the OEO to fund local employment and social programs that aligned with his conservative prerogatives. Hill's efforts were replicated elsewhere, in Houston and Atlanta especially, and other Republican leaders readily endorsed them. Houston's GOP stalwart George H. W. Bush stood out front in this effort, and throughout the 1970s he stressed the need for his party to endorse an "Open Door" policy and recruit a diverse base representative of his home's heterogeneous population. South Texas's black middle-class church folk responded to Bush's overtures and did what they could to advance a creative conservatism that had always had a hold on the heart of their town.[46]

The "Golden Buckle" of Evangelicalism

Bush's overtures, and Graham's and Hill's quest for a post-racial age, highlight a final progression in Houston evangelicalism's ambitions for impact. Already known as Baghdad on the Bayou and Heavenly Houston for its role as a crossroads of race, religion, and economy, Houston earned a new nickname in the late 1970s and early 1980s: "The Golden Buckle of the Sunbelt," a designation that bespoke its proliferating new money, technology, and corporate might, but that also alluded to its direct access to a world undergoing further revolutionary change. For Graham and his team, Houston now shone more brightly as America's (and evangelicalism's) bridge from the homogeneity of the midcentury to the dynamic heterogeneities of the century's end.[47]

Houston's emergence as the "premier Sunbelt city" was tied to its impressive demographic shifts. Attracted by its expanding job market and above-average income levels, five thousand persons migrated there each month during the late 1970s. By 1982, with a population over 1.6 million people, the city ranked as the nation's fourth largest. Although boosters tended to highlight gains made by Houston's white oil workers as proof of the city's unusual success, the city's spectacular expansion came via growth of its nonwhite communities, with African American and Hispanic constituents making up 45 percent of the total metropolitan population. In this period of ferment, Houston at once welcomed the world to its bustling environs and signaled to it a future of unprecedented pluralism.[48]

Graham's evangelical movement thrived more than ever in this milieu. Positioned on the southern edge of the country, white and nonwhite Houstonians alike sensed anew their unique opportunity to penetrate the global South with their gospel, and acted on it by supporting a plethora of transnational Christian organizations. Attentive to trends inside the country and their city's budding import to them, they also supported a range of ministerial innovations that redefined the theological and sociological compositions of their increasingly transnational constituency. Neo-Pentecostalism, the megachurch movement, Protestant-Catholic ecumenism—these and other phenomena shook this town with unusual intensity during the late 1970s and early 1980s and allowed their participants to envision a church not only unencumbered by black-white racial divides, but also enlivened by communion across a multicultural plane.[49]

Graham affirmed this gospel at the Houston-Gulf Coast crusade of 1981. Overseen by a familiar "who's who" list of white Houstonian business leaders, including Carloss Morris and veterans of earlier campaigns, this event was nonetheless different from what had come before. Gone, for instance, was any reference to politics. Chastened by Nixon's failed presidency, and disheartened by the fundamentalism of Jerry Falwell's Moral Majority, Graham arrived in Houston promising to avoid politicking of any kind. Gone too was some of the evangelist's unbridled awe with Houston's advancements. In its place was more unease with the accelerating pace of the metropolis's expansion. Most of all, though, Graham's 1981 event revealed his desire to promote a discourse of diversity beyond black-white lines, a race- *and* ethnic-neutral ecumenical evangelicalism as the heartbeat of the present church, and a charitable as well as enterprising spirit as the hope of the church's future. The pliable gospel of outreach that Graham had started applying across the Southwest a generation before was about to become even more pliant.[50]

The evidence of this inclusivity emanated from each facet of the eight-day crusade. In the lead-up to the event, the BGEA stressed ecumenical brotherhood as the key to success. Protestants of all persuasion embraced the charge. One Baptist minister reiterated Graham's challenge to "spark a citywide spiritual renewal . . . and work to bring the Christian community here closer together." "The Body of Christ . . . is divided in this town," he added repentantly. "At best, we are cousins who have never met. At worse, we are like competitors." Black, white, and Hispanic pastors agreed, and committed their churches to building an interfaith movement in advance of Graham's arrival. Their invitations were extended to Catholics as well. In the days leading up to the revival, Catholic leaders such as Reverend Bill Young, a local priest who sat on the crusade's executive board, served as liaison to the city's large non-Protestant population. During the crusade itself he helped strengthen a fellowship across Protestant-Catholic lines that was deemed remarkable by local media, but also understandable considering the recent demographic and religious trajectories (increased Hispanic presence, the rise of charismatic worship, grass-roots conservative politics) that had been redefining Houston since the 1970s.[51]

Urged on by these Houstonians, the Graham team also adopted its own innovations in order to meet the demands of multiethnic evangelism. With materials in hand from prior efforts in South America, Graham's associates recruited the city's large Spanish-speaking Pentecostal, Baptist, and Catholic constituents as campaign workers. Headed by "Hispanic Chairman" Alfonso Flores, a local Baptist, and Reverend Charles Ward, a veteran of BGEA activities in Mexico, the Graham team created a bilingual infrastructure. The system encompassed Spanish language classes and training programs held in Hispanic Pentecostal churches, the distribution of Spanish pamphlets and enlistment of Latino musicians, and, at the nightly services themselves, Spanish translation services cordoned off in a section of Rice University's football stadium, the site of the gathering. One of the Houston crusade's promotional magazines heralded the reach of the new Graham evangelistic team: "A world of ministries that ministers to the world."[52]

Graham's sermons celebrated this sentiment, as well as the changes that had occurred in Houston since his first appearance in the city three decades before. At a pre-crusade gathering of ministers in September 1981, he noted that during his visit in 1952, he and several of Houston's black clergy had met with the mayor to address race relations in the area. Despite the initiative and the "great strides" that followed, Graham told his 1980s audience, social injustice remained present in Houston. But other changes were afoot, transforming the town: the "decline of mainline churches," "rise of parachurch organizations" and "religious television," "evangelical resurgence," "new social emphasis," "the charismatic movement," and "changes in the Roman Catholic Church" were all shifting it (and America) in new and exciting directions, demanding a refreshed and "united evangelistic effort." In response to these conditions, Graham implored his pastor friends to sing loudly together as a larger, progressive, inclusive community of saints that could provide a more effective "witness to the world." The mechanisms of his evangelistic organizations, Graham added, had already been adjusted to make such witness possible, the wish to "move a city of [Houston's] magnitude" attainable.[53]

Moving a city is exactly what he attempted through the homilies he delivered on a nightly basis in early November. The sermons heard over the course of a week played off of the multiethnic spirit that Houston exhibited, and revealed Graham's intent to move beyond the sociopoliti- cal dichotomies of yesteryear (black-white, liberal-conservative), to a full embrace of multiculturalism's life-giving potentials. As vexing as race reform had been for all Americans during the 1950s and 1960s, and as challenging as it had been for Sunbelt evangelicals in the 1970s to pro- mulgate their corporate civil rights, ethnic pluralism seemed to supply a straightforward path to healthier relations across the spectrum of differ- ence. Migrants from Mexico and South America, workers and worshippers from across the world's oceans, brought with them to Houston a rags-to- riches ambition that harkened back to the wildcatters of an earlier time, and to those white and black merchants who had moved to the city from afar before making it big. The added worth of the new immigrants, Graham offered, was that their entrepreneurial spirit was neither squelched by an oppressive Jim Crow order, nor blind to the hurdles accompanying minor- ity status. Rather than see themselves as exploited, these new Houstonians considered their place in the city's melting pot as leverage for influence, their task to force their neighbors and churches to become attuned to the signs and wonders of the global.

Graham followed this reasoning in a number of his more colorful ser- mons. Though never as exhaustive in his homiletic treatment of Houston's ethnicity as he was of race, the evangelist used parabolic language to make his audience reconsider their new social condition. In a sermon labeled "SALT," for instance, he played off of a familiar Scriptural verse ("Ye are the salt of the earth") to highlight the different sources around the world from which this mineral was drawn, stress the wonder of its diverse "expression" in humanity, and savor its ability to flavor human existence. Theological application followed. It was up to the Christian, Graham charged, to "improve not only himself, but the lives of those he meets;

every experience, every relationship will be richer and better." It was up to the Christian to make Houston thirst (just as salt creates thirst) after God with renewed vigor. And it was incumbent upon evangelicals to embrace the zest of experience derived from diversity. "We are a very small minority in this great city," Graham proclaimed, and "yet God has always used minorities."[54]

His nod to the virtues of pluralism was repeated in other sermons, including one that he opportunistically titled "Roots." Using the popular television miniseries with the same title as his framework, Graham offered his listeners a walk through the historical foundations of their city and its origins as a place of new beginnings, then transitioned into exegesis about Americans' longing to rediscover their roots, and then to answers for this condition that rested in the Bible. According to Graham, for all of the positive dynamics that flowed from the identity revolutions of the era, the true rootedness for his multicultural congregation could only be recovered in the timeless truths of the Bible, and its one source of repentance: the cross. As he had done for decades, though with a multihued gaze, Graham closed his service by asking his audience to accept that redemption. As had been witnessed for decades, hundreds of people, but now with many languages, heritages, and identities in tow, walked the aisle toward his counsel.[55]

This procession in Houston's multiethnic evangelicalism continued long after Graham left town. It culminated in the BGEA's major undertaking of 1985, and one of the most memorable in its entire history: the first National Convocation on Evangelizing Ethnic America. Held in Houston over a four-day stretch in the spring, this touchstone event drew together seven hundred pastors, missionaries, lay leaders, and academics from around the country to "acknowledge the depth of the population shifts and to design strategy for turning 'unevangelized' ethnic families into Christians." The collective takeaway for those who attended the event was also one of renewal—a sense that American evangelicalism was itself crossing a threshold. Although Graham was not in attendance, the keynote address delivered by church-growth proponent and Fuller Seminary professor C. Peter Wagner redoubled the assertions he delivered in Houston four years earlier: that an ethnic revolution was offering the church a fresh chance to dismantle prejudices, stress unity over difference, and move forward into an epoch of unprecedented cooperation and growth. Even in this multicultural milieu, social injustice would not disappear easily, Wagner assured his audience. "We must work at it," he declared. But witnessed in this gathering, he continued, were signs that intercultural contact was enriching, and the necessity of the age, for Christians and the country. "Today's America is a multi-ethnic society on a scale that boggles the imagination. The teeming multitudes of all colors, languages, smells, and cultures are not just a quaint sideline in our nation; they are America." Had Graham been in attendance, surely he would have concurred, and singled Houston out as a city that imagined this America into being.[56]

Looking at Houston today, the most religiously, racially, and ethnically diverse metropolitan area in the country, one could commend Graham for being so farsighted in his vision for the place. In this epicenter of international exchange, where Nigerian roustabouts populate local oilrigs and Pentecostal pews, Mexican American Catholics enjoy authority in local Republican politics, stadium-sized megachurches broadcast their services to the world, and the religious expressions of the Third Ward shape white and black popular culture on a universal scale, the boosterism and corporate civil rights of yesteryear can be seen in abundance. Of course, anyone who studies Graham's career already knows how proficient he was at fastening the traditions of his evangelical doctrine to the currents of his day, and at anticipating and seizing upon new directions for the church and society.[57]

Still, his dealings with Houston, a city that could never stand still, are unusually striking and instructive, including where matters of race reform are concerned. When surveying Graham's interactions there, we encounter a man whose attachment to a particular space was profound and whose enchantment with its guiding principles and economic possibilities as the solution to injustice was unshakeable. To be sure, this enchantment and these principles certainly opened the door to other neglects. Too often the booster spirit that possessed Graham brushed over deeply engrained disparities in Texas's social order in the quest for the shiny and new, and allowed—even encouraged—evangelicals to move quickly ahead without pausing to grapple with the troubled histories and currencies of racism, with the destructive potentials of unbounded individualism and free-market capitalism, and with prejudiced power structures that still privileged white people. Its anti-statist biases and tendency to focus on the local without sensitivity to conditions further afield—in places like Harlem—further clouded its aims and effects. As witnessed in evolving electoral politics in contemporary Texas, where strands of a parochial and ill-tempered (white) boosterism emanate from some pulpits and pews (including Graham's former congregational home, First Baptist Dallas), the consequences of this limited attention span and purview still persist in evangelicalism today. Ironically, unsettlingly, Graham's own buoyant model of Christian corporate civil rights faces just as much (if not more) opposition in certain church circles today as it did at its inception.

Nevertheless, what is also obvious is that the entrepreneurial, race-bridging agenda Graham applied on the ground through relationship-building and constant outreach were, in his day at least, remarkably infectious, efficacious, and multilateral. During the 1960s and 1970s, while all Americans wrestled with the complexities of race and the real and proper yet uncertain extents of government-sponsored civil rights reform, Graham's philosophy was one that gained serious traction among a substantially large and increasingly pluralistic religious citizenry. In Houston, where the evangelist's message found especially fertile soil, this citizenry's collective actions at the grass-roots level produced some noteworthy moments of shared purpose and, in some cases, institutional and political mechanisms that would last. They also encouraged vital cultural turns with which the metropolis continues to live. By the 1980s, this city's white evangelicals, once Graham's gospel's chief proponents, were as much on the receiving end of its innovations and drive for change as they were its progenitors. By the end of the century, Houston's truly global population was dictating the flow of this ambition onto a global stage.

From these encounters, in short, we sense a man who was in his own way innovative in his pursuits of a fairer human order. Graham, like many of his vocational and political peers—and presidential allies—did not have all the answers to America's greatest dilemma, and the ones he offered did not always affect the change he desired. But he can still be appreciated as a catalytic figure who recognized sooner than most the need for church folk to acknowledge and attack the dilemma (publicly and politically, not simply rhetorically), and who understood quicker than many the wide repertoire of reformist weaponry needed to wage the war.[58]

Notes

1. "Evangelist Speaks to 43,691," *Houston Chronicle*, November 23, 1965, "Biog— Graham, Billy" file, Houston Metropolitan Public Library (HMPL), Houston, Texas.
2. Howard O. Jones, *Gospel Trailblazer: An African American Preacher's Historic Journey across Racial Lines* (Chicago: Moody Publishers, 2003), 139–140; Grant Wacker, *America's Pastor: Billy Graham and the Shaping of a Nation* (Cambridge, MA: Harvard University Press, 2014), 125–126.

3. Billy Graham, *Just As I Am: The Autobiography of Billy Graham* (San Francisco, CA: HarperCollins, 1997), 302–303. Niebuhr quoted in Richard Wightman Fox, *Reinhold Niebuhr: A Biography* (San Francisco: Harper & Row, 1985), 266. On King, Graham, and doubts of King's advisors, see David L. Chappell, *A Stone of Hope: Prophetic Religion and the Death of Jim Crow* (Chapel Hill: University of North Carolina Press, 2004), 96–98.

4. Tom McMahan quoted in Steven P. Miller, *Billy Graham and the Rise of the Republican South* (Philadelphia: University of Pennsylvania Press, 2009), 64.

5. See, for instance, Michael G. Long, *The Legacy of Billy Graham: Critical Reflections on America's Greatest Evangelist* (Louisville, KY: Westminster John Knox Press, 2008); Miller, *Billy Graham and the Rise of the Republican South*, 64–65. Martin's phrase taken from comments at Worlds of Billy Graham workshop, Kennebunkport, Maine, May 31, 2013.

6. On Graham's support of federal civil rights legislation, see Miller, *Billy Graham and the Rise of the Republican South*, 104–105.

7. Robert Wuthnow, *Rough Country: How Texas Became America's Most Powerful Bible-Belt State* (Princeton, NJ: Princeton University Press, 2014), 2.

8. David G. McComb, *Houston, the Bayou City* (Austin: University of Texas Press, 1969), 259.

9. Quoted in Wuthnow, *Rough Country*, 225.

10. Texas Historical Commission, *Texas in World War II*, thc.state.tx.us; US Census, County Data, 1947 and 1952, electronic data files; Wuthnow, *Rough Country*, 226.

11. Lawrence Goodwin, *Texas Oil, American Dreams: A Study of the Texas Independent Producers and Royalty Owners Association* (Austin: Center for American History, by the Texas State Historical Association, 1996), 76, 81.

12. Billy Graham, Address to Texas State Baptist Convention, October 10, 1951, Folder 24, Box 29, Collection 265, Records of the Billy Graham Evangelistic Association (BGEA), Billy Graham Center Archives (BGCA), Wheaton College, Wheaton, Illinois.

13. John P. Newport, "The Church Member," in *J. Howard Williams: Prophet of God and Friend of Man*, ed. H.C. Brown, Jr., and Charles P. Johnson (San Antonio, TX: Naylor, 1963), 121–125; National Council of Churches, *Churches and Church Membership in the United States: An Enumeration and Analysis by Counties, States, and Regions* (New York: National Council of Churches, 1956), electronic data file for states and counties, 1952; Leon Edgar Turesdell and Timothy Francis Murphy, *Religious Bodies, 1926* (Washington, DC: US Government Printing Office, 1929), electronic data file via Inter-University Consortium for Political and Social Research; Kenneth Dole, "Religious Roundup," *Washington Post*, March 28, 1953; Dole, "News of the Churches, *Washington Post*, June 13, 1953; Diana J. Kleiner, "H-E-B," *Handbook of Texas Online*, tshaonline.org/handbook/online/articles/fbu85, accessed June 25, 2015; on Butt and Graham, see hebff.org/, accessed June 25, 2014.

14. "Billy Graham Sets Premier of Western 'With Religion,'" *Indianapolis Times*, September 25, 1951, in Scrapbook 364, Collection 360, BGEA Scrapbooks, BGCA.

15. Sam Hodges, "Billy Graham Moves Membership from First Baptist Dallas," *Dallas News*, December 29, 2008, religionblog.dallasnews.com/2008/12/billy-graham-moves-membership.html/.

16. See "Table 2: Population and Territorial Growth of Selected Sunbelt Cities, 1940–1980," in Elizabeth Tandy Shermer, *Sunbelt Capitalism: Phoenix and the Transformation of American Politics* (Philadelphia: University of Pennsylvania Press, 2013), 201.

17. "Houston Was O. Henry's Baghdad-on-the-Bayou," *New York Times*, July 23, 1939. Jones quoted in Jordan A. Schwarz, *The New Dealers: Power and Politics in the Age of Roosevelt* (New York: Alfred A. Knopf, 1993), 61, 78.

18. John Pollock, *A Foreign Devil in China: The Story of Dr. L. Nelson Bell* (Charlotte, NC: World Wide Publications, 2010), 72–73; "Crossroads in the Life of Billy Graham," *Houston Chronicle*, October 10, 1965, "Biog—Graham, Billy" file, HMPL.

19. "Hugh Roy Cullen, Philanthropist and Oil Operator, Dies," *Dallas Morning News*, July 5, 1957. On Jones and LeTourneau, see Darren Dochuk, *From Bible Belt to Sunbelt: Plain-Folk Religion, Grassroots Politics, and the Rise of Evangelical Conservatism* (New York: Norton, 2011), 56–58; and "Moving Mountains: The Business of Evangelicalism and Extraction," in *What's Good for Business: Business and American Politics Since World War II*, ed. Kim Phillips-Fein and Julian E. Zelizer (New York: Oxford University Press, 2012), 72–90.

20. Barbara Elmore, "The Story of Oilman Earl Hankamer: Sharing the Wealth," *Baylor Business Review*, April 10, 2008; Billy Graham to Earl C. Hankamer, August 22, 1952, Papers of Earl Hankamer (EHP), BGCA.

21. "Billy Graham in *Oiltown, U.S.A.*, World Premier—Sam Houston Coliseum," Clippings File, BGEA; "'Oil Town' Story of Two-Fisted Sinner," *Houston Press*, June 2, 1952; "Graham Movie Jams Coliseum," *Houston Chronicle*, March 4, 1953; "Billy Graham Invites You to Meet the People who Live in OIL TOWN U.S.A.," Folder 3, EHP; Dick Ross to Mr. Earl C. Hankamer, May 15, 1952, May 20, 1952, and June 11, 1952, Folder 1, EHP.

22. "Church Builder, Dairy Founder Oldham Dies," untitled clipping, July 20, 1955; "Widow Carries on with Oldham Work," untitled clipping, September 14, 1957, "Biog—Oldham, Morris C." file, HMPL; Memorandum, November 17, 1965, Procedure Books—1965, Billy Graham Greater Houston Crusade (Houston, Texas), November 19–28, Collection 16, BGCA.

23. Dochuk, "Moving Mountains," 72–80. Shermer, *Sunbelt Capitalism*, 5, 10.

24. "Graham's Crusade to Open on Friday," *Houston Post*, October 10, 1965; "Oil Town, U.S.A.!" brochure, Folder 2, EHP.

25. While the 1953 Dallas crusade was segregated in principle, ropes preventing blacks from entering the revival did in fact come down prior to the meeting's

opening, though the specifics and reasons for this are somewhat unclear. Nels Hansen and Bill Coffey, "Criswell Rips Integration," *Dallas Morning News*, February 23, 1956; "Segregation Blast Lifted from Text, Criswell Says," *Dallas Morning News*, March 16, 1956; "Southern Church Leaders State Segregation Views," *Plaindealer* (Kansas City), October 5, 1956.

26. On Dallas's religion and politics, see Edward H. Miller, *Nut Country: Right-Wing Dallas and the Birth of the Southern Strategy* (Chicago: University of Chicago Press, 2015).

27. "Graham Rips 'Big Government," *Houston Chronicle*, October 28, 1963; "More Hope for Negro in the South, Says Graham," *Houston Chronicle*, October 28, 1963; "Four Days with Billy Graham," *Houston Chronicle*, October 31, 1963, Folder 1, EHP.

28. Billy Graham, "Message to Students," February 13, 1964, Folder 102, Box 28, Collection 265, BGCA.

29. Ibid.; Billy Graham, Address to Layman's Leadership Institute, Houston, Texas, January 25, 1967, Folder 91, Box 24, Collection 265, BGCA.

30. Billy Graham, Address to Ministers Meeting, October 14, 1965, Folder 91, Box 24, Collection 265, BGCA.

31. Billy Graham, "The Great Judgment Day," Houston Crusade, November 28, 1965, Folder 59, Box 23, Collection 265, BGCA.

32. Ibid.

33. See G.A. Lloyd, Coordinator of Public Affairs—Community Relations, Humble Oil & Refining Company, "The Private Sector's Role in Making All Systems Go," *Dateline: Church & Industry in the Current Scene* 12, no. 8 (May, 1968), 5–6, in "London, 1967," Folder 31, Box 9, Collection 285, BGCA.

34. "Graham Says Youth in Revolt," *Houston Post*, November 28, 1965, in "Biog— Graham, Billy" file, HMPL. Billy Graham, "The Great Judgment Day," Houston Crusade, November 28, 1965, Folder 59, Box 23, Collection 265, BGCA.

35. E. Franklin Frazier, *Black Bourgeoisie: The Rise of a New Middle Class* (Glencoe, IL: Free Press, 1957), 24–46. For critique of Frazier, with reference to Houston, see James M. SoRelle, "The Emergence of Black Business in Houston, Texas: A Study of Race and Ideology, 1919–45," in *Black Dixie: Afro-Texan History and Culture in Houston*, ed. Howard Beeth and Carty D. Wintz (College Station: Texas A&M University Press, 1992), 87–102.

36. Bernadette Pruitt, *The Other Great Migration: The Movement of Rural African Americans to Houston, 1900–1941* (College Station: Texas A&M University Press, 2013), 45; Lorenzo Greene and Jesse O. Thomas quoted in Pruitt, *The Other Great Migration*, 45; SoRelle, "The Emergence of Black Business in Houston, Texas," 105.

37. Wuthnow, *Rough Country*, 227, 253; US Census Bureau, *Statistical Abstract of the United States, 1952* (Washington, DC: Government Printing Office, 1952), 728–729, 732–734. "Texas: Hate in Houston," *Time*, May 26, 1967.

38. United States Department of Commerce, Bureau of the Census, *Negroes in the United States, 1920–1932* (Washington, DC, 1935), 518–519; Robert E. Weems Jr., *Business in Black and White: American Presidents and Black Entrepreneurs in the Twentieth Century* (New York: New York University Press, 2009), 71–73.

39. Clifton F. Richardson Sr., "Houston's Colored Citizens: Activities and Conditions among the Negro Population in the 1920," reprinted in Beeth and Cary Wintz, *Black Dixie*, 129; Robert D. Bullard, *Invisible Houston: The Black Experience in Boom and Bust* (College Station: Texas A&M University Press, 1987), 115–117.

40. "St. John Baptist Church," Houston-Churches, Standing Files, The African American Library at the Gregory School (AALGS), Houston, Texas.

41. Billy Graham Greater Houston Crusade, "Executive Committee, March 16, 1965," Folder 2, EHP. See also programs of the Houston Crusade in "Biog-Graham, Billy" file, HMPL.

42. "City of Houston Landmark Designation Report," 2009, houstontx.gov/planning/HistoricPres/landmarks/09L214_St_John_2222_Gray.pdf, accessed August 21, 2014; quoted from the Texas Historical Commission Landmark Plaque, entrance to St. John Missionary Baptist Church, (photographed and documented by author).

43. Hill quoted in Dochuk, *From Bible Belt to Sunbelt*, 327.

44. Nixon strategy quoted from and assessed in Dochuk, *From Bible Belt to Sunbelt*, 335.

45. Extensive treatment of Nixon and black Republican initiatives is provided in Leah Wright Rigueur, *The Loneliness of the Black Republican: Pragmatic Politics and the Pursuit of Power* (Princeton, NJ: Princeton University Press, 2015), 136–139, 159–162, 183–185, 194.

46. Wallace Best, "'The Right Achieved and the Wrong Way Conquered': J. H. Jackson, Martin Luther King, Jr., and the Conflict over Civil Rights," *Religion and American Culture: A Journal of Interpretation* 16, no. 2 (2006), 205; Rigueur, *The Loneliness of the Black Republican*, 147, 197.

47. Robert D. Bullard, "Black Housing in the Golden Buckle of the Sunbelt," *Free Inquiry* 8 (November 1980), 169–172.

48. Bullard, *Invisible Houston*, 7.

49. See, for instance, "16,000 Gather Here to Celebrate Pentecost with Rousing Tribute," *Houston Chronicle*, June 4, 1979, "H-Churches-Evangelical" file, HMPL.

50. Louis Moore, "A Billy Graham Crusade Doesn't Just Happen, It's Planned," *Houston Chronicle*, October 25, 1980; Louis Moore, "No Preaching in Schools, Graham Assures," *Houston Chronicle*, August 18, 1981; Louis Moore, "Graham Cites Concern over Moral, Spiritual Life in City," *Houston Chronicle*, November 9, 1981, Biog-Graham, Billy" file, HMPL.

51. Louis Moore, "Graham to Catholics: A New Fellowship," *Houston Chronicle*, September 12, 1981; Louis Moore, "Catholic Bishop May Hold Key to Graham's Crusade," *Houston Chronicle*, Undated, Biog-Graham, Billy" file, HMPL.

52. See Texas E. Reardon's letters to area pastors, written in English and Spanish, dated July 6, 1981 and undated; also letter from Gilbert Turner, chairman of Crusade Executive Committee, August 1981; also "A World Of Ministries That Ministers to the World"; all in Procedure Books—1981, Volume II, Houston-Gulf Coast Crusade, Collection 16, BGCA.

53. Billy Graham, Address to Ministers, September 18, 1981, Folder 37, Box 19, Collection 265, BGCA.

54. Billy Graham, "Salt," November 5, 1981, Folder 3, Box 7, Collection 285, BGCA.

55. Billy Graham, "Roots," November 13, 1981, Folder 8, Box 7, Collection 285, BGCA.

56. "Immigrants Called 'Ripe for Harvest Field' for Churches," *Los Angeles Times*, April 20, 1985; "C. Peter Wagner, "A Vision for Evangelizing the Real America," *International Bulletin of Missionary Research*, April, 1960, 59.

57. Jeannie Kever, "Diverse Houston Reflects U.S. Religious Changes," *Houston Chronicle*, February 26, 2008.

58. On evangelicalism's handlings of race, see Nancy D. Wadsworth, *Ambivalent Miracles: Evangelicals and the Politics of Racial Healing* (Charlottesville: University of Virginia Press, 2014); Michael O. Emerson and Christian Smith, *Divided by Faith: Evangelical Religion and the Problem of Race in America* (New York: Oxford University Press, 2001); and J. Russell Hawkins and Philip Luke Sinitiere, eds., *Christians and the Color Line: Race and Religion after "Divided by Faith"* (New York: Oxford University Press, 2013).

PART THREE

Culture

8

"You Cannot Fool the Electronic Eye"

BILLY GRAHAM AND MEDIA

Elesha Coffman

ACCORDING TO LEGEND, in 1949 the publishing magnate William Randolph Hearst boosted a young evangelist's Los Angeles crusade by instructing his editors to "puff Graham." In 2013, the Billy Graham Evangelistic Association (BGEA) amassed one million "likes" on Facebook. Between these milestones, Graham became one of the most recognized, televised, photographed, published, and quoted figures in America—and abroad—owing in large part to his adept engagement with media.[1]

The use of the word "adept" here is intentional. The intersection of media and evangelism is a tricky place in which to operate. There is a fine line between skillful and manipulative, between savvy and slick. Billy Graham, a media producer and media star, navigated that line adeptly as he advanced his two great goals: the evangelization of the world, and the advancement of the evangelical faith as a religious tradition. Graham's navigational skills were on vibrant display in his press conferences, so they constitute critical pieces of evidence for this chapter. The chapter will first situate Graham in the history of American revivalism and media. Next, it will sketch the growth of Graham's own media empire. Finally, it will explore ways in which the evangelist's media savvy, particularly his ability to convey sincerity across multiple platforms, helped him withstand the scrutiny of the spotlight and redirect its wattage toward his desired ends.

History

A direct ancestor to Graham emerged during the First Great Awakening: George Whitefield (1714–1770), who preached on both sides of the Atlantic, up and down the American colonies, attracting huge crowds through the power of his oratory and the efficiency of his marketing machine. Whitefield pioneered the use of all available media to generate interest before his arrival in a town, to publicize his meetings as they happened, to reinforce his message to those who had heard it in person, to expand his audience to include those who had not been present, to shape the reportage of his results, and to continue the revival after he moved on. All of that work required a lot of ink. An astonishing 30 percent of all titles printed in America in 1740 were written by or about the famous evangelist.[2]

Whitefield also engendered controversies that have flared ever since preachers began combining evangelism and commerce. He earned the scorn of the Boston blue-blood Congregationalist Charles Chauncy, who—prefiguring some of Reinhold Niebuhr's criticisms of Graham two hundred years later—found Whitefield's gospel hucksterism profoundly distasteful. Surely, Chauncy argued, it dishonors religion and the office of the clergy when Christianity is shilled on the street corner like some cheap commodity. A writer for the *Boston Weekly News-Letter* thought there ought to be laws constraining "Pedlars in Divinity." And if the content and delivery of peddled divinity were not bad enough, skeptics wondered where, exactly, all of that money in the collection plate went when the itinerant evangelist left town.[3]

Graham was acutely aware of the caricature of the traveling preacher. In interactions with reporters, he less often named one of his celebrated forebears—Whitefield; Second Great Awakening firebrand Charles Grandison Finney; Graham's personal hero, D. L. Moody; or the flamboyant Billy Sunday—than the fictional phony Elmer Gantry. The main character in Sinclair Lewis's bestselling 1927 novel, as well as a 1960 movie starring Burt Lancaster, Gantry did some preaching of his own, but he made an even bigger splash managing a female evangelist modeled on Aimee Semple McPherson. Among Gantry's clever moves as manager was hiring "a real press-agent, trained in newspaper work, circus advertising, and real-estate promoting" to sweet-talk city fathers into hosting revival meetings and then seed the local press with flattering, "exclusive" stories about the enchanting lady preacher. Gantry did not disbelieve the gospel, exactly, but he got into the God racket because it made him more money, and made him feel more important than his previous job of selling farm implements had.[4]

Graham acknowledged this stereotype in order to counter it. Following the real-life scandal of Marjoe Gortner, a fraudulent evangelist exposed in a 1972 documentary, Graham assured the assembled reporters at a Los Angeles press conference that "there was a time when we had some Elmer Gantrys. There's no doubt about it. I think that has been largely overcome. For example, in my own work I have some of the finest reporters from the major magazines, from the *Wall Street Journal* up and down, that cover us regularly every year or two to see what we are doing with the finances. So I don't think I could get by in my position with anything." Note here the use of one media source, the redoubtable *Wall Street Journal*, to counteract other sources: a novel, a feature film, a documentary, and, potentially, any negative stories that might be written or broadcast by the reporters at the press conference. Graham did not set himself up as the victim of a hostile press corps, as many conservative Christians did before and after him. Rather, he asserted that responsible journalists could corroborate his story and vouch for his character.[5]

George Whitefield and Elmer Gantry nicely illustrate the distinction between "savvy" and "slick" when it comes to media relations. Graham emulated Whitefield in the way he and his team used media to extend his evangelistic and movement-building work through time and space. At the same time, he distinguished himself from Gantry not just by being morally upright, but also by using media to verify his authenticity.

Media Empire

Graham's media empire grew out of the 1949 Los Angeles crusade and the meetings that followed in 1950. To keep the momentum of these crusades going, in November 1950 he launched the *Hour of Decision* radio program on 150 ABC stations. A few weeks into its still-continuing run, the weekly broadcast was heard on a thousand stations, and it topped all other religious programs in the Nielsen ratings. Producing the show required more sustained work than Graham's crusade team could handle, though, so the Billy Graham Evangelistic Association was born, complete with offices and a secretary. (There were also tax benefits to the creation of the nonprofit association.) Soon, the show spawned another challenge, as it generated a tidal wave of mail from listeners—more than 178,000 letters in 1951, and twice that volume the next year. The BGEA staff swelled to more than one hundred people, many of them handling correspondence. To address listeners' questions in a more public way, Graham started the "My Answer" syndicated newspaper column. Next, he moved into television, with a version of *Hour of Decision*, and into film, with the launch of World Wide Pictures. *Decision* magazine followed in 1960.[6]

Like his evangelistic forebears, Graham adopted new technologies as soon as they became available. His 1957 New York City crusade was broadcast on live local television, nightly, for an unprecedented sixteen weeks, and a weekly broadcast aired nationwide. His 1961 Philadelphia crusade was taped and then distributed to TV stations throughout the United States and Canada for later broadcast, an endeavor his press agency declared "a first in the history of television." A short film created by World Wide Pictures for the 1964 World's Fair, *Man in the 5th Dimension*, also deployed cutting-edge technology, which Graham gushed about in a press conference: "Stereophonic, the whole thing is in Todd AO's new process, the first time it's ever been used. It's the same as Cinerama." Whatever Graham meant by this quote, it captures his excitement about media technology. In 1993, when media like "the Internet" and "e-mail" were practically brand new, the seventy-five-year-old Graham participated in an hour-long live chat on America Online. And in 1995, with the help of 30 satellites, 160 digital editing machines, and 13 generators, he transmitted a sermon from San Juan, Puerto Rico, to nearly 3,000 sites across the globe in an effort to reach 1 billion viewers—approximately one-fifth the population of the planet.[7]

The bulk of the media generated by Graham and the BGEA was evangelistic and closely tied to Graham's signature mode of outreach, the urban crusade. *Hour of Decision* radio broadcasts featured crusade sermons. The TV specials often consisted of lightly edited crusade videos. *Decision* magazine included the kinds of testimonies featured at crusade meetings, and the magazine existed partly to raise funds for more meetings. World Wide Pictures releases might or might not include crusade scenes, but their intent was the same: to put a gospel message in front of an audience Graham could not address personally, whether that audience gathered in theaters, in front of their televisions, overseas, or in prison.[8]

Unlike several other high-profile evangelists, such as Oral Roberts and Pat Robertson, Graham opted not to sustain a regular TV broadcast, which would have required considerably more money. Not carrying that expense, but instead purchasing occasional airtime for specials, meant that Graham never needed to go into the hypercharged fundraising mode that contributed to the televangelist scandals of the 1980s. Though laborious, the practice of securing local sponsorship for radio broadcasts and TV specials also connected Graham to his audience while circumventing regulatory barriers.

In 1929 the Federal Radio Commission (precursor to the Federal Communications Commission) classified most independent religious broadcasters as "propaganda stations" and shut them down. Licensed commercial stations were then instructed to offer some free "sustaining time" for religious programs, but the Federal Council of Churches insisted that such time should only be used for programs bearing its imprimatur. The council's cartel-like hold on radio time loomed over the early era of television as well. An archived letter from Gordon Talbot, director of religious education at Union Park Baptist Church, in Des Moines, Iowa, dated September 2, 1961, illustrates how this system could be a barrier for Graham. Church member Ralph Lehman, a businessman and Graham supporter, wished to buy local television time for eight one-hour Sunday programs. However, "When Mr. Lehman called KRNT-TV, he was told this could not be done. The local area council of churches controls broadcasting time, which is free. The evangelical ministerial association, of course, has no time allotted to it for radio. If individual pastors want to go on the air, they must go through the area council of churches." Talbot sought advice from the head of the evangelical-affiliated National Religious Broadcasters, who brought Graham's public relations agent, Walter Bennett, into the conversation. Whether or not Lehman was ultimately successful in Des Moines (the archival record does not say), the paid-time model worked wonders for evangelicals. The media scholar Quentin Schultze called the FRC's discriminatory policies a "blessing in disguise," because they forced evangelicals to develop programming that people enjoyed so much they were willing to pay for it.[9]

One of Graham's media ventures stood outside this ecosystem: *Christianity Today* (*CT*) magazine. Launched in 1956 and headquartered in Washington, DC, before moving to Carol Stream, Illinois, *CT* was designed to speak for evangelicalism in the same way that its archrival, the *Christian Century*, spoke for mainline Protestantism. Neither magazine served as a house organ for any religious institution, such as the National Council of Churches, the National Association of Evangelicals, or the BGEA. Rather, each provided a center of gravity for its style of Protestantism—or, to use the sociologist Robert Wuthnow's terms, its party in the emerging postwar two-party system in American religion.[10]

Speaking for evangelicalism meant speaking to both insiders and outsiders. As editors stated in the inaugural issue,

> Christianity Today has its origin in a deep-felt desire to express historical Christianity to the present generation. Neglected, slighted, misrepresented—evangelical Christianity needs a clear voice, to speak with conviction and love, and to state its true position and its relevance to the world crisis. A generation has grown up unaware of the basic truths of the Christian faith taught in the Scriptures and expressed in the creeds of the historic evangelical churches.

The CT editors believed that a majority of American Protestants agreed with their rendering of "the basic truths of the Christian faith," but this majority lacked a "clear voice" in the churches or the public square. Graham made the same point in his memoir, Just As I Am, in which he wrote, "In mainline denominations where a significant number of leaders had liberal leanings, many rank-and-file clergy and lay leaders held more orthodox views and felt discontentment with the status quo. But they had no flag to follow. They had no counterbalance to the view presented in publications such as the Christian Century." As long as these liberal voices dominated, Graham and the CT editors feared, evangelicals would lack cohesion, confidence, or respect. CT, its founders hoped, would strengthen beleaguered evangelicals, rally undecided Christians to its banner, and counteract the sneering depictions of evangelicals in the Century and in secular media.[11]

Initially, CT was modeled fairly closely on the Century, with minimalist design and dense theological writing. By the 1980s, however, CT had become a consumer publication, with more pictures, more accessible content, and enough revenue from subscriptions and advertisements to launch or acquire new titles, including Leadership Journal, Today's Christian Woman, and the Youth for Christ magazine, Campus Life. Throughout its history, in addition to reporting on evangelical leaders and institutions, CT defined the boundaries of evangelicalism by publishing certain authors, but not others; carrying advertisements for certain books and academic institutions, but not others; and generally curating the biblical, theological, and political ideas that could carry the "evangelical" label. Graham's name remained on the masthead as founder and, eventually, honorary chairman of the board of directors, but he had little to do with the magazine's operations.

Christianity Today kept its distance from the BGEA media universe, but Graham himself was always both an evangelist and a movement-builder, and his press conferences found him switching constantly between the two roles. Indeed, the press conferences worked *because* Graham performed both roles. Graham and his team typically called a press conference to attract attention for an upcoming crusade. Graham would open by thanking local supporters, and saying a few words about how much he loved Cleveland, or Miami, or wherever he happened to be. Then he or a member of his media team would make sure the assembled reporters knew the logistical details on the upcoming meetings. In this phase of the press conference, Graham was using media—as George Whitefield had—as an extension of his own publicity efforts. In the Q&A phase, however, reporters would turn the press conference around to their own interests, using their audience with the international celebrity to get his (and, by extension, evangelicals') quotable opinion on the issues of the day. Thus, the resulting headlines were not just "Graham to Preach at Local Stadium"—though there were plenty of those stories—but also "Graham Deplores Distortion of Patriotism" or "Praises 'Jesus Freaks'" or, in a bout of selective, erroneous quotation in 1975, "Billy Graham Backs Ordaining Homosexuals."[12]

An exchange from a 1975 press conference in Lubbock, Texas, exemplified Graham's facility for using and being used by the media. Graham told the assembled journalists,

> You know, one of the things about being a well-known clergyman or a well-known evangelist is I'm supposed to be an authority on every conceivable subject. And I'm not an authority on many subjects. . . . And there are a lot of the problems that we face today that I haven't figured out the answer to. Except if everybody would turn to God, everybody would turn to Christ, I think we could approach our problems with new attitudes."

Having delivered that come-to-Jesus line, Graham proceeded to answer questions about Betty Ford's recent statements on sex and marijuana, college morality, Watergate, the Equal Rights Amendment, the Middle East, and the American divorce rate. And then he proceeded to fill Jones Stadium at Texas Tech University with crowds that were also glimpsed by television audiences watching taped broadcasts in Latin America, Africa, Europe, and Asia.[13]

Mediated Authenticity

Mainstream journalists understood that pretty much any Graham story would provide him with a platform for evangelization and for the promotion of evangelical Christianity. This preachiness could have been a problem, as reporters are not a particularly religious bunch (though they are not as hostile to religion as is sometimes assumed). Regardless of their personal feelings, journalists accepted Graham's terms of access for a number of reasons.[14]

First, Graham coverage fulfilled four of the seven classic news values: *prominence* (he was famous); *proximity* (Graham always got the attention of the local press when his crusade rolled into town); *impact*, or number of lives affected (many Graham stories led off with numbers—crowds of thousands, TV audiences of millions); and, thanks to the range of subjects touched upon in press conferences, *currency*, or relation to current events.[15]

Second, Graham was articulate and attractive. He made good copy and compelling airtime, even when he was not doing anything new. As a result, he was invited to write for publications ranging from *Family Circle* to *Cosmopolitan*, from the *New York Times* to the *National Inquirer*. He did guest spots on shows hosted by Johnny Carson, David Frost, Phil Donahue, and Woody Allen (an appearance now immortalized on YouTube). He was profiled, albeit against his wishes and with only minimal cooperation, in *Playboy*. He could have shared his thoughts on pornography and censorship in a publication called *Screw: The Sex Review*, but he declined the editor's invitation.[16]

Third, Graham enjoyed copious and strongly favorable media coverage because he was sincere—and sincere in ways especially suited to a media-saturated culture. Graham's personal sincerity and charisma certainly worked in his favor. Saul Braun, author of the 1971 *Playboy* profile, admitted, "I discovered that Graham in private discourse is friendly, responsive and alert. Everybody goes away from him liking him immensely and so did I." Many other journalists recorded similar impressions. Furthermore, Graham and his organizations operated strictly above-board, avoiding both sexual and financial disgrace. When Harold Fey, then editor of the *Christian Century*, asked an investigative reporter to follow the money flowing around Graham's 1957 New York crusade, all he found was a rumor that excessive payments had been made to an ad agency. Unsubstantiated, the story went nowhere.[17]

Personal probity, however, was not enough to endear Graham to everyone. The specter of Elmer Gantry lingered, renewed with each fresh televangelist scandal. Besides, not everyone could meet Graham personally. Most people encountered him through mass media, so that is the realm in which he needed most urgently to convey his authenticity.

Graham's methods of conveying authenticity varied by medium. The tone of the "My Answer" newspaper columns, along with the smiling thumbnail photo, lent a personal touch to highly repetitive, staff-written texts. Photo-rich magazine spreads of the Graham family at home, complete with witty comments from Ruth and self-deprecating remarks from Billy, brought the superstar down to earth. Radio, the longtime home of *Hour of Decision*, is an especially intimate medium—a "hot" medium in Marshall McLuhan's typology, grabbing listeners with a stream of high-definition auditory information. Television, for McLuhan a "cool" medium, required more active participation from the audience and thus allowed more room for nonparticipation—more room for doubt to seep into the gap between the evangelist and his audience. Though McLuhan's typology is confusing and contested, it helpfully recalls the audience experience during Graham's midcentury prime. Television pictures were blurry, and usually black-and-white. Audience members could not help but be conscious of the layers of technology between them and the evangelist. Clearer radio signals brought Graham's alternately forceful and reassuring voice near, as if he were speaking directly to the listener.[18]

Graham had his work cut out for him on television, but because it was the key medium of the second half of the twentieth century, he set out to conquer it. During a TV talk show appearance with Britain's Russell Harty in 1973, Graham put it this way: "[T]elevision is a medium of face to face communication. It's the most powerful medium we've ever known. And whether you're selling a bar of soap or whatever you're doing, television is the way to do it today." "So you're taking hold of the medium by the scruff of its neck?" Harty asked. "Well," Graham answered, "we're using the medium. I think that this medium has been given. It can be used for good."[19]

In order to use television for good, Graham also had to use it well. He and his organization needed to achieve technical excellence in sound, lighting, staging, and filming. Years of producing crusades offered a head start in this realm. Graham's team also found it useful to deploy a mixture of television shots—close on the evangelist's face for immediacy, and zoomed out to depict the enthusiastic, thoroughly convinced crowd. In his 1966 biography of Graham, John Pollock wrote,

> When the average, moral, reputable American sees Dr. Graham in a studio telling him he needs to be "born again," his first impulse will be to discredit him as a religious fanatic. But if the viewer sees thousands of respectable, normal people listening and consenting to all this he hears, and then sees hundreds voluntarily get up and walk to the front in response to a low-pressure request, he'll begin to consider the message and situation with some sincere, honest interest. It's much easier to say a single speaker is wrong than to discredit the conviction and decision of thousands.[20]

Because most of Graham's TV broadcasts sought to replicate the experience of attending a crusade as closely as possible, Quentin Schultze considered him a "holdout to itinerant revivalism" rather than a part of the "electronic church" phenomenon that garnered attention in the 1970s. Definitions of the electronic church varied, but the term was most often applied to television-centered ministries such as Pat Robertson's Christian Broadcasting Network and Jim and Tammy Faye Bakker's PTL (Praise the Lord) Network, which some observers feared would supplant rather than supplement Christian congregations. "What worries me about all this activity is not the financial success nor the big-business aspects of this evangelism—although I suspect it should worry *them*," wrote William F. Fore in *Ministry* magazine in 1979. "What worries me is whether this electronic church is in fact pulling people away from the local church. Is it substituting an anonymous (and therefore undemanding) commitment for the kind of person-to-person involvement and group commitment that is the essence of the local church?" Fore served as executive director of the National Council of Churches Broadcasting and Film Commission, so he had multiple reasons to look warily on conservative and charismatic TV ministries, but similar concerns were expressed outside mainline Protestantism as well, particularly as the televangelist scandals piled up. Both Graham's probity and the style of his broadcasts, depicting a crusade rather than a church service or talk show, kept him above the fray.[21]

Still, becoming too proficient at TV presentation put Graham perpetually at risk of being perceived as an Elmer Gantry, as all flash and no substance. Thinking along these lines, in 1972 a reporter asked Graham how much show business had influenced him. His response encapsulated the balance he sought. First, Graham listed ways, and reasons, that his presentation had become less showy over the years: "[W]e dress a little more conservatively now than we used to dress twenty years ago when we had bow ties that we could push a little button and they would light up on both sides," he said. "We don't do any of that any more. We have no gimmicks because you cannot fool the electronic eye of that camera and people can see whether you're sincere or not." But while Graham eschewed gimmicks, he explained that he and his team did tailor their approach to the medium: "It is true that our Crusades are partially designed because of the cameras. We have to. The timing has to be right. You have to have excellent personnel who do the singing and the music and that sort of thing. I suppose in that way we have adapted ourselves to television, but I would not call it show business."[22]

To be a George Whitefield in an Elmer Gantry world, Graham needed to adapt himself to television, and to an array of other media, without straying into show business. He needed to look good on TV, for example, without coming across as someone whose only talent was looking good on TV. His long record of popularity with scandal-hungry journalists and scandal-weary audiences alike indicates that he succeeded—though not perfectly.

Missteps

A man who attracted so much media coverage was bound to get some bad press, or at any rate some press that did not turn out the way he wanted. The first time Graham met with a president, Harry Truman, he later told reporters what they discussed and staged photographs of himself and his team kneeling on the White House lawn. Truman never forgave this breach of protocol. Graham quickly learned to be more careful, to draw some boundaries between his public and private actions, and to adopt the posture of one who lets the camera come to him, rather than thrusting his face in front of it. Still, he had a few very bad moments with the press in the course of his career. Sometimes, the fault lay mostly with the reporters, and sometimes it lay mostly with Graham.[23]

Wire-service reports posted from Graham's many trips overseas proved especially problematic. As mentioned, on July 24, 1975, a story ran in the *Atlanta Journal-Constitution* and elsewhere alleging that Graham approved

the ordination of homosexuals. This claim originated at a press conference in Brussels, Belgium. When asked by a reporter there if homosexuals
could be ordained, Graham replied that they could, if "they have accepted
Jesus Christ and have turned away from their sins." He continued, "After
repentance and training each should be considered on his individual
case." At least, this seems to be what he said. Different stories based on the
wire report selected different portions of Graham's comments, with some
anonymous editors isolating the parts about receiving training or being
considered on a case-by-case basis. These redactions made it appear that
Graham had no problem with the hypothetical candidates' homosexuality.[24]

A few days later, Graham addressed the subject again. Homosexuality
was a sin, he explained in articles that ran on July 27, because "[a]ny sex
outside marriage is a sin, according to the Bible." Homosexual marriage
would not help, because it was "not a natural state of affairs from a biblical point of view." Nonetheless, "homosexuals are people whom God loves
and whom God is willing to forgive if they repent." Thus far, Graham's
comments could all be read as amplifications of his earlier statement about
repentance being a prerequisite for ordination. But a few July 24 articles
had included another exchange: "Asked whether he thought a homosexual
could make a good preacher, Graham said: 'I don't know, I never met one.
No one has ever come up to me, and said, 'Hello, I'm a homosexual.'"
In comments reported on July 27, Graham said that he had homosexual
friends, but "I love them and don't treat them any different than my other
friends. There are worse sins." The incomplete and contradictory press
accounts of these two sets of remarks compound the mystery of what may
have transpired between them. What American readers understood to be
Graham's position depended on which version of the story appeared in
their local paper.[25]

Repackaged wire service reports ensnared Graham again during his
1982 trip to the Soviet Union. Much more than a journalistic game of
telephone was involved in that episode, but secondhand reporting made
a complicated situation worse. For example, when Graham visited three
well-attended Orthodox churches on a Saturday night, he quipped that he
would not find the churches so full on a Saturday back in Charlotte. The
Christian Science Monitor relayed that Graham had "jokingly suggested
churches in Moscow were doing better than in his hometown," which was
similar to what he said but not at all what he meant. Another wire service
report from the visit suggested that Graham had preached on Romans 13—
"Everyone must submit to the governing authorities"—to an audience of

oppressed Russian Baptists, when in fact Graham had only referenced this idea in a sermon on John 5. Rallying to Graham's defense in the *Saturday Evening Post*, Edward E. Plowman asserted, "It wasn't a clash of ideologies that sparked problems for Billy Graham on his Moscow trip, but a shocking short circuit in the Western press."[26]

A May 19, 1982, press conference in New York, conducted as soon as Graham got off the plane from Europe, found the evangelist in damage-control mode. The first question, posed by Jane Wallace at CBS, referenced previous coverage: "You were quoted in one article as saying that you saw no direct evidence of religious repression in Russia. And 'there is a lot more freedom here than I had been given the impression in the United States.' That seemed to be a quote that got you in a lot of trouble, it certainly received a lot of criticism. Do you stand by what you said?" Graham replied, "Yes and no, because I didn't say it quite that way." Graham explained that the reporter in Russia "pinned me down," demanding to know what the evangelist had personally seen. Graham had not personally seen repression. Instead, he had seen well-attended churches—on Saturday, not Sunday. "I think it was misinterpreted," Graham complained. A few minutes later at the press conference, another reporter asked if Graham felt he had been used as propaganda tool. Graham acknowledged the risk, but said he considered the trip worthwhile for the chances it afforded to preach the gospel and speak to leaders privately. This oblique mention of private conversations met the "propaganda tool" charge with a countercharge of press meddling, as Graham stated, "Now, if I made a big media event of it, I would never have gotten that opportunity."[27]

Graham's defense during this uncharacteristically hostile press conference took several forms. He clarified quotations and alluded to hidden aspects of the story. He contrasted what he saw personally with what reporters saw and wrote about. On topics about which he had no firsthand information, he repeatedly said that he did not know or was still trying to make up his mind. And he turned on the charm. When asked by George Cornell of the Associated Press whether he felt that the American media was treating him badly, Graham replied,

> No, I don't, George. You know, the press in this country has always dealt with me tremendously. I have used the press to get my message out, and the media to get my message out to millions of people. And I'm in great debt to the press. Very rarely in these 40 years that I've dealt with the press have I ever been misquoted. Sometimes a

text taken out of context causes some difficulties. And I have gone
through these periods several times in my life when there was a
situation prevails—like happens now, and always, it seems to me,
that divine providence was in charge of it.

The garbled syntax of that last sentence notwithstanding, Graham had
reasserted his media savvy, with a dash of gospel thrown in for good
measure.[28]

Unfortunately, using charm to sway a roomful of journalists was no
longer an option during Graham's last media crisis. In March 2002 the
National Archives released the audiotape of a conversation between the
evangelist and President Richard Nixon thirty years earlier, during which
Graham lambasted the Jewish "stranglehold" on American media. Graham
also claimed, on the tape, that many Jews in the media "swarm around me
and are friendly to me because they know that I am friendly to Israel and
so forth. But they don't know how I really feel about what they are doing
to this country." When the conversation became public, Graham quickly
apologized, saying that he did not remember making the remarks, that they
did not reflect his beliefs, and that he had always supported closer Jewish-
Christian relations. Two weeks after this initial apology, though, the scandal
still simmered, as the New York Times ran a long article with the callout, "An
evangelist's reputation called into question by a White House tape."[29]

There was no opportunity for Graham, then eighty-three, to share a room
with the journalists he had insulted on the tape, so reporter Cliff Rothman
sought out several leading media figures from the early 1970s and published
an article on their responses in The Nation. The harshest comment came
from Arthur Schlesinger Jr., not a journalist but a liberal public intellectual.
Graham "just showed that he was the pious hypocrite that we all knew that
he was anyway," Schlesinger said. "Sinclair Lewis wrote about all those fel-
lows in the great Elmer Gantry." Watergate reporter Carl Bernstein recalled
Graham with some admiration as a galvanizing, charismatic figure, but said
he had changed his mind after the "sickening" revelations on the tape. The
CBS news correspondent Daniel Schorr, who said that he was not hired by
the New York Times in 1953 because he was Jewish, observed that Graham
and Nixon "shared a subsurface of a lot of anti-Semitism in this country."
Other people contacted by Rothman chalked Graham's statements up to the
mood of the era, Nixon's baleful influence, or a momentary and ultimately
excusable lapse in judgment. Just two people disagreed with Graham's slurs
but admitted that he was not completely off-base in his assessment of Jewish

prominence in media. One, who spoke off the record, estimated that Jews had constituted 25 percent of the editorial staff of one leading newspaper in 1972, far above their proportion of the American population. The other was legendary television producer Norman Lear, who, when asked whether Jewish liberals like himself had any influence on the media, replied, "I would certainly hope so and believe so."[30]

However lamentable, Graham's comments on the White House tape did not make him an Elmer Gantry. They did betray some slippage between his private and public personas, and they did suggest that Graham was willing to remain friendly with people he disliked because they controlled access to things he needed, namely, headlines and airwaves. If this friendliness was as forced as the tapes indicated, was it savvy or slick? Is it reasonable to expect true camaraderie between the press and a public figure, or would such a bond actually signal a lapse on both sides?[31]

Some of Graham's comments in the testy 1982 press conference were forced, too, but they were nonetheless true. For more than forty years, the American press dealt with Graham tremendously. He used them to get his message out, and he appreciated their help. Sometimes a quote taken out of context caused difficulties. If charm and an otherwise sterling reputation could not turn that situation around, well, divine providence might yet use it for good.

Conclusion

The well-worn evangelical admonition to be "in the world but not of it" is a useful summation of Graham's relationship to mass media. He eagerly put himself in the media spotlight and utilized all available media technologies, from radio and print, to film and TV, to satellite and the Internet. He worked his way far enough into this world to be able to call reporters by name during a press conference, or to know exactly which camera to smile for onstage. These skills enabled Graham to broadcast the gospel—to scatter the seeds widely, like a modern-day sower—and to become the urbane, winsome face of once-maligned evangelicalism.

If Graham had crossed the thin line from savvy to slick, though, he likely would have followed other leaders of the electronic church into obscurity or disgrace. Because Hollywood delights in caricaturing itself, Americans are all too familiar with the types of the greedy mogul, the imbecile news anchor, the sexually predatory leading man, or the star who plays the hero on screen but loses battles to an array of demons at home.

These characters are all products of the world of media, created, nurtured, and eventually exposed under its bright lights. Graham could have become any of these types, but he did not. He probably knew people who fit all of them, but he was far too kind to call them out.

Perhaps the best way to appreciate Graham's insider-outsider poise is to watch his appearance on the 1969 *Woody Allen Special*. Allen introduced his guest as a "charming and provocative gentleman," with whom Allen disagreed about nearly everything but recognized as "the best in the world at what he does." Both men wore suits, sat in oddly ornate plush chairs, and did not touch the teacups on the table at their elbows. They bantered. They laughed. They fielded questions from the audience. As promised, they disagreed. Graham managed to convey both evangelicalism's stern morality ("the Bible teaches that premarital sex relations are wrong") and its open invitation (Graham told the self-deprecating Allen, "in God's sight, you are beautiful"). In another era, George Whitefield and his friendly antagonist Benjamin Franklin could have had a similar exchange. Elmer Gantry never had, nor did he deserve, such an opportunity.

Notes

1. The "puff Graham" legend has been reprinted numerous places but has not been substantiated by evidence of the original telegram. In *A Prophet with Honor* (New York: William Morrow, 1991, 95), William Martin cited secondhand evidence of an earlier "PUFF YFC" telegram sent by Hearst to his Chicago editor. In a November 7, 1983, wire story that ran in multiple newspapers (for one example, see "Hearst 'Anointed' Graham by Ordering Editors to 'Puff Graham,'" *Lakeland Ledger*, November 7, 1983, 2A), Graham was quoted alluding to the 1949 telegram and recalling that one of the reporters who suddenly showed up during the revival in Los Angeles told him that he had just been "kissed by William Randolph Hearst." Exactly how, and to whom, Hearst expressed his desire to see favorable Graham coverage has not been verified. On the Facebook statistic, see Trevor Freeze, "BGEA Social Media Reaches Million Milestone," http://www.billygraham.org/articlepage.asp?articleid=9186, accessed February 28, 2013.

2. Thomas S. Kidd, *George Whitefield: America's Spiritual Founding Father* (New Haven: Yale University Press, 2014); Harry S. Stout, *The Divine Dramatist: George Whitefield and the Rise of Modern Evangelicalism* (Grand Rapids, MI: Eerdmans, 1991); Gary David Stratton, "Paparazzi in the Hands of an Angry God: Jonathan Edwards, George Whitefield, and the Birth of American Celebrity Culture," *The Other Journal*, October 23, 2010, http://theotherjournal.com/2010/10/23/paparazzi-in-the-hands-of-an-angry-god-jonathan-edwards-george-whitefield-and-the-birth-of-american-celebrity-culture/.

3. Frank Lambert, "'Pedlar in Divinity': George Whitefield and the Great Awakening, 1737–1745," *Journal of American History* 77, no. 3 (December 1990): 812–837. For an example of Niebuhr's criticism of Graham, see Reinhold Niebuhr, "Literalism, Individualism and Billy Graham," *Christian Century*, May 23, 1956, 640–642.

4. Sinclair Lewis, *Elmer Gantry* (New York: Signet Classic, 1970 [1927]), 189. According to a long article he wrote for *Cosmopolitan*, Graham had not seen the Elmer Gantry film himself, but, based on what he read about it, he believed that it violated a section of the Motion Picture Code that disallowed films that "cast disrespect on religion." Graham, "Are Biblical Films Fit for Kids?" *Cosmopolitan*, May 1963, 14–18.

5. BG press conference, Los Angeles, August 25, 1972, Folder 5, Box 2, Collection 24, Billy Graham Center Archives (BGCA).

6. William Martin, "Giving the Winds a Mighty Voice," in *Religious Television: Controversies and Conclusions*, ed. Robert Abelman and Stewart M. Hoover (Norwood, NJ: Ablex Publishing, 1990), 63–70; Billy Graham, *America's Hour of Decision* (Wheaton, IL: Van Kampen Press, 1951), 55–56, 64–65.

7. Press release from William Bennett Agency, September 7, 1961, Folder 9, Box 22, Collection 54, BGCA; "Billy Graham a Convert to On-Line Preaching," *Los Angeles Times*, November 27, 1993; Laurie Goodstein, "Billy Graham Activates a Global Electronic Pulpit," *Washington Post*, March 14, 1995), A1; press conference transcript, Phoenix, April 23, 1964, Folder 12, Box 4, Collection 24, BGCA. On the adoption of new technology by fundamentalists in the early twentieth century, see Joel Carpenter, *Revive Us Again: The Reawakening of American Fundamentalism* (New York: Oxford University Press, 1997).

8. On prison showings of WWP releases, see Maurice Rowlandson, *Behind the Scenes with Billy Graham* (Buxhall, UK: Kevin Mayhew Limited, 2007).

9. Quentin Schultze, "Evangelical Radio and the Rise of the Electronic Church, 1921–1948," *Journal of Broadcasting & Electronic Media* 32, no. 3 (Summer 1988): 289–306; letter, Gordon Talbot to Dr. Eugene R. Bertermann, National Religious Broadcasters, St. Louis, Sept. 2, 1961, Folder 8, Box 22, Collection 54, BGCA.

10. Robert Wuthnow, *The Restructuring of American Religion: Society and Faith since World War II* (Princeton, NJ: Princeton University Press, 1988).

11. "Why Christianity Today," *Christianity Today* 1, no. 1 (October 1956); Graham, *Just As I Am: The Autobiography of Billy Graham*, rev. ed. (New York: HarperCollins, 2007), 284. On the history of *Christianity Today*, see Phyllis Elaine Alsdurf, "*Christianity Today* Magazine and Late Twentieth-Century Evangelicalism" (PhD diss., University of Minnesota, 2004). On the role of *The Christian Century* in establishing mainline Protestantism, see Elesha J. Coffman, *The Christian Century and the Rise of the Protestant Mainline* (New York: Oxford University Press, 2013).

12. Edward B. Fiske, "Graham Deplores Distortion of Patriotism," *New York Times*, June 24, 1970); "Praises 'Jesus Freaks,'" *Spartanburg Journal-Herald*, April 6, 1971; "Billy Graham Backs Ordaining Homosexuals," *Atlanta Journal-Constitution*, July 24, 1975).

13. Press conference, Lubbock, Texas, August 29, 1975, Folder 36, Box 3, Collection 24, BGCA.

14. On the religiosity of journalists, see Mark Silk, *Unsecular Media: Making News of Religion in America* (Urbana: University of Illinois Press, 1998); Doug Underwood, *From Yahweh to Yahoo! The Religious Roots of the Secular Press* (Urbana: University of Illinois Press, 2002).

15. Deirdre O'Neill and Tony Harcup, "News Values and Selectivity," in *The Handbook of Journalism Studies*. ed. Karin Wahl-Jorgensen and Thomas Hanitzsch (New York: Routledge, 2009), 161–174.

16. Letter, Heidi Handman to BG, Feb. 9, 1971, BGCA 345.50.13.

17. Saul Braun, "Nearer, Silent Majority, to Thee," *Playboy*, February 1971, 120, 134, 195–201; telegram, Everett C. Parker to Margaret Frakes, January 12, 1958, Christian Century Foundation Archives, Box 44, Folder 3. See also "Billy Graham Organization Is Exemplary, Charity Auditors Say," *Beliefnet*, October 17, 2002), http://www.beliefnet.com/News/2002/10/Billy-Graham-Organization-Is-Exemplary-Charity-Auditors-Say.aspx#.

18. Lou Orfanell, "Radio: The Intimate Medium," *The English Journal* 87, no. 1, *Media Literacy* (January 1998): 53–55; "The Playboy Interview: Marshall McLuhan," *Playboy Magazine*, March 1969, accessed online at http://www.digitallantern. net/mcluhan/mcluhanplayboy.htm.

19. *Russell Harty Plus*, August 26, 1973, transcript in Collection 24, BGCA.

20. John Pollock, *Billy Graham* (New York: McGraw-Hill, 1966), 238–239, cited in Martin, "Giving the Winds a Mighty Voice," 65.

21. Quentin J. Schultze, "Defining the Electronic Church," in Abelman and Hoover, *Religious Television*, 41–51; William F. Fore, "The Electronic Church," *Ministry*, January 1979, https://www.ministrymagazine.org/archive/1979/01/the-electronic-church. See also Stewart M. Hoover, *Mass Media Religion: The Social Sources of the Electronic Church* (Newbury Park, CA: SAGE, 1988).

22. Press conference, Southern Baptist Convention, Philadelphia, June 7, 1972, Folder 1, Box 2, Collection 24, BGCA. For an international perspective on Graham's mediated authenticity, see Judith Smart, "The Evangelist as Star: The Billy Graham Crusade in Australia, 1959," *Journal of Popular Culture* 33, no. 1 (Summer 1999): 165–175.

23. William Martin, *A Prophet with Honor: The Billy Graham Story* (New York: William Morrow, 1991), 131–133.

24. Among the sources reporting this story were the *Indiana* (PA) *Gazette*, "Billy Graham Says Gays Could Become Ministers," July 24, 1975, 14; the *Ottawa* (Ont.) *Journal*, "Graham Would Ordain Gays," July 24, 1975, 49; and *Jet*, "Billy

Graham Backs Gays, but Not Women Priests," October 2, 1975, 31. None of the stories carried a byline.

25. Quotes from the *Indiana Gazette*, July 24, 1975, and *The Argus* (Fremont, CA), July 27, 1975, 18.

26. Edward E. Plowman, "Billy Graham: The Gospel Truth in Moscow," *Saturday Evening Post*, September 1982, 68–69, 102, 110, 112.

27. Press conference, New York City, May 19, 1982, Collection 24, BGCA.

28. Ibid.

29. "Billy Graham Apologizes to Jews for His Remarks on Nixon Tapes," *New York Times*, March 2, 2002, 28; David Firestone, "Billy Graham Responds to Lingering Anger over 1972 Remarks on Jews," *New York Times*, March 17, 2002, 29.

30. Cliff Rothman, "Jewish Media Stranglehold?" *The Nation*, July 8, 2002, 22–24.

31. On the diligence with which Graham sought to distance himself from the Gantry stereotype, see Kurt A. Edwards, "Billy Graham, Elmer Gantry, and the Performance of a New American Revivalism" (PhD diss., Bowling Green State University, 2008).

9

Billy Graham's
New Evangelical Manhood

Seth Dowland

IN A 1971 article for *Playboy*, reporter Saul Braun described a brief encounter with Billy Graham. When Braun mistakenly left his tape recorder running during an off-the-record conversation, Graham "leaned forward sharply, his chin suddenly outthrust . . . his finger jabbing in the direction of my left hand," demanding Braun turn off the recorder. Convicted of his sin, Braun repented and sought forgiveness from the evangelist. At that, Graham "leaned forward and smiled, gripping [Braun's] forearm and squeezing it gently." The secular journalist admitted feeling like "Graham's child" and knew that "Graham loved me and would care for me." In the span of a few minutes, Graham transformed from an aggressive prophet into a caring father. Throughout the encounter, Graham maintained what Braun called "virile serenity."[1]

During this encounter—as in so many others—Graham displayed a type of masculinity that reflected his heritage and anticipated future trends. Reared among conservative evangelical Christians, Graham displayed the firmness and righteousness expected of a male evangelist. Yet he attenuated the stern masculine ideal of his upbringing. He accentuated the pastoral elements of his character. In so doing, he became a sort of proto-Promise Keeper. He displayed a new kind of evangelical manhood.

While manhood may not be the first thing one thinks about with regard to Billy Graham, his gender identity deserves consideration. Billy Graham's success as an evangelist derived partly from his personification of a new type of evangelical manhood. This characteristic displayed itself in three distinct ways. First, Graham constructed an identity as a desirable but off-limits icon. Second, he emphasized his certitude in both the Christian faith and his country. Third, he subtly modified his political and social views to embrace "softer" positions. All three aspects of Graham's masculinity capitalized on and anticipated cultural trends.

Over the last generation, scholars have come to understand gender as socially constructed and fluid. While most humans are biologically male or female, they construct their gender in a particular cultural context; that is, different societies expect different things of men and women. Appropriate dress, for instance, varies from the United States to the Middle East to Southeast Asia. Furthermore, gender norms change over time. While twentieth-century American evangelicals voiced "essentialist" understandings of gender that ascribed certain fixed roles to men and others to women, the "God-given" qualities of men and women actually changed over time. By the end of Graham's career, men could be more sentimental, more emotional, and more openly religious than their fathers and grandfathers had been.[2] Graham both capitalized on and accelerated these trends. He displayed a new evangelical manhood by constructing a persona that was at once desirable, strong, and adaptable. Put succinctly: Graham subtly changed what it meant to be a "real man" for millions of American evangelicals. These changes came about because Graham anticipated cultural trends and revised what it meant to be a man—but also because he knew which lines he could not cross.

Desirable but Off Limits

In 1948, thirty-one-year-old Graham was coming off a successful stint as a Youth for Christ evangelist and entering into a period of independent ministry that would last almost six decades. His revival team included Bev Shea, Grady Wilson, and Cliff Barrows. The quartet was young and charismatic. As Christianity entered its heady postwar boom, Americans flocked to revivals. Some sought salvation, but others had different aims. Politicians saw the revivals as a hedge against communism, and entertainers saw a chance to promote themselves. Given all the hangers-on surrounding him, temptations loomed on the horizon for Graham. American evangelists in the mid-twentieth century had to contend with the stereotype of Elmer Gantry, the title character of Sinclair Lewis's 1927 novel. In his cutting satire, Lewis portrayed Gantry as a narcissistic womanizer who became a minister accidentally and used his spiritual authority solely as a way to gain wealth, women, and power.

The Gantry stereotype exaggerated the sins of earlier evangelists, but its prevalence in American culture dictated the need for Graham to guard himself against allegations about abuses of money, sex, and power. The Graham team decided they needed to take concrete steps to avoid the slightest whiff of controversy. The team gathered in a hotel room in Modesto, California, in the fall of 1948. They drew up a compact that became known as the "Modesto Manifesto," though no written document was produced. The manifesto included provisions for distributing money raised by offerings, for working only with churches that supported cooperative evangelism, and for using official estimates of crowd sizes at evangelistic meetings in order to avoid exaggeration. These provisions would help Graham and his team avoid charges of financial extortion and hucksterism.

But nothing loomed larger than sex. The most famous provision of the manifesto (indeed, the only one most people cite) called for each man on the Graham team never to be alone with a woman other than his wife or another family member. Graham, from that day forward, pledged not to eat, travel, or meet with a woman outside his family, unless other people were present. This pledge guaranteed Graham's sexual probity and enabled him to dodge accusations that have waylaid evangelists before and since.[3]

The pledge also enabled Graham to capitalize on his good looks without worrying about an oversexualized image that might scandalize his fellow evangelicals. In coverage of Graham's breakout 1949 Los Angeles crusade, reporters mentioned the evangelist's "curly hair," "broad shoulders," and "blue eyes."[4] Several articles reported that Graham "has repeatedly turned down offers to go into the movies."[5] Nearly every piece commented on Graham's good looks. Unlike his most famous predecessors—the short, paunchy D. L. Moody and the balding Billy Sunday—Graham cut a dashing figure. He stood more than six feet tall and wore bold suits, belying stereotypes of evangelists as frumpy and weak. Moreover, Graham burst onto the nation's consciousness in southern California. By 1949, Hollywood had established itself as the heart of American popular culture. The filmmakers and newsmakers of Los Angeles had no trouble promoting the handsome young evangelist preaching in the "Canvas Cathedral," a massive, 6,000-seat tent constructed for Graham's revival. Yet evangelicals remained wary of the silver screen. Many churches prohibited moviegoing, and evangelicals had already begun honing jeremiads against the permissiveness and superficiality of Hollywood. Graham's good looks were both a blessing and a curse: they won him adulation, but that adulation came from an industry that few evangelicals trusted.

Graham managed to benefit from his all-American good looks by underlining his unavailability. Both the Modesto Manifesto and his marriage to Ruth Bell Graham made this possible. The manifesto ensured that Graham would avoid tempting situations with other women. Graham went so far as to have male associates "sweep" his hotel rooms, making sure they were free of other people before Graham would enter them. Ruth, for her part, seemed publicly content with a marriage full of long absences. In a line she would repeat frequently, Ruth said she "would rather have a little of Bill than a lot of any other man."[6] The remark spoke both to Ruth's contentment and to Billy's desirability. Standing in front of thousands, Graham's rapid-fire delivery and piercing stares won both converts and admirers. But Graham's provisions made it impossible for any of these admirers to catch him in a compromising situation. If anything, Graham's caution in this area made him even more desirable to evangelical women, who made up at least 60 percent of his audiences. The letters that flooded BGEA offices over the years testified to his wholesome appeal. His yearly presence on the Gallup "Ten Most Admired Men" list derived in no small part from his reputation for sexual fidelity.

Graham preached about sex periodically, usually confining his remarks to condemnations of premarital sex, adultery, and "immorality." Occasionally, he elaborated on this theme. In a crusade sermon about the biblical character Samson, Graham explained how sexual temptation could ensnare men. Graham said the longhaired Samson had "girl trouble. Everywhere he went, a crowd gathered around him, and hooted and hollered and whistled at him."[7] (It is not hard to see how Graham might have identified with Samson.) Samson fell for one of these admirers, Delilah, who eventually convinced Samson to divulge the secret behind his strength: his long, uncut hair. After Delilah cut Samson's hair while he slept, the Philistines were able to overpower him. Graham warned his listeners that such a fate could befall anyone who gave into sexual immorality. In private, Graham confided to friends that he feared that Samson's story "could happen to me."[8]

Given the frequency with which evangelists have fallen victim to temptations of the flesh, Graham's ability to dodge this particular landmine deserves both praise and analysis. Graham showed evangelicals that a man could be desirable, as long as he was off limits as well. To succeed

in modern America, evangelicals would have to shun the backward stereotypes ascribed to them by the satirist Lewis and the reporter H. L.
Mencken. Graham's good looks were an essential part of his appeal. But
evangelicals perceived danger in giving into the celebrity-obsessed culture of the twentieth century. Graham belied the notion that evangelical
men could be either virtuous or handsome but not both. During his 1949
L.A. revival, Graham showed evangelicals how to dive into Hollywood
without drowning one's virtue.

Graham also enhanced his appeal by showing an uncanny grasp of midcentury's most important technology, the television (as Elesha Coffman
details in her chapter). Graham's *Hour of Decision* television program
began broadcasting in the early 1950s, during a five-year stretch when television penetration of American households increased by 700 percent. Like
most early TV programs, *Hour of Decision* seems clumsy and dated when
viewed today. An episode from the fall of 1952 opens with Cliff Barrows,
the Campus Crusade founder Bill Bright, and UCLA football star Donn
Moomaw posed in an awkward studio set. Barrows perches on the arm of
an oversized chair, and Bright and Moomaw sit on a couch, looking pale,
uncomfortable, and blinded by the klieg lights. They proceed through
a chummy conversation about Moomaw's conversion and finish with a
clumsy reference to Moomaw as a "trophy" of Campus Crusade for Christ.

Then the camera cuts to Graham. He forsakes the studio furniture and
stands square to the camera. There is no pulpit between Graham and the
viewer. The living room setting creates the illusion of Graham being inside
one's home. For viewers, television creates a passive intimacy—they can
feel connection to the figures on the small screen without risking anything
themselves. Graham's evangelism fit perfectly in the passively intimate
setting of television. He preached dire warnings about the fate of America,
but those warnings never strayed far from generalities. Graham mastered
the art of what Andrew Finstuen has called "large-scale condemnation of
sin."[9] When it came to Graham's message for each viewer, redemption was
always close at hand. "The devil," said Graham on a pre-election broadcast
in 1952, "has voted against you, Christ has voted for you, and you have to
cast the deciding vote. . . . Won't you elect him as Lord and Master of your
life?"[10] Deliverance was only a short prayer away.

In *Hour of Decision* telecasts like this one, Graham showed an intuitive understanding of the demands of television. Whereas the football star Moomaw squirmed in a staged conversation with Bright and
Barrows, Graham came across as polished and confident. He modulated

the machine-gun preaching style that made him famous in revival tents. When Graham invited viewers to receive Christ, he was asking them to trust both the message and the messenger. Winning that trust on the television set required grace rather than bluster, smoothness rather than strength. Graham's early *Hour of Decision* telecasts suggested that a new type of manhood would be required of revivalists in the television age. Graham intuited that his podium presence would overwhelm the small screen, and that he needed to come across as reassuring. The soft lighting and domestic scenes created an intimacy that softened Graham. Television accentuated his desirability and brought him into his viewers' homes, albeit in a safe and sanctioned way. Graham's television presence featured the unbending rhetoric of his sermons, but it accentuated his pastoral tendencies. He came across as a patient and handsome father figure who wanted viewers to make the right decision.

Steadfast Believer

Graham could embrace the intimacy of the small screen without damaging his masculine credibility because he retained certitude in his faith. Graham's interpretive certainty—the lack of doubt he displayed about the teachings of the Bible—aligned him with earlier generations of evangelicals who equated conviction with masculinity. Some early twentieth-century evangelicals actually claimed that women were not "theological thinkers," making explicit a connection between females and theological uncertainty. Not all evangelicals shared this lack of faith in females' theological capacity, and plenty of women in their churches disproved the notion. But most evangelicals were sure that effeminate men populated the pews at liberal churches. Effeminacy went hand-in-hand with uncertainty, and uncertainty led to a loss of faith in the Bible. Christianity itself, said the evangelist Billy Sunday, was not a "pale, effeminate proposition." Rather, it involved commitment to Jesus, "a robust, red-blooded man."[11] Evangelicals like Graham trumpeted their masculine stripes by displaying surety.

Graham embodied this masculine surety. He steadfastly repeated the basic evangelical message: all have sinned, Christ died to save us from our sins, and only acceptance of Christ grants us redemption from sin. Graham's crusade sermons charted this path over and over and over again. His daily "My Answer" column addressed readers' concerns by providing firm and predictable advice, usually ending with a command to trust Jesus.[12] Graham preached on what "the Bible clearly says," showing unwavering conviction to a "straightforward" reading of the biblical text. Liberal critics of the evangelist marveled at his popularity in spite of what they saw as a simplistic and repetitive message. But his influence grew in part because he refused to alter the core of his thought over the years. Crusade audiences and newspaper readers wanted to listen to a man who knew what he believed.

In fact, Graham stated that he did away with doubt entirely at an early moment of his career. Just weeks before his breakout 1949 campaign in Los Angeles, Graham spent time with his friend and fellow evangelist Charles Templeton in the San Bernardino Mountains. On that trip, Templeton posed incisive questions about the authority of Scripture that Graham felt ill equipped to answer. Wracked by doubt, Graham wondered if he could preach the gospel in good conscience. On a midnight walk alone in the woods, Graham fell to his knees and prayed for direction. God answered. When he stood up, Graham said he felt the assurance of a faith that went "beyond [his] intellectual questions and doubts," and that he "knew a spiritual battle in my soul had been fought and won."[13]

This oft-told anecdote suggests that while uncertainty troubled Graham for a season of his early life, he left doubt behind in the San Bernardino Mountains. He entered Los Angeles's Canvas Cathedral later that fall, freed from Templeton's nagging questions and ready to face sin head-on. This posture was essential for a midcentury evangelist. In a Cold War world wracked by anxiety, Graham's sturdy faith proved alluring to countless hearers. While his loud suits and soft-focus television sets signaled important changes in the accouterments of an evangelist, Graham never wavered on the central convictions he preached night after night.

Note, too, how Graham described his grappling with doubt: he fought a spiritual battle and won. Graham frequently analogized the Christian life to either a battle or a sporting contest, suggesting a masculine striving for ultimate spiritual victory. Here Graham had to rely on his association with soldiers and sports stars in order to make the analogy work. He never fought in the army, nor did he play professional sports, as Sunday had done. But he frequently drafted athletes and military men to join him on the crusade platform, and they implicitly sanctioned Graham as one of the guys. For instance, Louis Zamperini, who ran in the 1936 Olympics and endured an ordeal as a POW in World War II, described Graham as a "tall, handsome, clean cut all-American athletic type."[14] This endorsement—from a celebrated former athlete and soldier no less—further enhanced Graham's manly reputation.

Indeed, Graham established a lasting connection with soldiers early in his career. Around Christmas 1952, Graham visited American troops on the front lines in Korea. Shortly after returning home, Graham published a slim book called *I Saw Your Sons at War*. The cover featured Graham's stern face alongside two soldiers rushing with rifles towards a firefight. The pages brimmed with Graham's admiration for soldiers. He noted that General Mark Clark was "very tall, every inch a man," and said every serviceman "was a rugged he-man . . . a courageous, red-blooded American." He spoke about signing Bibles "pierced and torn by bullets or shrapnel." Graham carefully noted how close he ventured to the front lines. According to BGEA accounts, soldiers loved that Graham risked his life to preach the gospel. Graham cherished the chance to rub shoulders with these "finest of American youth."[15] Like most Americans, Graham assumed the inherent nobility of soldiering (if not war itself), and he drew parallels between the live fighting he witnessed in Korea and the spiritual fighting between God and Satan.

A sense of "cultural custodianship," or the belief that God appointed Christians as guardians of America's values, facilitated Graham's identification with soldiers. Like soldiers, evangelicals saw themselves as uniquely called to defend liberty and morality. Both groups observed discipline and hierarchy that did not govern mainstream culture. If soldiers required a higher standard of discipline in order to fight the enemy, so too did evangelicals believe that strict standards were needed to guard against Satan. When Graham inveighed against communism, secularism, and immorality against a backdrop of American soldiers, he invited his readers to see him as a soldier of a different sort, drafted by God to fight agents of immorality.[16]

Yet even in this most masculine of venues, Graham indulged a tenderness that would enhance his reputation back home. In conversation with the Army chaplain Clayton Day, interviewer Doris Ferm asked Day about an incident in which Graham, preaching to a wounded soldier laying on a top bunk in a military hospital, caused the boy to cry. His tears fell from the top bunk onto Graham's face while Billy continued his tender preaching. "That would be such a beautiful picture," said Ferm, "with the boy's tears falling on Billy's face."[17] Graham's invitation to men, even to soldiers, required them to become vulnerable and emotional. He preached a message of total surrender. But men could take one look at Graham and see the power of assurance that lay beyond submission to God. Because he radiated certitude, they could trust that Christianity would not weaken them. In other contexts, the soldier's tears might have represented effeminacy. In Graham's presence, they signaled the first step toward strong faith.[18]

Graham managed to hold onto his rock-solid faith even as he waded into the currents of contemporary culture. In a mesmerizing 1969 interview with Woody Allen, Graham debated all manner of topics with the secular Jewish raconteur. Allen prodded Graham about strictures against premarital sex, the narcissism of the first commandment, and the foolishness in believing life had meaning. Graham deflected each of Allen's parries and even got in a few good lines of his own. After Allen said he was hoping to put his elderly parents "in a home," Graham replied, "I hope it's in a home with you." By the end of the interview, Allen seemed both befuddled and amazed by Graham's square-jawed sincerity.[19] Four decades later, Allen recalled his conversation with the evangelist. He said Graham told him, "even if I was right and he was wrong, and there was no meaning to life and it was a bleak experience and there was no god and no afterlife or no hope or anything, he would still have a better life than me."[20] Such steadfast faith stopped Allen short; it eventually inspired a character in Allen's 2010 film *You Will Meet a Tall Dark Stranger* (though Allen's character finds hope in a psychic rather than God). In a world rocked by sexual revolutions at home and wars abroad, faith was proving harder and harder to sustain. Graham showed Allen and his audience that evangelicals—unlike some of their fundamentalist forebears—could wade into the messy areas of modern life and yet retain their faith in God.

Audiences knew what they were going to get with Graham. Whether he was sitting down for an interview with a Jewish comic, talking with a wounded soldier, or preaching a crusade sermon in front of thousands, Graham could be counted on to state his convictions. In the turmoil of the 1960s, Graham declared, "I have a deeper conviction than when I began that the Bible has the answer to every moral situation known to man."[21] Critics scoffed. The Bible said nothing about birth control or capitalism or the war in Vietnam. Graham, however, plowed ahead, insisting that the Scriptures contained all the messages people needed to hear. Only rarely did he seem dogmatic; Graham had an acute social intelligence and regularly riffed on political events. His ability to engage with pressing social issues, along with his genial firmness, modeled the type of masculinity that late-twentieth-century evangelicals could embrace. Graham always stood where people knew he would.

"Soft" Politics

Graham's profession of absolute certainty in the unchanging truths of Christianity belied a subtle evolution in his social and political views. In particular, he announced in the 1970s that he had no problem with churches that chose to ordain women and that he opposed nuclear weapons. These announcements came at a cost, as hardline conservatives excoriated Graham, frequently calling him soft. Criticism of that sort could doom religious and political leaders, particularly those whose constituencies included conservative evangelicals. Yet Graham's popularity continued to grow. If anything, refusing to challenge women's ordination and opposing nuclear weapons attracted new supporters who found themselves surprised at Graham's evolution. How could someone so firm in his beliefs also be flexible? Graham, though, had his finger on the pulse of American culture. He swam against some currents but drifted with others. Billy Graham's masculinity depended on both the perception of unwavering belief and the ability to modulate his views. He never advocated for radical positions, but neither did he find himself left behind as the culture of American evangelicalism changed. He took new stances in the 1970s, but many evangelicals saw them as pragmatic responses to a changing world. If skepticism about nuclear war was "soft" in the 1950s, it was sensible by the late 1970s. Likewise, accommodating women in the workplace—even in the pulpit—reflected a measured response to a changing world. Graham's politics evolved alongside American evangelicalism, allowing him to embrace softer positions without seeming weak.

The majority of American evangelicals believed in essentialist notions of gender, and Graham initially shared that view. When a reader wrote Graham in 1961 to ask whether the reader should allow his wife to work, Graham suggested that she could work as long as doing so did not "cause her to neglect her first duty to her family."[22] Likewise, in a 1970 article titled "Jesus and the Liberated Women," Graham said, "I believe that the Bible teaches that women have . . . a God-given role, and they will be happiest, most creative—and freest—when they assume and accept that role. The same goes for men."[23] In this piece and elsewhere, Graham endorsed the notion that God had created men as fathers and breadwinners, while God wanted women to serve as mothers and homemakers. Graham's own marriage testified to this point: Ruth kept his home running smoothly while Billy went away for weeks or months at a time. (For more on Ruth Bell Graham, see Anne Blue Wills's chapter.)

In the late 1970s, however, Graham broke with many conservative evangelicals by admitting that plenty of women found fulfillment outside the home, and some even found it in the pulpit. In 1977 Graham told an interviewer that he didn't object to women's ordination because women had been ministers since the earliest days of the church.[24] This was a savvy way for Graham to articulate measured support for the growing number of evangelicals willing to ordain women. Although there have been women preachers throughout Christian history, there were a lot more of them in the late 1970s. Between 1974 and 1984, the number of ordained women grew twentyfold in Graham's denomination, the Southern Baptist Convention.[25] Perhaps more to the point, Graham's own daughter Anne launched a weekly Bible study in 1976 that attracted hundreds. Prodded by developments like these, Graham announced a new stance by claiming it had a long history. Refusing to challenge women's ordination placed Graham at odds with some conservative evangelicals. His evangelical tradition associated firmness with masculinity. But increasing numbers of evangelicals believed the gospel teachings on gender equality demanded support for egalitarian ordination practices. When critics called Graham soft, he deflected the criticism by saying he simply embraced a position that the Bible itself endorsed.

Graham displayed less subtlety in announcing his opposition to nuclear weapons, perhaps because his shift on that issue was more dramatic. Graham was an unlikely spokesman for nuclear disarmament. From the beginning of his public career in the 1940s, Graham had opposed "atheistic communism." In a 1947 evangelistic campaign in Charlotte, Graham warned, "Communism is creeping inexorably into . . . war-torn China, restless South America. . . . You should see Europe. It's terrible. There are Communists everywhere."[26] In 1952, during the height of the Korean War, Graham held an evangelistic crusade in Washington, DC, in which he criticized Harry Truman's handling of the Korean War, saying the president should have listened to General Douglas MacArthur's advice and taken whatever measures were necessary to win. Graham accused Truman of pursuing the war in a "cowardly" and "half-hearted" fashion, thereby costing American lives.[27]

By the late 1970s, his tune had changed. In a 1979 interview with the liberal evangelical magazine *Sojourners*, Graham admitted that through Bible study and prayer, he had come to regret his earlier, unqualified support of American military might. Specifically, Graham believed that Christians could not support the use of nuclear weapons. Furthermore,

Graham believed that Christians ought to work for universal nuclear disarmament. "We cannot afford to neglect our duties as global citizens," said Graham. "Like it or not, the world is a very small place, and what one nation does affects all others."[28] Graham's opposition to nuclear weapons won him the admiration of liberal evangelicals and Democrats; President Jimmy Carter asked the evangelist to testify before Congress on behalf of SALT II (a nuclear arms limitation treaty). As he did with all such presidential requests, Graham declined the invitation, but his outspoken support for disarmament did not go away even as the campaign for a "nuclear freeze"—a complete, bilateral moratorium on the development and production of nuclear weapons—became the key issue for political liberals in the early 1980s. In June 1982, 750,000 demonstrators flooded Times Square, demanding an end to the production of nuclear weapons in the largest political rally in New York City's history. A 1982 World Health Organization report estimated that nuclear war between the United States and the Soviet Union would result in two billion deaths, about half of the world's population. In response to this threat, hundreds of national organizations endorsed a nuclear freeze. The groundswell of popular support suggested public unhappiness with President Ronald Reagan's plans to augment America's nuclear arsenal. Freeze advocates argued that the only response to exponential nuclear proliferation over the past half-century was immediate and total cessation of nuclear weapons production, alongside commitments from both the United States and the Soviet Union to reduce their nuclear stockpiles.

As some American evangelicals sounded calls for bilateral disarmament, the Soviets invited Graham to visit Moscow in 1982 as part of a government-sponsored World Conference of Religious Workers for Saving the Sacred Gift of Life from Nuclear Catastrophe. The Soviets put on this conference even as they were engaged in one of the largest nuclear buildups in history. They played on Graham's documented opposition to nuclear weapons for maximum political advantage, using him to show how American religious leaders opposed nuclear weapons even as the Reagan administration continued its weapon stockpiling. The US ambassador in Moscow pleaded with Graham not to go, and the Reagan administration also intimated that the evangelist should reconsider his trip. Graham, however, thought the chance to preach the gospel in the USSR outweighed any potential diplomatic snafus. He visited the Soviet Union for a six-day tour in the spring of 1982. The Soviets outmaneuvered him throughout the trip, forbidding him to preach to anyone but carefully selected ticketholders and pressing him to engage in lengthy conversations about bilateral weapons reductions with government officials. Graham compounded the problem by saying, "I think there is a lot more freedom here than has been given the impression in the United States."[29] Moreover, he did not explicitly condemn the Soviets for suppressing religious dissidents.[30]

The reaction from conservatives was scathing. The political columnist William Safire said Graham made a deal with the devil. One article in Jerry Falwell's *Moral Majority Report* contended that the evangelist had "volunteered statements that on their surface appear to have been written by the KGB itself,"[31] while another said disarmament would "emasculate our defense buildup."[32] General Daniel Graham said, "Churchmen have been selling nuclear freeze for 15 years and that's not courage. . . . Any churchman who falls into the trap that cowardice replaces courage is wrong."[33] Even as his former detractors on the Left were lauding Graham's courage and change of heart, the Right was hammering him for his naïvete.[34]

Yet if Graham had made some missteps in Moscow, his opposition to nuclear weapons reflected both his increasingly urgent concerns about disarmament and his intuition about the changing beliefs of American evangelicals. The editors of *Christianity Today*, the flagship evangelical periodical, endorsed Senator Mark Hatfield's plan to initiate "a complete freeze on the development, testing, and deployment of strategic missile systems."[35] A subsequent issue of the magazine reported that readers largely agreed: 60 percent of evangelicals supported a bilateral freeze, while only 18 percent opposed it.[36] In the early 1950s, Graham had gone to Korea and lambasted President Truman for not taking General MacArthur's advice. At that point in his career, he was embodying a type of blustering masculinity that had deep resonance among pro-military evangelicals. But as the nuclear weapons became ever more destructive, growing numbers of Americans realized that bluster could lead to annihilation. Graham understood that. He modulated his views. Not surprisingly, many evangelicals reached the same conclusions Graham did. Graham weathered the attacks of opponents who called him soft, winning new admirers on the left and reassuring many conservative evangelicals that they could support peace and strength without pushing the world to the brink of Armageddon.

Softness and Certitude

A consistent message about sin and salvation provided the through-line in Graham's career, but his certitude on matters of faith contrasted with his subtle evolution on social issues. This flexibility allowed Graham to remain relevant throughout the social and political upheaval that marked the late twentieth century, even as he retained a reputation for fixity. Moreover, Graham's desirability and comfort with the small screen suggested to evangelical men that they could embrace the trappings of modern America without losing their faith, or their masculinity. He embodied a new type of evangelical manhood that contained apparent contradictions: desirable and off limits, certain but subtly changing with the times. Graham's ability to keep those contradictions in productive tension showed Christian men how to demonstrate their manhood in a modern age.

Graham's embodiment of a new evangelical manhood fed into the Christian men's organization Promise Keepers, whose meteoric rise became the most dramatic evangelical story of the 1990s. Founded in 1990 by the University of Colorado head football coach Bill McCartney, Promise Keepers urged men to make promises to their wives, children, churches, and communities. Giant Promise Keepers stadium rallies—which bore a striking resemblance to Billy Graham crusades—drew on the cultural residue of sport to preach a message of sin and salvation directed specifically to men. The group suggested that men had failed because they had abandoned their rightful roles as leaders. But leadership did not mean domination. Promise Keepers literature called for an open and inviting type of masculinity. Occasionally, the group even endorsed feminists.[37] But Promise Keepers—like Graham—acquired a reputation for firmness. The organization never wavered on its central message of the importance of men taking responsibility in their lives, even as it tried to embrace a host of competing models for evangelical manhood.[38]

Graham had laid down a path that Promise Keepers attempted to walk. He showed men how to hold onto something firm in the shifting sands of modern America. His good looks helped him win attention; his moral rectitude helped him keep it for decades. Graham was not afraid to venture into cultural realms that evangelicals had long avoided. But he always engaged with those realms—Hollywood, academia—on his own terms, insisting that God and the Bible provided the only answers to life's most pressing problems. Graham knew what he believed but was not afraid to bend on some issues. He offered a vision of how evangelical men could thrive in late-twentieth-century America.

Notes

1. Saul Braun, "Nearer, Silent Majority, to Thee," *Playboy*, February 1971, 134, 120.

2. Michael S. Kimmel, *Manhood in America: A Cultural History* (New York: Free Press, 1996).

3. William C. Martin, *A Prophet with Honor: The Billy Graham Story* (New York: William Morrow, 1991), 106–107; Billy Graham, *Just As I Am: The Autobiography of Billy Graham* (San Francisco: HarperCollins, 1997), 127–129.

4. Virginia MacPherson, "Graham Says 'No' to Movies," *Hollywood Citizen-Examiner*, November 11, 1949, 1, Collection 360, Billy Graham Center Archives (BGCA); "God Cuts in on Wire-Tapper: 'New Billy Sunday from Wheaton' Scores Sensational Conversion," *Chicago Herald-American*, November 8, 1949, 14, Collection 360, BGCA.

5. "God Cuts in on Wire-Tapper," 14.

6. Martin, *Prophet with Honor*, 92.

7. Billy Graham, "God's Delinquent," Sermon, Charlotte, NC, October 8, 1958, BGCA, http://www2.wheaton.edu/bgc/archives/docs/bg-charlotte/1007.html.

8. Marshall Frady, *Billy Graham: A Parable of American Righteousness* (New York: Simon & Schuster, 1979), 228.

9. Andrew S. Finstuen, *Original Sin and Everyday Protestants: The Theology of Reinhold Niebuhr, Billy Graham, and Paul Tillich in an Age of Anxiety* (Chapel Hill: University of North Carolina Press, 2009), 125.

10. Billy Graham, *Hour of Decision*, 1952, V54, Collection 54, BGCA.

11. Margaret Bendroth, *Fundamentalism and Gender, 1875 to the Present* (New Haven, CT: Yale University Press, 1993), 24. See chapter 3 of Bendroth for an extended discussion of the connection between effeminacy and uncertainty.

12. Finstuen, *Original Sin*, 143–150.

13. Graham, *Just As I Am*, 139.

14. Louis Zamperini, May 18, 1976, Folder 32, Box 10, Collection 141, BGCA.

15. Billy Graham, "I Saw Your Sons at War: The Korean Diary of Billy Graham," pamphlet (Minneapolis: BGEA, 1953), 20, 50, BGCA.

16. On cultural custodianship, see Grant Wacker, "Searching for Norman Rockwell: Popular Evangelicalism in Contemporary America," in *The Evangelical Tradition in America* (Macon, GA: Mercer University Press, 1984), 311–313.

17. Clayton Day, May 1, 1989, Folder 69, Box 47, Collection 141, BGCA.

18. James Gilbert, *Men in the Middle: Searching for Masculinity in the 1950s* (Chicago: University of Chicago Press, 2005), 106–134.

19. *Woody Allen Interviews Billy Graham pt. 1—Featured Video—GodTube Logged In.flv*, 2010, http://www.youtube.com/watch?v=K_poGsbBgpE&feature=youtube_gdata_player.

20. Scott Ross, "The Night Woody Allen and Billy Graham Argued the Meaning of Life," NBC Bay Area, *Popcorn Biz* (blog), May 30, 2012, http://www.nbcbayarea. com/blogs/popcornbiz/You-Will-Meet-a-Tall-Dark-Stranger-Pits-Woody-Allen-vs-Billy-Graham-102956239.html.

21. Quoted in Martin, *Prophet with Honor*, 316.

22. Billy Graham, "My Answer," n.d., Folder 10, Box 8, Collection 19, BGCA.

23. Billy Graham, "Jesus and the Liberated Woman," *Ladies' Home Journal*, December 1970, 114.

24. Martin, *Prophet with Honor*, 586–587.

25. Sarah Frances Anders, "Women in Ministry: The Distaff of the Church in Action, " *Review and Expositor* 80 (1983): 30; C.R. Daley, "Current Trends among Southern Baptists, " *Western Recorder*, August 5, 1976, 2. Both articles cited in Barry Hankins, *Uneasy in Babylon: Southern Baptist Conservatives and American Culture* (Tuscaloosa: University of Alabama Press, 2002), 311n.13. See also Leon McBeth, *Women in Baptist Life* (Nashville: Broadman Press, 1979), 16; Elizabeth H. Flowers, *Into the Pulpit: Southern Baptist Women and Power since World War II* (Chapel Hill: University of North Carolina Press, 2012).

26. Martin, *Prophet with Honor*, 101.

27. Ibid., 146–148.

28. "A Change of Heart," *Sojourners*, August 1979, 12–14.

29. "Graham Calls Soviet Church 'Free,'" *Christian Science Monitor*, May 14, 1982, http://www.csmonitor.com/1982/0514/051425.html.

30. Martin, *Prophet with Honor*, 491–513.

31. Ronald S. Godwin, "Why Did Graham Go to Russia?," *Moral Majority Report*, May 24, 1982, 7.

32. Walter Williams, "Nuclear Weapons Don't Make War Immoral," *Moral Majority Report*, January 1983, 15.

33. "General Graham: America Can Defend Itself," *Moral Majority Report*, November 1982, 8.

34. For more on Graham's trip, see Nancy Gibbs and Michael Duffy, *The Preacher and the Presidents: Billy Graham in the White House* (New York: Center Street, 2007), 269–275; Martin, *Prophet with Honor* 491–513.

35. "SALT II: The Only Alternative to Annihilation?," *Christianity Today*, March 27, 1981, 15.

36. "Evangelicals Are of Two Minds on Nuclear Weapons Issues," *Christianity Today*, August 5, 1983, 49.

37. Michael G. Maudlin, "Why We Need Feminism," *New Man*, December 1997.

38. John P. Bartkowski, *The Promise Keepers: Servants, Soldiers, and Godly Men* (New Brunswick, NJ: Rutgers University Press, 2004).

"An Odd Kind of Cross to Bear"

THE WORK OF MRS. BILLY GRAHAM, FROM "PRETTY WIFE" TO "END OF CONSTRUCTION"

Anne Blue Wills

RUTH BELL GRAHAM, in describing her courtship and marriage to Billy, repeated the prayer she recalled uttering after their first date: "God, if You let me serve You with that man, I'd consider it the greatest privilege in my life."[1] This chapter will consider several distinctive ways that Ruth Graham served God alongside Billy, how she participated in his work visibly or with clear effects. The oft-heard declaration that "he couldn't have been Billy without Ruth" has become a bromide. Yet the fact that the idea has staying power calls for a description of and an investigation into Ruth's contributions to Billy's public work. This chapter will not treat their domestic life, except as that life became raw material for constructing Billy's persuasive image. Instead, it will focus on her part in building that image; her revision of Billy's first book, in which her theological outlook and her commitment to reach new generations with the Gospel come to bear; and selected later public appearances in print and in person.[2] This evidence traces an arc of Ruth's growing comfort with sharing her views with the public—and perhaps the public's growing interest in Ruth as a woman with her own voice who nevertheless rejected second-wave feminism. The chapter will conclude, however, by considering Ruth's return—late in life and by virtue of circumstance—to an accessory role in Billy's (and his successor's) projects. This investigation has been complicated by Ruth's longstanding allergy to the limelight and her family's continuing desire to protect her.[3] But the attempt to detail her real impact on Billy's work must be made, or we risk losing track of an important tributary to his unequaled career.

Early Life

Ruth McCue Bell was born in China on June 10, 1920, to Dr. Lemuel Nelson Bell and Virginia Leftwich Bell, medical missionaries sent by the Presbyterian Church (US), the Southern Presbyterians. Together, Nelson Bell, who was a surgeon, and Virginia Bell, who was a nurse, ran the Love and Mercy Hospital in Tsingkiangpu (now Huaian), China, which had been founded in the 1880s by Absalom Sydenstricker, the novelist Pearl Buck's father.[4] Ruth joined an older sister, Rosa, born in 1918. The family eventually welcomed sister Catherine (called Maimai), born during the Bells' furlough in 1926, and brother Clayton (named for the Bells' Houston, Texas, bene-factor), born in 1932. (Nelson Jr. was born in 1925 but died of dysentery that same year.) The children all grew up under the energetic care and Christian parenting of Nelson and Virginia, various Chinese nannies, and a host of other mission workers.[5] Virginia, in addition to her nursing and supervi-sory duties in the women's branch of the hospital, oversaw her children's early education before they began tutoring with other missionary children. For high school, Rosa and Ruth headed for the Pyeng Yang Foreign School, in 1932 and 1934, respectively, in what is now North Korea. At the time, it was known as the best Christian boarding school in Asia.[6]

When the time came for college in 1937, Ruth again followed her older sister—to Wheaton College, outside of Chicago. She majored in Bible and minored in art, and at least early on aspired to become a missionary like her parents, aiming to evangelize nomads in Tibet. In her second year at Wheaton, however, Ruth met a new student, Billy Frank Graham (she always called him Bill), who had already established himself as a preacher of note. Academically rigorous Wheaton did not recognize his degree from a non-accredited Bible college in Florida, so although older, he was a class behind Ruth. By most accounts, Billy fell immediately in love with her on sight. So the accepted story goes. That canonical version of their courtship also notes that Ruth's curiosity about him was piqued, not so much by their first meeting—which she claimed not to recall—but by later hearing him pray.[7]

Although the asymmetry preserved in the courtship story underwrites a picture of Billy as a mix of helpless romantic and red-blooded American man, and Ruth as eye-catching but deeply spiritual, it also reflects some-thing about their dating relationship, which proceeded over the course of several years in fits and starts. Billy demanded an exclusive commitment, but Ruth still entertained thoughts of a missionary vocation. Billy insisted that God had brought them together and that she would find God's plan for her in following him as he responded to his vocation as an evangelist. They married on Friday, August 13, 1943, in Gaither Chapel at Montreat College. Ruth then began a lifelong process—typical for women married to clergymen—of negotiating the tensions experienced by generations of Christian women as they have tried to follow scriptural teachings about devotion to husband, devotion to vocation, and devotion to God.[8]

Wives of clergymen historically have lived in a unique space where public and private, or work and family, collide and collude. Over the American centuries, the role of the pastor's wife has stayed remarkably unchanged; from Sarah Edwards to Catherine Marshall, these women supported their husbands' work by handling domestic details, welcoming clergy visitors, and heading off—ever so gently—threats to the minister's authority. Her role has been unofficial, unpaid, but nevertheless essential, with severe penalties for her and her husband if she shirked. Ruth Graham lived during a period of incipient change for these expectations. As depicted in early press coverage of his work and family life, her marriage to Billy fit the historic pattern of clergyman-*pater*, head of congregation and protector of hearth, supported by his godly helpmeet. Significantly, Ruth never rejected that role. Hers is not a story of "liberation" in the usual sense of that word. In fact, during an appearance on the *Phil Donahue Show* in the late 1970s, Ruth declared, "I'm liberated from having to earn a living so I can devote my time to my family and home."[9] She rejected the feminist movement and held to what she understood as God's calling on her to be a faithful wife to a powerful public figure and mother to five. But like other evangelical Christian women, she acknowledged that her calling was "an odd kind of cross to bear."[10] Ruth Graham experienced both the empowering call of Christian vocation and the pain of the many sacrifices it involved. If we observe her activities on Billy's behalf, we get a sense of the texture, sophistication, depth, and ambiguity of what she understood as the helpmeet's role.

From Pretty in Pink to Public in Pantsuits: Ruth as Billy's Wife, 1949–1970

Part of Billy Graham's appeal, beginning with his surging popularity in the late 1940s and through his prime active years, came from the model of

Christian manliness that he offered postwar Americans, as Seth Dowland details in his chapter, "Billy Graham's New Evangelical Manhood."[11] Graham combined old, muscular modes of revival, emphasizing condemnation for sinners, with new, movie-idol methods, producing in his work and in his own physical presence exciting but finally reassuring results. Popular media coverage—in well-known publications such as *Cosmopolitan, Life, Look, Newsweek,* and *Time,* but also in myriad smaller religious and trade publications—put Graham before readers' eyes. The content of early coverage, particularly, is repetitive in the extreme. Reports extol his youth, attractive physical features, and use of modern methods to deliver a traditional "hot-gospel" message. Other topics included his modest salary, his expert management apparatus, his plain and godly parents, and his down-to-earth lifestyle.

Ruth, invariably described as Billy's "pretty" wife and the capable mother of his children, constituted a major focus of media interest. With Ruth prominently featured, Billy demonstrated how the manly Christian could navigate a modern postwar consumer-driven democracy. Grant Wacker has spoken of Billy Graham as uniting the modern, the Christian, and the American.[12] Over the decades, reportage consistently featured Ruth in the role of appealing homemaker, reinforcing Billy's embodiment of this complex of identifiers. In photos and descriptions, Ruth's beauty, domestic skill, and (by 1970) her up-to-date style were all imputed to Billy, shoring up his image as a modern Christian man with a modern Christian wife.

Lora Lee Parrott published a book in 1957 titled *How to Be a Preacher's Wife and Like It.* (Ruth Graham wrote a short foreword, to be discussed later in this chapter.) The book sums up midcentury expectations for women married to clergy: "[L]aymen have a standard of perfection for the pastor's wife. She needs to be neat, wise, happy, frugal, deft, strong, feminine, spiritual, etc. Such a standard of perfection is not even held for the pastor himself."[13] Parrott continued, "The responsibilities of a pastor's wife to her husband are like those of any other wife. It is her business to keep herself attractive, to abhor fretfulness and nagging, to create a happy home situation, and in general to do her part in keeping up the romance on which the marriage was first founded."[14] Parrott distilled expectations that, despite the contradictions—to be like every other good wife, only perfectly so—had not changed much over the centuries since her Reformation-era invention. Ruth fulfilled many of these expectations. Indeed, she embraced them and exhorted others to do so, explicitly resisting such constraints only very rarely in public, usually tempering any comment with a generous helping of humor.[15] She also was depicted as the epitome of the dedicated Christian wife.

The particulars of Ruth's image as feminine and home-focused shifted over the decades. During the early 1950s and through the mid-1960s, Billy and Ruth had a household of small children to manage, and stories about them attended to that busy scene. Bradford Wilcox notes how James Dobson, in his 1970 book *Dare to Discipline*, laid the burden of responsibility for the social chaos of the sixties at the door of " 'permissive' childrearing" in the 1950s.[16] News coverage of the Grahams' home life, however, evidenced none of the "overindulgence, permissiveness, and smother-love" that Dobson bemoaned.[17] Instead, the numerous early descriptions of the Grahams at home and the frequent pictures of "Papa's" presence there— even though he traveled sometimes a majority of the year—portray Billy Graham as a reassuringly strong patriarch, and Ruth as lovely to behold and resourceful (rather than resentful) at home.

Readers learned from many early reports that Ruth only "occasionally" traveled with Billy. In the absence of exciting accounts of their travels together, reporters returned again and again to their Wheaton College courting days and presented photographic evidence of their continued mutual devotion and domestic bliss. Descriptions of Ruth and images of her with the children and with Billy reassured magazine readers that American marriage, despite postwar insecurities, could be modern, grounded in faith, and even glamorous and romantic.

Readers also learned that, in keeping with expectations for a pastor's wife, Ruth was feminine and pretty.[18] Nancy Cott points out that "feminine" in this era signaled a woman's "modesty" rather than her sexual appeal.[19] An early feature promoting an upcoming Minneapolis crusade, probably around 1950, before their third child's birth, pictured Ruth with their eldest daughter, "Gigi," and second child, Anne. The two girls are strategically seated in front of Ruth, probably to hide her pregnant tummy, which that sexually conservative era deemed too risqué.[20] Ruth is a beautiful creature, maternal but asexual—embodying more midcentury paradoxes about gender and sexuality.[21] The caption describes Billy's "lovely wife, Ruth."[22] Her "loveliness"—which onlookers can enjoy and attest to—increases her contribution to Billy's persona. The *Youth for Christ* magazine from September 1961 described Ruth and Billy's meeting with Queen Elizabeth at Buckingham Palace. The article focused on Billy's activities and the excitement of the day, but added, "For you girls,

Mrs. Graham was dressed in pink from hat to shoes and wore a flared summery skirt."[23] Again, according to this account, Ruth's contribution to the occasion rested solely in the pleasing visual content she added. Another story, "Billy Graham: Has Bible—Does Travel," from 1962, repeats like a broken record Ruth's one salient attribute appreciated in early accounts of the couple: the evangelist "met a *pretty* coed" at Wheaton "who became his wife." Her beauty and his hard work all add up to the "private life . . . of a typical American. He loves his family and his *pretty* wife," even though the "[b]usy evangelist isn't able to spend as much time as he'd like with his *pretty* wife . . . and their family."[24] Even as late as 1969, a short retrospective on Graham's career in the *Baptist Messenger* captioned a ten-year-old photograph of the couple by reminding readers that "Billy married his college sweetheart, Ruth Bell."[25] Pretty in pink, Ruth adorned Billy's arm and enhanced his image by looking good at his side or by his hearth, looking like the era's ideal female complement to him.

Coverage of Ruth did not stop at appreciation of her physical attributes. Her seriousness about the vocation of being a wife and mother also garnered considerable press attention. In 1964, Ruth herself authored a report for *The Christian* titled "Love Begins at Home"—one of the earliest editorial pieces written by her. She reflected on the many large and small tasks involved in rearing a family and running a home. "It seems that we are expected to be chauffeurs, cooks, shoppers, housekeepers, mothers, wives, plumbers, cleaning men, yardmen—and so the list goes on ad infinitum." Yet she remained committed to what she understood as her most important responsibility. "Sometimes I feel that life does not tend so much to crush us as to distract us from the main purpose of being wives and mothers."[26] Another story boasts an eye-catching headline purporting to highlight Ruth's approach to discipline—"Mrs. Billy Graham: Rears Family with Switch in One Hand, Bible in Other." Yet the headline, for the most part, has nothing to do with the contents of the report. In the story, Ruth quotes Billy: "Bill says I raise them with a switch in one hand and a Bible in the other."[27] Note that the headline repeats *his* words about *her*, emphasizing Billy's centrality, even in a story about Ruth. Nevertheless, the story reflects the magazine's hopes that readers would admire Ruth's commitment to child discipline. A 1973 interview with daughter Bunny Graham that appeared in *Good Housekeeping* added to the picture of a woman who took the teaching role of mother very seriously and used whatever was at hand to accomplish that work. The reporter summarized Bunny's recollections: "Discipline

was firm. Rules were carefully spelled out and if they were broken, punishment followed swiftly—usually a shoe tree applied to the bottom."[28]
Through the decades, the persistent perception that Ruth was beautiful,
principled, and guided by the Bible embellished Billy's reputation as a
guiding light for modern America.

These feature pieces took on a somewhat different flavor beginning
in the 1970s, as the women's liberation movement embedded itself in
the culture.[29] Still attentive to Ruth's beauty and her devotion to home
and family, stories began to emphasize Ruth's individuality and her
accomplishments outside the domestic sphere. Her beauty still received
plaudits. But while early accounts read her "loveliness" as a sign of her
commitment to Parrott's standard of "keep[ing] herself attractive" for the
sake of a happy husband, later stories appreciated her striking appearance as an expression of her personal style. The *Christian Herald* ran a
story in early 1970 titled "Who's Whose? Can You Match the Wives with
Their Husbands?" Pictures crowded the page, Brady Bunch–style, one
page a checkerboard of men's faces, and the facing page one of women's.
Indicating an awareness of feminist challenges to conservative Christian
teaching about women's submission, the author declared, "Many of
these wives are lively, vital personalities who have carved careers and
made their own mark." The story devoted a paragraph to each wife, extol-
ling special qualities and unique contributions to Christian work. True
to the pattern established in decades past, the writer reported that "Ruth
Bell Graham (Mrs. Billy Graham) met her evangelist husband when she
was a brown-haired, hazel-eyed second-year student of twenty in the fall
of 1940." But the write-up went on to praise her as "indispensable to her
world-traveling husband's career." The writer offers evidence of Ruth's
"indispensable" work: she "has devoted her life to making a home for
her husband between crusades" and raising their children "in a secluded
mountain retreat she helped design with old timber." These accomplishments hew still to the "pretty wife" template. Yet he author also
describes attainments unrelated to appearance or domesticity, even if the
author relies on Billy to substantiate the information: "Some of my best
thoughts," Billy notes in the piece, "come from her." The piece details
her knowledge of the Bible, her poetry writing, and her co-authorship of
Peace with God, as well as her own book, *Our Christmas Story*, published
in 1957. Moreover, it credits her with naming the *Hour of Decision* radio
program and helping establish a "London institution for women narcotic

addicts." While a former Graham associate is quoted as describing Ruth Graham in banal and somewhat dismissive terms as "'utterly unconscious' of her own attractiveness and 'a perfect hostess,'"[30] this write-up otherwise extends the reader's understanding of Ruth's personal accomplishments and her contributions to Billy's public profile. In this account, Ruth gains dimension beyond her oft-noted attractive exterior.

Two other feature stories on Ruth, also published in 1970, continued to emphasize her pleasing appearance while at the same time filling column inches with her own opinions. This more dimensional picture of Ruth redounded to Billy's benefit by updating his image, too. *Parade* magazine reported that, "[a]t 50, [Billy's] wife, Ruth, mother of five and grandmother of four, is a slim, strikingly pretty woman, 5 feet 5 and 118 lbs., with warm and clear eyes, a quick and pleasing smile, her brown hair now turning gray." The story continued: "She dresses in gaily colored, fashionable clothes, nowadays *favoring* pantsuits. Drabness, *she feels*, isn't necessarily next to godliness."[31] Displaying an enduring interest in matters of wardrobe and style, the profile nevertheless allows Ruth some agency—she expresses a preference for pantsuits and a clear, even potentially controversial opinion that a good fashion sense is nothing to hide under a bushel.[32]

Woman's Day also featured Ruth in 1970 and emphasized her antipathy toward the drab. A caption on a photo of an admittedly beautiful, smiling Ruth reads, "Here, the woman who believes 'It's no credit to Christ to be drab' tells you some surprising details about her family, her life, her personal philosophy."[33] The story describes her as "warm, witty, worldly and a strikingly attractive woman" with a "youthfully slim figure that she dresses with a marked sense of taste and style," looking "as if she'd be more at home in a country club than in a Sunday-school class."[34] Yet both stories go beyond the briefly stated details of Ruth's beauty to devote pages to her own words (as we shall see below). By 1970, reportage still insists that being (or staying) pretty constitutes an "achievement" worth remarking. But by 1970, too, portraits of her take more interest in and appreciation of her agency and opinions. Moreover, Ruth herself seemed to grow more comfortable with a certain expanded public role—not exactly sharing the podium with Billy, but allowing herself to say more to those, including reporters, who cared to listen. In a year during which Billy dared to write about "Jesus and the Liberated Woman," Ruth's media profile helped him give new contemporary texture to his traditional stance on appropriate Christian gender roles.[35]

Writing and Revising Peace with God

Billy Graham published his first full-length book, *Peace with God*, in 1953.[36] John Pollock's 1966 biography of Billy gives one account of how the book came about: approached by a Doubleday editor, the young evangelist doubted his ability to write a book that would both satisfy a "big New York" publisher and effectively communicate the Gospel message to a popular audience. A ghostwriter came in, sifted through Billy's sermons, and, working from an outline Billy provided, began to produce a completely unsuitable manuscript; the ghostwriter apparently had no ear for Christian evangelism. Pollock quotes Graham: "I chucked the whole thing in the wastebasket, and Ruth and I wrote that book."[37] In the original preface, Billy acknowledged an unnamed Ruth—his "loyal and faithful wife"—not as his coauthor but as one "who has read and reread" the text.[38] But Pollock's version of events, coming more than a decade after the book's original publication, and when a successful Billy may have felt more comfortable acknowledging Ruth by name as a collaborator, may reflect more accurately the book's origins.

The account that describes *Peace with God* as coauthored by Ruth and Billy gains more credence in light of the evidence that Ruth almost single-handedly revised it for a second edition, published in 1984.[39] She had been evolving her understanding of nature, Scripture, and Providence in her poetry writing—an activity she started as a child and continued all her life[40]—and took on the revision project herself in November and December of 1983. Ruth's suggested edits—roughly 250 of them, most of which were adopted for the 1984 edition—indicate important aspects of her theology that were presented to readers as Billy's. Some of the changes merely demonstrate Ruth's penchant for precision—changing one sentence, for instance, to echo the book's title more closely.[41] The most significant modifications, however, reflect a woman eager to share, using the most effective language possible, her hard-won insights about the appropriate human response to God's immanence.[42] Ruth eschewed the obsolete in appearance and speech. She avoided a drab appearance, convinced that unbelievers would be turned off by "pale, frumpy Christians."[43] She also believed that drab or outmoded language did the Christian message no favors. In the early 1980s, as a sixty-three-year-old grandmother, having reared her children most of the way and worked with college students for more than a decade, Ruth tailored the book's message to remain scriptural but also be modern and approachable.[44] She wanted the new edition's readers to embrace a living relationship with God that saw the modern world realistically. Vague talk about "religion" or institutions and off-putting talk about rules missed the point she wanted the book to communicate: God's self-revelation to humanity in Jesus Christ.

She wanted to open the Christian message up to a new generation of readers in the 1980s by emphasizing the importance of a personal relationship of humans to God and Jesus, rather than emphasizing religious institutions or the abstract phenomenon of "religion" itself. Discussing Moses's faithfulness, for instance, she amended one sentence to reinforce the intimate connection at work in his calling: "Moses considered the claims and obligations of religion" (in the 1953 edition) becomes, in 1984, "Moses considered the claims and obligations of God."[45] The same impulse seems to be at work, too, when Ruth responded to the following line in the first edition with only a question mark in the margin: "It has been said, 'In practical terms this membership of the body of Christ must actually mean membership of some local manifestation of His body in the church.' "[46] While her puzzlement may be merely about the source of the quotation, which went unnamed, it more likely arose from her sense that church affiliation, while important, could not substitute for real intimacy with God. After all, Ruth's poems rarely, if ever, took church as a topic.[47] God's care for his beloved children, however, was her constant subject.

Ruth's almost genetic Presbyterianism obligated her to take the reality of human sinfulness seriously. Yet even as she grasped the acuteness of sin's consequences, she affirmed the unbounded grace of God. She recognized the delicate operation of encouraging readers toward repentance without shying away from the severe reality of human alienation from God. Her many changes to the text of *Peace with God* hammered home the inevitability of the unregenerate running to sin, and the hopelessness of human beings trying to work their way out of the consequences of sin as she (through the lens of John Calvin) understood them—"the curse" that people want to "reverse," as she put it.[48] "Isn't it strange," as the 1984 edition read, on her suggestion, "to recognize that the first sin was committed in the perfect environment?"[49] And for that sin, we deserve not just punishment (as in the 1953 edition), but, in 1984, "eternal punishment."[50]

Her emendations evidenced a real worry about the pervasive visibility of sin in the contemporary world. Ruth soberly assessed the contemporary world's situation: "How many wars in progress now in '83?" Ruth jotted, beside a 1953 mention of " 'peace in our time' . . . drawing closer." The query became, in the 1984 edition, this somber statement: "it appears that we are standing on the brink of Armageddon. We are told that there were hundreds of 'little' wars between 1945 and 1979 which caused between twelve and thirteen million deaths."[51] The "blasphemous words of punk rock" —a musical genre rooted in the mid-1970s—illustrated for Ruth in the mid-1980s the presence of the devil in the modern world.[52] Other new problems on the scene included diseases like AIDS and herpes, which she associated with the sexual revolution.[53] In the margins of the 1953 book's first chapter, Ruth listed myriad concrete examples of sinfulness and temptation facing contemporary Americans in the early 1980s: rampant divorce, drugs, pornography ("kiddie porn" appears in parentheses), "abortions, child abuse, soaring crime[,] wife abuse," as well as "surrigate [sic] mothers, 'adoptive dolls' couple flew to another country to pick up a 'cabbage patch' doll."[54] Ruth drew an arrow from "abortion" to this final phrase, noting perhaps the irony of dolls being adopted rather than unwanted children. "Sin is 'in,'" she penned, and "[t]oday, the general reaction is 'so what?'"[55] The devil (although he loses his capital D in the thirty years between the first and second editions) is bad; specifically, at Ruth's suggestion, he is described as "unrelenting and cruel. He is not, however, all-powerful, omniscient or omnipresent."[56] Ruth worried about contemporary reports of Satan worship, and mention of it appears in the revision.[57] Sin is bad. And punishment for sin is bad. On the question of hellfire's reality, Ruth's suggestion was adopted wholesale into the revised edition: "If [hellfire] is not literal fire, it is something worse. Jesus would not have exaggerated."[58] Humanity circa 1984 finds itself in a dire situation.

A fascinating moment reveals a key shift in emphasis that Ruth made between the first and second editions of *Peace with God*. The earlier version declared, "Two thousand years ago God invited the world to the gospel feast, and in the agonies of the cross, God held your sins and mine until every last vestige of our guilt was consumed." Ruth penciled in a change, adopted for the 1984 revision: "Two thousand years ago God invited a morally corrupt world to the foot of the cross. There God held your sins and mine to the fire until it was burned to ashes."[59] The locus of attention had moved from the "gospel feast" to the "foot of the cross."

Perhaps Ruth determined so firmly to keep the book's message approachable precisely because she saw the human situation in the early 1980s as so dire. Looking around her in late 1983, she saw national and international civil strife, cultural decay, and physical suffering on a massive scale. So she recalibrated some language in the book to sound more welcoming and familiar, and reshaped its claims in order to emphasize relationship rather than regimentation. For instance, she renamed the book's first part so that it stated not the "Problem," as in the 1953 edition, but the "Situation."[60] The "*Rules* of the Christian Life," the 1953 edition's title for chapter 14, was renamed "*Principles* (Rules)," which became finally a more inviting set of "*Guidelines* for Christian Living" in chapter 15 of the new edition.[61] As seriously as Ruth took the human situation of inevitable sin, she worked to produce an inviting rather than condemning picture of the Jesus she believed in. She showed a perfect horror of the verb "demand" when applied to God or Christ. Jesus can "expect" or "command" or "require" but in the second edition, only infrequently does he "demand."[62]

Another part of Ruth's motivation as she revised *Peace with God* rose from her own poetic vision that saw God continuously acting in the everyday world. She held in mind a new generation of readers who lived in a rapidly changing, ever more technological world. This generation may also have had more confidence in its own power, and it certainly expressed a jaded view about admonitions to Christian obedience. In light of her audience, Ruth pursued a rage for "updating" illustrations and references.[63] To avoid the earlier edition's frozen-in-time quality, Ruth referred to the "moon shot" frequently; Ruth uses the moon missions of the late 1960s and 1970s, and the even more recent NASA shuttle program of the 1980s, to reinforce Billy's argument that "[i]n the wonders of nature we see God's laws in operation."[64] Even the field of genetics became raw material for Ruth's illustrative hand: a first-edition comment about Adam's sinfulness spreading to the whole human race gets recast in the 1984 edition: "Just as we inherit characteristics, such as intellect, coloring, body size, temperament, etc., from our parents and grandparents, mankind inherited its fallen, corrupt nature from Adam."[65] Determined never to be stodgy or out of touch, Ruth drew on the image of a "gambler—a 'High Roller'" and (somewhat confusedly) "Russian Roulette" to illustrate the eternal chances a nonbeliever takes. In the 1984 edition, Ruth's suggestion becomes a reference to a *People* magazine story about "one of the nation's leading gamblers, Lem Banker," who never bet more than he could afford to lose.[66] The wide world, from the sublimities of outer space to the banalities of gossip magazines, offered up material for Ruth's editorial eye.

The Lady Doesn't Vanish

Ruth rarely made formal appearances or gave talks—"I think one speaker in the family is enough," she told *Parade* magazine in 1970.[67] She preferred to avoid center stage and either stay put on the home front or, if accompanying Billy on the road, blend in with crowds of listeners.[68] During the pivotal London crusade at Harringay Arena in 1954, Billy put Ruth at the microphone with only a few hours' warning. She struggled mightily with what to say. When her turn came, Patricia Cornwell reports, "she moved to the podium, turned to her husband, her mouth strategically placed close to the microphone. 'I could kill you,' she said."[69] Although the audience's delighted laughter drowned out her comments, Ruth reflected in her journal that night that "God helped me through without my throwing up on the platform or falling up the steps."[70]

Another early and perhaps less jarring foray into the public realm came when Ruth penned a very brief foreword for the 1957 advice manual previously mentioned, Lora Lee Parrott's *How To Be a Preacher's Wife and Like It*. This piece may be the earliest published writing by Ruth Graham. True to form, she kept it short (so short that she may have omitted a key word). The foreword, in its entirety, reads as follows:

> If you are like I am you will be tickled to death to discover a book that is both inspirational and very, very practical as a sort of guide book for us preachers' wives. All of us get to the place where we feel the job is just too big for us. That's [not?] a good way to feel, I know, but we need something practical to help us to be better wives and mothers. This little book will do just that. It has helped me and I know it will help you too.

Lora Parrott's book offers instruction about proper helpmeet attitudes and the way to create a loving Christian home for husband and children. This book is of a piece with the "pretty wife" coverage of Ruth in the early years of Billy's work.

Later in Billy's career, however, Ruth did take one crusade-related stage or another, probably always reluctantly, but also in service to spreading an encouraging gospel message.[71] As part of the buildup to the September 1969 Anaheim crusade, for instance, Nancy Reagan (then First Lady of California) hosted a large luncheon for Ruth on September 15 at the Anaheim Convention Center.[72] The *Washington Post* reported a crowd of eleven thousand women, with five thousand more listening to Ruth's remarks through a closed-circuit television broadcast—as the report notes, "the largest gathering she had ever addressed."[73] The *Christian Times* noted that "observers described [the gathering] as one of the greatest public tributes ever accorded any woman anywhere."[74] In her comments, Ruth offered winsome humor and pithy insight. Beards on young men did not bother her, she declared, because they set the long-haired boys apart from the long-haired girls. She proudly reported her continued resistance to being baptized by immersion—a desire of Billy's, at least for a time—in spite of his imposition of a bounty to anyone who could persuade her: "[N]ever in my life have I met so many fee-splitting Baptists." She also offered advice for wives, later often repeated: "Make [your husband] happy and leave it to God to make him good." She advised unmarried women to "marry someone you don't mind adjusting to."[75] And she expressed compassion and even admiration for the current generation of teenagers, who were committed to resisting "the hypocrisy of their elders."[76] The *Christian Times* reporter observed, "Her speech was a mixture of homey personal anecdotes and an astonishing variety of literary resource material."[77] The Ruth who later, in revising *Peace with God*, wanted to keep Billy's message approachable and vital was already discernable here in her traditional views, but also in her wit and pragmatism.

Ruth Graham also spoke at a women's luncheon at the North American Congress on Evangelism, held in Minneapolis at the end of 1969. According to one account, her "speech was not eloquent" or carefully prepared, but "a collection of little things she'd jotted down along the way to help her."[78] Her comments again focused on being supportive as a wife and mother, but she also offered thoughts, drawn from that home front, about how to evangelize. Illustrating the point with a story about an unnamed son (probably Franklin) and his "wildly enthusiastic" devotion to both rock music and the comedy of Bill Cosby, Ruth cautioned against "tun[ing] out people who need us before we understand them." She declared, "You can't make a person commit himself to Christ or make him want to change his way of life. That's the Holy Spirit's work." Refusing to reject her son's (and his generation's) interests, she again showed herself committed to a welcoming Christianity that would meet young and old where they were. God's agency—a phenomenon she explored constantly in her poems and would revisit in *Peace with God*—did not shy away from long hair, loud music, or a good time.

A May 1970 piece in the *Knoxville News-Sentinel* featured words and pictures of Ruth "in one of her rare appearances at one of Dr. Graham's crusades."[79] The story conveyed Ruth's extensive comments on marriage and motherhood and the importance of communicating God's love at home and beyond. Perhaps most significant, the reporter also acknowledged the "reputation" that "the wife of one of the world's foremost voices of Christianity" must "live up to"—shades of *How to Be a Preacher's Wife*. Yet Ruth had by this time gained some perspective on those expectations. The author quoted Ruth: "Do people expect perfection from me? Not people with good sense!" The comment marked a significant public acknowledgment by Ruth of the impossible clergy-wife perfection extolled by Lora Lee Parrott twenty-plus years before. Parrott bemoaned those standards but exhorted readers to meet them nonetheless, and Ruth had given Parrott's book her imprimatur. More than two decades on, with fewer children to occupy her at home, and "estimat[ing] that [Billy] is home only one-fourth of the time," Ruth openly expressed a certain detachment from pretty perfection. Nevertheless, she also acknowledged that "I don't think God ever really called me to be a missionary," a comment that in some ways reflects her acceptance of the "pretty coed" role. Here, she seems content to see her central accomplishments as having happened hearthside, rather than in the mission field.

As noted earlier, the *Parade* and *Woman's Day* stories about Ruth that also appeared in 1970 held to a modified "pretty wife" script. Both stories featured more of Ruth's own words than any of the early stories about her and Billy did. The *Woman's Day* piece pointedly noted that Ruth broke with the stereotype of "prudish churchwoman strangers often expect her to be."[80] With all their upbeat patter, however, these two stories point to one of the challenges in studying Ruth: the image of pretty helpmeet that contained her in the early years did, and continued to, partake in reality. She embraced the supporting role—and the embrace, ironically, became easier to see in later years precisely because she talked about it more. Yet Ruth did embrace her role in her own way. She hollowed out space for herself even as a "clergy wife." Ruth was both sophisticated and a dedicated Christian, worldly and devoted to husband and home. This evolving image redounded to Billy's benefit, "updating" his own look somewhat and allowing him to marry, for his followers, the modern, the Christian, and the American.

Ruth took her message of appealing Christian sophistication global in 1983. At the first International Conference for Itinerant Evangelists (ICIE), held in 1983 in Amsterdam, programming focused on practical training for evangelists around the world, but especially those identified as high-potential evangelistic workers in the developing world. The conference also featured what William Martin called a "special wives program;" one source calls it the Women's Program.[81] This part of the proceedings featured some of the Graham "team wives"— Millie Dienert, Jean Ford (Billy Graham's sister), Patricia Palau, and Mary Helen Wilson, among others. One session billed in the schedule as a "Q&A" featured Ruth alone; Hanspeter Nüesch summarizes what he sees as her main points in an appendix to his book about the couple.[82] For the assembled wives, Ruth emphasized the priority of the husband's evangelistic work. The wife, as his partner and the caretaker of his children, played an essential part in making it possible for him to focus fully on spreading the gospel. In Nüesch's paraphrase, Ruth observed that "the main task as the wife of a spiritual leader was to joyfully stand beside him and support his ministry with all one's strength. As a mother, the task was to raise children with love and biblical guidelines and provide a happy home."[83] The implication, "that one had to put one's own wishes as a wife on the back burner for a certain time," could be borne, she declared, with God's help.[84] She exhorted her audience to be in what she called "constant fellowship" with God throughout the day.[85]

In her talk, Ruth also acknowledged the help she gave to Billy unrelated to her domestic role, "reading for him, doing research for his sermons, and proofreading his books."[86] She was his "assistant . . . free to do her part" because he shouldered the main responsibilities of his evangelistic calling.[87] Nüesch noted a verbal "wink at the women's liberation movement" as Ruth asserted that Billy "allowed her to be herself so she could be truly liberated"[88] and help him in his work. For other women, however, with "the gift of teaching before big audiences," Nüesch reported Ruth said that "she should do it, and her husband should back her up."[89] Indeed, the Grahams' second daughter, evangelist Anne Graham Lotz, spoke at the conference that year, both in plenary session (the only woman to do so)[90] and the Women's Program; she also spoke at the 1986 follow-up conference.

Ruth's emphasis in her 1983 comments landed on both the difficulty of being an evangelist's wife and the ever-present strength available in Scripture and from God through the Holy Spirit. Martin reported that Ruth also spoke at another Q&A session at the 1986 Amsterdam conference, "drawing warm appreciation for such frank and commonsensical observations as 'I find Christian parents without problem children can be stuffy. If you have a prodigal, you will love all prodigals.' "[91] Such comments reflected Ruth's own experiences with Franklin and Ned (Ruth and Billy's youngest child), experiences she grew more comfortable about disclosing as the decades passed.[92]

Back in the Spotlight's Shadow

A short ten years after the second Amsterdam conference, on May 2, 1996—the National Day of Prayer—Ruth and Billy together received the Congressional Gold Medal at a ceremony in Washington, DC. With a frail Senator Strom Thurmond (SC) playing a small part in his capacity as president pro tempore of the Senate, North Carolina senators Jesse Helms and Lauch Faircloth presented the medal to the Grahams in a Capitol rotunda ceremony attended by many national dignitaries and emceed by Speaker of the House Newt Gingrich.[93] Speaker Gingrich announced the speakers and honorees as they filed in to their front-row seats; they met Ruth, seriously weakened by illness, already seated but barely visible to cameras.[94]

Screened from the view of cameras for most of the ceremony, Ruth was also obscured in the encomia offered. They focused on Billy's accomplishments almost to the exclusion of Ruth's. Gingrich briefly mentioned her authorship of six books, and Vice President Al Gore praised Billy and Ruth's connection "with ordinary mothers and fathers and families throughout this nation." Yet amid mentions of Ruth's partnership with Billy, the speakers gave few details about her work and public contribution to his activities. Even the citation, read in alternating lines by Helms and Faircloth, only mentioned Ruth specifically in relation to the children's hospital project the Grahams started.[95] The exception to vague Ruth references came in Senator Bob Dole's remarks. (His presidential campaign against Bill Clinton constituted part of the political backdrop for the event.)[96] Dole described unusual congressional unanimity in approving the Grahams' award. Unlike the others, Dole spoke from longtime friendship with Ruth and Billy, describing her as "Billy's remarkable partner of 53 years and a distinguished communicator of God's power and peace in her own right." He also revealed the topic of her seventh book, "a humorous look of the life [sic] with Billy." He continued, "[Y]ou can see the constant twinkle in Ruth's eyes in the title she has given the book: *How to Marry a Preacher and Remain a Christian.*"[97] The line received the biggest laugh of the day.

Onstage during the actual presentation of the medal, Ruth, bedeviled by a cough she struggled to suppress, could hardly be seen behind Billy and the other men surrounding her. Vice President Gore hurriedly brought a chair up to the platform so that she could sit—again, out of view. The best images of her came when Billy spoke and the camera could focus on her gazing at him.

The audience, a critical Colman McCarthy wrote, "applaud[ed] itself numb" over the award, paying tribute in his view to a presidential lackey for the political benefit of everyone who could squeeze into the Rotunda.[98] Fair enough. McCarthy's indignant reaction to the occasion, true to the day's proceedings, also failed to notice how the ceremony treated Ruth as both essential and accessory. Congressional leaders and their invited guests applauded an idea of Ruth Graham as a supportive helper without thinking too hard about how she actually had "helped" Billy over the decades. The applauding crowd recognized her without really seeing her depth of thought and work. The pretty helpmeet, immortalized on the gold medal's face as the benign chignoned granny, returned that day, at the behest of ambitious political partisans, in order to burnish the upright image of the man they all gathered around as a fetish of their legitimacy.

Nancy Gibbs and Michael Duffy wrote about another episode in which Ruth played a pivotal but passive role, true to the oldest traditions of clergy-wifedom. Events continued to draw power from Ruth's significance, as his pretty helpmeet, to burnish Billy's image and legacy. During their final visit with the revered evangelist, in January 2007, Gibbs and Duffy noted that while Billy was "smiling and looking as strong as eighty-eight years allow," Ruth was not well. Worry about her increasing frailty—owing to painful spine degeneration—had "consumed" Billy all the previous autumn.[99] Increasingly aware that she most likely would not live much longer, the Graham family divided over where Ruth (and Billy) would be buried, with Franklin pushing for the soon-to-open Billy Graham Library—a museum with an evangelistic pitch offering multiple opportunities to connect with the Billy Graham Evangelistic Association, which Franklin now led. Their youngest child, Ned, meanwhile, defended his parents' long-held decision to be buried in Asheville at the Cove, a retreat and lay training center the Grahams dedicated in the early 1990s. In late 2006, Ned dispatched Ruth's protégé and biographer, Patricia Cornwell, to the almost completed library to assess it and give the Grahams her opinion. The reporter Laura Sessions Stepp of the *Washington Post* was present, at Ned's invitation, to hear Cornwell's negative impressions and Billy and Ruth's responses; her stories made the disagreement public.[100]

Ruth sighed, "It's a circus . . . a tourist attraction."[101] Ned encouraged his mother to make her preferences clearly known; she dictated a statement that he recorded and had signed by his mother and notarized by one of the witnesses present.[102] In part, Ruth declared in the statement that "the Memorial Garden at Chatlos Chapel"—the chapel at the Cove— "was prepared for" the "very purpose" of receiving her and Billy's remains. "Under no circumstances," she stated, "am I to be buried in Charlotte, North Carolina."[103] After China, Ruth considered "the beautiful mountains of North Carolina" to be her home.[104] After all, she had never lived in Charlotte. The BGEA had only moved its headquarters to the city after Franklin took over from his father. Sessions Stepp painted this episode as a tangle of conflicts—primarily between, on one side, the headstrong but physically weakened mother and her younger son and caretaker Ned, and on the other, the elder son and scion Franklin.

The fact that so many readers responded to Sessions Stepp's *Washington Post* stories about the controversy (and Tim Funk's *Charlotte Observer* stories) evidenced the continued significance of the Grahams for the public.[105] Moreover, some of their comments hit on some of the paradoxes of the episode. The question of where to be buried should be a private, family matter, several respondents observed—although many other events in the Grahams' lives, including births of children and nightly story time, had been opened to public scrutiny over the decades. Ruth and Billy's marriage was never a completely private matter. Moreover, Billy, somewhat notorious for never wanting to offend, found himself in another quandary, trying impossibly to honor his beloved wife's wishes without squashing his son's ambitions, which he would have, in characteristic fashion, charitably interpreted as ambitions for the gospel and not for personal power or financial gain. Although it took some convincing, Billy eventually accepted Franklin's idea of the Billy Graham Library as a tool for Christian witness.[106] Still further, Ruth, disciplined her whole life long for sacrifice, typically deferred to Billy's determination to read things this way, even if she disagreed. She would never have asked him to pull back from an opportunity to attract people to the gospel, even if doing so meant using the lure of a kind of evangelical reliquary.[107]

Of course, Ruth was buried in 2007 at the library. In a December 2007 interview with the *Guardian* newspaper, Cornwell said she would most like to apologize to Ruth Graham, "because," she explained, "I swore that I would ensure she was buried in the mountains of Western North Carolina."[108] But perhaps Cornwell can take some solace from Ruth's final flourish. Her headstone famously bears the comment, "End of Construction—Thank you for your patience," something Ruth once saw on a road sign.[109] The cheeky inscription perhaps closes the lifelong round of practical jokes mother and elder son played on one another. If Franklin planned to construct a solemn memorial to the giants of twentieth-century evangelism, Ruth wrinkled up the blueprint a bit. She also had the Chinese symbol for "righteousness" included on the marker, reflecting—right up alongside the jokey epitaph—Ruth's utter seriousness about the Christian's duty and the nature of God.[110] The marker therefore captures at least "two sides of Mrs. Graham"—the woman who saw God in the most ordinary places and who devoted herself wholeheartedly to God's service, even to the point of almost disappearing.

A final episode bears witness to Ruth's vanishing: *Sitting by my laughing fire . . .*, her poetry collection originally published in 1977, was reissued in 2006 by the Billy Graham Evangelistic Association with a new cover and layout. As the dust jacket declares, "Numerous family photos taken over the years—including some never before published—add a rich context to this edition, creating a treasured memory book of the life of this remarkable woman." The photographs and layout, which includes pictures of pressed flowers and leaves, create the illusion of a scrapbook. Leafing through this volume appears to bring one into intimate contact with Ruth, Billy, their children, and the whole family's life together. (It also, not incidentally, includes pictures of Franklin doing Samaritan's Purse work, perhaps subtly arguing visually for his legitimacy as Billy's successor.) Just as the poems focus on Ruth's particular, even idiosyncratic, religious vision, the book as a whole constructs the reader's experience of private encounter. The evangelistic appeal comes as the book leads readers from quietly conversing with Ruth to encountering the redeeming Jesus in a vivid, intimate way.

This 2006 edition of *Sitting by My Laughing Fire* also highlights the clergy-wife paradoxes that I have tried to take seriously here. On the back flap of the dust jacket, where biographical information on a book's author usually appears, Ruth is described as "the daughter of Presbyterian missionaries." The text continues, with questionable accuracy, more myth than fact: "She traveled extensively with her husband, Billy Graham, on his many Crusades around the world." Without any transition, the mini-biography concludes: "While their five children were growing up, she took

on the responsibilities of managing the household to give Billy the freedom to travel and preach wherever God called him." These two final sentences seem out of chronological order. At the very least, they seem an odd
summation of her life.

The two sentences provide a digest of the public and the private duties
performed by perhaps all wives of prominent men, clergy or not. In public,
she traveled with him (and indeed they are pictured together at the end of
the paragraph, well-dressed, smiling, without the children),[111] certifying
his family-man bona fides and providing him with important support and
companionship—yet the crusade project was his and the BGEA's, and it
certainly continued on the many occasions when Ruth was not with him.
In private, she handled home and children, attending to the countless,
often uninteresting, but insistent details of upkeep and nurture—unpaid
and publicly unacknowledged (except in the breach). These spheres are
mutually exclusive. Where, in this write-up's view, was the most important
place for Ruth to be? What was the most important task for her to accomplish? Did Billy's adjutant serve him best by his side or at home with the
children? She could not do both the public and the private work at once,
yet both were essential. The author of the dust jacket bio had a difficult
time solving this equation as well. And so Ruth's identity is left suspended,
duck-rabbit-style, confounding and so describable only in platitudes.[112]

Notes

For research assistance, thoughtful questions, and encouragement, my deep
appreciation goes to Peggy Bendroth, Edith Blumhofer, David Bratt, Caroline
Brooks, Julia Capalino, Amy Colombo, Andrew Finstuen, Katie Kalivoda, Bob
Shuster, Laura Spencer, Grant Wacker, and students in my "Married to the
Ministry" seminar (fall 2012 and spring 2015).

1. Patricia Cornwell, *Ruth: A Portrait. The Story of Ruth Bell Graham* (New York:
   Doubleday, 1997), 83.
2. Ruth Bell Graham honed her theological perspective over decades of writing
   poetry. I consider that subject separately in " 'The Heavens are Telling': Nature
   and Scripture in Ruth Bell Graham's Poetry" (unpublished manuscript).
3. I must, however, express my sincere gratitude to family members and friends
   who have opened their homes to me and shared their memories of Mrs. Graham.
4. G. Thompson Brown, *Earthen Vessels and Transcendent Power: American
   Presbyterians in China, 1837–1952* (New York: Orbis, 1997), see chap. 11, "Healing,
   Mending, Caring." Buck created a portrait of her single-minded missionary father
   in *Fighting Angel: Portrait of a Soul* (New York: John Day, 1936).

5. Cornwell, *Ruth*, 25.

6. David Aikman, *Billy Graham: His Life and Influence* (Nashville: Thomas Nelson, 2010), 176.

7. Cornwell, *Ruth*, 81, 82–83.

8. The historical literature on the role of the clergy wife in the United States needs updating, but some idea of the particularities of the role can be gleaned from Wallace Denton, *The Role of the Minister's Wife* (Philadelphia: Westminster, 1962); William Douglas, *Minister's Wives* (New York: Harper & Row, 1965); Marilyn Brown Oden, *The Minister's Wife: Person or Position?* (Nashville: Abingdon, 1966); and Leonard Sweet, *The Minister's Wife: Her Role in Nineteenth-Century American Evangelicalism* (Philadelphia: Temple University Press, 1983). Margaret H. Watt, *The History of the Parson's Wife* (London: Faber and Faber, 1943), focused on the European context, gives useful background on the Reformation-era origins of the minister's wife's role and its development in the subsequent centuries. Jane Hunter, *The Gospel of Gentility: American Women Missionaries in Turn-of-the-Century China* (New Haven, CT: Yale University Press, 1984), esp. chaps. 3 and 4, explores the distinctive experience of missionary wives.

Sweet, *Minister's Wife*, provides the current exploration with the useful category of "helpmeet," which he discusses in chap. 4, " 'What Women These Christians Have!' Lydia Finney and the Assistant Model" (76–106). In addition to Lydia Finney—Charles Grandison Finney's first wife—Sweet's typology makes use of, among others, Peggy Dow (wife of Lorenzo Dow) and Elizabeth Finney (Finney's second wife). The influence two other women had on the lives and thought of their respective husbands are examined in Edythe Scott Bagley with Joe Hilley, *Desert Rose: The Life and Legacy of Coretta Scott King* (Tuscaloosa: University of Alabama Press, 2012); and Elisabeth D. Dodds, *Marriage to a Difficult Man: The Uncommon Union of Jonathan and Sarah Edwards* (Laurel, MS: Audubon, 2003; originally published in 1971).

A few works in which women record experiences they had as wives of ministers or missionaries add to this catalogue. For instance, Mrs. Henry Ward [Eunice] Beecher, *From Dawn to Daylight; or, The Simple Story of a Western Home* (New York: Hurst & Co., 1859), lightly fictionalizes the Beechers' life at his first pastorate in rural Indiana; Rosalind Goforth, *Climbing: Memories of a Missionary's Wife*, 3rd ed. (Nappanee, IN: Evangel, 2008), contains a short introduction by Ruth Bell Graham; see also Catherine Marshall, *A Man Called Peter: The Story of Peter Marshall*, Anniversary Edition (Grand Rapids, MI: Chosen, 2002; originally published in 1951); and Helen Smith Shoemaker, *I Stand by the Door: The Life of Sam Shoemaker* (Waco, TX: Word, 1967).

Two helpful archival sources that illustrate the relative stasis of the clergy wife's role through the nineteenth and much of the twentieth century are Catherine L. Adams, *Daily Duties Inculcated in a Series of Letters, Addressed to the Wife of a*

Clergyman (1835); and Mary Schauffler Platt, *The Home with the Open Door: An Agency in Missionary Service* (1920).

9. Jhan Robbins, *Marriage Made in Heaven: Billy and Ruth Graham* (New York: Putnam, 1983), 108–109, recounts Ruth's statement on the *Phil Donahue Show* (October 11, 1979?).

10. Quoted in Cornwell, *Ruth*, 133.

11. This section of the chapter draws on work I presented as "Billy Graham, Man of God, 1949–1954," at the winter meeting of the American Society of Church History, January 8, 2010, San Diego, CA.

12. Grant Wacker, Opening Remarks, Worlds of Billy Graham Conference, Wheaton College, Wheaton, IL, 26 Sept. 2013.

13. Lora Lee Parrott, *How to Be a Preacher's Wife and Like It*, 2nd ed. (Grand Rapids, MI: Zondervan, 1957), 27, emphasis in original.

    The how-to literature advising pastors' wives includes such titles as the above-listed Adams, *Daily Duties*; and Schauffler Platt, *Home with the Open Door*, which I take as shaping the later texts from the middle of the twentieth century, among them, Martha Hickman, *How to Marry a Minister* (Philadelphia: Lippincott, 1968); Donna Sinclair, *The Pastor's Wife Today*, Creative Leadership series (Nashville: Abingdon, 1981); and Alice Taylor, *How to Be a Minister's Wife and Love it* (Grand Rapids, MI: Zondervan, 1968).

    In the current millennium, the production of how-to literature for pastor's wives shows no sign of slowing: see, for example, oft-cited works such as Lorna Dobson, *I'm More Than the Pastor's Wife: Authentic Living in a Fishbowl World*, rev. ed. (Grand Rapids, MI: Zondervan, 2003); Jeana Floyd, *10 Things Every Minister's Wife Needs to Know* (Green Forest, AR: New Leaf, 2010); Lisa McKay, *You Can Still Wear Cute Shoes: And Other Great Advice from an Unlikely Preacher's Wife* (Colorado Springs: David C Cook, 2010); and Jane Rubietta, *How to Keep the Pastor You Love* (Downers Grove, IL: InterVarsity, 2002), esp. chap. 7, "The Paragon of the Pews (or, How to Really Love Your Pastor's Spouse)."

14. Parrott, *How to Be*, 28.

15. More frank, yet still coded, assessments of her "odd cross" appear in Bell Graham's poetry, some of which reflects profound loneliness, fatigue, even despair. See, for instance, the poems in the section of *Sitting by my laughing fire* . . . titled "The Closing of a Door"; Ruth Bell Graham, *Sitting by my laughing fire* . . . (Waco, TX: Word Books, 1977), 149–158. The fact that she did not publish these poems until 1977 suggests that they revealed too much of a struggle with her role during the years when Billy needed her to appear completely content in order to establish his credibility as a successful Christian man.

16. W. Bradford Wilcox, *Soft Patriarchs, New Men: How Christianity Shapes Fathers and Husbands*, Morality and Society Series (Chicago: University of Chicago Press, 2004), 21.

17. Dobson quoted in Wilcox, *Soft Patriarchs*, 21.

18. Some of this material was presented in a public lecture at Wheaton College, March 21, 2013.

19. Nancy F. Cott, *Public Vows: A History of Marriage and the Nation* (Cambridge, MA: Harvard University Press, 2000), 160.

20. The Grahams had five children: Virginia Leftwich (nicknamed "Gigi"), born in 1945; Anne McCue, 1948; Ruth Bell (nicknamed "Bunny"), 1950; William Franklin III, 1952; and Nelson Edman (nicknamed "Ned"), 1958.

    See http://www.avclub.com/articles/more-than-60-years-ago-a-pregnant-lucille-ball-cou,100629/, accessed 26 September 2013. In a 1952 episode of *I Love Lucy*, in deference to the television censors, Mrs. Ricardo (Lucille Ball) was spoken of as "expecting," not "pregnant."

21. See the discussion of conservative evangelical understandings of the God-given differences between female and male sexual appetites and behavior in Seth Dowland, *Family Values and the Rise of the Christian Right* (Philadelphia: University of Pennsylvania Press, 2015), chaps. 4 and 6. Stephanie Coontz, *The Way We Never Were: American Families and the Nostalgia Trap* (New York: Basic, 1992), chap. 2, explores the tension that arose during the 1950s, an era that emphasized the importance of family and childbearing —and therefore acknowledging and encouraging sex within marriage—while at the same time stressing the important role women played in "containing" or "holding out" against men's advances (40).

22. Microfilm, "A Day with Billy Graham," n.p., ca. 1950, Reel 61, Collection 360, Billy Graham Evangelistic Association Clippings File, Billy Graham Center Archives (BGCA). Unless otherwise noted, news items come from this microfilm collection and will be designated by the reel number and BGCA.

23. Mel Larson, "The Queen and Billy Graham," *Youth for Christ Magazine*, September 1961, 48, Reel 74, Collection 360, BGCA.

24. Stanley Pieza, "Billy Graham: Has Bible—Does Travel," *Chicago's Sunday American Leisure Magazine*, May 27, 1962, n.p., Reel 77, Collection 360, BGCA. Emphasis added.

25. Gil Stricklin, "Twenty Wonderful Years," *The Baptist Messenger*, September 25, 1969, Reel 99, Collection 360, BGCA.

26. Ruth Graham, "Love Begins at Home," *The Christian*, March 20, 1964, n.p., Reel 82, Collection 360, BGCA.

27. Originally published in *Grit Magazine*, republished in *Christian Times for a Changing World*, December 10, 1967, n.p., Reel 94, Collection 360, BGCA.

28. Joan Rattner Heilman, "Billy Graham's Daughter Answers His Critics," *Good Housekeeping*, June 1973, 156, Reel 107, Collection 360, BGCA.

29. See Coontz, *The Way We Never Were*, chap. 7; also Sara M. Evans, *Tidal Wave: How Women Changed America at Century's End* (New York: Free Press, 2003), esp. chap. 3, "The Golden Years."

30. Jo-Ann Price, "Who's Whose? Can You Match the Wives with Their Husbands?" *Christian Herald*, January 1970, 22–27, Reel 100, Collection 360, BGCA.

31. Viviane Peter, "Mrs. Billy Graham: Crusader's Wife," *Parade*, March 8, 1970, 7, Reel 100, Collection 360, BGCA. Emphasis added.

32. On the connection between women's pantsuits and expressing female agency, see, for instance, Jo Barraclough Paoletti, *Sex and Unisex: Fashion, Feminism, and the Sexual Revolution* (Bloomington: Indiana University Press, 2015); and Betty Luther Hillman, *Dressing for the Culture Wars: Style and the Politics of Self-Presentation in the 1960s and 1970s* (Lincoln: University of Nebraska Press, 2015).

33. Hallie Burnett, "The Two Sides of Mrs. Billy Graham," *Woman's Day*, December 1969, 53, Reel 100, Collection 360, BGCA.

34. Ibid., 88.

35. Billy Graham, "Jesus and the Liberated Woman," *Ladies' Home Journal*, December 1970, 40, 42, 44, 114, Reel 101, Collection 360, BGCA.

36. Billy Graham, *Peace with God* (New York: Doubleday, 1953). Future references to this first edition will be to B. Graham, *PWG*.

37. John Pollock, *Billy Graham: The Authorized Biography* (New York: McGraw-Hill, 1966), 102. Much appreciation to Mary Thornberry for giving me her late mother's copy of this book. Cf. George Burnham, "Graham Book, *Peace with God*, Puzzles Author Janet Baird," n.p., n.d. The ghost-writer appeared in a photograph with B. Graham and noted in the story how the book seemed to write itself. BGCA.

38. B. Graham, *PWG*, 8.

39. The copy of *Peace with God* that contains Ruth Graham's marginalia and handwritten notes, hereinafter cited as *PWG* (RBG), is in Folder 2, Box 2,Collection 15, BGCA. Archivist Bob Shuster made me aware of its existence, for which I am most grateful. *PWG* (1984) will denote the 1984 print edition of *Peace with God*.
    Something to note: some of Ruth's comments reflect more of her own devotional sensibilities exploring for the truth than those of an editor revising a manuscript. She conducted a ceaseless, serious quest for greater intimacy with God and greater freedom as a Christian.

40. As noted, I explore this lifelong poetic quest in " 'The Heavens are Telling': Nature and Scripture in Ruth Bell Graham's Poetry" (unpublished manuscript).

41. I indicate adopted changes in the notes by citing first the page in the 1953 edition and then the corresponding page in the 1984 edition; e.g. *PWG* (RBG), 44: "we shall find peace with ourselves and with God" becomes, after Ruth's suggestion to "reverse order," in *PWG* (1984), 43, "we shall find peace with God and with ourselves."

42. On patterns in women's responses to divine immanence, see Mary Farrell Bednarowski, "The Immanence of the Sacred: Women's Religious Thought Comes Down to Earth," in *The Religious Imagination of American Women* (Bloomington: Indiana University Press, 1999), 44–85.

43. Cornwell, *Ruth*, 104, uses this phrase to describe how Ruth felt after a 1946 episode in Belfast, during which Billy and partner Cliff Barrows insisted that their

wives remove all traces of makeup in order to avoid alienating the conservative Irish crowd.

44. I treat this topic at length in my forthcoming biography of Ruth Graham, so I will note here simply that the Montreat mountainside house that Ruth built, Little Piney Cove, appears to run counter to her preference for a fresh style. She had the home constructed using salvaged log cabins and fixtures she scoured from the surrounding mountain communities. The house emerged from a complex of motives—to recreate the cozy feel of her childhood home in China, to imitate the kind of creativity that her mother and father deployed in building and furnishing that home, to express what was indeed a fresh style—the rustic—in the mid-1950s, when architectural fashions ran to the sleek and space-age. Many of the mountain folk who sold Ruth logs or lanterns could not understand her desire for such old things; many of the craftsmen who worked on the house bridled at her repeated instructions to make their work look rustic.

45. *PWG* (RBG), 123; cf. *PWG* (1984), 126.

46. *PWG* (RBG), 176. In the 1984 edition, the paragraph has been deleted; *PWG* (1984), 181.

47. More typically, Ruth wrote poems about nature and its power to reveal God's power and Providence.

48. *PWG* (RBG), 45, appears again at 47. See *PWG* (1984), 47.

49. *PWG* (1984), 45.

50. *PWG* (RBG), 49.

51. *PWG* (RBG), 57; *PWG* (1984), 55.

52. *PWG* (1984), 62.

53. *PWG* (RBG), 70; cf. *PWG* (1984), 73.

54. *PWG* (RBG), 17.

55. *PWG* (RBG), 50; cf. *PWG* (1984), 50.

56. *PWG* (RBG), 60; *PWG* (1984), 58.

57. *PWG* (RBG), 63; *PWG* (1984), 61, 62, and again, with recommendations from Ruth for reading about demon possession and cults, at 64.

58. *PWG* (RBG), 77; cf. *PWG* (1984), 81.

59. *PWG* (RBG) 97; *PWG* (1984), 100.

60. *PWG* (RBG), 9; *PWG* (1984), 7.

61. PWG (RBG,) 9; *PWG* (1984), 7. Emphasis added.

62. Perhaps the best example is at *PWG* (RBG), 118, where the poet once again foregoes the effectiveness of a repeated "he demands . . . he demands . . . he demands" for the verbs noted. See *PWG* (1984), 122. Also *PWG* (RBG), 119.

63. For example, *PWG* (RBG), 7. Similarly, a statistic on the amount spent by Americans on "fortunetellers" in 1952 prompted another "update" note from Ruth; *PWG* (RBG), 16; in *PWG* (1984), 16, the two sentences about the statistic have been deleted. Other "update" notes in PWB (RBG), 16–17 (suicide statistic), appears in PWG (1984), 17, with new emphasis on teenage suicide but

less precise numbers; 19 (Satan described as "he of the cloven hoof"), in PWG (1984), 19, becomes a less literal "great deceiver"; 20 (helicopters and jets as marvels), in PWG (1984), 20, the space shuttle becomes the new marvel. Note that the book originally came out before the Apollo moon landing, and would be reissued during the early years of NASA's space shuttle program, which began flying in 1981. Several of Ruth's "updates" refer to space exploration, travel, and technology. See Henry C. Dethloff, "The Space Shuttle's First Flight: STS-1," accessed 22 September 2013, http://history.nasa.gov/SP-4219/Chapter12.html.

64. PWG (RBG), 27; see also 32; cf. PWG (1984), 32.

65. PWG (1984), 46; cf. PWG (RBG), 46.

66. PWG (RBG), 76; cf. PWG (1984), 80.

67. Peter, "Crusader's Wife," 7.

68. See, for instance, Cornwell, Ruth, 120.

69. Ibid., 126.

70. Ibid., 126.

71. Another "stage" that bears study is Ruth's work for many years as a Sunday school teacher at Montreat Presbyterian Church. Her class probably attracted hundreds of Montreat College students over the years.

72. "Mrs. Billy Graham: Lunching with 11,000," Christianity Today, October 24, 1969, 45, Reel 99, BGCA; the item reported that the "sit-down meal was the largest ever served under one roof west of the Mississippi." Date given in [Helen Kooiman?], "11,000 California Women Hear Mrs. Billy Graham," Christian Times, November 9, 1969, 12, Reel 99, BGCA. The Christian Times also detailed the grocery list for such a gathering: "540 pounds of kumquats, 1,400 pounds frozen melon balls, 500 pounds grapes, 750 pounds sliced peaches, 2,000 pounds cottage cheese, 16,000 strawberries, 900 gallons coffee and 50 gallons milk." The story also notes that Christian Times reporter Helen Kooiman sat at the head table with Mrs. Graham and Mrs. Reagan, as well as President Nixon's sister-in-law, Clara Lemke (Mrs. Donald) Nixon.

    See also "At Home with the Angels," Christianity Today, October 24, 1969, 40, Reel 99, BGCA.

73. Lael Morgan, "Mrs. Billy Graham Speaks Out," Washington Post, September 28, 1969, 136. ProQuest Historical Newspapers. William Martin, A Prophet with Honor: The Billy Graham Story (New York: William Morrow, 1993), 381–381, notes that Melvin Graham, Billy's brother, participated in a Graham crusade for the first time in Anaheim, an experience that led to more speaking engagements for him.

74. "11,000 California women."

75. "Bend a Little, Love a Lot," The Standard, November 3, 1969, 18, Reel 100, BGCA. Cf. this advice with the poem discussed above, SLF, 106, "Love / without clinging": "the heart will adjust / to being the heart, / not the forefront of life."

76. Christianity Today has this last item as part of a pre-luncheon press conference.

77. "11,000 California women."

78. "Bend a Little." Millie Dienert, wife of team member Fred Dienert, introduced her at this event.

79. Charla Haber Sear, "'Life Isn't Lonely with Christ in the Home,'" *Knoxville News-Sentinel*, May 22–31, 1970, 14, Reel 101, BGCA.

80. Burnett, "Two Sides," 88.

81. Martin, *Prophet with Honor*, 532; cf. Records of the 1983 International Conference for Itinerant Evangelists (Amsterdam 83).csv. Dave Foster, *Billy Graham, A Vision Imparted, Amsterdam 82: A Pictorial Report* (Minneapolis: World Wide Publications, 1984), also refers to this part of the conference as the "Wives' Program" (62).

82. "Ruth Graham's Message to Wives," in Hanspeter Nüesch, *Ruth and Billy Graham: The Legacy of a Couple* (Grand Rapids, MI: Baker, 2014), 359–363. He did not attend the program but obtained an audio recording of Ruth's comments.

83. Ibid., 360.

84. Ibid., 360.

85. Ibid., 361.

86. Ibid., 361.

87. Ibid., 361.

88. Ibid., 361.

89. Ibid., 362.

90. Foster, *Amsterdam 83*, 45.

91. Martin, *Prophet with Honor*, 539; see also Records of the International Conference for Itinerant Evangelists (Amsterdam '86)-Collection 560.csv.

92. Franklin Graham, *Rebel with a Cause, Finally Comfortable with Being Graham: An Autobiography* (Nashville: Thomas Nelson, 1995), details the sometimes meandering path he took to the leadership of Samaritan's Purse. Less well known, Ned has nevertheless acknowledged his own meanderings; Martin, *Prophet with Honor*, 599–600, summarizes these.

93. Nancy Gibbs and Michael Duffy, *The Preacher and the Presidents: Billy Graham in the White House* (New York: Center Street, 2007), 315–316, discusses the political one-upmanship that drove congressional Republicans to let "Republican Revolution" leader Gingrich rather than President Clinton award the medal to Graham; they do not mention Ruth's inclusion in the citation.

94. Video available at http://www.c-span.org/video/?71572-1/congressional-gold-medal. Two reports revealed that planners originally hoped to have Graham address a joint session of Congress, which no religious leader had ever done before; see Lucy Howard and Carla Koehl, "A Gold Medal for Graham," *Newsweek*, April 8, 1996, 6; and John W. Kennedy, "Politicians Pay Homage to America's preacher," *Christianity Today*, June 17, 1996, 65. See also the emphasis on Billy, to the exclusion of Ruth, in Roxanne Roberts, "A Host of Voices Lifted in Praise; Gala Caps a Day of Tributes to the Gospel of Billy Graham," *Washington Post*, May 3, 1996, D01; and Colman McCarthy, "For Services Rendered unto Caesar," *Washington Post*, May 21, 1996, C09, which excoriates Billy for quietism regarding racism and ignores Ruth completely.

95. The building appears on the reverse side of the medal presented to the Grahams and serves as the focus of the hospital's Gold Medal Endowment Fund, which helps pay healthcare costs of low-income rural children in the Asheville, NC, area. See http://www.missionfoundation.org/content/ruth-and-billy-graham.

96. Kennedy, "Politicians Pay Homage"; Gibbs and Duffy, *Preacher and the Presidents*, 315.

97. I first learned of this project from Gigi Graham; the book has never been published. Interview with Gigi Graham, June 3, 2014, Black Mountain, NC.

98. McCarthy, "For Services Rendered."

99. Gibbs and Duffy, *Preacher and the Presidents*, 345, 346. Laura Sessions Stepp, "A Family at Cross-Purposes: Billy Graham's Sons Argue over a Final Resting Place," *Washington Post*, December 13, 2006, A01. LexisNexis Academic. Katie Kalivoda provided indispensable research assistance on this topic.

100. Laura Sessions Stepp, "On Billy Graham: Live Web Chat," *Washington Post*, December 15, 2006, Liveonline (transcript).

101. Sessions Stepp, "Family at Cross-Purposes," A01.

102. Ibid., A01; Session Stepp, "On Billy Graham."

103. Sessions Stepp, "Family at Cross-Purposes," A01.

104. Ibid., A01.

105. Laura Sessions Stepp, e-mail to the author, 12 June 2014. Letters to the editor appeared in the *Charlotte Observer* after coverage of the story broke.

106. Sessions Stepp, "Family at Cross-Purposes," A01.

107. Indeed, the remains of Billie (Mrs. Cliff) Barrows were moved from the Cove to the Library's Memorial Garden in March 2009; see http://www.findagrave. com/cgi-bin/fg.cgi?page=gr&GRid=50547250. George Beverly Shea was buried there in April 2013; see http://billygraham.org/story/george-beverly-shea-laid-to-rest-in-angola-casket/.

108. Rosanna Greenstreet, "Weekend: Starters: Q&A: Patricia Cornwell," *The Guardian* (London), December 15, 2007, 10. Cornwell also indicated that her "most treasured possession" was "a bracelet that Ruth Graham wore," adding, "She died last June."

109. The story appears on a marker beside Ruth Bell Graham's grave.

110. The symbol also appears on Dr. Bell's grave marker.

111. The photograph appears to be a cropped version of a larger one that appears in *SLF*, 125; the couple was posing with none other than a somewhat stiff Richard Nixon. Incidentally, the poem on this page is one that Ruth wrote about Lyndon Johnson's funeral in 1973—the date even appears at the bottom of the page.

112. Referring to the American psychologist Joseph Jastrow's (1863–1944) famous duck-rabbit illustration, which is not an "illusion" that appears to be one thing while disguising its reality, but a "bistable," "ambiguous," or

"reversible" figure—two things coexisting but also excluding one another. See John F. Kihlstrom, "Joseph Jastrow and His Duck—Or Is It a Rabbit?," accessed 17 July 2013, http://ist-socrates.berkeley.edu/~kihlstrm/JastrowDuck. htm. My thanks to colleague Greta Munger for sharing her expertise in perceptual figures.

II

Complicated Innocence

A CASE STUDY OF THE BILLY GRAHAM IMAGE

Steven P. Miller

MARSHALL FRADY WENT looking for the soul of Billy Graham. Instead, the Graham biographer found a sailor named Billy Budd. The latter Billy appears in the epigraph of Frady's 1979 book, *Billy Graham: A Parable of American Righteousness*. Billy Budd is the title character of Herman Melville's classic tale of an impressed British sailor "hung at the yard-arm" for a single fatal blow to a scheming superior. With his "welkin eyes," Billy Budd is a symbol of ingenuous beauty. Like heaven itself, the strapping young sailor is a sight to behold. Yet he lives on earth—more specifically, at sea—where a celestial countenance can drive lesser men to "envy," "antipathy," and "disdain of innocence." Billy is hardly prepared to account for the machinations of the ship's master-at-arms, John Claggart. In "welkin-eyed" Billy's righteous repulsion at a false accusation of malfeasance, he fails to understand that the hanging noose relies on human timber.[1] In the end, he did not grasp the ways of the world.

What did Billy Budd, the sailor, share with Billy Graham, the evangelist, other than a nickname? For Marshall Frady, Graham was a modern-day Billy Budd—"the apotheosis of the American Innocence itself." In Frady's telling, his Billy Budd epiphany occurred immediately after his inaugural conversation with Graham. "I have to tell you, I've never gotten off of anyone I've ever met such a feeling of natural goodness—sheer elemental goodness," Frady quoted himself stating to a Graham aide on the drive down from the evangelist's mountainside home in Montreat, North

Carolina: "What a wickedness it would be to ever visit mischief on a soul like that."[2]

Frady's biography appeared at the close of a rare fragile moment in Graham's remarkable reign as an American icon. The Watergate scandal, and Graham's inability to distinguish the forest of presidential corruption from the trees of Richard Nixon's profanity, gave critics ample material. Soon, a new wave of politicized televangelists distorted popular perceptions of evangelical Christianity. Graham confided to Frady his fear of a "frame-up" that would leave the evangelist looking the part of Elmer Gantry. When the book appeared, Graham's appalled supporters surely noted the irony. In their eyes, Frady himself had framed the evangelist. Future biographers had to contend with the fallout, as Graham's personal papers remained largely off limits.[3]

The mid-1970s encounter between Graham and Frady produced a peculiar and problematic book. This was to be the grand biography of America's flagship evangelist. Instead, its five-hundred-plus pages came wrapped in metaphors and entangled in a literary experiment. Both Frady and Graham were products of the traditional evangelical South. However, their divergent responses to this shared background meant that they occupied contrasting places within the emerging New South. Their differences led to fundamental tensions within the biography. The assertive pushback against the book by the evangelist and his handlers suggested the high stakes surrounding the Graham image.

Frady may have authored a failed study, but it was also a telling one. The most consistent thing about Billy Graham has been his message of salvation. The second most consistent thing has been his popularity. Both continue to distract from the changing and contested nature of Graham's image. Scholars, pundits, and others with access to the published word have written Graham into roles that defied his self-conception. Graham always insisted that he was one thing—an evangelist—but his detractors and admirers alike have demonstrated that he was many other things, too. Ultimately, the meaning of Billy Graham cannot be separated from the stories that Marshall Frady and others have told about him. Graham proved to be an elusive subject even for a writer of Frady's talents, in no small part because of the latter's ambivalence about the former's contribution to the South they both shared and loved. Frady was not able to penetrate the apparent innocence of Graham, so he chose to make it the main theme of his book. Frady was onto something, and the theme he selected made his book significant. The evangelist and his welkin eyes have alternately charmed, frustrated, and befuddled those who have tried to elucidate him and his place in American society. Billy Graham is perhaps America's most complicated innocent.

When Marshall Met Billy

The Graham-Frady collaboration seemed incongruous in later years, but it made a little more sense in the mid-1970s. At that point, Graham still awaited a definitive biography. Countless journalists and a handful of scholars had treated him, first, as an emblem of the postwar religious revival, and, second, as an enabler of Richard Nixon's "silent majority." Frady wrote at the end of the latter, Nixon-centered wave of Graham analysis. Frady was a rising practitioner of the "new journalism," the catch-all term for the 1960s and 1970s vogue of long-form journalism marked by novelistic flourishes and self-reflexive authorship. He made his name as a *Newsweek* correspondent during the mid-1960s, and then gained renown for a lively, unconventional 1968 biography of Alabama governor and presidential aspirant George Wallace. Not yet forty when the Graham book appeared, Frady was at a transitional stage in a career that would culminate with turns in broadcast journalism and screenwriting. The Graham biography confirmed Frady's arrival as a professional writer; it netted him a $100,000 advance.[4]

Graham and Frady sprouted from similar southern soil, but they moved in quite different circles as adults. To be sure, Frady knew the evangelical South on a personal level. The son of a Southern Baptist minister, he grew up in small towns and cities throughout South Carolina and Georgia. His paternal ancestors hailed from western North Carolina, "that complex of religious compounds" where Frady recalled going to a Baptist gathering as a child. In 1948, at age eight, he even attended a Graham revival in Augusta, Georgia, one year before the young evangelist became a certifiable phenomenon. Frady's writerly interest in Graham began with a magazine assignment to cover the evangelist's 1973 crusade in Raleigh, North Carolina. The author soon commenced the tortuous task of finding face time with the perpetually busy Graham. Access arrived after Graham, an avid newspaper browser, took note of a *Charlotte Observer* profile of Frady. They first talked at Graham's home in the spring of 1976 and then conversed intermittently during his San Diego crusade later that year. The bulk of Frady's interview material came from "two marathon sessions over two separate days in Montreat, both of which lasted almost literally from breakfast straight through on past dusk." Meanwhile, Frady sought out Graham's family and relatives. Frady took care to keep Graham's chief gatekeeper, T. W. Wilson, in the loop. He joked with Wilson about rumors of the Graham aide's "right combustible temper—it seems you're coming into focus as sort of the Simon Peter of the whole operation." "I do hope to emerge from all this with my ears intact," Frady added.[5]

Southern charm aside, Frady was in many respects an unconventional choice to write a biography of someone like Graham, who was notoriously protective of his public image. For starters, their brands of Christianity were only marginally compatible. In a 1967 essay for the *Atlantic Monthly*, Frady criticized the white southern church, especially his own Southern Baptist Convention, for its "predominantly passive role" during the civil rights struggle. He called Graham "the South's folk preacher." Frady's identity as a writer derived from his abandonment of southern-style faith (although not, he insisted, the Christian faith as a whole). He juxtaposed his childhood conversion story with his decision as a teenager to walk out of his father's Wednesday evening prayer meeting. Frady's literary commitments likewise made for an awkward fit with the typical modes of biographical writing. In his first book after the Graham biography, Frady described the process by which one gets to "actually *experience*" subjects and "to feel you know them better than your own family, better even than you know yourself." Then the writing process begins. "No matter how intense your empathy with your subjects while you were with them, it is when you sit down at the typewriter that the real understandings take shape. . . . And your only loyalties at that point are to the important meanings in the story." Frady's writing amounted to what he termed an "odd unchurched coupling between the novel and journalism." Under the heavy influence of William Faulkner, Frady's prose style was a character unto itself. More sacrament than ornament, it was meant to house the truth. As such, the Graham biography constantly risked literary excess. (In one instance, Frady described Jell-O as "that chill translucent abstraction of fruit that had always been Billy's most passionately cherished of savors.") Frady believed that journalism had become the highest art form and that his "own errant star was to be that of a forestalled, unbegotten novelist left with journalism to do it all in." The Atlanta-based author wrote the biography during "two years of solitary confinement and high concentration in a Buckhead attic."[6]

The result was a book with a structure more like a screenplay than a traditional biography. Frady opened and closed with references to

Nixon, whom Frady believed resembled Billy Budd's nemesis. For both, in Melville's words, the appearance of "reason" was but an "implement for effecting the irrational." Frady wrote that his first talk with Graham occurred "over a year after Nixon's fall." The author then flashed back to Graham's youthful antics in the Carolina Piedmont and bumbling escapades as a young preacher overseas. Frady paid particular attention to early romances, including onetime fiancée Emily Cavanaugh. The writer was taken by the future evangelist's experience with jilted love, describing it to friends as "Graham's Gethsemane of the flesh." Frady also featured a previous girlfriend, Pauline Presson, whose teenage relationship with Billy did not survive his distinct but hardly unpredictable turn toward fundamentalist probity. Presson was "indisputably the transport of his life" for a few years. She "was just built for this world," in the memorable words of Graham's childhood friend and evangelistic associate Grady Wilson. Frady contrasted these spirited flourishes of desire with Graham's sober courtship of his future spouse, Ruth Bell, "a singularly ethereal and conscientious soul." A missionaries' kid turned "patient Penelope," she grew up in a compound in China and now passed her days in a "mountainside aerie." The upshot of such "pretty solitude" was unsettling: an insulated Billy and an isolated Ruth.[7]

Despite its obvious limits, Frady's book offered some insightful character analysis. It was not a full biography. Frady overlooked whole aspects of Graham's career, not least a global influence that extended well beyond his heady days as an innocent abroad. Still, by comparing Billy Frank, the Carolina flirt, with Billy Graham, the evangelist to the world, Frady briefly peeled back the sticker narrative of Graham's story. The author found past neighbors and associates who, while admiring of Graham, remained "vaguely mystified" by how slightly above average Billy became slightly below a saint. Frady had a gift for disarming approaches. He had learned how to pal around with George Wallace's unsavory entourage, and he knew how to finesse good Christian folks, too. His interview with Graham's mother went well, and Ruth even sent him poems to critique. On numerous occasions in the book, Frady allowed these and other outside voices to define the evangelist. While Frady was surprised at how close he got to Graham himself, he never quite received the candor he hoped to elicit. On one occasion, Frady quoted *Billy Budd* to Graham, wondering if it might shed light on Nixon. Graham, ever generous when fending off a curveball, exclaimed that the passage "sounds like it could have come right out of the Scriptures!"[8]

Graham and his associates did not care for the book, for understandable reasons. Billy Budd was not the only metaphor that Frady pushed to the fore. At times, Frady appeared unsure whether Graham was a holy innocent or an *Übermensch*. He kicked off the main text with a quotation from *Billy Budd*. Then, two pages into the prologue, he described the singing at the Raleigh crusade as having "a certain fugitive Nuremberg grandeur." Frady went on to summon that city's association with both authoritarian effervescence and postwar reckonings, alluding to a "Nuremberg mystique," "Wehrmacht Christianity," and "judgment at Nuremberg." At the very least, he was wary of large crowds.[9]

The biography received mostly positive reviews, sometimes even glowing ones, in prominent and prestigious publications. Many reviewers took advantage of the chance to get in their own shots at Graham—a fact that distressed Frady. Reviewers called Graham "a carny barker for God" and "perhaps the most remarkably contrived leader of our time—a hollow man stuffed with publicity." Another line of criticism departed from the conventional complaint that Graham's call for national repentance really amounted to a national blessing. Rather, argued journalist Tracy Early, Graham was an artful mimic man. "If America ever develops a better conscience," Early wrote, "Graham will be the first to pick it up on his radar and proclaim it, without compromise." On the other hand, *Christianity Today*, the flagship evangelical magazine that Graham had helped found more than two decades earlier, published an extended, collectively authored attack on Frady. The attempted riposte was "not solely in defense of Mr. Graham, but also in defense of evangelicalism" as a whole. More neutral reviewers generally liked the book, if not the loosely wound bundle of conceits that constituted Frady's writing style. Such "purple" prose was "a reminder that William Faulkner's influence on southern writing was not entirely benign," even if Frady's straining was "perhaps the result of a desperate effort to compensate for Graham's prosaicness." Many reviewers were as conflicted about the book as Frady was about Graham. They saw just how much Frady had struggled with his subject, yearning for a more reflective Graham. The author had "measured Graham against himself, and said, Why can't you ponder as I do? Why must you be 'God's own divine bumpkin?' How can you be so critical, yet still so self-deceived?"[10]

As several reviewers noted, Graham and his team did not keep their complaints to themselves. They beat most reviewers to the punch. Concerns surfaced even during the writing process. Graham's attorney for literary matters, the Manhattan-based Harriet Pilpel, was not someone to take lightly. Her well-known work for both the American Civil Liberties Union and the Planned Parenthood Federation made her a savvy choice on the part of Graham. With lawyers serving as intermediaries, Frady agreed to send Graham (and, eventually, numerous Graham associates) a draft manuscript. In Frady's telling, the formal response to the draft noted some minor factual concerns and complained about a vaguely eroticized description of Graham's preaching as "making love to whole multitudes." (In the passage in question, Frady was trying to capture a past Graham associate's understanding of what happens during an evangelistic service.) Meanwhile, a letter from Graham to Frady stated that the manuscript contained inaccuracies and, much more pointedly, recalled "how few notes" were taken during interviews. In a series of written exchanges, Frady tried to assure Graham that the book would not damage the evangelist's reputation. The controversy was enough to dissuade the *Atlantic Monthly* from running an excerpt, although one did appear in *Esquire*. Additional pushback came with the book's publication. The *Asheville Citizen* quoted Graham as suggesting that Frady had taken no notes at all.[11]

Frady was alternately incredulous and pensive in the face of such attacks. He surely had suspected that T. W. Wilson would not appreciate his take on Graham. In the book, Frady shook his head over the "polite, unflagging defensiveness" of Graham's handlers, "acute to the point of neurosis." He remained steadfastly mystified by the more sweeping charges, which clearly stung. "In short: *of course I took notes*," Frady declared in a fifteen-page letter sent to *Christianity Today* editor Kenneth Kantzer (The line did not surface in the four-paragraph version that the magazine printed). Frady had indeed taken copious notes, even though his application of them revealed a biographer who prioritized essence over precision. He came to at least some of his talks with Graham toting 117 pages of typed questions, often of a detailed nature, with ample space to scrawl responses, which he did. Many of the recorded anecdotes appear in the book, but often not precisely as transcribed. Frady apparently embellished quotations, if not the details themselves. Afterwards, Frady claimed that the whole experience had strengthened his Christian faith. Still, as Frye Gaillard of the *Charlotte Observer* suggested, Frady's highest loyalty was to his typewriter.[12]

Southern Crossings

Frady's self-pity and propensity for overreach overshadowed the question of why he was drawn to Graham in the first place. Frady had a genuinely divided mind about his subject. His ambivalence about Graham was rooted in a discomfort with what was becoming of the region that he and Graham called home. The biography appeared during a transitional moment for both the South and for the image of Graham. Frady's interpretation of one influenced his take on the other.

Frady saw his work as part of a conversation about the South. He became a southern writer as soon as he joined the Atlanta bureau of *Newsweek* toward the end of its run as a leader in civil rights coverage. He found himself thrown into the tense mid-1960s crest of the civil rights movement, traveling to cover Martin Luther King Jr. in Saint Augustine, Florida. Quickly, though, Frady moved from the "race beat" to the "Southern Literary Mafia." He owed his literary reputation to his southernness, a fact that made him aware of history as both a tragic burden and a precious commodity. Unlike many southern liberals of his generation, he never imagined that a new, better South might follow the violence at Birmingham and Selma. Yet he held on to the belief that there was something of lasting value that could be said about the South, even as the region's presumed authenticity was rapidly disappearing. Frady interviewed Graham in a Blue Ridge Mountain retreat and wrote the resulting biography in a thriving Sunbelt metropolis. Yet, quite curiously, he failed to finger the evangelist's role in the very kind of southern modernization that, in other forums, Frady so poignantly decried.[13]

Graham, in Frady's mind, was the product of a bygone South. This was a South that Frady believed he could remember, despite the fact that he had fled his father's prayer service at the same stage in life when Graham had answered Mordecai Ham's altar call. "[A]s the son of a Southern Baptist preacher in much the same religious barometrics that made up Graham's world," Frady wrote in the preface to the biography, "I felt in a way that I already knew him, in a sense that I'd known him all my life." Before discovering John Steinbeck and the *New Yorker*, Frady read "the same sort of books . . . that Billy grew up with." Graham's childhood in rural Mecklenburg County, Frady knew, predated the emergence of Charlotte as one of the South's "glassy metropolises." Rather, it was like the South Carolina and Georgia towns of his youth, "the South's outback . . . the old plain primeval South of roadside gas pumps and rusted R-C Cola signs and brief flat-roof main streets fragrant with popcorn and pretty perfume on dreamy mellow Saturday afternoons." In such places, "rigorous religious-ness was simply one of the natural elements, like heat or lightening, of the surroundings." Frady understood how much of the rural inland South—the "bland midlands" of Graham's upbringing or the "buzzard-floated emptiness" of Jimmy Carter's—resembled the austere prairie West, only with pine trees. Graham's South was "molten green," but not lush. It was more Mayberry than Charlotte, more Nebraska than Tara. Its prototypi-cal resident was Billy's younger brother Melvin, with his "hominy-plain face." Frady had made a conscious pivot from rank-and-file southerner to southern writer. Graham, by contrast, had made an improbably seamless progression from a "genial and lambently handsome but sturdily uncom-plicated country youth" to a modern proselytizer. Like Graham's onetime evangelistic partner Charles Templeton, whom Frady profiled extensively in the biography, Frady wondered that a man of Graham's accomplish-ments could remain so unchanged.[14]

What had changed Frady was the civil rights movement, and the same could not be said of Graham. "By lucky accident," Frady wrote, "like others of my colleagues during the civil rights movement in the Sixties, I hap-pened to be writing about the South at one of those climactic moments of truth when everything—past and present, inward and outward—suddenly glares into a resolution larger and more urgent than its ordinary aspect." It proved "the Damascus Road event in more lives than mine." Graham's relationship to the Movement was hardly comparable, even if the evan-gelist's racial moderation surprised Frady when he looked into it. In the biography, Frady ably demarcated the significance and limits of Graham's witness in the area of southern race relations. Graham's relatively early criticism of segregation was "without question his handsomest hour." Frady understood what it meant to grow up a segregationist. The evange-list's decision to hold desegregated crusades in the late Jim Crow South—a policy enforced on a consistent basis by 1954—thus was no small thing. Yet Frady also understood that such gestures were only indirectly related to the actual question of civil rights and who should have them. Despite Graham's generally friendly relationship with fellow southerner Martin Luther King Jr., the evangelist was quite removed from civil rights activ-ism and its "untidy affronts to the ethic of discipline and order." King and Graham both served as "the conscience of America," but King called for "a national New Birth" more meaningful than the evangelist's patriotic platitudes. Frady saw King as central to southern history in a way that

Graham could never be. The sacrifices of protesters in Birmingham and Selma made possible the successful presidential run of Jimmy Carter, who presented himself as a born-again agent of national redemption. "Without King," Frady wrote, "there would have been no Carter—it could only have been out of the kind of redeemed and regenerated South which King principally brought to pass that any serious presidential aspirant could have emerged." Carter represented "the South's whole incorporation at last into America Proper."[15]

Frady resisted seeing Graham's place in what he unflatteringly termed the "Brave New South." To Frady, Carter was a modernizer, while Graham hardly seemed modern at all. The evangelist's remote location in Montreat, North Carolina, deceived Frady, not unlike how the Billy Graham Evangelistic Association's longtime headquarters in Minneapolis distracted casual observers from the southern qualities of Graham himself. The novelist Walker Percy, another restless denizen of the New South, offered a contrasting contemporaneous image of the Montreat milieu. Percy's *The Second Coming*, which appeared in 1980, is set in the wealthier confines of western North Carolina. The protagonist, Will Barrett, lives in the golf enclave of Linwood (likely based on Highlands, not the real-life town of Linwood). That is, he lives "in the most Christian nation in the world, the U.S.A., in the most Christian part of that nation, the South, in the most Christian state in the South, North Carolina, in the most Christian town in North Carolina." This is not far from the site of a regular ecumenical gathering nicknamed "the Montreat mafia." Barrett spends his days "deep in the woods, socking little balls around the mountains, rattling ice in Tanqueray, riding $35,000 German cars, watching Billy Graham and the Steelers and M*A*S*H on [a] 45-inch Jap TV." His daughter Leslie is a born-again Christian with charismatic proclivities. She is intent on using the family fortune to support a "love-and-faith community." Barrett remains the bumbling lapsarian, a "once-born in a world of the twice-born." He watches Graham on television, but his daughter embodies what Frady called "that pandemic evangelical mystique over America," of which Graham was "the elder statesman."[16]

While Frady never fully made the connection, his reservations about the Graham phenomenon were of a piece with his critique of the contemporary South. For Frady, Seventies born-again chic and related trends signaled the end of southern history as such. With the close of the civil rights movement, the South ceased being, as Frady wrote elsewhere, "profoundly . . . like another country within the United States . . . wholly outside the general American sensibility of rationality and optimism." Frady idolized the regionally transformative role of King, his intended next subject for a biography. At the same time, in a 1975 *Newsweek* essay titled "Gone with the Wind," Frady lamented the loss of southern distinctiveness. His bittersweet tone betrayed more than a little romanticism. For so long, "the South lingered on as a civilization of villages." In the decades since World War II, though, "the South has been mightily laboring to mutate itself into a tinfoil-twinkly simulation of southern California." All that was left was the "dullness" of concrete and chain stores, humming a "comfortably monotone note of middle C." The South was being "trivialized." The result was a kind of "spiritual impoverishment," as the "tabernacle evangelists" of yore yielded to bumper stickers declaring, "PEOPLE OF DISTINCTION PREFER JESUS." This was a far cry from the gory "romance about the Cross," which Frady described as the central theme of his own Christian upbringing in the South. It was not a far cry from Graham's celebrity-centered brand of evangelism, even though readers were left to draw that conclusion for themselves.[17]

Nearly four-hundred pages into the biography, Frady dedicated an eighteen-page aside to profiling what one reviewer called his "alternative to Graham." Will D. Campbell, the Southern Baptist "free-form guerilla gospel minister," was also Frady's alternative hope for the South. Campbell represented, as Frady later wrote, "a last . . . possibility that the South still holds at least potentially, within its past and its folk character, its own native answer to what has lately been happening to it." Frady sought to evaluate Graham "against the nature and implications of Jesus' own ministry and message," but Campbell proved a more accessible standard. Campbell was best known for his unconventional work in the area of racial reconciliation. He had a remarkable story. He began his ministerial career as a classic white southern liberal (selectively pushing envelopes), evolved into a civil rights activist (helping to found the Southern Christian Leadership Conference), and then made a dramatic pivot amid the rise of Black Power (ministering to Klan members). He remained a favorite among southern creative types, including the Catholic Percy. Campbell's notion of grace figured sin and salvation as one garment; he took his Bible with a swig of Tennessee mash. As pithy as he was provocative, his mantra was, "We're all bastards, but God loves us anyway." In Campbell's mind, this was a far cry from Graham's brand of faith. In the early 1970s, Campbell and his editorial partner, James Y. Holloway, published "An Open Letter to Billy Graham" in which they charged their "Baptist brother" with being a "court prophet" in the Nixon White House. The editorial page of the *Charlotte Observer* soon cited the letter in a strongly worded piece accusing Graham of abetting Nixon's "Southern Strategy" of racially tinged appeals to disgruntled whites. The occasion was Charlotte's 1971 Billy Graham Day, the festivities of which included a Graham-Nixon motorcade and what Frady described as a "Belshazzarian" reception.[18]

The Nixon-Graham alliance weighed heavily on Frady's evaluation of Graham, to the point of distraction. Frady saw it as the most telling story about Graham. As such, he missed the place of Graham in numerous narratives that proved impervious to the evangelist's Nixon problem. For example, Graham's South did not end with the civil rights movement and the Southern Strategy. Rather, it became ground zero for new series of headlines with names like "Sunbelt," "Christian Right," and "Reagan Revolution." The traditionalist proclivities of Graham—what Frady called his "staggering obsession to transform and pasteurize the whole world . . . into a Sunday afternoon in Charlotte"—were actually also signs of the New South. Graham's innocence surely struck Frady as one of the evangelist's least southern characteristics. Yet if the New South ideal was anything, it was an attempt by a long-stained region to reclaim the American Dream. Graham was not just a postwar holdover, not just "the last hero of the old American righteousness." Much more than Frady could perceive, Graham was indicative of themes that would predominate in American culture for the next quarter century.[19]

Beyond Billy Budd

Ultimately, both Graham and Frady survived the biography—not that the evangelist's position was ever much in doubt. But Frady kept trying to make sense of the "niceness of righteousness" that he saw in Graham. In the 1990s, Frady circulated sketches of a movie script about the famous evangelist. There, Frady made more explicit the narrative arc of the much longer biography. The framing events of Graham's life are his two youthful romances and the crushing revelations of Watergate. In between, Graham "says farewell to the earth." Confronted with human evil in the form of his beloved President Nixon, Graham "survives by merely contracting further into the simple certitudes of his lifetime's message." In this respect, as Frady conceded in the final leg of his book, Graham was not really a Billy Budd, after all. By keeping his innocence, the evangelist escaped the noose of modernity. In Frady's imagination, Graham's emptiness was a world-shaped hole. While Frady wanted to see Graham as a tragic figure, the biographer's own writing demonstrated a similar imbalance between ambition and self-understanding. Frady was one of the few authors who spent personal time with Graham and then managed to distance himself from the internal logic of Graham's work. Rarely had such a likely critic gotten so close to the evangelist. What beguiled Frady was, in the words of one otherwise sympathetic reviewer, Graham's status as "a resistant object for Frady's intense contemplation." More than a decade later, the biographer Edmund Morris had a similar and much more public struggle to explain Ronald Reagan. Morris turned himself into a fictional character who then waxed speculative about Dutch. Frady's approach, while less eccentric, produced similarly mixed results.[20]

The image of Graham evolved in ways that Frady could not anticipate. *Billy Graham: A Parable of American Righteousness* stood as the definitive biography of Graham until the appearance of William Martin's more authoritative, reliable, and readable work in 1991. Graham's candid, if not especially revealing, 1997 autobiography further dated Frady's book. In the aftermath of Carter and in the age of Reagan, Graham-style evangelicalism could no longer plausibly be presented as cultural detritus. It was, as the futurist Jeremy Rifkin and others contended, a trend-line. Graham emerged as a comforting voice during the culture wars of the 1980s and 1990s. He contrasted favorably with Jerry Falwell, James Dobson, and other spokespersons for right-wing evangelical politics. In the decade between Frady's biography and Martin's, Graham went "from being a cold warrior and celebrant of capitalism to being a critic of the arms race and of the injustices of a market economy," as one admirer asserted in a letter to the *New York Times*. At the start of a new century, Graham was a national "source of unity."[21]

Both Billy Graham and Billy Graham's image thus came of age. To Frady, Watergate was the central conflict in Graham's life, the event that should have changed him but did not. Subsequent releases of the Nixon White House tapes were a reminder of the Graham that had preoccupied Frady.[22] To others, though, those tapes showed how far Graham had come. Indeed, a fundamental divide in interpretations of Graham has concerned the question of how much he really changed in the years after Frady's book appeared. There has been a tendency to see Graham as a kind of consensus figure who cracked the Iron Curtain, criticized the Christian Right, and said nice things about Bill and Hillary Clinton. Yet, for every clear point of difference between Graham and Falwell or Dobson, there were enough anecdotes involving Reagan, the two Bush presidents, and Mitt Romney to suggest that Graham's personal preferences bore a striking resemblance to the establishment wing of the Republican Party.

The elasticity of Graham's image is a testament to the simultaneity of continuity and change within any major historical figure. Graham can be seen as an emblematic actor in manifold narratives. As a historical subject, he has usually been "Billy Graham *and*—." For Frady, the most important *and* was the American myth of innocence, which Vietnam and Watergate had put on trial. As such, it is worth remembering how Graham appeared to a sympathetic skeptic back in the mid-1970s, before the Christian Right came along and made the evangelist look more moderate. The Graham-Frady encounter was a profound case of two southerners talking right past each other. Their miscommunication produced an enduring conceit: Graham's innocence and all that it has meant for his cause, his country, and our world.

Notes

1. Marshall Frady, *Billy Graham: A Parable of American Righteousness* (New York: Simon & Schuster, 2006 [1979]), 1. The version of *Billy Budd* that Frady used can be found in Herman Melville, *Billy Budd, Foretopeman*, 224–304 (quoted in 288, 257, 256, 257, 227), in *Billy Budd and Other* Stories (London: John Lehmann, 1951).
2. Frady, *Billy Graham*, 15, 11.
3. Ibid., 493.
4. Wolfgang Saxon, "Marshall Frady, 64, Journalist Who Wrote Wallace Biography," *New York Times*, March 11, 2004 (Lexis Nexis); Marshall Frady, *Wallace* (New York: Meridian Books, 1968); Steve Dougherty, "The Marshall Frady Show," *Atlanta Constitution*, June 5, 1979, 1B, 5B; David Halberstam, "Marshall Frady: A Son of the South," in Frady, *Billy Graham*, xiii-xxiii.
5. Marshall Frady, "Growing Up a Baptist," *Mademoiselle*, March 1970, 156, 225–229; Frady, *Billy Graham*, 54, vii, ix; Dougherty, "The Marshall Frady Show"; T. W. Wilson to Frady, April 19, 1974, Emory University Manuscript, Archives, and Rare Book Library (EUMARBL), Marshall Frady Papers (MFP), Box 18 (as of February 2013, this collection was unprocessed. Thus, only box numbers are listed here); Frye Gaillard, "In Search of Billy Graham," *Charlotte Observer*, April 29, 1979, EUMARBL, MFP, Box 23; Frady to Wilson, July 18, 1976, EUMARBL, MFP, Box 18.
6. Marshall Frady, "God and Man in the South," *Atlantic Monthly*, January 1967, 37–42; Frady, "Growing Up a Baptist"; Frady, *Southerners: A Journalist's Odyssey* (New York: New American Library, 1980), xxv, xxvi, xxvii, xxiv; Frady, *Billy Graham*, 109; Dougherty, "The Marshall Frady Show."

7. Frady, *Billy Graham*, 486, 8, 108–114, 74–77, 89–90, 100–105, 135–144, 148, 117, 347; Gaillard, "In Search of Billy Graham."

8. Frady, *Billy Graham*, 64, 486; Gaillard, "In Search of Billy Graham"; undated yellow notepad, EUMARBL, MFP, Box 23.

9. Frady, *Billy Graham*, 1, 4, 288, 405, 467.

10. Frady to Kenneth Kantzer, December 29, 1979, EUMARBL, MFP, Box 18; Bob Terrell, "Billy Graham: Frady Book Is Filled With Inaccuracies," *Asheville Citizen*, August 10, 1979; Bill McVicar, "A Carny Barker for God," *Toronto Star/Toronto Sun*, undated clipping; Robert Sherill, "The Magic Christian," *New York*, undated clipping; Tracy Early, review of books by Frady and John Pollock, *Worldview*, September 1979; "The Graham Image: A Parable of America's Blindness?," *Christianity Today*, November 16, 1979; Jonathan Yardley, review of *Billy Graham*, *Washington Star*, May 27, 1979; Michael Barton, review of *Billy Graham*, *USA Today*, May 1980; all in EUMARL, MFP, Box 23.

11. On Graham and Pilpel, see the content of Harriet F. Pilpel Papers, Schlesinger Library, Radcliffe Institute, Harvard University, Folder 50. On Pilpel, see Leigh Ann Wheeler, *How Sex Became a Civil Liberty* (New York: Oxford University Press, 2013), 94–96; Gaillard, "In Search of Billy Graham"; Frady to Kantzer, December 29, 1979; Frady, *Billy Graham*, 163; Frady, "The Use and Abuse of Billy Graham," *Esquire*, April 10, 1979, 25–44; Terrell, "Billy Graham: Frady Book Is Filled with Inaccuracies."

12. Frady, *Billy Graham*, 277; Frady to Kantzer, December 29, 1979; Frady, letter to the editor, *Christianity Today*, February 22, 1980, 8–9. I compared portions of the published version of Frady's manuscript with portions of the content in a folder titled "Graham—Interviews," EUMARBL, MFP, Box 18. Steve Hill, "Despite the Bitterness, Marshall Frady Says Billy Graham is 'Righteous,'" *Tampa Tribune*, June 16, 1979; Gaillard, "In Search of Billy Graham"; both in EUMARBL, MFP, Box 23.

13. Gene Roberts and Hank Klibanoff, *The Race Beat: The Press, The Civil Rights Struggle, and the Awakening of a Nation* (New York: Knopf, 2006), 377; Frady, *Martin Luther King, Jr.: A Life* (New York: Penguin, 2002), 2–3, 6–7; Dougherty, "The Marshall Frady Show"; Steven P. Miller, "Whither Southern Liberalism in the Post-Civil Rights Era? The Southern Regional Council and Its Peers, 1965–1972," *Georgia Historical Quarterly* 90, no. 4 (Winter 2006): 547–568.

14. Frady, *Billy Graham*, viii, 11, 45, 34, 13, 178–191; Dougherty, "The Marshall Frady Show"; Frady, "Growing Up a Baptist," 156; Frady, *Southerners*, xv, 338.

15. Frady, *Southerners*, xiv, xxiv, 326; Frady, *Billy Graham*, 407–416; Frady, "Why He's Not the Best," *New York Review of Books*, May 18, 1978 (nybooks.com).

16. Frady, *Southerners*, 355; Frady, *Billy Graham*, 489; Walker Percy, *The Second Coming* (New York: Ballantine, 1990 [1980]), 12, 124, 17, 115, 138. Georgann Eubanks, *Literary Trails of the North Carolina Mountains: A Guidebook* (Chapel Hill: University of North Carolina Press, 2007), 53.

17. Frady, *Martin Luther King, Jr.*, 1; Frady, "Gone with the Wind," *Newsweek*, July 28, 1975, 11; Frady, *Southerners*, xv; Dougherty, "The Marshall Frady Show."

18. Frady, *Billy Graham*, 374, x, 377–395, 461; Frady, *Southerners*, 285, 361; Barton, review of *Billy Graham*, *USA Today*, May 1980; Steven P. Miller, "From Politics to Reconciliation: *Katallagete*, Biblicism, and Southern Liberalism," *Journal of Southern Religion* 7 (2004), http://jsr.fsu.edu/Volume7/Millerarticle.htm; Miller, *Billy Graham and the Rise of the Republican South* (Philadelphia: University of Pennsylvania Press, 2009), 159–160, photo insert.

19. On the South and recent American history, see, for example, Matthew D. Lassiter, *The Silent Majority: Suburban Politics in the Sunbelt South* (Princeton, NJ: Princeton University Press, 2006); Daniel Kenneth Williams, "From the Pews to the Polls: The Formation of a Southern Christian Right" (PhD diss., Brown University, 2005); and Joseph Crespino, *In Search of Another Country: Mississippi and the Conservative Counterrevolution* (Princeton, NJ: Princeton University Press, 2007). Frady, *Billy Graham*, 318, 500.

20. Halberstam, "Marshall Frady," xxi; Frady, "Billy Graham" (screenplay summary faxed on 29 September 1998); see also "*STORY ELEMENTS FOR GRAHAM FILM*" (undated draft, likely from late 1990s); and *The Odyssey of Billy Graham* (undated, likely from late 1990s); all in EUMARBL, MFP, Box 23. Frady, *Billy Graham*, 491; Edmund Morris, *Dutch: A Memoir of Ronald* (New York: Random House, 1999); Elizabeth Hardwick, "The Portable Canterbury," *New York Review of Books*, August 16, 1979, nybooks.com.

21. William Martin, *A Prophet with Honor: The Billy Graham Story* (New York: William Morrow, 1991). Billy Graham, *Just As I Am: The Autobiography of Billy Graham* (New York: HarperCollins, 1997). Jeremy Rifkin with Ted Howard, *The Emerging Order: God in the Age of Scarcity* (New York: G. P. Putnam's Sons, 1979); Eugene McCarraher, letter to the *New York Times*, January 26, 1992, http://www.nytimes.com/1992/01/26/books/l-the-evolution-of-billy-graham-245292.html.

22. See, for example, John Boyle, "Nixon Tapes Detail Billy Graham's Encouragement," *Charlotte Observer*, August 24, 2013, http://www.charlotteobserver.com/2013/08/24/v-print/4260685/nixon-tapes-detail-billy-grahams.html.

Afterword

BILLY GRAHAM'S LEGACY

Margaret Bendroth

"SPLIT-SECOND SALVATION IS Promised All," the newspaper headlines ran in 1950, desperately seeking superlatives for the "outspoken wonder boy of American Evangelism," Billy Graham. Many more adjectives have piled up since then, as have the books, articles, and essays assessing Graham's impact on American evangelicalism and the wider realm of American culture. He was, after all, "The Man Who Won't Go Away," as a Roman Catholic admirer once described him, "an institution, an organization, a trademark," "a rallying point and spearhead," an enduring symbol of spiritual revival.[1]

No one has ever doubted his importance. Graham's penetrating gaze and platform cadences are known around the world; at last estimates, he evangelized over two billion people during his sixty-year career. But crusades and conversions are just the beginning point. Here was a man culturally nimble enough to stay in the public eye through all the tumultuous years of the late twentieth century. Yet Graham was more than simply famous. He remains an important and intriguing figure because of his "extraordinary agency," to use Grant Wacker's phrase. Billy Graham did not just reflect his times—he also changed them.[2]

Exactly what that means is a matter of debate. Despite the evangelist's durable popularity, his long-term impact, both on American evangelicalism and on American culture more generally, is surprisingly difficult to assess. Did he usher fundamentalism into a meaningful relationship with the world it hoped to save, opening the way for a vigorous and self-aware neo-evangelical movement? Or was he an "enabler" of evangelicalism's worst traits, a man with "a rather average moral imagination" complicit in a legacy of intellectual shallowness and moral opportunism? These are questions not just about Graham, but about the larger trajectory of evangelical religion in the decades since World War II—a narrative that is far from settled.[3]

Beyond all this is the possibility that the evangelist might not be remembered at all. In a Gallup poll conducted in 2007, only 30 percent of adults under thirty could even identify him, much less explain his importance. Ironically, the generational divide is most visible in the monument built to preserve his memory. Most of the visitors to the Billy Graham Library, which opened near his home in Charlotte, North Carolina, in 2007, arrive in buses from nursing homes and churches and shuffle the grounds on canes and walkers. "We're so thrilled when we see a group of kids on a school group come through," a tour guide confessed. For his part, Graham seemed intent on receding gracefully from the public spotlight. He was visibly uncomfortable at the library's opening ceremonies—not so much a library as an enormous devotional tribute to his storied career, housed in a theme-park-sized barn and silo complete with hay bales and a mooing mechanical cow. "'It was too much Billy Graham,'" he said.[4]

Another complexity is the nature of Graham's public persona, always more oblique than his strident platform rhetoric and vivid media profile seemed to imply. Unlike many other high-profile evangelicals, he never established a college, founded a church, or organized a nonprofit ministry. His institutional imprint rests almost solely in the Billy Graham Evangelistic Association (BGEA) and *Christianity Today*, the magazine of record for much of the evangelical reading public, which he helped found in 1957. This light footprint is not an accident. Like many evangelists before him, from George Whitefield and Charles Finney to Dwight Moody and Billy Sunday, Graham's overriding goal was winning converts. According to the thoroughly pragmatic ground rules of American revivalism, campaigns against social evils like slavery or intemperance or institutional racism were important, but they were always deemed secondary to the central aim of saving souls.[5]

Given the ambiguities of Graham's career, the persistent conversation about "what will happen next" is all the more telling. A one-time phenomenon does not leave a legacy worth analyzing, or achieve enough cultural traction to require a successor. Discussions about the "next Billy Graham" have been going on at least since the early 1980s, when he was in vigorous health and leaders of the Moral Majority were regular visitors to the Reagan White House. At the time a seamless transition seemed possible, with one of Graham's children appointed to take his ministry into the future. Over the next several decades, however, the conversation grew more difficult, tapping into nagging uncertainties about the future of the evangelical world Graham helped shape and about the long-term prospects for religion in American society.

Indeed, despite years of concerted opposition to homosexuality and gay marriage, feminism, and abortion, evangelicals are not winning the culture wars. In fact, survey after survey confirms that most Americans dislike "intense religiosity of any sort." "Even in the midst of high levels of religious belief and practice in American society," says the sociologist Mark Chaves, fewer and fewer believers are willing to claim their own faith as "uniquely true." As these percentages grow with each rising generation, realistic pessimism is definitely warranted. "Beyond the diversity created by people of different religions," Chaves concludes, "America now has a significant minority of people with no religion at all."[6] Add to this genuinely dire predictions about global warming and the threat of terrorism, now deeply woven into the daily lives of millions, and there are many good reasons why so many people are wondering what will happen next.

A Hard Act to Follow

Evangelicals do not choose their leaders lightly. They have always craved heroes, larger-than-life martyrs and missionaries, high-profile preachers and teachers. But upstanding morals, an unshakable faith, and even personal charisma have never been enough to inspire a genuine following. Indeed, it is one thing to be "quick with the quote," as the evangelical pundit Ted Olsen wrote in 2005, but something more to command the moral respect that inspires enthusiasm.[7] At bottom, perhaps, evangelicals want a prophet, someone with an intuitive grasp of the "signs of the times" and the rhetorical talent to make them look spiritually promising. This unique kind of charisma was the core of Graham's appeal in 1947, and, for good or ill, it has become the standard for judging his successors since then.

That summer William Bell Riley lay uneasily on his deathbed, an old fundamentalist warrior worrying about his own legacy. Some twenty years before, Riley had rallied the Christian troops into battle as the head of the World Christian Fundamentals Association, the organization behind the notorious Scopes Trial. Northern Baptists also knew him well. After forcing a schism in the denomination, he had built his own Baptist empire in the Upper Midwest, a network of Bible institutes and churches led by a cadre of loyal disciples, all graduates of the schools Riley had established. But the future of Riley's empire was by no means set. Fundamentalism was an unstable mix at best, with a constant tendency toward internal warfare, and each faction claiming to be theologically and spiritually purer than the rest.

A reluctant young Billy Graham sat at Riley's bedside. The dying patriarch had been pursuing him for some years now, after seeing the young evangelist on the platform at a Youth for Christ rally. As a summer thunderstorm raged overhead, Riley made his last altar call, declaring in no uncertain terms, "Billy, you are the man to succeed me." This was not an invitation—it was an order. Billy Graham was to be the next president of the Northwestern Schools. "You will be disobeying God if you don't," Riley warned him, promising a full accounting "at the judgment-seat of Christ."[8]

Graham took the Northwestern presidency, but only briefly. Both he and his supporters knew he was needed elsewhere. Indeed, what looked like a manipulative ploy by a bitter old man rang true in one respect: the fundamentalist world in 1947 was clearly ready for a new prophet. "After years of alienation," Joel Carpenter writes, "the fundamentalists, at least the more moderate and mannerly ones, were back." They found themselves in odd and unprecedented times, both promising and frightening. World events, from Cold War politics to the return of the Jews to Israel, seemed to be falling in line with fundamentalist readings of biblical prophecy, confirming the accuracy of predictions once scorned by liberal scholars and secularists. Even more encouraging were signs that the looming threat of atomic warfare was turning American hearts and minds to hear the gospel. With some astonishment, evangelicals began to prepare for a national revival. Well before Graham's first memorable crusade in Los Angeles, the spiritual infrastructure was already humming, a vigorous network of churches and parachurch organizations—the Gideons, the Christian Business Men's Committee, and the National Association of Evangelicals—offering prayers in unison.[9] Graham's evangelical supporters understood the moment: he was a new leader, anointed by God to bring the world to Christ. Graham did, too. Tellingly, he preached often from the Hebrew Scriptures, especially the books of Amos and Isaiah, not just quoting from them, says Carpenter, but "reenacting their message in contemporary context and idiom."[10]

Sixty years later, as Graham's career wound toward its conclusion, anointing had become a much more complicated business. No longer a beleaguered sect reveling in its unpopularity, evangelicalism was a multimillion-dollar network of megachurches and media figures, thoroughly in tune with American popular culture. Estimated at one-quarter of the American public, this unwieldy "nexus of fundamentalist-evangelical-Pentecostal-Baptist-conservative Protestant denominations"—Martin Marty's description in 2004—had gained "more media attention, more governmental access and influence, more popular cultural expression" than any other group in American society.[11] How could any one person represent, much less lead, this "quirky and vibrant mosaic"? As a sympathetic observer concluded, evangelicalism is "not a giant ship as much as a fleet of rowboats and boogie boards," all in pursuit of an "authentic personal experience with God."[12]

Yet even in the midst of prosperity, evangelicals united around one core conviction, that they were more hated and misunderstood than any other group in American society. It did not matter that study after study confirmed the opposite was true, that the average American had no particular grudge against "born again" believers. According to the sociologist Bradley Wright, "The feeling of being disliked and alienated has worked its way deep into the evangelical consciousness. We feel it deep in our bones." In fact, the best explanations of the movement's surprising success emphasize this dual self-image, as both "embattled and thriving." Evangelicalism is a faith of both the margins and the center.[13]

Within this dynamic setting, it is not surprising that Graham's heir emerged as such an important question. As uncertainties mounted, visible symbols of continuity, especially in public leadership, carried more weight than ever. But fear was not the only factor. The conversation about the next Billy Graham, like evangelicalism itself, is a blend of the movement's own contradictory impulses. It is a mixture of anxiety and optimism, deep-seated social conservatism and love for innovation, a long list of resentments about the past and an enthusiastic embrace of a limitless future.

From the very beginning of the discussions about Graham, the most obvious successors to his ministry were his children. Many high-profile evangelicals have turned thriving ministries over to their sons and, less frequently, their daughters, a practice providing the appearance, if not always the reality, of institutional stability. Keeping one generation's success within the family makes good sense in business as well as religion, but in an evangelical culture built around "family values," a smooth father-son transition is an important proof of spiritual sincerity and good parenting.

But the results are decidedly mixed. The shining example is Joel Osteen, who took over his father's Houston church in 1999, days after John Osteen had died of a heart attack. Under the younger Osteen's leadership, the Lakewood Church grew from a respectable 5,000 members to become the single largest American megachurch, with 43,500 attending weekly services and a worldwide presence through television programming and best-selling books. Counterexamples have been more numerous, however. Serious financial mismanagement led to the ouster of Richard Roberts from the presidency of Oral Roberts University, and Robert Schuller's children filed for bankruptcy after the celebrated Crystal Cathedral became an unwieldy and unsustainable burden. But the practice persists. Ironically, Oral Roberts said it best: "Success without a successor is failure."[14]

In fact, despite all the risks involved, nothing beats a returning prodigal. Perhaps this is why speculation about Franklin Graham, the son with the most dramatic story of wild ways and personal redemption, took root so early. Fond of dirt bikes, Scotch, and cigarettes, the youthful Franklin was a challenge to his parents, especially during his father's prolonged absences from home. As he admitted to an interviewer, "I gave my mother her gray hair." When Franklin was twenty-two years old, he finally had a decisive conversion experience, a long-awaited moment that did not necessarily dim his edgy style or his predilection for motorcycles and cowboy boots. Talk about an evangelistic career began in the early 1980s, when Franklin's subsequent ordination to the ministry marked his full return to God and to his family's graces. In an article in *People* magazine, however, he was quick to deny being "groomed" as a successor, declaring that "I believe God has called me to my own work" with Samaritan's Purse, the broad-based nondenominational Christian relief agency he took over in 1979. His achievements in that role certainly bore out his claim: Franklin was not only a successful executive, he was also a compassionate advocate for victims of HIV/AIDS, even bringing staunch social conservative politicians like Jesse Helms and William Frist to an international conference he organized.[15]

There were certainly other contenders among the Graham siblings, who were for their part reluctant to endorse Franklin. In the early 1980s, Anne Graham Lotz, one of Graham's three daughters, was already appearing in public events alongside her father, who described her as "the best preacher in the family." She was by then already a gifted speaker with many of the Graham pulpit mannerisms, and over the next several decades she became a nationally recognized figure as the author of some fourteen books and the host of a daily radio program airing on more than seven hundred stations. Lotz was not self-effacing about her public career either, describing herself as an "evangelical feminist," a "woman who knows what she believes, has strong convictions and the courage to stand up for them regardless of the glass ceilings or boundaries that other people may want to place upon us."[16]

Would evangelicals anoint a woman? There is ample historical prec-edent for female preachers and evangelists in the conservative Protestant world, going back more than two hundred years. But none of it amounts to a ringing endorsement; at best, evangelicals are solidly ambivalent about women in leadership. Lotz's own denomination, the Southern Baptist Convention, has made no bones about "male headship" and rarely ordains women—at one of her early denominational speaking engagements, eight hundred ministers literally stood up and turned their backs to her—but the biblical injunctions are only part of the problem. Within the tangled world of evangelical gender politics, where male and female roles are strictly complementary, a woman in charge is usually a sign of spiritual trouble. The most well-known example comes from the Promise Keepers, the evangelical men's movement popular in the 1990s, and Dallas pastor Tony Evans's call for men to "take their role back" from women, whom he said were "carrying responsibilities God never intended them to bear." "Don't misunderstand what I'm saying here," Evans declared. "I'm not suggesting that you ask for your role back, I'm urging you to take it back."[17] It is not surprising that Lotz has consistently described herself as a Bible teacher rather than a preacher, insisting she did not "feel called" to the national pulpit.[18]

In the end, as Franklin grew to look more and more like a fresh young image of his visibly aging father, inevitability prevailed. One signal moment came in 1995 at a crusade in Toronto, when the elder Graham collapsed with a bleeding colon. Though his hosts called a Canadian evangelist to step in, he insisted that Franklin preach in his place. Within months the BGEA officially named Franklin as its first vice chairman, the next in line when his father stepped down as chair and chief executive, which he did in 2001. The following year Franklin moved the BGEA from its Minneapolis headquarters closer to his home to Charlotte, North Carolina, signaling not only a final break with William Bell Riley, but also an intention to exercise far more direct leadership of the organization than his father had ever attempted or desired.[19]

Franklin quickly proved himself just as sensitive to the twenty-first century prophetic moment as his father had been in 1947—but these were far uglier times. His public agenda was already clear in 2001, when he gave the opening prayer at the inauguration of another redeemed prodigal taking on the family mantle, George W. Bush. Though Franklin was acting once again in place of his ailing father, he pointedly ignored the ecumenical courtesies of the occasion—rules that the elder Graham was adept in following—and prayed in "the name of Christ Jesus." The prayer was a deliberate rallying signal to the evangelical public, and in the months after 9/11, Franklin's rhetoric took on an increasingly provocative tone. In short order he published a best-selling book, *The Name*, defending his inaugural prayer as a countercultural act of courage. He also stoked a growing sense of persecution among evangelicals with warnings about the rise of Islam, "a very evil and wicked religion," a dangerous force, knowingly or unknowingly enabled by politically correct liberal sympathizers. "If I mention the name Muhammad," he told *Christianity Today*, "people go: Okay. You mention the name Buddha: Oh, that's nice. You mention the name of Jesus Christ, and it divides a room. People scowl."[20]

In deeply partisan times, Franklin walked a militant Tea Party Republican line. The elder Graham was no stranger to the political limelight, serving as a personal counselor to presidents from Dwight D. Eisenhower onward; but in the wake of the Nixon Watergate debacle, he learned to remain above the political fray. There was nothing oblique about Franklin, however, who fanned political passions by endorsing Sarah Palin and Mitt Romney, decrying the "war against Christmas," and hinting that Barack Obama was a secret Muslim and a Kenyan citizen. He also campaigned against gay marriage in North Carolina, most controversially by bringing his aging father to a rally and implying his support. "Supporters and critics of Franklin Graham agree on little except this," two journalists concluded in 2002, that "the man who now runs one of Christianity's most famous ministries is no Billy Graham."[21]

If Graham's children do not carry on his mission, then who might? For at least one segment of the evangelical public, the ideal successor would be as unlike Franklin as possible, a gentle, nonconfrontational leader without a political ax to grind. Graham was, after all, "America's pastor," more than just a public figure, a trusted spiritual friend to all kinds of people: presidents, business leaders, and the thousands of ordinary citizens who wrote letters addressed to him by name. The evangelical world certainly has no shortage of candidates for this role, nationally known clergymen with a warm and comfortable style, and a few have been nominated for pastor-in-chief. In 2004, *Christianity Today* gave its explicit endorsement to the Texas minister Max Lucado, the author of best-selling books with titles like *You Are Special, Just the Way You Are,* and *You'll Get through This.*[22]

But if anyone were to fill the role of America's pastor it would be Rick Warren, a California pastor/author with a more sharply defined public presence than Lucado, and an even more influential bestseller, *The Purpose-Driven Life.* Published in 2002, this simple, direct, and inspirational book had sold over thirty million copies by 2007, and it is the second most-translated book in the world after the Bible. By that time Warren was a regular on lists of "most influential people" and "top leaders," named by his ministerial peers the second most influential figure in American church life, right behind Graham. In 2005, *Time* magazine declared him "America's New People's Pastor." Warren is beyond doubt an international representative of evangelical Christianity, invited to speak at the United Nations, the World Economic Forum in Davos, Switzerland, and Harvard's Kennedy School of Government. During the 2008 election, Warren hosted presidential candidates John McCain and Barack Obama at a Civil Forum on the Presidency at his Saddleback Church. But, especially for well-connected white evangelicals, political confrontation has become the default mode, and staying clear of the culture wars has been difficult if not impossible. When Warren delivered the benediction at Obama's first inauguration, he was already a controversial figure mired in a public campaign against gay marriage legislation in California. He went on to oppose the Affordable Care Act, wading into the court battles over its provisions for birth control and abortion, and declaring the president "absolutely unfriendly to religion."[23]

But Warren was not the only possibility. When the *New York Times* published its own list of possible successors to the "national pulpit" in 1999, the most significant figures were Latino and African American. Though less familiar to the secular public, these candidates reflected both the new demographics and shifting theological center of modern evangelicalism.[24] One of the best known, in fact, was the Argentina native Luis Palau, a Graham convert who gave the traditional crusade model a crossover appeal to multiethnic audiences.[25] The Luis Palau Evangelistic Association (LPEA), formed in 1978, now holds "festivals" rather than stadium-style campaigns, family-oriented events with evangelistic speakers, popular

Christian bands, and extreme sports. "We began to realize," Palau explained, "that the classic campaign model—uniformed choir, the suits on the platform, the old hymns—wasn't the way to go for us."[26] In 2002 the LPEA formed a partnership with the Festival con Dios, an enormous road show featuring everything from motorcycle stunts and bungee jumping to contemporary Christian music. Though Palau is nearly as old as Graham and not likely to stay on the public stage much longer, he has forged connections with important new audiences that will play an important role in the future direction of American evangelicalism—about 16 percent of Latinos are evangelical Protestants, many of them recent immigrants, and the proportion is growing. As one Latino pastor put it, the evangelist's message of hope, hard work, and moral integrity helps "make sense of what for many is a hard and confusing life in the United States."[27]

If twenty-first-century evangelicalism is becoming less white and Anglo, it is also, like much of Christianity worldwide, becoming more Pentecostal. The evangelical mosaic today bears scant resemblance to the buttoned-down fundamentalism that gave rise to the neo-evangelical revival and to Graham's career in the 1940s and 1950s.[28] The new Pentecostalism, which Graham by his ecumenical example helped bring into the evangelical fold, is boldly supernatural, media savvy, and attuned in its own way to particular currents in American culture. There is no better example than the popularity of the "prosperity gospel" among Pentecostals, the teaching that God wants everyone to prosper, not just spiritually but materially. Not all Pentecostals, and not all evangelicals, are adherents, but the numbers are significant. A recent *Time* magazine poll found that 17 percent of American Christians identified themselves as believers in the prosperity gospel, with many more in agreement with its central tenet (over 40 percent in a recent Pew survey, including 75 percent of Latinos), that God rewards faithfulness with health and wealth.[29]

The leading advocate of the prosperity gospel—also high up on the *New York Times* list—is T. D. Jakes, the African American pastor of The Potter's House, one of the nation's largest megachurches, seating over thirty thousand worshipers every Sunday. Indeed, in 2001, *Time* magazine featured Jakes on the cover, under the caption, "Is this man the next Billy Graham?" Without doubt he is a formidable media presence, with best-selling books on timely topics like weight loss and healing from abuse. But would evangelicals anoint an African American? The black churches, about 10 percent of the whole, certainly share a deep affinity with the biblically based, conversion-oriented faith Graham represented.

But their relationship to white evangelicalism is a historically ambivalent one, given the movement's record of support for slavery and segregation and its indifference or opposition to the civil rights movement. The highly individualistic piety characteristic of American evangelicals is another hurdle, reducing structural social evils to spiritual ones, and contributing to sharp differences with black Protestants about racial inequality. By large margins, white evangelicals believe that the problem can be met by being neighborly and personally friendly across racial lines—not by demanding social justice or structural change. True, Jakes does have a theological problem—besides his identification with the prosperity gospel, he belongs to a "oneness" branch of Pentecostalism that emphasizes the importance of baptizing in "Jesus' name," and departs from traditional orthodox teaching on the Trinity. Yet, given the racial divide, Jakes would have difficulty becoming a consensus figure like Graham once was. He may well be "too black," as the *Time* magazine religion reporter David Van Biema observed, to represent the broader evangelical world.[30]

Indeed, if the "next Billy Graham" is to be black or brown, he will most likely not be an American. He will instead represent the vast and growing majority of Christians living in the Global South. " 'I fully expect major personalities to come forward from Christendom,' " Lonnie Allison, director of the Billy Graham Center at Wheaton College, told the *New York Times* in 2004, and " 'my hunch is they will be either Chinese, Korean, Nigerian or Brazilian.' "[31] For its part, the BGEA has publicly endorsed the possibility of a geographic "torch-passing." Advance publicity for "Amsterdam 2000," a gathering of over ten thousand evangelists from 190 countries, most from the Southern Hemisphere, used that exact phrase. The other even more telling one was "swan song," all the more significant when Graham's planned appearance was canceled because of another health crisis.[32]

Curtain Falling

Closer to home, however, many North American historians and journalists—and evangelicals themselves—are beginning to doubt that Graham will have any successor at all. And with good reason. Some of the problems are obvious: story after story of televangelist sex scandals and horrific revelations about sex abuse by Roman Catholic priests have made religious leaders deeply suspect across the general public. Only a quarter of respondents to a 2008 survey expressed much confidence in the clergy, ranking them well below military leaders, scientists, doctors, teachers, and even the US Supreme Court.[33]

The larger obstruction, however, has to do with belief itself, and the waning of the basic convictions that made Billy Graham–style revivalism such an enduring presence in American Christianity. The problem goes beyond the old model of "split-second salvation," itself an increasingly remote possibility in a culture accustomed to therapeutic language and personal journeys of self-discovery. Billy Graham's power came from his rock-bottom confidence that the evangelical message was true, that sinners were bound for hell and the saved for heaven. But now many evangelicals, not just their liberal and secular counterparts, are far less certain.

One especially telling moment came in 2011 with the publication of *Love Wins,* a small book by young megachurch pastor Rob Bell. In simple, accessible language, Bell posed evangelicalism's thorniest question: was Mahatma Gandhi, or any other righteous non-Christian for that matter, in hell? True, the Bible taught that salvation through Christ was the only way to salvation, but did an exemplary figure like Gandhi really deserve eternal punishment? The orthodox evangelical answer—"unfortunately, yes"—was not the only alternative, Bell argued. It rested not only on relatively thin biblical evidence, but also on a limited and self-contradictory view of God. God wants all people to be saved, he said, and "God gets what God wants."[34]

Bell was not the first Christian to question eternal damnation—intermittent speculation goes back to the early days of Christianity—but even before his book was released by HarperOne, conservative opponents were racing into battle, armed with the instantaneous tools of social media. When Justin Taylor, a blogger and editor at conservative Crossway Books, declared Bell far from "anything resembling biblical Christianity," his post received 250,000 hits and hundreds of responses. Southern Baptist Theological Seminary president Albert Mohler was no less adamant. "We have read this book before," he fired from his personal website. "This is just a reissue of the powerless message of theological liberalism." Baptist stalwart John Piper simply tweeted, "Farewell Rob Bell." Even mainstream critics took note. In a cover story for *Time* magazine ("What If There's No Hell?"), Jon Meacham generally agreed with Bell's critics, that his book "raise[s] doubts about the core of the Evangelical worldview." [35]

Intriguingly, many evangelicals did not seem unduly alarmed. Asked to comment on the Bell controversy, the North Park Theological Seminary professor Scott McKnight told the *New York Times* that most conservative

Christians "more or less believe that people of other faiths will go to heaven." Statistical evidence seemed to bear this out: though most evangelicals continued to profess belief in heaven and hell, they did not appear willing to follow their belief to its logical conclusion. In one popular survey, even when researchers asked the question as specifically as possible— "can non-Christians go to heaven"?—a majority said yes.[36]

Disputes are nothing new for evangelicals. If anything, the regular stream of debates about biblical inerrancy, women's ordination, and homosexuality have been a kind of lifeblood, defining and maintaining the boundaries of a movement rife with ambiguities. But this controversy was different, arising within an atmosphere of doubt about evangelicalism's viability in a postmodern and increasingly post-Christian American world. At the very least, the coalition that gathered around Graham in the 1940s and 1950s had passed, and along with it their entrepreneurial zeal and passionate certainty about national revival.[37] "Evangelicalism is constantly under the burden of re-inventing the wheel," as the theologian Stanley Hauerwas observed in a conversation with Albert Mohler, and at some point, "you just get tired."[38]

Many evangelicals, especially younger ones, are simply done arguing. "After ten years, I'm getting tired of trying to convince fellow Christians that I am, in fact, a Christian," Rachel Held Evans wrote in 2011, "even though I may vote a little differently than they vote, interpret the Bible differently than they interpret it, [and] engage with science a little differently than they engage with it. And I think a lot of other young evangelicals are growing weary of those arguments too."[39] The journalist Christine Wicker, author of *The Fall of the Evangelical Nation*, agreed. "Their politics have hurt them tremendously," she told an interviewer in 2008, "so much so that even the word evangelical is now in bad odor and many don't want to claim it."[40]

The 2015 Supreme Court ruling on gay marriage may be a last straw. *Obergefell v. Hodges* was, to many evangelicals, a decisive sign that conservative Christians would never win the battle for American culture. They would have no choice but to accept a society in which gay marriage was legal, along with a sexual ethic entirely at odds with evangelical morality on abortion and premarital abstinence. As one insider noted ruefully, "We've gone from being the home team to the away team." For some, this has been an occasion for mourning, for others, anger and denunciation, but there are also signs that evangelicals may be ready to adopt a quieter social presence. "Rather than lecturing the world," the journalists Michael Gerson and Peter Wehner wrote in *Christianity Today* in 2015, "we need to show a different and better way to live in the world." The next generation of evangelicals, they predicted, would do best as moral exiles, a minority working for change from within.[41]

It is probably too early to know what the ferment might mean in the long run. Is the next stage an "emerging church" or an entirely new paradigm in the history of Christianity? Is the present moment simply a pause before the next evangelical prophet ascends to the platform?[42] Paradigms shift less often than we think they do, however, and what some are calling the end of evangelicalism might in the end turn out to be an updated version of the old. Indeed, the next Billy Graham may be waiting in the wings, this time in skinny jeans and an ironic T-shirt.

But even if in fifty years no one knows who Graham was or why he was important, they will still feel his impact. Not just evangelicals, but Americans in general, will have inherited a complex legacy of spiritual certainties and missed opportunities, of ecumenical cooperation and narrow clannishness, of grand visions and pragmatic compromises. In all these ways and more, they will be living in a world he made possible.

Notes

1. Stanley Eames, "Graham Converts 300 More at Rally: Split-Second Salvation is Promised All," *Boston Herald* April 19, 1951, 1, 14; Charles W. Dullea, *A Catholic Looks at Billy Graham* (New York: Paulist Press, 1973), 3, 8.

2. Grant Wacker, *America's Pastor: Billy Graham and the Shaping of a Nation* (Cambridge, MA: Harvard University Press, 2014), 28, 29.

3. See, for example, David Hollinger's review of *America's Pastor* in the *Christian Century*, October 15, 2014, 36–38; and Molly Worthen, "Evangelical Boilerplate: Billy Graham's Innocuous Blend of Showmanship and Salvation," *The Nation*, February 4, 2015, www.thenation.com/article/evangelical-boilerplate.

4. Ken Garfield, "Billy Graham's Legacy Is Fading 'Into the Mists of History,'" *Religion News Service* October 1, 2013, ; Edward Rothstein, "At Billy Graham Library, Man and Message Are One and the Same," *New York Times*, November 10, 2007; Neela Bannerjee, "Accolades, Some Tearful, for a Preacher in His Twilight Years," *New York Times*, June 1, 2007; Ken Garfield, "Visitors Retrace Paths of Faith at Billy Graham Library," *New York Times*, March 8, 2008.

5. See, for example, Charles Hambrick-Stowe, *Charles G. Finne y and the Spirit of American Evangelicalism* (Grand Rapids, MI: Eerdmans, 1996).

6. Mark Chaves, *American Religion: Contemporary Trends* (Princeton, NJ: Princeton University Press, 2011), 38, 11, 21. See also Robert D. Putnam and David E. Campbell, *American Grace: How Religion Divides and Unites Us* (New York: Simon & Schuster, 2010), 1–23.

7. Ted Olsen, "Who's Driving This Thing?" *Christianity Today*, February 21, 2005, 76, http://www.christianitytoday.com/ct/2005/februaryweb-only/12.0c.html.

8. William Vance Trollinger, *God's Empire: William Bell Riley and Midwestern Fundamentalism* (Madison: University of Wisconsin Press, 1990), 151–154; Joel Carpenter, *Revive Us Again: The Reawakening of American Fundamentalism* (New York: Oxford University Press, 1997), 219–220.

9. Matthew Sutton, *American Apocalypse: A History of Modern Evangelicalism* (Cambridge, MA: Harvard University Press, 2014), 293–303; Carpenter, *Revive Us Again*, 231. See also Andrew S. Finstuen, *Original Sin and Everyday Protestants: The Theology of Reinhold Niebuhr, Billy Graham, and Paul Tillich in an Age of Anxiety* (Chapel Hill: University of North Carolina Press, 2009), 129.

10. Carpenter, *Revive Us Again*, 212–231.

11. Martin Marty, "At the Crossroads," *Christianity Today*, February 1, 2004, 38.

12. Randall Vander Mey quoted in Philip Yancy, "A Quirky and Vibrant Mosaic," *Christianity Today*, June 3, 2005, 37–39.

13. Bradley R. E. Wright, "They Like You: What Americans Really Think about Evangelicals, and Why We Don't Believe It," *Christianity Today*, August 2011, 22; Christian Smith, *American Evangelicalism: Embattled and Thriving* (Chicago: University of Chicago Press, 1998).

14. David Edwin Harrell Jr., *Oral Roberts: An American Life* (New York: Harper & Row, 1985), 491.

15. Leila C. Albrecht and Rick Lanning, "Billy Graham Has a Son, If Not a Successor, at Work in the Fields of the Lord," *People*, January 25, 1982, in Scrapbook 38, Collection 360, Billy Graham Center Archives (BGCA); Billy Graham Chooses Son as Likely Successor," *New York Times*, November 9, 1995; Gustav Niebuhr, "A Onetime Rebel is Handed a Cause as Likely Successor to Billy Graham," *New York Times*, November 26, 1995; "Christians Called to Wage War on AIDS: Billy Graham's Son to Host Conference," *Cincinnati Inquirer*, February 21, 2002, in Scrapbook 962, Collection 360, BGCA.

16. Lisa Miller, "The Fight over Billy Graham's Legacy," *Newsweek*, May 5, 2011; Gustav Niebuhr and Laurie Goodstein, "The Preachers: A Special Report; New Wave of Evangelists Vying for National Pulpit," *New York Times*, January 1, 1999; "Taking the Reins of Billy Graham's Legacy," NPR Interview with Anne Graham Lotz, October 10, 2011, http://www.npr.org/2011/10/10/141215977/billy-grahams-daughter-takes-the-reins-of-his-legacy.

17. Tony Evans, "Spiritual Purity," in *Seven Promises of a Promise Keeper* (Colorado Springs: Focus on the Family Publishing, 1994), 74.

18. Anne Graham Lotz, "Jesus Calls Women to Serve and Lead," OnFaith, http://www.faithstreet.com/onfaith/2008/09/17/jesus-calls-women-to-serve-and/4015. On gender politics see Sally Gallagher, *Evangelical Identity and Gendered Family Life* (New Brunswick, NJ: Rutgers University Press, 2003); on Southern

Baptists, see Elizabeth Flowers, *Into the Pulpit: Southern Baptist Women and Power since World War II* (Chapel Hill: University of North Carolina Press, 2012).

19. Richard Ostling, "Franklin Graham's Era Has Begun," *Gastonia Gazette*, January 12, 2002, in Scrapbook 962, Collection 360, BGCA).

20. "Jesus Freak," *Christianity Today*, November 18, 2002, 58.

21. Adam Bell and Ken Garfield, "Charting Own Path, with No Apologies," *Charlotte Observer*, January 20, 2002, in Scrapbook 962, Collection 360, BGCA.

22. Cindy Crosby, "America's Pastor," *Christianity Today*, March 1, 2004, 63.

23. "About Rick Warren," accessed January 3, 2017, http://pastorrick.com/about; "Rick Warren," *Time*, February 7, 2005.

24. Niebuhr and Goodstein, "The Preachers."

25. On festival crusades, see "Beach Blanket Rebirth," *Christianity Today*, February 1, 2003, 25; "Evangelistic Circus in a Box," *Christianity Today*, February 7, 2002, 18.

26. Luis Palau Association, "History," accessed January 9, 2015, http://www.palau.org/about/history/item/lpa-history.

27. Blaine Harden, "Hispanic Evangelicals Flock to Hear a Force in Their Faith," *New York Times*, September 5, 2000. On demographics, see http://www.pewforum.org/topics/hispaniclatino-demographics.

28. Figures vary, but the numbers are impressive. A study conducted in the 1980s found nine million American Pentecostals and charismatics; another in 2000 put the number at eleven million. See "Church Growth," in *Dictionary of Pentecostal and Charismatic Movements*, ed. Stanley M. Burgess and Gary B. McGee (Grand Rapids, MI: Regency Reference Library/Zondervan, 1988), 181–195; "Appendix," in Grant Wacker, *Heaven Below: Early Pentecostalism and American Culture* (Cambridge, MA: Harvard University Press, 2001), 271–272.

29. On Graham's role regarding Pentecostals, see Harvey Cox, "The Lasting Imprint of Billy Graham," in *The Legacy of Billy Graham: Critical Reflections on America's Greatest Evangelist*, ed. Michael G. Long (Louisville: WJKP 2008), 223. On statistics, see Kate Bowler, *Blessed: A History of the American Prosperity Gospel* (New York: Oxford University Press, 2013), 6.

30. The primary work on this subject is Michael O. Emerson and Christian Smith, *Divided by Faith: Evangelical Religion and the Problem of Race in America* (New York: Oxford University Press, 2000); see also the helpful summary in Barry Hankins, *American Evangelicals: A Contemporary History of a Mainstream Religious Movement* (Lanham, MD: Rowman and Littlefield, 2008), 122–131. On the elder Graham's own record, see Steven P. Miller, *Billy Graham and the Rise of the Republican South* (Philadelphia: University of Pennsylvania Press, 2009), 59, 123.

31. "Billy Graham, A Hard Act to Follow," *New York Times*, June 26, 2005.

32. Gustav Niebuhr, "At Conference, Billy Graham's Torch Moves South," *New York Times*, July 30, 2000; "Is Amsterdam 2000 Graham's 'Swan Song'?" *Christianity Today*, July 10, 2000, 28.

33. Chaves, *American Religion*, 75–79.

34. Rob Bell, *Love Wins: A Book about Heaven, Hell, and the Fate of Every Person Who Ever Lived* (New York: HarperOne, 2011), 1–2. See also Kelefa Sanneh, "The Hell-Raiser: A Megachurch Pastor's Search for a More Forgiving Faith," *New Yorker*, November 26, 2012.

35. Justin Taylor, "Rob Bell: Universalist?," *The Gospel Coalition* (blog), http://thegospelcoalition.org/blogs/justintaylor/2011/02/26/rob-bell-universalist/; Albert Mohler, "We Have Seen All This Before: Rob Bell and the (Re)Emergence of Liberal Theology," March 16, 2011, www.albertmohler.com; Lauren F. Winner, "An Evangelical Pastor Opens the Gates of Heaven," *New York Times*, April 22, 2011. The previous discussion was as recent as 2000 and equally strident, with the published debate between a liberal Anglican and the well-known evangelical John Stott, in which Stott opted for the argument that the dead are simply annihilated (annihilationism) and do not face torment. See Robert A. Peterson, "Undying Worm: Unquenchable Fire," *Christianity Today*, October 23, 2000, http://www.christianitytoday.com/ct/2000/october23/1.30.html.

36. Erik Eckholm, "Pastor Stirs Wrath with His Views on Old Questions," *New York Times*, March 4, 2011; Jon Meacham, "Is Hell Dead?" *Time*, April 14, 2011. See also Putnam and Campbell, *American Grace*, 534–540.

37. According to recent data, evangelical numbers are no longer keeping pace with population growth. Some groups, including most notably Southern Baptists, have reported actual decline. See http://www.bpnews.net/44914/sbc-reports-more-churches-fewer-people.

38. Albert Mohler, "Nearing the End: A Conversation with Theologian Stanley Hauerwas," April 28, 2014, www.albertmohler.com.

39. Rachel Held Evans, "The Future of Evangelicalism: A Twenty-Something's Perspective," March 24, 2011, http://rachelheldevans.com/blog/future-of-evangelicalism.

40. "Interview with Christine Wicker, Author of *The Fall of the Evangelical Nation*," *Patheos* (blog), June 4, 2008, http://www.patheos.com/blogs/friendlyatheist/2008/06/04/interview-with-christine-wicker-author-of-the-fall-of-the-evangelical-nation. See also Christine Wicker, *The Fall of the Evangelical Nation: The Surprising Crisis within the Church* (San Francisco: HarperOne, 2008).

41. Michael Gerson and Peter Wehner, "The Power of Our Weakness," *Christianity Today*, November 2015, 46.

42. James Bielo, *Emerging Evangelicals: Faith, Modernity, and the Desire for Authenticity* (New York: New York University Press, 2011), 8.

Epilogue

WHAT NOW?

Ken Garfield

BILLY GRAHAM'S LEGACY fills the pages of this book, as well as the hearts of millions of Christians whose lives were turned around or touched in some way by his simple call to salvation. While a growing number of people under the age of about forty answer "Billy Who?" when asked to identify Graham, there can be no doubt that the lessons of his half-century of evangelism will endure. For goodness sake, this lanky farm boy from Charlotte, North Carolina, grew up to preach in person to 215 million people around the world, and who knows how many millions more via TV, radio, and the Internet. He built and maintained a ministry largely unsullied by scandal, one that harnessed the power of the media and technology and blended spirituality and spectacle better than any other. He admitted his faults, rare in the realm of evangelists, confessing to having gotten too close to conservative politics and presidents, most notably Richard Nixon. With the advance of age, his message became gentler as he began to fade from public life after his last crusade in 2005 in New York. Perhaps because of his softer tone, and his obvious physical struggles to stand up and preach at the end, he seemed to connect with a broader audience. Once fiery, frail at the end, Graham inspired a deepening tenderness. More than anything, Billy Graham convinced an untold number of broken souls in every corner of this challenging world that second chances are possible. As a result, Billy Graham will undoubtedly resonate through the ages.

That last Graham crusade came in 2005, however. The ministry has long been in the hands of his controversial son, Franklin Graham, who is likely be followed by his son, Will Graham, and who can say after that. What does the future hold for the organization that bears the name of the father (and grandfather)? Can it continue to command Christendom's attention and dollars as Billy Graham's older followers pass away and some of the younger ones perhaps turn away from Franklin Graham's fiery partisanship on matters of politics and culture? Even more broadly, what is the future of mass evangelism? In this age of declining interest in organized religion, can one man (or woman) rise above humanity's angst to give hope to the lost and, while he or she is at it, fill stadiums and raise enough money to pay for it all?

With these essays on Billy Graham's life and work fresh in our minds, we close by venturing into the future, asking three questions whose answers are far from definitive.

Will Billy Graham's Legacy Endure?

This is probably the easiest one to address. Larry Eskridge, American religion historian and author of God's Forever Family: The Jesus People Movement in America, makes a good point when he says evangelical Christians today tend to worship at the "Church of What's Happening Now." His point applies on a broader level, for ours, like never before, is a culture with a short attention span and far more options for our time than ever before. That holds true in the realm of religion, where we seem to lift up a Joel Osteen or T. D. Jakes for a season of sold-out followings and best-selling books before turning the spotlight on someone else the next season.

But Graham, even in this atmosphere of inattentiveness and spiritual fads, will endure on every level we can think of: In works like this one; in the thirty-plus books that he wrote; and in classes of all kinds that will study him for generations to come in schools, colleges, churches, and beyond. We will flock to the Billy Graham Library in his native Charlotte, North Carolina—more than 1.1 million visitors since it opened in 2007—to see old crusade clips and reminisce. Students writing their theses on most any dimension of modern American religion will pore over research material at the Billy Graham Center at Wheaton College. Historians and preachers wanting to see how it's done will linger over old clips on YouTube and elsewhere, transfixed as Graham electrifies the masses. Want to smile nostalgically? Google Billy Graham and Woody Allen and enjoy their 1969 TV interview that will endure on the Internet, a timeless illustration of faith, doubt, grace, and whimsy.

Death will claim some of Graham's most ardent followers. Time will dim the memory of others. But his name will endure in religious history, and in the public consciousness beyond the faith realm. Leaders from all movements will seek to learn the lessons Graham leaves behind—of building an honest ministry, reaching people across multiple platforms, blending faith and entertainment, and holding fast to the same message. And evangelical Christians will hand down from one generation to the next the story of the man who brought their particular blend of belief and emotion into the mainstream of American life. Even people of other faiths or no faiths—mention the name Billy Graham and they will see in their mind's eye the lanky silver-haired preacher, and hear again the Southern drawl that swayed millions.

Dr. Jim Goff, who teaches American church history at Appalachian State University in Boone, North Carolina, puts it this way: "He became the person who allowed America to become comfortable with evangelicalism." That is part of a legacy too powerful to fade, even with time.

What about Franklin Graham?

This is the question I am asked most frequently, and it is the most complicated to answer in terms of his impact on the future of the ministry, and indeed on his father's legacy. Since taking over as CEO of the Billy Graham Evangelistic Association in 2000, Billy and Ruth Graham's once wild child of a son has rebranded the BGEA in his unabashedly conservative, combative image.

Franklin Graham's father admitted getting too close to politics, and he sought to move away from partisanship in the later years of his public life. In contrast, Franklin Graham charges right in. His early and unrelenting condemnation of Islam, his attacks on homosexual practice, his support of conservative candidates and his more recent allegiance to President Trump—all of it has pushed the BGEA to the right in the public's consciousness. Indeed, the older among us may most immediately identify Franklin Graham with his humanitarian work with Samaritan's Purse, and the Operation Christmas shoeboxes sent to needy children all over the world. At one point, he partnered with rock star Bono to raise the world's consciousness around HIV-AIDS. But those in their 30s, and certainly younger, will largely know Graham first from his political outbursts in favor of conservative causes; his praying in Jesus' name (repugnant to a more moderate constituency) at President Trump's inauguration; his telling a Trump "Thank You" rally in Alabama that the President-elect's victory was God answering the prayers of hundreds of thousands of people. Today, to many, Franklin Graham is more a culture warrior than a theological figure, one with 5.2 million followers following his partisan posts on Facebook.

Can people see through the political fog that Franklin Graham has created to clearly see his father's very different legacy?

No one can say.

It's not just Franklin Graham's stances that have cast the Graham name in a new light. The aggressive lengths to which Franklin Graham goes to make his point make him a lightning rod to many. Before the 2012 election, for example, an ad campaign by the BGEA featured a photo of a young Billy Graham and a call to elect candidates with biblical values—meaning those who oppose abortion and homosexuality. Given the elder Graham's frail health and remorse over past partisanship, Franklin Graham was compelled to deny that he put his father up to this. "Nobody kidnaps my Daddy," he told the *Charlotte Observer.* Then there was the ninety-fifth birthday party for Billy Graham in Asheville, North Carolina— a dinner that drew a ballroom full of old ministry friends, mixed in with the conservative leaders Rupert Murdoch, Donald Trump, and Sarah Palin. Franklin Graham used the occasion to call right-leaning Fox News, which had the exclusive on the festivities, the world's greatest news channel. And his attacks on gay marriage are unrelenting. In a video interview in March of 2014 with the *Observer's* Tim Funk and Todd Sumlin, he claimed that adopting children is part of a "gay lesbian agenda."

Even those who would agree with Franklin Graham can appreciate that this is language that inflames rather than unites. Franklin says he's only preaching what's in the Bible, and he reminds his critics that his father railed against communism in his younger days. "He's been active in politics since the 1940s," Franklin has said. "People need to remember that." If gays can get involved in politics, he asks, why can't Christians?

Goff, the Appalachian State professor who lives about a mile from Franklin Graham in Boone, North Carolina, doesn't buy the argument that the son is politicizing the father's ministry, or that he's a firebrand. "When I see him and hear him," Goff says, "I think to myself that it's mainstream, evangelical thought. I've met him behind the scenes. He's really a pretty nice guy." Goff says that being an evangelical in the twenty-first century, and running counter to so much of the modern cultural standards, is by its nature controversial. He echoes Franklin Graham's reminder that Billy

Graham was just as fiery in his younger days, railing against communism and the secular culture in that rat-tat-tat preaching style of his. He says all this talk about Franklin's conservative politics tends to overshadow the good he has done through his Samaritan's Purse ministry and now the BGEA, reaching out to those rocked by tsunamis, earthquakes and the like. "Who's on the ground first? It's almost like people forget that about him."

Eskridge is among those with a different perspective. Billy Graham, he says, focused on the greater good, seeking to save souls for Christ and build up the church universal one altar call at a time, in a spirit of hoped-for unity. Indeed, in an article in *Christian Century* magazine in 1960, Billy Graham wrote about the need for Christians to disagree agreeably, that "what is most needed in the church today is for us to show an unbelieving world that we love one another." Franklin Graham seems to be working to prove that he is on the right side (no pun intended) of the battles he fights, Eskridge says. The father seemed more at home inviting those on the last row of the stadiums to come and commit your life to Christ, we will wait for you as the mass choir sang that gentle anthem of invitation, "Just As I Am." The son rails against Muslims and President Obama, and takes the stage at his father's ninety-fifth birthday party and sings instead the praises of Fox News.

There is another more practical question raised by the way Franklin Graham is running the family ministry: How will it impact fundraising and the financial viability of the BGEA? Goff says raising money is difficult for any and all evangelists, given the cynicism that the industry inspires, and some might say earned. "That's a part of the (Jim) Bakker legacy you'll never get back," he says, referring to the PTL sex-and-money scandal of the 1980s.

The BGEA under Franklin Graham has been forced to lay off employees over the years to reduce the budget. The ministry has acknowledged that many of its older Billy Graham supporters have passed away, and it's not at all clear that their sons and daughters and others of a younger generation will take their place as loyal givers. Billy Graham biographer William Martin told me for a piece in *Christian Century* that Franklin Graham may have trouble holding onto the support of mainline Protestants because of his partisan brand.

To his credit, the BGEA under Franklin Graham, and perhaps Will Graham to follow, is harnessing the power of technology to spread the gospel and raise money. The BGEA website is full of bells and whistles. Franklin Graham has mastered the use of Facebook and other social media platforms to continually push out his partisan views. Such is the nature of our never-ending hunger for something new and different online these days that Franklin Graham generated headlines with his post about going to a vegetable-dominated diet. And it's all done with the quality demanded by twenty-first-century consumers. The production values of BGEA videos are first-class—indeed, Billy Graham's last official ministry appearance was not at a crusade but in a slickly produced *My Hope* video. Franklin Graham's live events exude the same sophisticated production values, because the BGEA knows that to win souls they first have to win their attention. When I speak to groups about all this, I tell them that if Billy Graham was still preaching, he'd probably be tweeting. "Every communications device the secular world uses, I'm going to use it, too," Franklin Graham told me for my *Christian Century* piece.

But no matter how sophisticated the means of communication, the questions persist: If the BGEA is permanently recast in the more fiery image of Franklin Graham and perhaps CEOs to follow, will it flourish as it did under the father? Will it even survive?

What Does the Future Hold for Mass Evangelism?

This last question is cosmic in nature, for its answer hinges on where we will turn our hearts in the days, years, and generations to come. Will we look to one great evangelist above all others for comfort and counsel? After Billy Graham, will one man, woman, or movement be touched by God or some other great force, imbued with the gifts to rise up and touch the world, one soul at a time?

I was asked this question hundreds of times in the dozen years I covered Billy Graham for his hometown newspaper, the *Charlotte Observer*. My response, based on experience, instinct, and a dab of cynicism, was "No, I don't think any one person will command the world's attention the way he did. He came along at precisely the right moment, after World War II, when American Christendom was searching for a symbol of assurance and hope. He filled the role with distinction. But the times have changed. We are far too distracted, diverse and busy, and far too suspicious of celebrity, to embrace anyone to that degree of devotion."

Cynicism? It seemed as if each summer, some evangelist would roll into town, pack our coliseum, sell some books, and attract some buzz about him being "The Next Billy Graham." Greg Laurie, Rick Warren, Luis Palau, T. D. Jakes, Joel Osteen, even Franklin Graham and his sister, Anne Graham Lotz—these megachurch pastors, authors and cable TV news-supported personalities all had the spiritual equivalent of fifteen minutes of fame before the spotlight turned to someone else, or just turned off. Another Billy Graham? I didn't see one coming then, and I highly doubt it now.

Eskridge says not so fast, however. He speaks of satellites, smart phones, and the like sapping us of our time and energy and making it difficult to get our attention. But what if we rise up against what he calls "the tyranny of this constant barrage of images, information, and cyber-connectivity?" What if the culture changes on a dime and suddenly we look for that one great figure to galvanize us, unite us, promise us heaven on earth, then heaven after this life? Could it be that years from now, Will Graham becomes that galvanizing force, with the weight of his father's and grandfather's ministry behind him? Could it be another whose name we do not know yet, or someone who has yet to be born?

"If there is any constant in the development of evangelical mass evangelism over the last 300 years," Eskridge says, "it's that predictability of style, emphases, strategies and personality profiles cannot be forecast. . . . Right now, it looks like we may be in some sort of lull, but it would not be surprising to see 'another Billy Graham' come along—but someone and something none of us can envision now."

Maybe here is the best place to end our consideration of a man and movement that took flight a lifetime ago under a tent in Los Angeles—with a question about the future for which there can be only one sure answer. Another Billy Graham? Nobody knows. But certainly the next Billy Graham will not look like the old one.

Index